MW00803840

Baptists Worldwide

Baptists Worldwide

Origins, Expansions, Emerging Realities

EDITED BY
Erich Geldbach

FOREWORD BY
Elijah Brown

CASCADE *Books* · Eugene, Oregon

BAPTISTS WORLDWIDE
Origins, Expansions, Emerging Realities

Cascade Books
An Imprint of Wipf and Stock Publishers
199 W. 8th Ave., Suite 3
Eugene, OR 97401

www.wipfandstock.com

PAPERBACK ISBN: 978-1-6667-9587-5
HARDCOVER ISBN: 978-1-6667-9586-8
EBOOK ISBN: 978-1-6667-9588-2

Cataloguing-in-Publication data:

Names: Geldbach, Erich [editor]. | Brown, Elijah [foreword writer].

Title: Baptists worldwide : origins, expansions, emerging realities / Edited by Erich Geldbach .

Description: Eugene, OR: Cascade Books, 2022 | Includes bibliographical references.

Identifiers: ISBN 978-1-6667-9587-5 (paperback) | ISBN 978-1-6667-9586-8 (hardcover) | ISBN 978-1-6667-9588-2 (ebook)

Subjects: LCSH: Baptists | Church | Baptists—History | Baptists—Doctrines

Classification: BX6231 G45 2022 (print) | BX6231 (ebook)

This book is gratefully dedicated to all General Secretaries of the Baptist World Alliance for their invaluable service to the mission, ecumenical challenge, and unity of the worldwide community of baptized Christian believers, commonly known as Baptists

Table of Contents

E. Baptists on All Continents

List of Contributors

Ayanrinola, Isaac Duro, PhD, was a missionary of the Nigerian Baptist Convention for eight years in Sierra Leone before he earned a doctor of missiology degree in the United States. Until 2021 he served as general secretary of the All Africa Baptist Fellowship.
aabfgs@gmail.com

Bebbington, David, PhD, was Professor of History at the University of Stirling, Scotland and Visiting Professor of History at Baylor University. He is a Fellow of the Royal Society of Edinburgh and the Royal Historical Society.
d.w.bebbington@stir.ac.uk

Belding, Julie, a journalist and author from New Zealand, was president for one term of the Baptist Women's Union of the Southwest Pacific.
julie@belding.co.nz

Brackney, William, PhD, is Professor of Baptist Theology and Ethics at Carey Theological College in Vancouver, BC and the retired Millard R. Cherry Distinguished Professor of Christian Thought and Ethics Emeritus at Acadia University in Wolfville, NS. He is a prolific author on Baptist history and thought.
whbrackney@gmail.com

Briggs, John, PhD, was Professor of History at Keele University, Rector of Westhill College (1997–99), Vice Chancellor of the University of Birmingham (1999–2001), member of the Central and Executive Committees of the WCC, and active in various committees of the Baptist Union;

he is research professor at Regent's Park College, Oxford, and IBTS Centre, Amsterdam.
jhy.briggs@virgin.net

Bowers, Faith, an English Baptist historian, has been a member of Bloomsbury Central Baptist Church in London since 1961 and is author of two books on this congregation.
faithbowers@btinternet.com

Callam, Neville, PhD, received his education from the United Theological College, University of the West Indies, and Harvard Divinity School, was pastor and teacher at theological institutions in the Caribbean, member of the Faith and Order Commission of the WCC, founded Christian radio and TV stations, and held several leadership positions in the Baptist Union of Jamaica and the BWA which he served as General Secretary from 2007 to 2017. He is author of several books.
nevillecallam@yahoo.com

Cross, Anthony, PhD (May 1, 1962–July 22, 2021) was pastor in Baptist churches, lectured at Roehampton and Oxford Universities, and published books and articles with emphasis on the sacrament of baptism. He was an Adjunct Supervisor at the IBTSC Amsterdam.

Dick, Devon, PhD, was president of the Jamaica Baptist Union and currently serves as pastor of the Boulevard Baptist Church, Kingston, Jamaica.
boulevard.baptist@gmail.com

Durso, Pamela, PhD, was executive director of Baptist Women in Ministry in Atlanta, Georgia and is now President of Central Baptist Theological Seminary in Shawnee, KS.
pdurso@cbts.edu

Geldbach, Erich, Dr. theol., University Professor of Ecumenical Studies, Ruhr University Bochum (ret.), has published numerous books and articles and is a member of the Commission on Christian Unity and the Commission on Religious Freedom of the BWA.
Geldbach@t-online.de

Goodwin, Everett C., PhD, pastored churches in Rhode Island, Connecticut, Virginia, and Washington, DC, where he was senior minister of the historic First Baptist Church. He authored several books on Baptist topics.
ecgoodwin1@aol.com

Gouldburne, Ruth, PhD, taught at Bristol Baptist College before being called as co-minister of Bloomsbury Central Baptist Church; since 2018 she has pastored the Grove Lane Baptist Church in Cheadle Hulme.
ruth@grovelane.org

Gushee, David, PhD, is Distinguished University Professor of Christian Ethics and Director of the Center for Faith and Public Life at Mercer University. He was President of the Society of Christian Ethics, is involved with initiatives to end torture and save the climate, serves as columnist for various news organizations, and was appointed as a member of the Church Relations and the Holocaust Committee of the US Holocaust Museum; he has authored important books on ethical issues.
gushee_dp@mercer.edu

Hankins, Barry, PhD, is Professor of History and Graduate Program Director at Baylor University in Waco, Texas. He is an expert in religion and American society. Barry_Hankins@baylor.edu

Harmon, Steve, PhD, Professor of Historical Theology, School of Divinity at Gardner-Webb University in Boiling Springs, NC, USA. He is a member of the Faith & Order Commission of the WCC and the Commission on Christian Unity of the BWA.
sharmon@gardner-webb.edu

Ishola, Solomon Ademola, PhD, was general secretary of the Nigerian Baptist Convention (2001–11), pastored many churches, and is heavily involved in the national life of Nigeria.
osofoishola@gmail.com

Kretzschmar, Louise, PhD, has been professor of Christian Ethics since 1991 in the Department of Philosophy, Practical and Systematic Theology of the University of South Africa, Pretoria.
louise@konkie.co.za

Mackey, Tómas, PhD, an ordained Baptist minister from Argentina, is President of the Baptist World Alliance for the 2020–25 quinquennium.
tomasjmmackey@gmail.com

Manley, Ken R., PhD, was principal and professor of church history at Whitley College, the University of Melbourne, Australia.
kmanley@iprimus.com.au

McSwain, Larry L., PhD, was associate dean of the doctor of Ministry degree program and held the Watkins Christian Foundation Chair of Ministry, at McAfee School of Theology, Mercer University, now retired.

Mendez, Dinorah, PhD, Professor of Theology and Christian Heritage at the Mexican Baptist Theological Seminary, member of the Heritage Commission of the BWA.
dmendezo@hotmail.com

Msiza, Paul Ngwedla, was general secretary of the Baptist Convention of South Africa (2001–10), President of the All Africa Baptist Fellowship (2006–11) and President of the BWA (2015–20). He pastors Peniel-Salem Baptist Church in Pretoria.
npmsiza@polka.co.za

Nash, Robert N., is Associate Dean of the doctor of Ministry degree program and Professor of Missions and World Religions, McAfee School of Theology, Mercer University in Atlanta, USA.
nash_rn@mercer.edu

Osephashvili, Ilia, Bishop of the Evangelical Baptist Church of Georgia, responsible for the region of Kakheti in Eastern Georgia.
Ilia.osefashvili@gmail.com

Randall, Ian, PhD, pastored Baptist churches, taught church history simultaneously at Spurgeon's College London and at IBTS in Prague and is now a Research Associate, the Cambridge Center for Christianity Worldwide, a Senior Research Fellow at Spurgeon's, and at the IBTS Center, Amsterdam. He has also been a hospital chaplain and has written many books on evangelical and Baptist topics.
ian.m.randall@gmail.com

Rubboli, Massimo, PhD, Professor em. of North American History at the Department of Political Science of the University of Genoa (Genova, Italy). One of his current projects is 'The legacy of the Radical Reformation'. maxrubboli@gmail.com

Schulze, Dietmar, Dr. theol., Associate Professor of Missions at Southwestern Baptist Theological Seminary, lecturer at Bible Seminary Bonn (Germany) and adjunct professor at Liberty University as well as Truett McConnell University. He is also an associate team member of the International Mission Board. dschulze@swbts.edu

Sessions, Erin M. received a prestigious scholarship and is working toward her PhD on Song of Songs as a model for prevention of domestic violence. She is a lecturer in Integrative Studies at Excelsia College, accredited with Australian Baptist Ministries. She is an errant poet and arrant academic. erin@commongrace.org.au

Sutherland, Martin, PhD, was until January 2020 Dean and CEO of the Australian College of Theology. He now resides in his native New Zealand. msutherlanded@gmail.com

Wheeler, Edward L., PhD, an ordained Baptist minister, was President of the Interdenominational Theological Center in Atlanta, Georgia from 2015 to 2019; he had previously served as President of Christian Theological Seminary (CTS) in Indianapolis, Indiana for fourteen years. He has been active in numerous academic, church, and civil organizations and has been an outstanding representative of the Afro-American community. anklehigh1960@gmail.com

Wheeler, Mary Susan earned her BA from Spelman College and her MA from Troy State University in American History and Adult Education. She has served as an adjunct professor in the African Studies Program at Indiana University/Purdue University/Indianapolis (IUPUI) for fifteen years. maryw7509@gmail.com

Foreword

As a Christian Worldwide Communion that draws upon a shared history of over 400 years, the Baptist movement has grown from the humble origins of a few gathered people of conviction as religious minorities in Europe to a truly worldwide ecclesial family. At the 22nd Baptist World Congress held in July 2021, over 4,500 delegates registered from 146 countries and territories as the most globally diverse gathering of Baptists who, amid a global pandemic, joined in worship with Baptist believers from 75% of the nations of the world. In *Baptists World-Wide*, Professor Erich Geldbach helps weave together this story of transformation and offers powerful insights from across Baptist history, doctrinal teachings, and from every continent in the world.

I am honored to commend this project as an important and substantive contribution to understanding the Baptist movement as a multinational communion that reflects our various cultures within a common commitment to Jesus Christ and to one another. Pastors, theologians, denominational leaders, and members of churches around the world will gain fresh insight into the work of God through the Baptist family and will be challenged again to live with missional conviction.

Professor Geldbach helps reorient Baptists from western only dominated themes and histories to a truly worldwide perspective. While demographic projections are notoriously fluid, every indication is that Baptist demographics are increasingly shifting to Asia, Latin America, and most especially Africa, where the BWA family has grown 134% over the preceding ten years. *Baptists World-Wide* will be an enduring legacy that helps illuminate the path to a future that celebrates Baptists in every country working in an essential oneness in Jesus Christ.

Today such shared commitment is necessary. As wars continue to rage, millions are forced to flee as refugees, religious freedom remains denied to significant portions of Baptists and other people of faith and conviction, environmental challenges loom, and where there are still many who have never heard the hope of salvation in Jesus, there is an urgency to rediscovering and recommitting afresh to living – as was affirmed at the very first BWA Congress in 1905 – in the spirit of Pentecost.

At the BWA, we believe Baptists belong together because we belong to Jesus Christ. Because we belong to Jesus Christ, we are called, in the Holy Spirit, to God's global mission. In *Baptists World-Wide*, Professor Geldbach helps show us the way.

Rev. Elijah M. Brown, Ph.D.
General Secretary and CEO
Baptist World Alliance

Preface

THIS BOOK WAS A long time in the making. When the first preparations were under way, I lost my wife, Dr. med. Ursula Geldbach, of more than fifty-one years of a happy partnership. The weeks and months that followed were very difficult, and the book project was somewhat on the back burner, but always on my mind. Through an unexpected turn of events, the sadness gave way to unforeseen happiness as Dr. med. habil. Renate Kammerer and I entered an adventure which we both thought unimaginable only a few years ago. This volume appeared in Germany within a series of books on present-day Worldwide Christian Communities.[1] The coeditor of this collection, my long-time friend Dr. theol. Walter Fleischmann-Bisten, remarked that he knows of no professor of theology who was married twice by the same minister over a time span of more than fifty-three years: It is Rev. Hermann Woock to whom we both are very grateful for his inspiring words at our wedding, and we would like to send him our best wishes. Renate both encouraged me and put pressure on me to complete the project. My sincere gratitude goes to her for invaluable help.

My heartfelt thanks also go to all the authors for their diligent and innovative work. Some who promptly responded to my initial invitation to take part in this project had to wait excessively before the manuscripts could go to the printer. To them I apologize. Health problems prevented some contributors from completing their assignments, so others came on board. To them I am especially grateful.

---

1. Geldbach, Erich, ed., *Baptisten weltweit. Ursprünge, Entwicklungen, Theologische Identitäten* (Bensheimer Hefte 118 = Die Kirchen der Gegenwart 7; Göttingen: Vandenhoeck und Ruprecht, 2021). An Italian version is also available thanks to the work of Professor Massimo Rubboli and his associates: *I Battisti. Una communità mondiale, a cura di Erich Geldbach* (Bologna: Società editrice il Mulino, 2021).

Modern technology is both a blessing and a curse. My hard drive had to be replaced only a few weeks before the completion of the German version, and some of my translations were lost and had to be done again. As all but two essays had been submitted in English, I thought that an English edition of the book might be easy to accomplish. However, the guidelines of the publisher Wipf & Stock were quite demanding so that I sent all essays plus the guidelines back to the authors. It took much time before all contributors had returned their pieces, and even then I needed to read each chapter carefully before it could be incorporated into the final manuscript. Therefore, I am responsible for any mistakes or inaccuracies that may be found in the book. In the English edition, the American spelling is used, perhaps to the dismay of individual authors who are used to British spelling and punctuation. Some essays have extensive footnotes; other authors did not include these or reduced them to a minimum. Each essay is presented as each author wanted it to be.

It is a great pleasure for me to express my gratitude to Professor Dr. Gury Schneider-Ludorff and my friend of many years Dr. Walter Fleischmann-Bisten for including this book in the series on present-day Christian denominations which both colleagues are coediting in Germany. It is done on behalf of a unique ecumenical study and research institute called "*Konfessionskundliches Institut*" in Bensheim (thirty miles south of Frankfurt). It is well-known by its publications, especially a series of books which are called "*Bensheimer Hefte.*" The present volume on the Baptist community is number 118 overall and is also number 7 within the series of books on the Christian denominations. The outline of the books are to follow the same pattern: after a short historical introduction, the major teachings are to be presented, to be followed by exemplary descriptions of the expansion on the world map. I took the liberty to add two chapters: one is on "mission" as Baptists are known (and sometimes feared) as "missionary people," the other is on "Baptist women" as this particular topic is widely discussed in all denominations.

Thanks to the work of Professor Dr. Massimo Rubboli and his team of translators, Corrado Grottoli, Susanna Chiarenzi, Raffaele Volpe, Dario Monaco, Simona Rizzardi, and Nicola Pantaleo, plus the proofreading by Patrizia Necci, Massimo Rubboli, and Fabrizio Tartaro, this book also appeared in an Italian version under the auspices of the Historical Commission of the Italian Baptist Union. The publisher is Società editrice il Mulino in Bologna (www.mulino.it), and I am grateful to Ms. Annalena

Monetti of this publishing house for a friendly email exchange before and while the book was produced.

Finally, I am thankful to the team of experts of the American publisher Wipf and Stock in Eugene, OR, for accepting this volume in the Cascade Books imprint.

A Spanish version is pending and may appear in 2022.

Erich Geldbach
Magdeburg/Marburg, Easter 2020

List of Abbreviations

AABF	All Africa Baptist Fellowship
ABCUSA	American Baptist Churches (USA)
ABCW	American Baptist Churches of the West
ABFMS	American Baptist Foreign Mission Society
ABHMS	American Baptist Home Mission Society
ABK	Afrikaanse Baptist Kerke
ABWU	Asian Baptist Women's Union
ABPAid	Asia Pacific Baptist Aid
APBF	Asia Pacific Baptist Federation
APBY	Asia Pacific Baptist Youth
BASA	Baptist Association of South Africa
BBCF	Bangladesh Baptist Church Fellowship
BCHK	Baptist Convention of Hong Kong
BCP	Baptist Conference of the Philippines
BCSA	Baptist Convention of South Africa
BCV	Baptist Convention of Vietnam
BGAV	Baptist General Association of Virginia
BGCT	Baptist General Convention of Texas
BMS	Baptist Missionary Society
BMSA	Baptist Mission of South Africa
BSF	Baptist Student Fellowship

BTS	Baptist Theological Seminary (in Singapore)
BUA	Baptist Union of Australia
BUGB	Baptist Union of Great Britain
BUSA	Baptist Union of South Africa
BWA	Baptist World Alliance
BWUSWP	Baptist Women's Union of South West Pacific
CBCNEI	Council of Baptist Churches in North East India
CBF USA	Cooperative Baptist Fellowship (USA)
CBF	Caribbean Baptist Fellowship
CCT	Twelfth District of the Church of Christ in Thailand (TKBC)
CLC	Christian Life Commission
CBPC	Convention of Philippines Baptist Churches
EBF	European Baptist Federation
EBM (I)	European Baptist Mission (International)
EBWU	European Baptist Women's Union
FGBFI	Full Gospel Baptist Fellowship International
FMB	Foreign Mission Board (SBC)
IBTS	International Baptist Theological Seminary
IMB	International Mission Board (SBC)
IVF	Inter-Varsity Fellowship
IWM	Interchurch World Movement
KJV	King James Version (of the Bible)
JNBMS	Jamaica Native Baptist Missionary Society
LMS	London Missionary Society
MBC	Malaysia Baptist Convention
MBC	Myanmar Baptist Convention
MBTS	Malaysian Baptist Theological Seminary
MIT	Myanmar Institute of Theology

NABF	North American Baptist Fellowship
NABWU	North American Baptist Women's Union
NBC-USA	National Baptist Convention USA
NBC	Nigerian Baptist Convention
NBCC	Nepal Baptist Church Council
NRSV	New Revised Standard Version
NSW	New South Wales
NZBMS	New Zealand Baptist Missionary Society
PNG	Papua New Guinea
PNBC	Progressive National Baptist Convention
SABMS	South African Baptist Missionary Society
SBC	Southern Baptist Convention
SBTS	Singapore Baptist Theological Seminary
SCM	Student Christian Movement
STBC	Samavesam of Telegu Baptist Churches
TBC	Telangana Baptist Convention
TBC	Thailand Baptist Convention
TEC	Theological Education Committee (APBF)
TLBC	Thailand Lahu Baptist Convention
TKBC	Thailand Karen Baptist Convention
UBLA	Unión Bautista Latino-Americana
UCA	Unione Cristiana Apostolica Battista
UCEBI	Unione Cristiana Evangelica Battista d'Italia
WCC	World Council of Churches
WCTU	Women's Christian Temperance Union
WFBMF	World Fundamental Baptist Missionary Fellowship

Introduction

ERICH GELDBACH

THE BAPTIST MOVEMENT IS a post-Reformation group of churches in the Reformation tradition as received by seventeenth-century English Puritanism in its separatist wing.[1] Since its inception, the Baptist movement has not been tightly unified, but very diversified. Most followed the Calvinistic expression of the Reformation principles or what seventeenth-century Baptists perceived Calvin had taught. Even then, there were differences as to the anthropological question who was privileged, predestined or "called" to be a Christian. Some questioned the traditional observance of the Sunday as the Lord's Day and began to assemble on the Sabbath or the Seventh Day.

As the Baptist movement spread and grew, other hotly debated issues arose, and the four-hundred-year history revealed that Baptists with their emphasis on freedom of the individual and of the local congregation had a preference "to split when in doubt." The urge to unify came with two tendencies within Protestantism in general: the missionary movement and the ecumenical movement. Even though both began roughly a century apart, they are nevertheless intertwined as mission strategists have argued that the credibility of the Christian faith suffers when it is presented in multiple ways and when "sheep stealing" takes place on the "mission field." Both movements, however, also elicited mixed reactions within Baptist circles: Some ministers positioned Baptist churches as "anti-missionary" as they found no examples of missionary societies,

---

1. For a very helpful tool and source of information consult Brackney, William H., *Historical Dictionary of the Baptists* (3rd ed., Lanham, MD: Rowman & Littlefield, 2021).

organizational and geographical planning, or other modern developments in the New Testament. The same is true for the ecumenical movement: some welcomed the quest for Christian unity, others stayed aloof and followed their separate ways. Within the larger Baptist community and as part of the ecumenical movement, the call to more intra-Baptist unity came with the founding of the Baptist World Alliance (BWA) in 1905. For one hundred years the BWA was the one Baptist organization to hold the major manifestations of Baptist faith, order, life, and work together. However, one year prior to the centennial celebration in 2005, the Southern Baptist Convention decided that it was theologically important for this organization to withdraw from the BWA. The Convention had been in "Baptist Battles" (Nancy Ammerman)[2] between fundamentalists and moderates over control of the denomination which ended in a complete victory of the fundamentalist, inerrantist wing. When the inerrantists failed to take over the BWA as well, the notion of separateness and splitting proved more important than the unity even in one faith tradition.

As mentioned in the preface above, the outline of this book follows the pattern of the other books in the German series on different Christian denominations. After a historical introduction, emphasis is on Baptist teachings. However, before these topics are taken up, an essay that covers the missionary endeavors of Baptists is inserted as Baptists have always been known as a "missionary people."

The section on the teachings first takes up the ecumenical issues as brought forth in the "Lima convergence papers" on *Baptism, Eucharist and Ministry* (BEM). The Lima document BEM of 1982 (Faith and Order Paper No. 111) is the most widely translated and distributed ecumenical document thus far and highlights the growing agreement ("convergence") and also the remaining differences in the faith and life of the churches. Baptist teachings on these issues are important for the ongoing conversations among and between the churches within the ecumenical movement. The Baptist teaching on the ordinance or sacrament of baptism is of particular importance as many non-Baptist or paedo-Baptist theologians and church leaders find the Baptist practices to be church-dividing. The author of this segment, Dr. Anthony Cross, had recently

---

2. Ammerman, Nancy Tatom, *Baptist Battles: Social Change and Religious Conflict in the Southern Baptist Convention* (New Brunswick, NJ: Rutgers University Press, 1995).

published extensively on the topic. Unfortunately, he passed away on July 22, 2021.[3] His untimely death is a great loss for the Baptist community.

The BEM section is followed by an essay on religious liberty. This concept has been throughout Baptist history a major eccleciological and political strength in the life of the denomination. One might, in fact, claim that in the Baptist tradition the four time-honored "notions of the Church," the *notae ecclesiae*, i.e., *una, sancta, catholica et apostolica*, must be expanded to include a fifth: *libertas*, the liberty of the church. It is from this point of departure that the section on sociopolitical involvement follows logically and brings out the best in Baptist traditions. The entire section on Baptist teachings can be read as an exercise in "Baptist distinctives."

Some women scholars urged me not to include a special chapter on "women." The original outline also did not call for this topic. However, as the place of women in the church, especially in leadership and pastoral positions, is highly debated in the entire Christian community, it seemed suitable to introduce some Baptist views on these issues. Besides, in some essays such as the one on missions, those on black churches or on geographical descriptions, special subsections are also devoted to women.

The second part of this book is on the expansion of the Baptist movement throughout the world. Needless to say that this section cannot be exhaustive. This is especially true for the continent of Africa and for the very diverse situation in India. However, an effort was made to give an overview and present exemplary situations and countries, including India. The largest Baptist groups are to be found in North America and hence this portion of the book is the longest. Special additions were made for Europe as the situation in Georgia reflects a unique experiment in contextualizing the Baptist tradition in the culture which for centuries has been dominated by the Orthodox Church.

The other addition was to be Ukraine, but the intended article had been written almost four years before the war broke out when Russian troops crossed the border into Ukraine on February 24, 2022. Therefore, the difficult decision was made not to publish this pre-war essay at this time.[4] The independent country of Ukraine was illegally attacked and invaded by the Russian military contrary to international law as laid down in the UN Charta. The ensuing suffering and uprooting of people,

---

3. Rev. Dr. Anthony R. Cross (May 1, 1962—July 22, 2021).

4. The reader can find the article on the internet: https://www.yoder.de/2018/09/17/ukrainian-baptists-since-2014/.

especially the elderly, women and children, the vast number of refugees who are seeking shelter within the Ukraine, but mostly in neighboring countries[5], the senseless bombing of apartment complexes, hospitals, schools, theaters, and other non-military facilities, in addition to railroads and stations, as well as the bombing of vital infrastructures are horrific. All of these and the long-range effects on the economy and agriculture, especially grain production and grain export bring to mind that the war is, indeed, a turning point in recent European history. Notions of mutual security and non-interventions to move borders by force are no longer in place. The "European House" is on fire. Mikhail Gorbachev's metaphor of a European House meant that the new house which he wanted to see being built after the Cold War was to have many rooms (nations) with easy access (no walls or barbed wired fences) to all inhabitants. Free interchange of ideas and mutual dependability on economic terms were to replace East-West tensions. Putin's military erased all these, perhaps too idealistic, expectations.

True, there can be long debates whether or not Putin's Russia felt betrayed by the West as NATO moved ever closer to the Russian border, whereas Secretary of State James Baker in his negotiations with Russian leaders, especially with Gorbachev, had vowed not to move NATO "one inch eastward"[6] beyond the border of the former German Democratic Republic. Likewise, debates can take place about the events leading up to and carrying out Kyiv's 2013/14 Maidan revolution. The late Senator John McCain (1936-2018) and Under Secretary of State for Eurasian Affairs, Victoria Nuland, were in Kyiv during the Maidan upheaval with lots of money. Why were they in Ukraine and where did the money go? After pro-Russian President Viktor Yanukovich was ousted and fled to Russia, a new government was installed, and some high-profile Baptists were involved in the new administration. Most exposed was Baptist lay preacher Oleksandre Turchynov who served as Acting President of Ukraine from February until June 2014.

The reasons for the invasion of Ukraine as given by President Putin and Foreign Minster Lavrov include the absurd and baseless claims to de-nazify Ukraine and to prevent a further genocide of Russian-speaking

---

5. As of mid-April 2022 reports are that two-third of Ukrainian children are uprooted and refugees, mostly with their mothers as their fathers are enlisted in the Ukrainian army to defend their country against the Russian invaders.

6. https://usarchive.gwu.edu/briefing-book/russia-programs/2017-12-12/nato-expression-what-gorbachev-heard-western-leaders-early

people in Donbas where Putin "recognized" the two "People's Republics" of Luhansk and Donetsk. Despite Ukrainian troops being largely outnumbered as concerns both manpower and ammunition, Russian troops failed to obtain large territorial gains. Instead, upon retreating from the outskirts of the Ukrainian capitol to regroup, the horrific violence and the enormous sufferings inflicted by the invaders became obvious. The aim now is to bring the two "People's Republics" and the second largest Ukrainian city of Kharkiv completely under Russian control.

It seems that Putin had expected his military to perform a *Blitzkrieg* to take Kyiv within a few days. The atrocities that were committed, more than anything else, united Ukrainians in their determination to defend the independence of their country. The national unity that Putin's armed forces provoked in Ukrainian citizens, proved Putin wrong as far as his ideological basis is concerned upon which he acts. He is strongly and unequivocally backed by the Patriarch of Moscow of the Russian Orthodox Church, Kyrill I. The Byzantine concept of "symphonia", i.e. a mutual interdependence of church and state, draws the heads of state and church ever closer together. Who is whose sycophant? What are the two trying to achieve?

The ideology behind the war is a mythological reading of history. Foreign minister Lavrov told a state-owned TV channel that the "special military operation" is to put an end to the expansion of NATO and the "drive towards full domination by the US and its Western subjects on the world stage."[7] Lavrov's political comments can be transformed into religious language: ". . . the most important thing that distinguishes Russia from other countries is its history, its tradition and system of values, which have been preserved in this country by the grace of God." The civilization which is based on this "system of values" is called "*Russkij Mir* = the Russian world" by the Moscow Patriarch, and he goes on to explain that this Russian world is derived from "the Kiev baptismal font.[8] The Russian world is a special civilization to which belong people who today call themselves by different names—Russians, Ukrainians, and Belarusians."[9] When asked at a press briefing April 12, 2022 about the

7. See https://www.rsn.org/001/sergei-lavrov-says- courtesy Reader Supported News (RSN)

8. This refers to the baptism of Vladimir and the Kiev Rus'. The mass baptism was followed by Vladimir's marriage with a Byzantine princess, thus establishing a close tie between the Kievan Rus' and the Byzantine Empire.

9. Cited in a press release www.patriarchia.ru/db/text/3730705

relationship between Russia and Belarus, Putin responded: "We do not actually know where Belarus ends and Russia begins. We are one people – Russians, Belarussians and Ukrainians." The secular and the religious concept of the "Russian World" go hand in hand and support each other. In both cases the enemy is the "West", its liberalism, secularism, and a value system which supports gay parades instead of family values as the Patriarch states and as Putin echoes. Both also comfort Russian soldiers as they march into battle by citing Holy Writ: "No one has greater love than this, to lay down one's life for one's friends" (John 15:13). The conflict is a "metaphysical war" between two friends, and one friend had no other choice than to try to save the other from the impact of Western decadence and pseudo-values even as the rescuer risks his life.

These utterances demonstrate to everyone who has ears to hear that the credibility of His Holiness hit a low mark, and he was heavily criticized by the Patriarch of Constantinople, Bartholomaios I., who in the Orthodox tradition is the "first among equals". The war is not waged "for the sake of truth, but with lies, and these are one of the main weapons of the evil one." Hence he characterized the war as "diabolical".[10] He was not the only critical voice in the Orthodox orbit: more than five hundred Orthodox scholars of the Eastern Christian world, issued a *Declaration on the "Russian World" Teaching*. The Orthodox scholars flatly call this teaching a "heresy" from which have sprung "the shameful actions of the Government of Russia in unleashing war in Ukraine with the connivance of the Russian Orthodox Church." When communicating with a patriarch, it is highly unusual to come across this kind of language, but the *Declaration* does not stop here. It rejects "any teaching that seeks to replace the Kingdom of God . . . with a kingdom of this world, be that Holy Rus', Sacred Byzantium, or any other earthly kingdom." Obedience to Christ must be placed above any obedience to a "leader vested with ruling powers and claiming to be God's anointed, whether known by the title 'Caesar', 'Emperor', 'Tsar', 'or 'President.'" No particular civilization may be divinized or demonized, hence "a holy Orthodox Eastern culture" is not "above a debased and immoral 'West.'" The *Declaration* reminds Russian Orthodox leaders to be "truth-tellers". Should they decline to speak the truth about the "evils that are perpetrated against the Gospel of Christ in Ukraine", they condemn themselves as cowards, liars, or both.[11]

10. As quoted in the German Catholic Press release KNI-OeI April 12, 2022.

11. See https://publicorthodoxy.org/2022/03/13/a-declaration Public Orthodoxy is a publication of the Orthodox Christian Studies Center of Fordham University.

The *Declaration* and its biblical language is a stark reminder that the war which Russia unleashed has changed the world in which we live. Nothing seems to be the same as before the war which had actually been going on ever since Russia annexed the peninsula Crimea and sent troops into the Donbas. It is, therefore, impossible to follow the usual path of narrating the story of the All-Ukrainian Union of Churches of Evangelical Christians-Baptists. Before the hostilities this Union was one of the strongest within the European Baptist Federation (EBF), and in 2018 it hosted the Council meetings of the EBF in Lviv. At this time a resolution was passed which reads:

The European Baptist Federation Council meeting in Lviv, Ukraine on 26th–29th September 2018: Takes note of the Resolution of the Baptist World Alliance, on Religious Freedom in the Lugansk Region of Eastern Ukraine, agreed at the BWA Gathering in Zurich, July 2018, and commends it to the EBF member unions.

And further: DEPLORES the worsening situation in the "Lugansk People's Republic" (LPR), and also in the "Donetsk People's Republic" (DPR) for all people of any or no religious persuasion.

STANDS as a European Baptist community with our Ukrainian brothers and sisters as they persevere in serving the internally displaced persons from those regions, and the churches there in the struggle to maintain their identity and religious freedom.

COMMIT ourselves as leaders and members of the EBF to pray for, and speak truth in love, to those in positions of authority, and to promote Freedom of Religion or Belief for all in the LPR and DPR.[12]

The All-Ukrainian Union has a total membership of roughly 130,000 believers. Where are they now? How many had to flee their homes to avoid the shellings and bombings? Where did these refugees find a place to stay? What happened to young families and their children?

The missiologist Johannes Reimer reported that the Union sent out missionaries in great numbers into neighboring countries.[13] How are they looking at the disaster at home, and did they return or could they not come back?

---

12. It is reported that not a single church other than Russian Orthodox remained open in the LPR and only a few in the DPR. This is the immediate effect of the "Russian World" theory as Baptist churches are "Western" and will lead Ukrainians astray. They cannot enjoy religious liberty as this is an alien concept in the "Russian World".

13. Johannes Reimer, "Home, Mission Field and the Great Commission", Evangelical Focus Europe, 15 March 2022. https://evangelicalfocus.com/features/15875/

The Union and the Seminaries were on the ambitious path to ordain 120 new ministers per year. Are the seminaries still teaching? Are the buildings still standing? One casualty is certain: The dean of the Seminary in Kyiv was shot in the street.

The Union in conjunction with local congregations built more than 50 foster care homes and are now helping about 1,200 orphans.[14] Can this work be upheld as the war situation continues or worsens?

What is happening to the buildings of the congregations? If they are still in usable condition, the congregations open their houses of worship and try, as much as they can, to distribute food, water and other articles if, indeed, they have any. In some cases refugees who are on a westward course may stay over night to catch some sleep. The EBF keeps updates on its website with heartbreaking stories.

Johannes Reimer cites Vasyl Ostryi of Kyiv Theological Seminary:

> "We will shelter the weak, serve the suffering, and mend the broken. And as we do, we offer the unshakable hope of Christ and his gospel. While we may feel helpless in the face of such a crisis, we can pray like Esther. Ukraine is not God's covenant people, but like Israel, our hope is that the Lord will remove the danger as he did for his ancient people. And as we stay, we pray the church in Ukraine will faithfully trust the Lord and serve our neighbors."

The country that happens to be the last in this book is New Zealand. Baptists in that beautiful part of the world should not be disappointed as this was a "geographical" decision rather than a value judgment.

---

14. Communication by Elijah Brown, secretary general of the BWA after his recent trip to Eastern Europe.

A. Origins and Development of the Baptist Movement

1

Origin and Development of the Baptist Movement in the Seventeenth and Eighteenth Centuries

JOHN BRIGGS

ENGLISH BAPTISTS, WITH CONTINUOUS history from the beginning of the seventeenth century, have the longest history of any Baptist group in the world and because of this their early history necessarily becomes part of the history of the whole family. Overall, English Baptists find their origins among those who were not content with the limited, even though profound, achievements of the mainstream reformation. For them, something more was necessary. Whether this took them into the camp of the Radical Reformation or into the tradition of Puritan Separatism has been hotly contested. Most likely both movements played their part.[1]

More recently it has been argued that certain early General Baptist congregations derive from the Lollards, the followers of John Wycliffe (1320–84). Called General (Arminian) Baptists, they argued that Christ died for all, not just the elect. Scrutiny of church court records shows that far from dying out before the Reformation, Lollard activities continued well into Tudor England. More particularly, analysis of the surnames of those who signed the (General Baptist) Orthodox Confession of 1679, suggests that these signatories had Lollard family backgrounds.[2]

---

1. Manley, "Origins of the Baptists," 34–46.
2. Baines, "Signatories."

3

In 1608, John Smyth (ca. 1570-1612), sometime Fellow of Christ's College, Cambridge, went into exile in Amsterdam with fellow puritans from the covenanted congregation which he had gathered in Lincoln-shire, a congregation which existed separate from the established church. Whilst in Holland, he and his lay supporter, Thomas Helwys (ca. 1550-ca. 1616), together with those they led, broke with the other English puritan exiles, convinced that the infant baptism they had received in the estab-lished church was invalid and that only those who confessed the faith for themselves were the fit subjects for baptism. Then in 1609 Smyth first baptized himself and then baptized the others: hence his nickname of the "Se-Baptist."

Doubting the wisdom of this, Smyth later decided that the Water-lander Mennonites, notwithstanding the bad press that haunted Ana-baptists, were not as heretical as he first supposed. With the majority of his group, therefore, he sought membership of the Waterlander church, thereby identifying his followers directly with the radical reformation. For his part, Helwys opposed the joining of the Waterlanders, believing this to be a going back on Smyth's new beginning reflected in his inde-pendent baptism, mistakenly now seeking baptism of another Christian church, rather than making the clear breach with the past symbolized by his earlier action. Leading the rump of the Lincolnshire group back to England, Helwys formed the first Baptist Church on English soil in Spitalfields, London, in 1612.

Smyth and Helwys, it can be argued, notwithstanding later associa-tions formed in Holland, came to Baptist views independently of Menno-nite influence, as they sensitively studied the Scriptures from a reformed and separatist perspective. It is equally clear that the early Baptists, like the Anabaptists before them, rejected the Constantinian identification of church and state, embodied in the folk and state churches of the main-stream reformation, in favor of a Believers' Church arising from a per-sonal experience of new birth, and this was powerfully illuminated by confining baptism to believers only, hence their underlining of the need for a regenerate church.

The first Particular or Calvinistic Baptists, that is those who believed in Christ's death as effective for the elect only, emerged from an Indepen-dent congregation in London, some of whose members came to believe that believers' baptism was the right way of Christian initiation. Thus they had even clearer continuity with other Calvinistic separatists. Anxious to secure a Biblical pattern of baptism, they sent one of their number,

Richard Blunt, to Holland to confer with a group committed to baptism by immersion. Again, the English deputation chose not to seek baptism of that group, but rather, in January 1642, Blunt baptized himself, this time by immersion, and then baptized fifty-three others. Both groups suffered much persecution. Although in 1612 Helwys penned a remarkable plea for toleration and freedom of worship, indeed the first to be written in the English language, *The Mistery of Iniquity*, his life ended in prison some time before 1616. The General Baptists developed a pattern of ministry which embraced not only local elders but also inter-church officers called "messengers." These might just be elders chosen to deliver a message or represent a church in a larger conference, but clearly on other occasions it indicated an evangelist and church planter, who later on came to exercise some wider *episkopé* or oversight within the life of the churches. Thus persecution notwithstanding, initial growth was considerable.[3]

Very soon these infant Baptist churches were hurled into the fury of the debate about the proper relationship of church and state, as the controversy over royal power and the divine right of kings developed in the latter years of the reign of King Charles I (1600–1649), leading to what has variously been called the English Civil War and the English Revolution. Suffice it to say that the nation was bitterly divided, and Charles I lost both his throne and his head. This was followed by the turmoil of the protectorate and the commonwealth, with such experiments in politics as government by the saints. For his part, Oliver Cromwell (1599–1658) allowed an established church to continue, staffed with non-royalist Anglicans, Presbyterians, and Congregationalists. Even such a reformed state church, however, attracted few Baptists.

Towards the end of the commonwealth, other more internal threats to Baptist life emerged. In these uncertain times, millenarian speculations were rife among extreme puritans. Baptists like others thumbed the pages of Daniel and Revelation, seeking the texts that would help them interpret what was happening in the world around them. Daniel 2 became the key text and the execution of Charles I in 1649 was identified with the end of the fourth monarchy, which would usher in the fifth monarchy of Christ's return. Initially, Cromwell was seen as implementing the prophecy, but when he accepted the title of Lord Protector in 1653, he was seen as obstructing God's purposes. "Fifth Monarchism" was not a sect so much as an attitude, which captured the imagination

---

3. Nicholson, "Office of 'Messenger,'" 206–25.

of a considerable number of Baptists, both General and Particular, who thereby set themselves against the state.[4]

If they represent "the church engaged," even "over-engaged," the Quakers, who in the years following 1655 secured the support, not only of individual Baptists but of whole congregations, represented "the church withdrawn." The appeal was not now to outward rules of church membership or even the written word of Scripture, but the inner testimony of the Spirit. Much ground was lost; by 1660 there remained only around three hundred churches across the two traditions of Baptist life, and the restoration of the crown in 1660 brought a quarter of a century of intermittent persecution by the state. Local records, such as The Broadmead Records, for what became the principal Baptist Church in Bristol, give vivid details of what it cost to be a Baptist in these years. Thus it is recorded that when King Charles II (1630–85) was restored in 1660, "then Satan stirred up adversaries against us, and our trouble or persecution began." It was not until 1687 that the record was able to look back upon "the times of our late troubles."[5]

However, in some senses, worse was to follow. The accession of the protestant sovereigns, William III (1650-1702) and Mary II (1662-94), brought only limited toleration. Oppressive laws remained on the statute books, though protestant dissenters of trinitarian faith, who subscribed to the principal points of the 39 Articles of the Church of England, were nearly always exempted from the penalties prescribed. However, even within this limited toleration, there was a dilution of commitment and a tolerance for a wider range of theological opinions. Both General Baptists and Particular Baptists suffered.

The General Baptists suffered a division between the General Association who roughly corresponded to those General Baptists with Lollard origins, who lived in the inland counties of Buckinghamshire, Hertfordshire, Northamptonshire, and Cambridgeshire, and who remained orthodox, and those churches in Kent and Sussex particularly, who had more contact with Dutch Mennonites. It was these churches that, under the leadership of the Sussex messenger, Matthew Caffyn (1628-1714), adopted the heterodox Christology of Melchior Hoffman (1495-1543), which *de facto* denied the reality of the incarnation. These were churches which over the next half century would lapse first into Arianism and

---

4. Capp, *Fifth Monarchy Men.*

5. Hayden, *English Baptist History and Heritage*, 51-59.

then into Unitarianism, with little distinctively Baptist remaining by the middle of the nineteenth century.[6] Indeed when Methodism came to offer a more attractive Evangelical Arminianism, many ministers and members transferred their affections, and many General Baptist congregations simply died out. The record is of preachers traveling to appointments only to find zero congregations, with the consequence that General Baptist churches began to issue prohibitions to their members about attending Methodist meetings.[7]

If the General Baptists suffered from a "rationalism of the left," then the Particulars were vulnerable to a "rationalism of the right." By this I mean the impact of high, or more properly hyper, Calvinism, which prohibited the preacher from both offering Christ and inviting a response to him, the entry of what the Baptist historian Joseph Ivimey (1773-1834) was to call "the non-invitation, non-application system John Skepp (1675-1721), a London hyper-Calvinist Baptist minister, complained of preachers who engaged in a kind of "moral persuasion" to try to influence their hearers to put their trust in Christ. So to do, he argued, would be to reflect a half-hearted Calvinism, and to exercise "a piece of robbery against the Holy Spirit." You do not have to read far in the sermons of such preachers to realize just how far their speculative theology hampered effective gospel ministries.[8]

This issue of whether or not to invite the uncommitted to respond to a gospel message became known as "the modern question." It clearly had to be addressed for the sake of effective mission. It should, however, be understood that not all Calvinists were made in the hyper mold. George Whitefield (1714-70) wrote to Philip Doddridge (1702-51) in 1748 affirming that "sweet invitations to close with Christ" were "the very life of preaching," and some of those converted by Whitfield became influential among the Particular Baptists.[9]

From the pessimism of the mid-eighteenth-century life it is right to look at the ways in which Baptist work was reborn, though it should be noted that it took some time for the new life of the Evangelical Revival to revitalize Baptist life. In the first place, on the Arminian side, a new denomination came into being. As the Old Connexion became ever more

6. Bass, *Caffynyte Controversy.*

7. Brown, *English Baptists,* 66-67.

8. Ivimey, *History,* 262-74.

9. Ivimey, *History,* 290-305.

tolerant of views which moved towards Unitarianism, so in 1770 a New Connexion of General Baptists was founded, very largely out of people with a Methodist background who, reading their Bibles, had come to see Believer's Baptism as the only proper form of baptism. The leader of this movement was a Yorkshire man named Dan Taylor (1738-1816). Because of its Methodist background, it is not surprising that this became the best organized group of Baptists. The Particular Baptists all too often put too much emphasis on local independence to work together effectively. In the administrative structures of the New Connexion are to be found the origins of much of the organization that would subsequently underpin the work of the whole denomination.[10]

On the Particular Baptist side, a number of factors made for renewal. First, a number of pastors converted in the revival came into denominational leadership. Secondly, new educational institutions came into being to train men for ministry, more or less modeled on the Countess of Huntingdon's College at Trevecca (e.g., Rawdon, Stepney). Training also took place in the homes of certain senior ministers such as John Sutcliffe (1752-1814). Thirdly, at the same time in several parts of the country disciplined programs of itinerancy were initiated. These were conducted by teams of ministers/ministerial students/evangelists, often college-based, traveling from preaching station to station, preaching the gospel and hoping to lay the seedbeds for the emergence of future churches. The fourth mark of the changed temperature of Baptist life was the development of new associations with a clear missionary purpose, of which the Northamptonshire Association (1764), though not confined to the county of that name, was particularly noteworthy. Finally, the period also witnessed the foundation of many other pan-evangelical endeavors designed to further the mission of the church, such as the forming of Tract Societies, Sunday Schools, the Bible Society, etc., in which Baptists shared the leadership.[11]

Three developments within the Northamptonshire Association are of particular importance. First, in 1784 John Sutcliffe, influenced by the experience of Jonathan Edwards (1703-58), issued his famous call to united prayer on the first Monday of every month, "that sinners be converted, the saints edified, the interest of religion revived, and the name of God glorified. . . . Let the whole interest of the Redeemer be affectionately

---

10. Briggs, "New Connexion," 57-75.

11. Morden, "Continuity and Change," 1-28.

remembered, and the spread of the Gospel to the distant parts of the habitable globe be the object of your most fervent requests." Sutcliffe's challenge was taken up not only by Baptists but also by Independents, and in continental Europe as well as Great Britain. In 1785 Andrew Fuller (1854-1915) finally published his *Gospel Worthy of All Acceptation*, a book he had been working on for some five years. In this volume Fuller worked out in an English context some of the insights of Jonathan Edwards from America and provided a theology which he believed would provide a proper answer to "the modern question." Fuller argued against the hypers that "faith in Christ is the duty of all who hear or have opportunity to hear the gospel." The goodness of God, properly presented, almost contained within itself a moral demand "for a return of gratitude." Every preacher, according to Fuller, ought to govern his preaching by the understanding that every sinner, whatever his character, was "warranted to trust in the Lord Jesus Christ for the salvation of his soul."

Prayer and theology came together in a revived denomination: Nineteenth-century historian Joseph Ivimey spoke of it as "a new era in the history of our denomination," for the third Northamptonshire Baptist to contribute to this story was William Carey (1761-1834), who provided an answer to the prayer call initiated by Sutcliffe and translated the new theology into new missionary action, with Fuller heading up the support in England. In 1792, after a lot of persuading undertaken by William Carey, not least in his *An Enquiry into the Obligation of Christians to use means for the Conversion of the Heathen*, the Particular Baptist Missionary Society for Propagating the Gospel among the Heathen was founded. The foundation was accompanied by an apology for a denominational initiative, but indicated that the divided state of Christendom, as then existing, could not be allowed to delay effective mission. Hard on the heels of the overseas initiative came the founding in 1797 of the London Baptist Society for the Encouragement and Support of Itinerant and Village Preaching, later to be known as the Home Missionary Society.

Thus, whilst Europe was engaged in revolution and war, British Baptists were engaged in strategizing about world mission. Taking the initiative here was to bring rich dividends not only overseas but in the renewal of the denomination at home in what was to become a century of conspicuous growth, for 1792-1892 saw English and Welsh Baptists grow from around 20,000 church members to something like 320,000.[12]

---

12. Morden, "Continuity and Change," 16-23.

The process described in this account of Baptist origins and early development may be allowed to find its focus in two architectural images which focus two ongoing compulsions in Baptist life. First, come inside a seventeenth-century meeting house. Note the language: this is not a church, for such high language is for people, not for bricks and mortar. The building is domestic in scale, perhaps with thatched roof. It will be twice as wide as it is deep, with the pulpit set against the long wall opposite the entrance. In front of the pulpit will be the big pew encircling the communion table, where the deacons may well have had their seats. John Betjeman says it will have the quality of a well-scoured farmhouse kitchen, for this is a building built for business: it is where the saints meet around the open Bible and the Table for their nurture and growth in grace. All is good quality, the best that men and women of modest means can provide, but, above all, this is a place where the saints, well-versed in Scripture, meet together to discern the mind of Christ.

Contrast with this a Tabernacle or a Salem Chapel of the late eighteenth century or early nineteenth century. The language has changed, and although this may be a Baptist Tabernacle it will be found to be far from temporary or portable, especially if equipped with classical portico to spell out a proper defiance of Catholic Gothic. The interior is changed as well. The scale and the orientation have both been altered. The pulpit, or perhaps now more correctly a rostrum, to house the preacher's supporters as well as himself, is set against the short wall opposite the entrance. Behind it are ranged, in commanding fashion, an array of impressive organ pipes, as if these trumpets, great and small, were of major theological significance. The model is now not so much the domesticity of farmhouse, but the performance of a theater, with the preacher lifted six feet high above contradiction. Everything is done to accommodate as many hearers as possible, in serried ranks of pitch pine pews, with galleries taking the seating up the rear and side walls. There is much less sense of sharing here: the preacher has the message and the people, many of whom may be here for the first time, are present to receive it, not to engage in theological debate. This is a building for mission, a building to accommodate the unbeliever as much as the committed disciple, this is a house for sinners. What may appear like a communion rail is there for a different purpose, for this is the penitents' bench, where those seeking Christ may make public display of that intention. The invitation, now called an "appeal," will surely both be made and pressed, so that we can legitimately speak of it as a part of the liturgy, especially at the Sunday evening service, when among those present the preacher will be anticipating the presence of those needing conversion. He is preaching for a verdict. Indeed the whole service will be constructed to lead up to a climax which will be found as those present respond to the gospel appeal.[13]

Those two pictures spell out the dialectic of church and mission which must always be an essential part of the Baptist calling, and which each generation has to heed, and in so doing find a way of faithfulness living in inter-relationship between the two, for if the church loses its vision of mission, then its days are numbered as witnessed by the loss of initial strength by English Baptists at the beginning of the eighteenth century. But mission needs to be rooted in the life of the church community, the believers' church, in which faith and service are gently nurtured, freely assembling under the "Crown Rights of the Redeemer," free from all external interference from secular authorities, free to decide its own priorities in vocation and purpose, to appoint its own officers, not isolated from other congregations but seeking their advice and associating with them in serving others both locally and in worldwide mission.

In summary, the first two centuries of Baptist history reflect the impact of three movements: the radical dissatisfaction with the established order in church and state seen in the countercultural activity of the Anabaptists, the puritan nurture of a theologically literate covenant community of Christian disciples and their families, and the dedicated concern of those whose faith had been reawakened in the Evangelical Revival for gospel outreach, both at home and abroad.

Bibliography

Baines, Arnold H. J. "The Signatories of the Orthodox Confession of 1679." *Baptist Quarterly* 17 (1957) 170–78.

Bass, Clint C. *The Caffynyte Controversy*. Oxford: Regent's Park College, 2020.

Betjeman, John. *First and Last Loves*. London: John Murray, 1952.

Briggs, John H. Y. "New Connexion General Baptists, 1770–1813." In *Challenge and Change: English Baptist Life in the Eighteenth Century*, edited by Stephen Copson and Peter J. Morden, 57–75. Didcot: Baptist Historical Society, 2017.

Brown, Raymond. *The English Baptists of the Eighteenth Century*. A History of the English Baptists 2. London: Baptist Historical Society, 1986.

Capp, Bernard. *The Fifth Monarchy Men: A Study in Seventeenth-Century English Millenarianism*. 1972. Reprint, London: Faber, 2011.

13. Betjeman, *First and Last Loves*, 97–105.

Hayden, Roger. *English Baptist History and Heritage.* Didcot: Baptist Union, 1990.

———, ed. *The Records of a Church of Christ in Bristol, 1640–1687.* Bristol: Bristol Record Society, 1974.

Ivimey, Joseph. *A History of the English Baptists.* Vol. 3, *The Principal Events of the History of Protestant Dissenters, from the Revolution in 1668 till 1760 and of the London Baptist Churches, During that Period.* London: Holdsworth, 1823.

Manley, Ken R. "Origins of the Baptists: The Case for Development from Puritanism-Separatism." *Baptist History and Heritage* 22 (1987) 34–46.

Nicholson, John F. V. "The Office of 'Messenger' amongst British Baptists in the 17th and 18th Centuries." *Baptist Quarterly* 17 (1957) 206–25.

2

Developments in the Nineteenth and Twentieth Centuries

David Bebbington

At the opening of the nineteenth century the Baptists remained a relatively small community on both sides of the Atlantic Ocean. In England they had no more than 445 churches; and in America, according to a survey of 1813, 2,633 churches. They were divided by the central doctrine of salvation into the Particular Baptists (or Regular Baptists in America), who held that Christ died only for the elect, and the General Baptists (or Free Will Baptists in America), who held that Christ died for all. The former were self-conscious Calvinists, the latter Arminians. There were also a small number of Seventh Day Baptists who maintained that the Jewish sabbath should still be observed by Christians.

Though rather few in number, nearly all the Baptists had been reinvigorated by the Evangelical Revival of the previous century. The Regular Baptists of the United States had been augmented by the Separate Baptists, those whose origins went back no further than the Great Awakening and who were notably revivalistic in practice. In the American South the spirit of revival, with open-air preaching and expectations of emotional response, was particularly strong. In England the General Baptists had in many cases lapsed into an unappealing rational theology and so were growing only slowly, if at all, but a New Connexion of General Baptists, thoroughly Evangelical in temper, was making rapid progress, especially in the East Midlands. The Particular Baptists, a much larger body, were increasing in numbers at a similar rate. Like the Methodists, with whom they shared their evangelistic principles, the Baptists were advancing.

Their practice was deeply affected by another legacy from the previous century, the Enlightenment. It used to be supposed that the Enlightenment, with its appeal to reason, was uniformly hostile to the Evangelical Revival, with its reliance on revelation. More recent work, however, has shown that the Enlightenment and the revival were closely bound up together. Thus John Wesley (1703–91), the founder of Methodism, insisted on the importance of reason in religion. The features of enlightened thinking therefore became prominent among the Baptists. The empiricism of the age, encouraging inquiry and investigation, marked their thought during the nineteenth century. In philosophy Baptist theologians generally followed the Scottish "common sense" school of Thomas Reid (1710–91). This approach was based on an investigation of the properties of the human mind, an empirical technique. The philosophers of this school claimed that the mind always assumes certain truths such as the existence of God. What is assumed is common sense. This was the method of Francis Wayland (1796–1865), the president of Brown University, the premier Baptist institution of learning in the new world, and was widely taught in Baptist colleges. Natural science, furthermore, was seen as a proper investigation of God's creation.

In the era before the publication, in 1859, of Charles Darwin's (1809–82) *Origin of Species*, there was little sense that science and religion were in competition. On the contrary, a synthesis of science with Christian faith was widely upheld as "natural theology." God's works, it was often said, confirmed God's word. Baptists, like their Evangelical contemporaries, saw science and religion as being in harmony. Thus empiricism reigned among Baptists in the life of the mind.

The temper of the Enlightenment affected theology itself. The Evangelical counterpart of the idea of progress, the expectation of human improvement under the guidance of reason, was postmillennial doctrine. The millennium, a time of peace and prosperity on earth, was anticipated before the last judgment. Accordingly the second coming of Christ would take place after ("post") the millennium. Before that time there would be a steady spread of the gospel and its values. The *General Baptist Magazine* for 1854 carried an article about the advances that could be expected as the millennium approached. These would include, among other strides forward, the total abolition of taxes, though that might not take place until the year 2016. An optimism pervaded Baptist life since the triumph of the gospel was assured in the Scriptures. Again, the moderation typical of the Enlightenment transformed Calvinism among the Particular/Regular Baptists. The theological views of Jonathan Edwards (1703–58), the great Congregational theologian of New England in the middle years of the eighteenth century, were widely embraced. Edwards taught that the Creator did not make human beings unable by nature to accept the gospel. Instead the unconverted showed a moral inability to believe the gospel, a result of their own wickedness. Hence they, and not the Almighty, were responsible for their own perdition. This more moderate form of Calvinism was expounded by Andrew Fuller (1754–1815), the leading theologian among the Baptists at the opening of the nineteenth century. Fuller was also willing, unlike earlier Calvinists, to grant that the atonement was universal in scope, though not universal in application. Further, he modified the inherited idea of penal substitution, accepting substitution but not a penal element because Christ was without sin, and only the guilty could be punished. Fuller's stance became the normal one among Baptists in the United States as well as in Britain long into the nineteenth century. Baptist theology reflected the enlightened thinking of the age.

The pragmatic spirit of the Enlightenment also made inroads into Baptist attitudes. Instead of constantly asserting principle, they became more flexible. Whereas previous generations of Baptists had held that churches must obey all the commands of Scripture, they now became less punctilious. Thus the General Baptists, who had long required the laying on of hands after baptism on the ground that was taught in Hebrews chapter 6, dropped the practice. Francis Wayland was even prepared to assert that Christians were free to adopt "any form of church government which they may esteem most for their edification."[1] That was to concede that traditional Baptist claims for the exclusive rightness of their church order were mistaken. The most marked change was over the Lord's Supper. In 1815 Robert Hall (1764–1831), a leading English Baptist minister, questioned the inherited view that only those baptized as believers should be admitted to communion. Hall contended, on the contrary, that even if Christians were not baptized, it was still expedient that they should remember Jesus at the Lord's Supper. Hall urged the admission to the table of any converted person, a policy of "open communion." That rapidly became the prevailing stance in England, though in Wales and

1. Wayland, *Salvation by Christ*, 321.

America it was resisted as an unjustified concession of the basic principle of the denomination that believers ought to be baptized. The new policy was a typical symptom of the pragmatism of the Enlightenment.

Missions formed a prominent instance of agencies not prescribed by Scripture that Baptists sponsored. The Baptist Missionary Society, founded in 1792, was modeled on joint stock companies, not biblical examples. Missionary cooperation, soon imitated in the United States, inspired greater coordination of Baptist life. The Baptist Union of Great Britain and Ireland, first commenced in 1813, was put on a much stronger basis in 1832. The American national body, set up in 1814, though usually called the Triennial Convention, was actually named the General Missionary Convention of the Baptist Denomination in the United States. Other institutions multiplied. Baptists, eager in the spirit of the Enlightenment to ensure that members of the wider public could develop their powers of reasoning, specially favored education. They founded a series of colleges, primarily for the training of ministers, but also, particularly in America, for supplying a liberal education to layfolk. Sunday schools, usually associated with churches, gave a basic education to the working population. All these ventures called for more generous giving and the rising prosperity of the age made them possible.

There was, however, resistance. Some Baptists were alarmed by the fresh developments. It was not just that they were being asked to pay for the new institutions, though many resented that. The fundamental problem was dismay that the early Baptist concern to ensure that the church was patterned in the correct way was being modified. The critics were right that seventeenth-century Baptists would not have recognized the style of church life that had grown up under the impact of the Enlightenment. Many rejected the idea of open communion, insisting that the table should be restricted to the baptized. They denounced missions and colleges as innovations alien to the word of God, and so came to be known in America as "anti-missionary Baptists." These agencies actually seemed to infringe the prerogatives of the Almighty, who, according to traditional Calvinism, would call the elect by his own methods. The theology of Andrew Fuller was dismissed as too close to, or even identical with, Arminianism. The defenders of the old paths who refused to open the Lord's table to the unbaptized were called "Strict." Those who asserted older and higher forms of Calvinism kept the label "Particular." Hence in England the traditionalists came to be known as "Strict and Particular Baptists." Their equivalents in the United States were the "Primitive Baptists," those who preferred the earliest, or primitive, ways of the movement. The first Strict and Particular Baptist association in England was set up in 1829; the first Primitive Baptist association in America was formed in 1828. On both sides of the Atlantic the staunch opposition to innovations occasioned schism in the ranks of the denomination. The splits were a sign of the drastic degree of change that was being introduced in the early years of the nineteenth century.

Yet the fresh developments generated growth. The number of churches in mainstream associations in England increased from 445 to 1,080 during the first half of the century; and membership expanded from around 100,000 at the middle of the century to 516,000 by its end. In America the number of members swelled from about 100,000 at the opening of the century to 313,000 at mid-century and to over three million by 1900. In the past English Baptists had often been confined to market towns, but now, like the Methodists, they sent out preachers to small villages to gather new congregations. Special itinerant societies were formed for the Highlands of Scotland and the remoter parts of Ireland. In America, especially in the South, Baptist pioneers moved westward with successive waves of settlers. Largely because of the unresolved issue of slavery, the Baptists of the South split away from the Northern Baptists in 1845, creating a new Southern Baptist Convention with its own centralized denominational apparatus. In the maritime region of what is now Canada, the spiritual descendants of Henry Alline (1748–84), a late-eighteenth-century revivalist, divided into Regular and Free Christian Baptists, Calvinist and non-Calvinist respectively. In central Canada, Regular Baptists occupied the field. Australia, divided until 1901 into six distinct colonies, drew Baptists as immigrants from Britain, as did New Zealand and South Africa, the other major settler colonies. In continental Europe Baptists spread out from Germany to other nations, eventually becoming strongest in Russian Ukraine. Meanwhile the Baptist Missionary Society was carrying the gospel to fresh lands: To India, where William Carey (1761–1834) labored in the early years of the nineteenth century, to the West Indies, to West Africa from the 1840s, and to China and the Congo later in the century. The Americans of the North undertook work in Burma, Siam, Assam, southern India, China, and Liberia; and the Southern Baptist Convention created fields in Nigeria, China, and Brazil. The Baptist world was growing.

The theological views of these various Baptists were uniformly Evangelical. They were strongly attached to the Bible, made the cross their central doctrine, aimed for conversions, and were dedicated to energetic gospel work. Thus they were marked by what have been seen as the four salient characteristics of the global Evangelical movement: biblicism, crucicentrism, conversionism and activism. But the Calvinism of the Particulars and the Arminianism of the Generals were upheld with less tenacity than in the past. The preaching of the gospel seemed so much more important than any specific formulation of it that there was a growing sense that the other party had merits in its case. The Enlightenment view that old types of theological expression could be discarded played its part too. Accordingly members started to transfer between the two bodies without question and General Baptist ministers began to train at Particular Baptist institutions. From its refoundation in 1832, the Baptist Union, though primarily a Particular Baptist body, permitted General Baptist churches to join. Although the eminent Baptist preacher at the Metropolitan Tabernacle in London, Charles Haddon Spurgeon (1834–92), maintained a doughty Calvinism in his ministry and at his college down to his death in 1892, the numbers professing a distinctive Reformed faith dwindled. By 1891 the New Connexion of General Baptists was wholly absorbed into the Baptist Union, only a few years before equivalent events in Canada and the United States. The blending of General and Particular bodies was possible because they shared an ethos that was generically Evangelical rather than specifically Arminian or Calvinist.

A slow process of theological change, however, began to affect Baptists, as it gradually transformed the whole Evangelical world. Influences associated with the Romantic movement in the early years of the century steadily infiltrated the mind of the population at large. Ideas beginning in Germany were transmitted to the English-speaking world through innovators, of whom the poet Samuel Taylor Coleridge (1772–1834) was the chief. Instead of the Enlightenment's stress on reason as the supreme human faculty, the Romantics emphasized will, spirit, and emotion. The cold temper of scientific investigation gave way to warm human imagination as the avenue to truth.

The impact on theology was primarily to foster liberal tendencies. Instead of conceiving the Almighty as essentially an upright ruler of the universe, as Fuller had done, advanced thinkers began to picture him as a kindly Father caring for his wayward family. The atonement became not a demonstration of divine justice but an exhibition of the eternal generosity of the Father towards his children. Hell was called into question, for what father would consign his offspring to such a fate? The earliest Evangelical ministers to express these ideas were usually Congregationalists, but by the 1870s a few Baptists on both sides of the Atlantic were taking the same path. Samuel Tipple, a minister in south London, for example, taught that Christ came to reveal that God was "the perfection of Fatherliness."[2] At the same time German critical methods were applied to the Scriptures. The Bible began to be seen as no different in kind from any other book. In America Crawford H. Toy (1836–1919) reached the view that the Old Testament recorded the natural evolution of the religious spirit of mankind and so, in 1879, resigned from Southern Baptist Theological Seminary. Although the views of Tipple and Toy were at this time highly unusual among Baptists, liberal theology was beginning to find its way among them.

It was Spurgeon who complained loudest against these developments. In 1887–88 he launched the "downgrade controversy," criticizing the tendency to modify the atonement and even abandon the doctrine of hell. Although Spurgeon failed to lead many out of the Baptist Union in protest, his objection slowed the process of theological drift in a liberal direction. His efforts were seconded by other changes, also associated with the rising tide of Romantic sentiment, which reinforced conservative tendencies. In particular beliefs about the last things began to shift away from the previous postmillennialism. In its place there arose premillennialism, the expectation that the second coming of Christ would take place before ("pre") the millennium. If so, the end of the age might be imminent. The most widespread version of this outlook was dispensationalism, contending that the present dispensation was about to end with the rapture of the saints to heaven and the ensuing chaos of the great tribulation. Dispensationalism became immensely popular in America, especially after the notes of the Scofield Bible of 1909 codified its teachings. Its spokesmen condemned the rising social gospel movement, expressed supremely in the American Baptist Walter Rauschenbusch's (1861–1918) book *Christianity and the Social Crisis* (1907), as a futile attempt to improve an order that was about to be swept away. Dispensationalism also encouraged a sense that theological decline was to be expected but that a remnant would retain its grasp on the truth. By critiquing the social engagement as well as the doctrines of more liberal leaders, it fostered suspicions of contemporary tendencies in Baptist life. The newer way of

2. Tipple, *Echoes of Spoken Words*, 184.

looking at prophecy contributed a great deal to the conservative side of the growing polarization among Baptists.

The outcome was the Fundamentalist controversy that broke out after the First World War. It was preceded by the distribution to ministers of all Protestant denominations in America and Britain, between 1910 and 1915, of a series of pamphlets called *The Fundamentals*, vindicating traditional attitudes to the Bible and asserting the dispensational scheme. In 1917 William Bell Riley (1861–1947), pastor of First Baptist Church, Minneapolis, published *The Menace of Modernism*, in which he identified modern teaching at the colleges as the source of dangerous liberal opinions. Three years later controversy broke out among the Baptists of the North in the United States over the type of teaching at their colleges. During its course the term "Fundamentalists" was first coined to apply to those who acted with Riley. In 1922 Harry E. Fosdick (1878–1969), the Baptist pastor of a Presbyterian church in New York, preached a pugnacious sermon, *Shall the Fundamentalists Win?*, arguing that the Bible was a record of progressive revelation. Although the initial attempt to rein in the colleges failed, the Fundamentalists maintained a campaign of sniping at heresy over subsequent years. Eventually it led to schism. In 1927 there was a division in central Canada and in 1932 a separate General Association of Regular Baptist Churches was created in the northern United States. There was no split over this issue in the American South, Britain, or Australia, but the same Fundamentalist/Modernist strains were felt there. In Britain its most obvious enduring expression was over whether one's sympathies lay with the Student Christian Movement, which was ecumenical in temper and broad in theology, or with the Inter-Varsity Fellowship, which was separatist in practice and conservative in doctrine. A study outline issued by the Baptist Union of Great Britain in 1990 still recommended SCM and IVF titles in rough balance. During the twentieth century the Baptists were constantly conscious of liberal/conservative tensions.

Partly in consequence of a weakened sense of the united purpose that had marked the previous century, numbers fell in many lands. In Britain Baptist church membership was at a peak in the first decade of the twentieth century, but fell slowly until the 1960s, when, in company with most measures of church allegiance, it collapsed. During the twentieth century the figure declined from over 500,000 to under 200,000. Likewise Australian census returns show that the proportion of the population claiming a Baptist allegiance reached its highest in 1901, at 2.37 percent, falling thereafter. Baptists in New Zealand and Canada did rather better, but were still losing ground relative to population. In the USA, however, religion flourished during the twentieth century. The Northern Baptist Convention, created in 1908 and renamed the American Baptist Convention in 1950 and the American Baptist Churches in the USA in 1972, was numerically successful overall, with about 1,413,000 members in 1928 and 1,607,000 in 1982, though the number of affiliated churches dropped. The outstanding success was the Southern Baptist Convention, which adopted a "cooperative program" in 1925, ensuring that resources were kept within a tight-knit organization, and remained much more theologically conservative than its Northern counterpart. From the 1940s the Southern Convention began to accept affiliations from the North as well as the South, becoming a universal but distinctive brand throughout the United States. Its membership mushroomed from 3,150,000 in 1920 to 15,900,000 in 2000. Meanwhile African American Baptist denominations, which had emerged towards the end of the nineteenth century, also flourished in the United States. A broad contrast could be drawn between the relative weakness of the churches in much of the English-speaking world and their vigor in America.

Fresh impetus came in the 1960s from charismatic renewal, a movement bringing a rejuvenating sense of the work of the Holy Spirit, but also reflecting the spirit of the age. Already by 1981 most of the candidates for ministry in the Baptist Union in Britain were from charismatic churches. Although not reversing the statistical decline, renewal introduced a fresh style, especially in worship, that appealed to young people. New Zealand proved especially receptive, but Southern Baptists were largely resistant to its distinctive theology, though not in many of the larger churches to its ethos. At the same time a recovery of sacramental theology emerged among Baptist theologians and there was a resurgence of Calvinism, largely in congregations outside the Baptist Union in Britain, but substantially within them in the Southern Convention. The most marked development, however, was a successful struggle during the 1980s to gain control of the Southern Convention by a section of opinion professing biblical inerrancy—conservatives to their friends and Fundamentalists to their foes. Although a great majority in the denomination was not aligned with the policies of this party, by the next decade all the seminaries and virtually all the state conventions were in its hands. The backbone of by far the largest Baptist body in the world had been stiffened.

Baptists had therefore emerged from relative obscurity at the opening of the period to play a major role in English-speaking Protestantism. Deeply swayed by Enlightenment assumptions, their predominant theology became a moderate form of Calvinism, and they adapted their practice to the temper of the age. Missions and colleges were organized, and, despite the resistance of traditionalists, they contributed to rapid expansion during the nineteenth century. At that period Baptists were united by a common Evangelicalism. Under the influence of the Romantic cultural mood, however, more liberal theologies began to spread and more conservative convictions became increasingly entrenched. The resulting Fundamentalist controversy in America, together with its echoes elsewhere, divided the denomination. The twentieth century saw decline among English-speaking Baptists outside the United States, but there growth was sustained. Charismatic renewal had a revitalizing effect, but the Southern Baptist Convention plunged into controversy. Thus the Baptist story during this period shows the healing of the old division between Calvinists and Arminians but the creation of a new fracture along conservative/liberal lines. It also demonstrates the power of the cultural context to mold Baptist attitudes. The Baptist record displays a constant attempt to remain loyal to the deposit of faith while adapting to the changing setting. It is a revealing study in the relationship of gospel and culture.

Bibliography

Bebbington, David W. "Baptists and the Gospel in the Twentieth Century." *Baptist Quarterly* 52 (2021) 2–20.

———. *Baptists through the Centuries: A History of a Global People.* 2nd ed. Waco, TX: Baylor University Press, 2018.

———. "British Baptist Crucicentrism since the Late Eighteenth Century." *Baptist Quarterly* 44 (2011) 223–37; 44 (2012) 278–90.

Briggs, John H. Y. *The English Baptists of the Nineteenth Century.* Didcot, Oxfordshire: Baptist Historical Society, 1994.

Dix, Kenneth. *Strict and Particular: English Strict and Particular Baptists in the Nineteenth Century.* Didcot, Oxfordshire: Baptist Historical Society, 2001.

Heath, Gordon L., et al. *Baptists in Canada: Their History and Polity.* Eugene, OR: Pickwick, 2020.

Hopkins, Mark. *Nonconformity's Romantic Generation: Evangelical and Liberal Theologies in Victorian England.* Carlisle: Paternoster, 2004.

Kidd, Thomas S., and Barry Hankins. *Baptists in America: A History.* New York: Oxford University Press, 2015.

Manley, Ken R. *From Woolloomoolloo to 'Eternity': A History of Australian Baptists*. 2 vols. Milton Keynes: Paternoster, 2005.

Marsden, George M. *Fundamentalism and American Culture: The Shaping of Twentieth-Century Evangelicalism, 1870–1925*. New York: Oxford University Press, 1980.

Minus, Paul M. *Walter Rauschenbusch: American Reformer*. New York: Macmillan, 1988.

Randall, Ian M. *The English Baptists of the Twentieth Century*. Didcot, Oxfordshire: Baptist Historical Society, 2005.

Sutherland, Martin. *Conflict & Connection: Baptist Identity in New Zealand*. Auckland, NZ: Archer, 2011.

Tipple, Samuel A. *Echoes of Spoken Words*. London: Sampson Low, Marston, Searle, and Rivington, 1877.

Torbet, Robert G. *History of the Baptists*. 3rd ed. Valley Forge, PA: Judson, 1973.

Trollinger, William V. *God's Empire: William Bell Riley and Midwestern Fundamentalism*. Madison: University of Wisconsin Press, 1990.

Walker, Michael. *Baptists at the Table: The Theology of the Lord's Supper amongst English Baptists in the Nineteenth Century*. Didcot, Oxfordshire: Baptist Historical Society, 1992.

Wayland, Francis. *Salvation by Christ*. Boston: Gould & Lincoln, 1859.

B. Baptist Missionary Endeavors

3

Baptists and Mission: A History

Robert N. Nash

Introduction

Baptist mission origins and history are as challenging to trace as the origins and history of the Baptist tradition itself. The Baptist mission story is a complex story dominated in its first 150 years by Baptist missionaries from England, the United States, and other Western nations, who, motivated by the Great Commission in Matt 28, as well as by their own colonial aspirations, shared the gospel of Jesus Christ in the Caribbean, Asia, Africa, and Latin America. As this gospel, framed in Western and Baptist theology and form, took root outside its old strongholds, or built upon roots that already existed in the new contexts, it became something far different from what its Western European and North American bearers imagined.

A monumental shift occurred as these new contexts transformed Baptist missiology, theology, and practice, and missionaries and immigrants from these places arrived in the United States and Western Europe in the mid to late twentieth century bringing with them revitalized expressions of the gospel that have renewed the faith and practice of those who first sent it out. Baptist mission in much of the world now is the work of Baptists from the majority world who may or may not be professional career missionaries.[1] Their mission efforts provide an opportunity for the

1. The majority world is that part of the world outside Western Europe, Australia,

27

reassessment of the privileged status accorded to Western European and North American missionaries, generally male, while often overlooking the contributions of African Americans, Baptists from the Southern and Eastern hemispheres, and women. At the same time, North Americans and Europeans in the earlier era made significant contributions that must not be minimized, including enabling Christianity to become a major religion of the world and extending the influence of Christian and democratic principles of spiritual and political freedom and individual human rights.

Robert G. Torbet (1912–95), a historian of Baptist missions, identifies the origins of the Baptist missionary movement in "a series of religious awakenings which broke out spontaneously in many quarters and which moved out along several different currents within the sixteenth, seventeenth, and eighteenth centuries."[2] Among these awakenings were the Protestant Reformation including Puritanism in England and the Radical Reformation of the Anabaptists, Pietism in Germany, and the Evangelical and Great Awakenings in England and the United States.

Some significant personalities and movements who contributed both theological and missiological foundations for this Protestant world mission were Felix Manz (1498–1527) and the Anabaptists (baptism of adult believers by immersion), Philipp Jacob Spener (1635–1705) and the Pietists (heart faith), Nikolaus von Zinzendorf (1700–1760) and the Moravians (methodologies and early missionaries), John Eliot (1604–90) and the Puritan mission to Native Americans (sacrificial devotion), John Wesley (1703–91) and the Methodists (evangelical preaching), and Jonathan Edwards (1703–58) and the American revivalists (experiential faith). Another powerful influence was the Catholic world mission that exploded in the aftermath of the Council of Trent and the age of exploration as such European nations as Spain, Portugal, France, and Italy sent missionaries of various religious orders around the world. In some ways, concerns that Catholicism would triumph globally spurred the Protestant world mission.

New Zealand, and the United States where most of the world's population resides, including specifically Asia, Africa, and Latin America.

2. Torbet, *Venture of Faith*, 5–6.

Jamaica: The First Baptist Mission Field

These religious and political forces set the stage for the launching of the Baptist world mission. The unlikely source of that launching was an African American and former slave named George Liele (1750–1820) who had converted to the Christian faith in a Baptist church in Georgia in the United States and who eventually made his way to Jamaica as the first Baptist missionary.[3] To pay for his voyage to Jamaica in 1783, Liele became an indentured servant, eventually paying off his debt. By the end of his ministry, some eight thousand Jamaicans had become Christians and Baptists, many as a direct result of Liele's preaching. His successful mission in Jamaica, along with that of another former African American slave, Prince Williams (ca. 1760–1840) in Nassau in the Bahamas, preceded that of William Carey in India by several years.

India

William Carey (1761–1834) was a humble shoe cobbler from a small village near Northampton, England. Like Liele, he was largely self-taught. Despite only about six years of formal education, Carey possessed a remarkable proclivity for languages and a passion for knowledge. He served as pastor of Particular Baptist churches at Moulton and Leicester where he became convinced that the Great Commission in Matt 28 was intended for the church across history and not simply as a command to the disciples in Jesus's day.

In 1792, Carey published his views in *An Enquiry into the Obligation of Christians to Use Means for the Conversion of the Heathen*. This publication would serve as the foundation for the theology and the organizational structure of the Protestant world mission in the modern world. The book was a remarkable apology for a Protestant and Baptist world mission, answering Calvinist arguments against such a mission on the grounds that God should do the saving and not human beings. In it, Carey summarized the work of missions across nearly two thousand years of church history and then provided an analysis of the mission field itself by identifying the sizes and locations of the major religions of the world. For the next two centuries, most missionary-sending agencies

---

3. The word "missionary" refers in this chapter to persons who cross international borders for the purpose of sharing the gospel of Jesus Christ in order to bring persons to faith in Jesus Christ and to establish churches in the new cultural context.

would follow Carey's model that called for the establishment of a board to oversee the financing of the missionary movement, the selection and training of missionaries, and the oversight of their work. Carey proposed the following structure:

> Suppose a company of serious Christians, ministers, and private persons, were to form themselves into a society, and make a number of rules respecting the regulation of the plan, and the persons who are to be employed as missionaries, the means of defraying the expense, &c. &c. This society must consist of persons whose hearts are in the work, men of serious religion, and possessing a spirit of perseverance; there must be a determination not to admit any person who is not of this description, or to retain him longer than he answers to it. From such a society a *committee* might be appointed, whose business it should be to procure all the information they could upon the subject, to receive contributions, to enquire into the characters, tempers, abilities, and religious views of the missionaries, and also to provide them with necessaries for their undertakings.[4]

Stirred by Carey's work, his contemporaries invited him to preach at the next associational meeting held at Nottingham in May of 1792. Subsequently, the association founded the Particular Baptist Society for Propagating the Gospel among the Heathen, later known as the Baptist Missionary Society. William Carey and John Thomas (1757–1801), together with their families, went to India in 1793 as the Society's first missionaries. Carey served in India for the rest of his life, devoting considerable energy to the translation of scripture into the vernacular languages and dialects of India and to the establishment of Serampore College. The devotion of the people of India to the Hindu religion surprised him, and it would be seven years before the first converts embraced Christianity.[5] Carey's wife, Dorothy, who had never understood her husband's call to India, would suffer from mental illness and depression, passing away in 1807. The challenges she faced, in terms of both physical and mental health, presaged the struggle of many Baptist missionaries, both male and female, over the next two hundred years.

Other missionaries of the Baptist Missionary Society, including William Ward (1769–1823), Joshua Marshman (1768–1837), Daniel Brunsdon (1777–1801), William Grant (d. 1799), and their respective

---

4. Carey, *Enquiry*, 82–83.
5. Leonard, *Baptist Ways*, 106.

families arrived in India in 1799. William Ward (1769–1823) and Joshua and Hannah Marshman (1767–1847) would join the Careys at Serampore and live together in intentional community modeled after Moravian mission communities, holding all property in common and sharing income equally.[6] This model was the earliest form of mission "stations" and missionary compounds in Baptist life, in which missionaries lived together and provided support and encouragement to each other. The strategy of mission stations was an effective method by which new missionaries, appointed to unreached populations, could live within range of a support system. By the time of Carey's death in 1834, nineteen such stations existed with both British missionaries and Indian nationals cooperating in the work.[7] In time, mission stations became the sole province of Western missionaries, something the Serampore Trio, as Carey, Marshman, and Ward were known, had not envisioned. These stations ensured missionary "control" in local contexts, yet often separated missionaries from the people they served.

The Serampore Trio established the foundation for the work of future Baptist missionaries in their focus upon Bible translation, evangelism, education, and the creation of a national church, combating perceived moral ills like the caste system and the immolation of widows. Serampore College, established in 1818 to train Indian church leaders, focused primarily upon evangelism and upon assisting students to understand their cultural context in order to share the gospel with Hindus and Muslims. It became a model for future universities founded by Western missionaries.

In 1806, Carey proposed "'a meeting of all denominations of Christians at The Cape of Good Hope somewhere about 1810.'" Ruth Rouse rightly referred to this idea for an ecumenical gathering as "the most startling missionary proposal of all time."[8] She imagines what such a gathering might have accomplished some one hundred years before the 1910 Edinburgh Conference that paved the way for the ecumenical movement within the Protestant tradition and how such a gathering might have provided the opportunity for the coordination of mission strategy and missionary appointments. Unfortunately, Carey directed his proposal to

---

6. Stanley, *History of the Baptist Missionary Society*, 39–43.

7. Stanley, *History of the Baptist Missionary Society*, 52–53.

8. Rouse, "William Carey's 'Pleasing Dream,'" 181.

Andrew Fuller who considered it one of Carey's "pleasing dreams," but did not see the wisdom in pursuing it.[9]

The West Indies

In 1813, British Baptist missionaries joined George Liele, the first Baptist missionary, in his work in the West Indies. Liele had requested assistance from British Baptists as early as 1791 reporting to John Rippon (1751–1836) of London that his church in Kingston, Jamaica had nearly 350 members. This appeal for support occurred at least two years before British Baptists formed the Baptist Missionary Society. Liele's work complemented that of Moses Baker in northwestern Jamaica who formed a congregation and appealed to British Baptists for support in combating opposition to religious instruction by British plantation owners. John Rowe, a member of John Ryland's (1723–92) church in London, arrived in Jamaica in 1814 under appointment of the Baptist Missionary Society.[10] The effort by missionaries and national Jamaicans over the next few years to eradicate slavery in Jamaica would create considerable political tension with planters who even undertook legal action against some missionaries. Eventually emancipation was granted to slaves in the British West Indies in 1834.

Other work in the West Indies by the BMS included efforts in the Bahamas, Haiti, Trinidad, and British Honduras (later Belize). For the most part, a Baptist presence already existed in each of these islands, except for Belize.[11] Significant tensions occurred between British missionaries and local Baptist pastors and leaders who often disagreed over worship practices and theology. Disagreement emerged primarily over the enculturation of such practices and theology in ways that were quite different from that familiar to white Euro-Americans. Similar tensions would emerge in other parts of the world.

West Africa

Jamaican Baptists formed the Jamaican Baptist Missionary Society in 1842 with the intention of sending missionaries to West Africa in cooperation

9. Rouse, "William Carey's 'Pleasing Dream,'" 181.

10. Stanley, *History of the Baptist Missionary Society*, 70.

11. Stanley, *History of the Baptist Missionary Society*, 91.

with the Baptist Missionary Society.[12] Encouraged by funding from their British Baptist partners and determined to combat the slave trade at its source, a community of forty-two Jamaican Baptists, including John Clark and G. K. Prince, arrived in Fernando Po in Cameroon in 1842. Also in the group were British Baptist missionaries Alfred (1814–80) and Helen (1816–86) Saker.[13] The mission often seemed at the point of collapse as the result of serious illness and death among the missionaries but the work of missionary Joseph J. Fuller (1825–1906), a Jamaican under appointment by the British board, provided much needed stability and some considerable success.

Burma

The Serampore Trio had hoped to establish a missionary presence in several countries around India, including Nepal and Burma. Four missionaries had attempted work in Burma between 1807 and 1812 but none had been successful. Carey's son, Felix, had moved to the country at his father's insistence and with the intention of serving as a missionary, but he lacked the evangelical zeal of his father.

Ann (1789–1826) and Adoniram (1788–1850) Judson, the first American Baptist missionaries under US agency appointment, would successfully launch a mission to the Burmese. Appointed by a board of the Congregational church, the Judsons determined once they were in India that baptism by immersion as adult believers was the only legitimate form and they presented themselves to the Serampore Trio for baptism. After considerable deliberation about a field of service, they decided to go to Burma. Their colleague, Luther Rice (1783–1836), another Congregationalist missionary who had sought baptism as a Baptist, returned to the United States to raise financial support for the Judsons from Baptist churches. With Rice's encouragement, Baptists in the United States organized in 1814 the General Missionary Convention of the Baptist Denomination in the United States of America for Foreign Missions, later known as the American Baptist Foreign Missionary Society.

The work of missionaries Ann and Adoniram Judson among the Burmese was challenging and difficult. Adoniram was imprisoned for a time and Ann died in 1826. Later and together with his second wife,

---

12. Russell, "Question of Indigenous Mission," 86.

13. Stanley, *History of the Baptist Missionary Society*, 107–9.

Sarah Boardman Judson (1803–45), Adoniram began a highly successful mission effort among the Karen people of Burma. The Karen embraced an ancient belief that was remarkably similar to the story of the fall in Genesis chapter 2 and chapter 3, in which the first man and woman were removed from the presence of God as a result of disobedience. Karen prophecy foretold a day in which white wings would bring a white man in possession of a book that would enable them to return to God. Confident that Adoniram Judson was this man, the Karen converted to Christianity and became hugely Baptist. For centuries until their expulsion from Burma in the late 1970s, they practiced a deeply committed faith, waiting for that moment when they might fulfill the Great Commission by carrying the gospel to the world.

Nineteenth Century Baptist Mission Efforts

Three significant Baptist missionary-sending agencies, the Baptist Missionary Society in England, the American Baptist Foreign Missionary Society, and the Richmond African Missionary Society, were in place by late 1815. Black Baptists in Richmond, Virginia pooled their resources to form the Richmond Society in 1815 in order to support Lott Carey, the first Baptist missionary to Africa. Its constitution stipulated that all its funds would support missionary efforts on that continent and, together with the General Missionary Convention and the American Colonization Society, it sent Carey, along with Collin Teague (1780–1839), to West Africa in 1821.[14] Both men had worked to secure their own freedoms and the freedoms of their families. Prior to their departure, they constituted a church composed of seven members of their families. That church would become the first Baptist church in Liberia and, by extension, in Africa.[15]

In 1840, black Baptists in New York City at the Abyssinian Baptist Church organized the American Baptist Missionary Convention, the first national black Baptist missionary-sending agency.[16] The limited income of African Americans made it necessary for this board to cooperate with the American Baptist Foreign Missionary Society and later the Southern Baptist Foreign Mission Board in order to appoint missionaries.[17]

14. Poe, "Lott Cary," 50–51.

15. Poe, "Lott Cary," 52.

16. Martin, *Black Baptists and African Missions*, 16.

17. Fitts, *History of Black Baptists*, 112.

In 1845, the Baptist Convention of the Maritime Provinces in Canada sent missionaries Richard (1810–53) and Leleah (1820–93) Burpe to Burma, and Canadian Baptists later formed the Canadian Baptist Foreign Mission Board in 1912. Earlier nineteenth-century efforts by Canadian Baptist missionaries focused primarily on India and Bolivia. Four Canadian Baptist unions and conventions merged in 1995 to form Canadian Baptist Ministries that continues to send missionaries and to coordinate the mission efforts of Canadian Baptist congregations.[18]

Other European Baptists, and particularly German Baptists, soon joined British, American, and Canadians in missionary outreach, particularly within Europe itself and later in Africa and Asia. Bill J. Leonard has pointed out that "in 1800 there were no Baptist churches on the European mainland" but soon thereafter, Johann Gerhard Oncken (1800–1884), a German Baptist, established Baptist churches in the countries of Germany, Denmark, Russia, Switzerland, Lithuania, and a host of other nations. His work influenced dozens of other missionaries who began Baptist churches and unions in their own countries.[19]

British Baptist mission efforts in the nineteenth century focused primarily upon the Cameroons, Congo, India, Ceylon (now Sri Lanka), China, and Japan. Between 1814 and 1845, the American Baptist Foreign Missionary Society, also popularly known as the Triennial Convention, served as the major sending agency for Baptists in the United States. Its history during these decades included the formation of the American Baptist Home Missionary Society and the establishment of a Baptist missionary presence in Siam (Thailand), South India, Assam, Liberia, Europe, Haiti, and China.[20]

From 1820 to 1845, American Baptists found themselves increasingly divided over the issue of slavery. Many Baptists in the North championed the abolition of slavery while Baptists in the South responded that such matters were the concern of individual states. Tensions increased with the creation of anti-slavery societies in New England and New York. By 1840, some missionaries in Burma were refusing to work with slaveholding missionaries and, by 1843, abolitionists in the North founded the American and Foreign Free Baptist Board of Foreign Missions for "the

18. See "Our History."

19. Leonard, *Baptist Ways: A History*, 306–7.

20. Torbet, *Venture of Faith*, 57–90.

expressed intention of not cooperating with the Southern churches."[21] In 1844, the Triennial Convention refused to appoint a slaveholder from Georgia as a missionary to the Cherokee, and the stage was set for the creation of the Southern Baptist Convention and a new Baptist mission-ary-sending agency. Southern Baptists gathered in Augusta, Georgia in May of 1845 and declared the creation of the new denomination as well as the establishment of its Foreign Mission Board.

The separation of the two conventions was remarkably amicable. The Northern board allowed its missionaries to choose the board under which they would serve, and this generous offer set the tone for future collaboration and cooperation between the two Baptist bodies.[22] Imme-diately, the Southern board approved China as its first mission field and sent a letter to missionaries in China inviting them to come under the new board's appointment. Missionary J. Lewis Shuck (1812–63), appointed with his wife Henrietta (1817–44) as the first General Missionary Con-vention appointees to China in 1835, at once accepted the invitation, and Lewis Shuck[23] became the first missionary of the Foreign Mission Board of the Southern Baptist Convention.[24] The board also conferred with Is-sachar J. Roberts (1802–71) of Canton, China, a missionary supported by the small China Mission Society of Kentucky. The China Mission Society dissolved, and Roberts became the second FMB missionary in China.[25] By 1850, eight SBC missionaries were serving in Canton and Shanghai. Prior to the Civil War, the Foreign Mission Board would expand its work to include already established fields in China and Africa, building upon the work of both the BMS and the American Baptist Foreign Mission Society. It would also attempt to open work in Japan and Brazil, but the declining health of missionaries and the financial challenges created by the outbreak of the Civil War hindered these efforts.

African American Missionaries in the Nineteenth Century

For African Americans, the Protestant foreign mission movement pro-vided opportunity for the evangelization of Africa while also perpetuating

21. Ray, *Southern Baptist Foreign Missions*, 30.
22. Ray, *Southern Baptist Foreign Missions*, 30.
23. Henrietta Shuck had recently passed away.
24. Hall, *I Give Myself*, 68.
25. Nash, *Influence*, 75.

and institutionalizing racist attitudes on the part of primarily white boards. Euro-American white culture, infused with a confidence in its own chosenness and superiority, believed it played a central and divinely ordained role in the evangelization of the world. The British Missionary Society, while at first reluctant to enter the political arena to fight the abolition of slavery, did eventually support such efforts and, as has already been described, cooperated with black Baptists in Jamaica in a mission to West Africa. In the United States, the larger and better-financed boards were overwhelmingly supported by white Baptist churches and black Baptists were precluded from full and equal participation as missionaries. In the interest of the evangelization of Africa however, black Baptists were more than willing to serve under white boards, at least until African American denominations formed stronger mission organizations after the Civil War.

The appointment of African Americans by the Foreign Mission Board of the Southern Baptist Convention prior to the Civil War provides an example of both the successes and challenges of the cooperation between white and black Baptists in missions. The FMB insisted upon appointing only freed slaves and that black Baptists should serve in Africa for several years under appointment by the American Baptist Missionary Convention or another African American agency before appointment by the FMB. Black Baptist missionaries were appointed to both Liberia and Nigeria, but white missionaries or supervisors who visited from the United States generally supervised their work. All American missionaries serving in Africa in 1849 were black and consisted of thirteen missionaries, seven ministers, and six teachers serving in eight different locations.[26]

Black Baptists had formed the Baptist Foreign Mission Convention in 1880 in Montgomery, Alabama with the stated purpose of evangelizing Africa. After the Civil War, the FMB and ABFMS continued to appoint black missionaries to Africa until the creation of the National Baptist Convention in 1895 as a partnership between the Baptist Foreign Mission Convention, the National Baptist Convention of America, and the National Baptist Education Convention. The Foreign Mission Board of the NBC would serve as the missionary arm of the new denomination. Its work is still focused upon Africa with ten mission stations there as well as one in Nicaragua. The Lott Carey Baptist Foreign Mission Society,

26. Martin, *Black Baptists and African Missions*, 21.

established in 1897, also supported African American missionaries to West Africa.

Women and Missions

The influence that women have had in Baptist mission history includes service both as missionaries and as financial and prayer supporters of mission agencies and missionaries. In the late eighteenth and early nineteenth century, women organized societies for the support of missionaries like William and Dorothy Carey and Ann and Adoniram Judson. In 1800, Mary Webb (1779–1861) organized the Boston Female Society for Missionary Purposes that included both Baptist and Congregational women in its membership. The Female Missionary Society of Richmond, Virginia was founded in 1814. Other such societies included the Female Baptist Society for Foreign Missions and the Black Swamp Female Foreign Mission Society.[27] Briefly stated, the cause of Baptist missions would have failed without the financial support of women, their promotion of the work of missionaries, and their own service as missionaries.

Baptist sending agencies like the BMS, and the American Baptist Foreign Mission Society generally only sent married women to the field, but in 1815, the ABFMS appointed Charlotte H. White (1782–1863), a widow, as the first single woman missionary. In 1850, the Foreign Mission Board of the SBC appointed Harriet Baker, a single woman, to Shanghai.[28] Her male colleagues opposed her presence and, consequently in 1853, a missionary physician diagnosed her slight cough as consumption, and she was forced to return to the United States. No single woman would be appointed again until 1871 when Edmonia Moon (1851–1908) was sent by the FMB to China.[29] The Board defended its refusal to appoint single women by citing several highly paternalistic reasons that, in its estimation, precluded such appointments:

> their unprotected condition in heathen lands—the difficulty and expense of their coming to Richmond to be examined—the difficulty of conducting the examination before the board—of

27. Barnes, *Southern Baptist Convention*, 141.
28. Bebbington, *Baptists Through the Centuries*, 224.
29. Cullather, "Laborers Are Few," box 785.

supervising their outfit and embarkation and the danger of their being incited to the work by romantic and immature views.[30]

Two women, one married and one single, serve as stellar examples of the work of women in foreign missions and provide incontrovertible evidence that women were as capable as men of international mission service. Ann Judson served as a missionary to Burma from 1813 until her death in 1826 at the young age of thirty-eight. During this relatively brief span of time, she learned the Burmese language, began a small school for girls, developed a friendship with the wife of the local viceroy, and translated the books of Daniel and Jonah into Burmese. She also was the first Protestant missionary to translate a portion of Scripture, the Gospel of Matthew, into the Thai language. In addition, she published an account of the American mission in Burma and used the proceeds to free Burmese girls from servitude.[31]

Appointed to China in 1873, Lottie Moon (1840–1912) eventually became an iconic name in the annals of Baptist mission history, perhaps achieving greater name recognition than most any other Baptist missionaries except for William Carey and the Judsons. Focusing her energies in rural areas of China in Shandong province, she sent accounts of her work to Southern Baptists in the United States. Her reports and letters chronicled her maturation from that of a recent arrival who objectified the Chinese people to that of a seasoned veteran who understood their struggles and empathized with their plight.[32] The Woman's Missionary Union of the Southern Baptist Convention would respond to her appeal for an offering for missionaries, establishing the Lottie Moon Offering for Foreign Missions in the late nineteenth century. The focus that Ann Judson and Lottie Moon placed upon education and raising the status of women in both Burma and China would have a profound effect upon the future work of missionaries, women, and men alike.

Twentieth-Century Baptist Mission Efforts

Baptists in Western Europe and North America entered the twentieth century with optimism about the possibilities that it brought for mission

30. Minutes, Foreign Mission Board of the Southern Baptist Convention, July 4, 1859. Manuscript Collection, FMB, Richmond.

31. Robert, *American Women in Mission*, 44–46.

32. Harper, *Send the Light*, xii–xiii.

advancement and accomplishment. The underlying assumption on the part of most Western missionary-sending agencies was that the Christian faith would soon emerge as the dominant religion of the world. Coupled with this assumption was the subtle racist ideology of Anglo-Saxon supremacy that emerged because of the fears of immigration from Eastern Europe in the late nineteenth and early twentieth centuries. Josiah Strong published *Our Country: Its Possible Future and Its Present Crisis* in 1885, warning of the threat of immigration to the advancement of Anglo-Saxon ideals.

This optimistic attitude toward world evangelization was tempered considerably by the outbreak of World War I and by the emergence of the racist ideology of Anglo-Saxon supremacy. James Franklin Love (1859–1928), corresponding secretary for the Foreign Mission Board of the SBC, argued in 1920 that the evangelization of the world would be accomplished more rapidly if the aggressive white races were evangelized first. He defended his desire to increase the number of missionaries in Europe and to reduce the number of missionaries in the rest of the world with the following words:

> Let us not forget that it is to the white man God gave the instinct and talent to disseminate His ideals among other people and that he did not, to the same degree give this instinct and talent to the yellow, brown, or black race. The white race only has the genius to introduce Christianity into all lands and among all people.[33]

While other missionary-sending agencies may not have touted the perceived genius of Anglo-Saxons so boldly, nevertheless the confidence of Western Europeans and Americans in their own cultural and religious superiority resulted in an increasing number of missionary appointments throughout much of the century. Motivations to missionary service are difficult to assess. Certainly, many Western Baptist missionaries entered career mission service with pure motivations, driven by a commitment to sharing the gospel with the world. At the same time, cultural motivations, while less obvious, had profound influence.

The British Missionary Society intensified its efforts in India, West and Central Africa, the Caribbean, and China and began new work in Latin America. Northern and Southern Baptists expanded their work in

---

33. Love, *Appeal*, 14–15. Love added that "this is not a ground for spiritual pride nor of contempt for any colored race. It is a solemn fact."

Asia, Africa, and Latin America. By 1980, some five thousand missionaries were serving under appointment by the Foreign Mission Board of the Southern Baptist Convention, and it had become the largest missionary-sending agency in the world.

A number of global realities spurred these appointments. At the end of World War II, Baptists responded to Douglas MacArthur's call for missionaries in Japan and, at the end of the Korean War, the missionary presence in South Korea increased. By the mid-1970s, mission strategists described South Korea as the most responsive country to the Christian faith in the world. Mao Tse-tung's victory over the Nationalist forces and the creation of the People's Republic in China resulted in the expansion of a Baptist missionary presence in the rest of Asia. The new Communist government expelled missionaries from China in 1949 and missionaries undertook new work, primarily with displaced Chinese in such areas as Hong Kong, Taiwan, the Philippines, Malaysia, Singapore, and other parts of East and Southeast Asia. Eventually this work expanded beyond only the Chinese who had fled the Communist revolution.

European Baptists created the European Baptist Mission in 1954. Its first members were the Baptist unions of Germany, France, and Switzerland. Each of these unions had carried out missionary efforts prior to 1954 and primarily in Africa. In an effort to overcome the divisions of World War II, they combined their efforts to form the new Mission. In 2010, it became EBM International, and twenty-six Baptist unions from Europe, Latin America, and Africa are now members. Its work includes about eighty-five development and mission projects in Africa, Latin America, and India.[34] It continues to appoint European missionaries and staff to work both in Europe and beyond.

The decade of the 1960s was a watershed moment in Baptist mission history though it was hardly noticed at the time by the major Baptist missionary sending agencies. The growth of Baptist denominations in particular, and of the Christian faith in general in such countries as Korea, India, Brazil, and the Philippines occurred at the same time that the relaxation of immigration laws, numerous technological advances, and inexpensive air travel made it possible for people to move around the world easily, either by choice or by necessity. Samuel Escobar (b. 1934) has documented this increased mobility of Christian peoples from all

34. Rosner, "European Baptist Mission."

regions of the world as well as the resulting theological and missiological implications:

> The *migration model* that has functioned admirably through the centuries is also an avenue for mission in our days. Migrants from poor countries who travel in search of economic survival carry the Christian message and missionary initiative with them. Moravians from Curazao moved to Holland, Jamaican Baptists emigrated to England, Haitian believers went to Canada, Filipina Christian women go to Muslim countries, and Latin American evangelicals are going to Japan, Australia, and the United States.[35]

The globe shrank in the sixties, as the primary means of transportation for missionaries became planes instead of boats. About this same time, many Western nations opened their borders to immigrants from various parts of the world. Control of Baptist denominational work in various countries shifted from Western missionaries to local Baptists who insisted upon control of the work in their own contexts. This postcolonial world became the source of a powerful global vision for Baptists beyond the West that has exploded onto the world scene.

This pivotal decade served as the climax of the work of Western missionary agencies and the missionaries that they have sent. Their work should be affirmed for the powerful role they played in carrying the gospel of Jesus Christ to the world. Christianity became a major world religion, and because of their work, now claims about one-third of the world's population among its followers. The structures and methodologies that they put in place were highly effective in a world that valued pragmatism, denominationalism, doctrinal conformity, and carefully structured worship and practice.

The pooling of denominational resources allowed for the sending of missionaries to the ends of the earth at a time in which travel was difficult and unaffordable. These missionaries carried with them the best and the worst of Western cultural traditions. Robert Woodberry has recently documented the ways in which the work of Protestant missionaries resulted in the establishment of democratic governments around the world, largely because of the evangelical focus upon individual rights,

---

35. Escobar, *New Global Mission*, 67–68.

the defense of religious liberty and the emphasis upon education for the purpose of understanding scripture.[36]

With the decline in loyalty to denominations, many Baptist mission-sending agencies have implemented cost-cutting measures, including bringing missionaries home from the field and reducing the number of appointments that they can make. At the same time, Baptist churches around the world have taken center stage as the leaders of a new era in global missions. In the United States in particular, millions of local Baptist church members are now participating in short-term mission experiences around the world and partnering with Baptist churches and other institutions in Africa, Asia, Latin America, and even in the Middle East.[37] The future of Baptist global mission efforts will be largely dependent upon the effective cultivation of networks of global Baptists who are able to bring various assets to the table that can be leveraged to transform global communities and to share the gospel all over the world.

The Future of Baptist Missions

Walbert Bühlmann (1916–2007), a Swiss Roman-Catholic missiologist, has divided global mission history into three distinct stages or Churches. The First Church was the Eastern Church that shaped the growth and expansion of Christianity in its first millennium. The Second Church has been the Western Church that has shaped that expansion through most of the second millennium. Now the Third Church, generally understood to be the church of the Southern and Eastern hemispheres, stands poised to take its place as the missionary center of the future.[38]

In 2007, I visited the Mae La refugee camp in Thailand. The camp has been the home of Karen refugees from Burma for more than thirty years as the Karen have fled oppression and persecution by the Burmese government. Hugely Baptist due to the work of the Judsons, the Karen are a deeply committed Christian minority whose future looked very bleak until about 2005 when several countries agreed to receive Karen refugees

36. Woodberry, "Missionary Roots," 244–45. This chapter has already drawn attention to the debilitating effects of Anglo-Saxon supremacy upon missionary attitudes and mission strategies.

37. Priest et al., "Researching the Short Term Mission," 432. This excellent essay traces the rapid growth of short-term mission experiences (under four weeks) in the United States.

38. Bühlmann, *Coming of the Third Church*.

and assist them to gain citizenship. I was visiting Mae La to consider ways in which a US missionary-sending agency, the Cooperative Baptist Fellowship, might assist the Karen in their integration into American cities and towns.[39] From my perspective, I was there to help a group of poor refugees who had lost everything and who were fortunate to receive the assistance of governments, missionary agencies, and other social services to relocate, find jobs, and establish their own churches and homes in a new land.

We gathered with the self-governing Karen Council in a small room at the camp. I wanted to hear from the Council about its hopes and dreams in the resettlement. I expected words of appreciation and thanks and expressions of relief about how happy the refugees were to resettle after so many years. Instead, I found a group of Baptist Christians celebrating the opportunity that they had been given by God to carry the gospel of Jesus Christ to the ends of the earth. They told me the Karen story of Adoniram Judson who had shared the gospel with the Karen on an evangelistic tour of Burma in 1831.

Upon resettlement, their Baptist connection led them to Baptist churches in the United States, England, and other European countries where they joined local congregations in huge numbers, refusing to become mission churches in the basement. In turn, their deep commitment to such practices as singing, tithing, worship, and evangelism led to the rejuvenation of many United States and European Baptist congregations.

The next two hundred years of Baptist mission history will rest solidly in the hands of this Third Church. It is now the most creative and expansive Baptist missionary force in the world. The Baptists of this Church will provide the missionary force of the future. Baptists in such contexts as Brazil, South Korea, India, Southeast Asia, Nigeria, Uganda, the Middle East and North Africa, Kazakhstan, Uzbekistan, Moldova, Romania, Hungary, Russia, and a host of other locations, have revolutionized mission theology, methodology, and practice by creating innovative centers for missionary training and by sending missionaries across international borders. Often these missionaries go with few resources but with enormous conviction and determination to carry the gospel of Jesus Christ to the world, including to the now spiritually depleted European and North American Second Church.

39. The Cooperative Baptist Fellowship was formed in 1991 in the wake of increasing tensions in the SBC over biblical inerrancy and the ordination of women. It now has about 90 US missionaries serving in some 30 countries.

Perhaps most importantly, the Third Church in its Baptist expression, moves into the new millennium with a deep missiological understanding of its calling, one that is shaped by the weight of two-hundred years of Western Baptist mission history and yet unhindered by it. The Third Church beckons the Baptist tradition toward renewed spirituality and deeper convictions about mission. Karen Baptists influence the worship and practices of Baptist churches in the United States. Brazilian Baptist students travel to Sub-Saharan Africa with nothing but a backpack and a Bible. Baptists from Syria, Jordan and Iraq gather to train at a seminary in the Middle East. Vietnamese Baptists form a Bible School in the rainforest for a time and then quickly disband. A ministry training center in Moldova prepares Baptist church planters for work in Kazakhstan and Uzbekistan. Filipina Baptist domestic servants teach Scripture and music to Middle Eastern children. Ugandan Baptists minister to refugees in Uganda and then ensure that they relocate to places where the gospel can take root and grow. The largest Baptist church in the United Kingdom is now a church of West African Baptists. In all these ways, the diaspora mission of the Third Church is the foundation of Baptist mission in a new day.

Perhaps more than any other Protestant tradition, Baptists have shaped the global mission movement over the last 250 years. This chapter expresses the full cycle of the Baptist missionary movement across those years. Black Baptists in the Caribbean who were formerly slaves in the United States served as the very first Baptist missionaries and shared a vision for their own context that was significant enough to result in the sending of missionaries to West Africa. British Baptists, stirred by the fires of the Evangelical Awakening in England, provided the theological justification for world mission, the structure for its implementation, and many of its first missionaries. White Baptists in the United States, motivated by the accomplishments of British Baptist missionaries and utilizing British methodologies, would establish some of the largest missionary-sending boards and agencies of the nineteenth and twentieth centuries. As a result, a huge portion of the world received the gospel and embraced it. Influenced by these new contexts, the gospel took on deeper theological and missiological expression, shedding some of its European and American ethos. Now, the gospel moves from everywhere to everyone, as Samuel Escobar has expressed it, enabling Baptists from Asia, Africa, and South and Central America to transform the old missionary-sending cultures who gave birth to the Baptist mission movement in the first place and to engage in new forms of mission in ways its founders could never have imagined.

Bibliography

Barnes, William Wright. *The Southern Baptist Convention, 1845–1953*. Nashville, TN: Broadman, 1954.

Bebbington, David W. *Baptists Through the Centuries: A History of a Global People*. Waco, TX: Baylor University Press, 2010.

Bühlmann, Walbert. *The Coming of the Third Church*. Maryknoll: Orbis, 1977.

Carey, William. *An Enquiry into the Obligations of Christians to Use Means for the Conversion of the Heathen*. Leicester, UK: Ann Ireland and Other, 1792.

Cullather, Nick. "Laborers Are Few: Southern Baptist Missionaries in China, 1846–1865." Unpublished Manuscript, International Mission Board Manuscript Collection, Box 785.

Escobar, Samuel. *The New Global Mission: The Gospel from Everywhere to Everyone*. Downers Grove, IL: InterVarsity, 2003.

Fitts, Leroy. *A History of Black Baptists*. Nashville, TN: Broadman, 1985.

Hall, Thelma Wolfe. *I Give Myself: The Story of J. Lewis Shuck and His Mission to the Chinese*. Richmond: Thelma Wolfe Hall, 1983.

Harper, Keith, ed. *Send the Light: Lottie Moon's Letters and Other Writings*. Macon, GA: Mercer University Press, 2002.

Leonard, Bill J. *Baptist Ways: A History*. Valley Forge: Judson, 2003.

Love, James Franklin. *The Appeal of the Baptist Program for Europe*. Richmond: Foreign Mission Board of the Southern Baptist Convention, 1920.

Martin, Sandy D. *Black Baptists and African Missions: The Origins of a Movement, 1880–1915*. Macon, GA: Mercer University Press, 1989.

Nash, Robert N., Jr. *The Influence of American Mythology on Southern Baptist Foreign Missions, 1845–1945*. PhD diss., The Southern Baptist Theological Seminary, 1989.

"Our History: Embracing Global Mission Since 1874." https://web.archive.org/web/20190524055242/https://www.cbmin.org/our-story/our-history/.

Poe, William A. "Lott Cary: Man of Purchased Freedom." *Church History* 66 (1970) 49–61.

Priest, Robert J., et al. "Researching the Short Term Mission Movement." *Missiology* 34 (2006) 431–50.

Ray, T. Bronson. *Southern Baptist Foreign Missions*. Nashville, TN: Sunday School Board of the Southern Baptist Convention, 1910.

Robert, Dane L. *American Women in Mission: A Social History of Their Thought and Practice*. Macon, GA: Mercer University, 1996.

Rosler, Klaus. "European Baptist Mission Is Now Called EBM International." https://web.archive.org/web/20200131004747/http://www.ebf.org/european-baptist-mission-is-now-called-ebm-international.

Rouse, Ruth. "William Carey's 'Pleasing Dream.'" *International Review of Mission* 38 (1949) 181–92.

Russell, Horace O. "A Question of Indigenous Mission: The Jamaican Baptist Missionary Society." *Baptist Quarterly* 25 (1973) 86–93.

Stanley, Brian. *The History of the Baptist Missionary Society, 1792–1992*. Edinburgh: T. & T. Clark, 1992.

Torbet, Robert G. *Venture of Faith: The Story of the American Baptist Foreign Mission Society and the Woman's American Baptist Foreign Mission Society, 1814–1954*. Philadelphia: Judson, 1955.

Woodberry, Robert D. "The Missionary Roots of Liberal Democracy." *American Political Science Review* 106 (2012) 244–74.

C. Baptist Teachings

4

Baptism

Anthony R. Cross

(May 1, 1962—July 22, 2021)

For Baptists, faith and practice is grounded in Christ as witnessed to in the New Testament, and this is why, from their beginning, they sought to recover the New Testament church as the baptized community, in which there were *no* unbaptized believers (1 Cor 12:13). John's baptism of repentance and confession (Matt 3:1–2, and Acts 19:4) was the precursor of Christian baptism, anticipating the gift of the Spirit at Pentecost in fulfillment of the Baptist's prophecy (Matt 3:11). In his baptism Jesus identified himself with humanity (Matt 3:13–17).

The origins of Christian baptism is Christ's command (hence "ordinance") to "Go and make disciples of all nations, baptizing . . . and teaching them" (Matt 28:19; cf. Mark 16:16), and in the primitive, apostolic church it was an integral part of the *kerygma*. All who repented and accepted Christ were baptized immediately (e.g., Acts 8:12; 8:36–38; 10:44–48; 16:14–15; 18:8) and were assured of the forgiveness of their sins and the gift of the life-giving Spirit (Acts 2:38, 41). New Testament baptism was conversion-baptism into the Trinity, and new converts were discipled in their faith in what they should believe (doctrine) and how they should "live a new life" (ethics, cf. Rom 6:3–4). Baptism is, therefore, inseparably linked with discipleship, and whether baptism is administered before any teaching can take place, it must be followed by a life of learning and following Christ.

Because baptism is an ordinance of Christ and the God-ordained response to the preaching of the gospel, it is not an optional extra, but the initial, faithful response to the gospel. In the New Testament Spirit and water baptism were the humanward and Godward dimensions of becoming a Christian (Acts 2:38; 1 Cor 12:13; John 3:5), but they were separated in the fourth century. We should, then, avoid the spirit-matter dualism characteristic of the Hellenistic world, and restore a healthy view of God as creator and matter as the means in and through which he works for the salvation of his bodily creation, humanity, something he has done through the incarnation. With this understanding of the goodness of God's creation and the way he uses ordinary, material means as vehicles of his grace we can see that baptism becomes the meeting place of the initiating divine-human encounter, the grace of God meeting the faith of the repentant believer.

Though the first Baptists baptized by affusion/pouring, they quickly realized that the Greek word that gives us baptism/baptize means "to dip, to plunge," that is, total immersion, expressing the dying and rising of the Lord Jesus: both Philip and the Ethiopian eunuch "went *down* into the water" (Acts 8:38), while Jesus "went *up* out of the water" (Matt 3:16). The physical act of going down into the water and then being raised up from it provides baptism with its powerful symbolism and makes it a visible word. Paul uses this symbolism of a watery grave to show us that "all of us who were baptized into Christ Jesus were baptized into his death" and were "buried with him through baptism into death in order that, just as Christ was raised from the dead . . . we too may live a new life" (Rom 6:3–4). It also ties in with baptism in the New Testament being the occasion where the forgiveness of sins are first experienced (Acts 2:38) and its washing us clean (Acts 22:16; 1 Cor 6:11; Eph 5:26) by the working of the Spirit (Titus 3:5).

Yet baptism is more than a symbol, it is an *effective* symbol. The understanding of baptism as an ordinance does not prevent it from also being a sacrament. In fact, these two understandings are complementary, a sacrament being a divinely appointed *means of grace*. New Testament baptism is faith-baptism, and this is clearly shown in the fact that the full range of the gifts of salvation that are attributed to faith in the New Testament are also attributed to baptism: forgiveness, cf. Rom 4:5–8 with Acts 2:38; justification, cf. Rom. 3:28 with 1 Cor 6:11; union with Christ, cf. Eph 3:17 with Gal 3:27; being crucified with Christ, cf. Gal 2:19–20 with Rom 6:2–11; death and resurrection, cf. Rom 8:12–13 with Col 2:12;

sonship, cf. John 1:12 with Gal 3:26–27; the Holy Spirit, cf. Gal 3:2–5, 13–14 with Acts 2:38 and 1 Cor 12:13; entry into the church, cf. Gal 3:6–7 with Gal 3:27; regeneration and life, cf. John 3:14–16, 20:31 with John 3:5 and Titus 3:5; the kingdom and eternal life, cf. Mark 10:15 and John 3:14–16 with 1 Cor 6:9–11; and salvation, Rom 1:16 and John 3:16 with 1 Pet 3:21. However, this is *not* to succumb to the idea that baptism acts mechanically—from our perspective faith is *always* essential, otherwise the actions are meaningless. Any suggestion of the automatic operation of baptism is excluded in 1 Pet 3:21, where we read that "baptism now saves you," but it is "not the removal of dirt" as happens in an ordinary bath, but "the pledge/prayer of a good conscience towards God." In fact, "It saves . . . by the resurrection of Jesus Christ." Elsewhere, Paul tells us that we are "saved . . . through the washing of rebirth and renewal/ regeneration by the Holy Spirit" who is poured out through Jesus Christ so that "having been justified by his grace, we might become heirs having the hope of eternal life" (Titus 3:5–7; regeneration is Paul's expression for what John records as rebirth/birth from above, see John 3:3 and 5).

Baptism normally takes place in the baptistery in a church build-ing, but it can also take place in a river, lake or the sea, wherever there is water. When this is not possible, and, for example in drought areas, valid baptisms have been performed where there is no water at all, or, if only a little water is available, baptism can be performed by affusion. As baptism is into the name of the Trinity (Matt 28:19), this baptismal formula is spoken at the moment of immersion, but it is more than this. It is a Semi-tism that means that in baptism a person is brought into an existence that is fundamentally determined and ruled by the triune God. Use of the trinitarian formula is not at odds with the testimony of Acts that the earliest baptisms were into the name of "Jesus Christ" (e.g., Acts 10:48; Rom 6:3; Gal 3:27) or "the Lord Jesus" (e.g., Acts 8:16, 19:5), because the Persons of the Trinity cannot be divided, and to be baptized into Christ is to be baptized into the triune God. There are some who baptize "into the name of (the Lord) Jesus Christ," and this is quite legitimate. The norm for Baptists appears to be a single act of immersion using the trinitar-ian formula, but it can equally follow the ancient practice of a threefold immersion with each person of the Trinity named at the corresponding immersion.

Baptism is an occasion where the baptized believers profess/confess their faith in Christ (Rom 10:9–10; 1 Tim 6:12), and this is why the bap-tized believers either respond to questions and/or give their testimony of how they came to faith in Christ. First Tim 6:12 shows us that this normally happened "in the presence of many witnesses," so baptismal services are not private affairs, but usually take place in the context of the church's worship and often this will include many non-Christians, so providing an evangelistic opportunity for the declaration of the gospel.

This raises the question of the age for baptism. From what we have seen of the New Testament's faith-baptism it is not age that determines whether someone should be baptized, but whether they have come to faith in Christ. Many Baptists insist that baptism should not be administered until teenage years, sometimes early (thirteen or fourteen), sometimes later (seventeen or eighteen). But this upper age range changes baptism altogether from believer's baptism to adult baptism. Many people become Christians before their teenage years—sometimes earlier. If this is the case then, as far as the New Testament is concerned, they are eligible for baptism. To separate baptism from conversion is to depart from New Testament baptism. However, the younger the child the more complicated matters become pastorally, requiring knowledge of the young person, discernment as to whether their request comes from a true commitment to Christ or from peer pressure, the desire for attention or some other reason. If the young person comes from a Christian family, then the pastoral decision is more straight forward than if the young person comes from a family where either one or neither of the parents are believers. In all such cases, the pastor and the church need to consult with the parents and the candidates themselves before the decision to baptize is taken. There might also be legal reasons why care needs to be taken. There are other reasons often given as to why baptism should be postponed. If it is because "they are too young to be baptized," then the answer is "if they are old enough to believe in Christ, they are old enough to be baptized." If it is "because it will mean more to them when they are older," this is to divorce baptism from conversion, and it thereby becomes something other than New Testament baptism. Sometimes young people are deterred from baptism on the grounds that they might backslide, but this is true of anyone at any age in life. Since Baptists ground their theology and practice in the New Testament, we must seek to be faithful to it even when Baptist tradition says something different.

Baptism normally takes place within the church's worship also shows us that baptism has a corporate dimension—it is not just an individual's act. According to Paul, "we [are] all baptized by one Spirit into one body" (1 Cor 12:13) and enter God's family ("children of God through faith in

Christ Jesus," Gal 3:26). Baptism is the initiating rite through which we enter the church. Here Baptists have frequently understood baptism in covenantal terms. We are in covenant relationship with the triune God, and in and through this relationship we are in covenantal relationship with all other members of the body of Christ. This is a great privilege, but with it comes responsibility to be fully committed to the work of Christ in the local church. This is why Baptists, who are antipaedobaptists, have frequently practiced closed membership—though there have always been Baptists who have not excluded others who understand baptism differently to ourselves (i.e., infant baptism). In New Testament times, however, when all believers were conversion-baptized, it was true that baptism was initiatory into the body of Christ, the church, but as soon as baptism is separated from conversion (by paedobaptists who put it before conversion, and by most Baptists who put it after conversion) then it becomes less easy for us to claim the fullness of the New Testament theology of baptism for our baptismal practice because it is different from that of the earliest church.

For many years Christians have understood conversion to be punctiliar, happening at a specific, datable moment in time. But for such a widespread view the records of the conversions in the book of Acts have always been problematic. Which is the normative order of conversion: repentance, water baptism, forgiveness, and reception of the Spirit (Acts 2:28, 41); or believing, water baptism, the laying on of hands, and reception of the Spirit (Acts 8:12–17); or reception of the Spirit, speaking in tongues, and water baptism (Acts 10:44–48); or believing, and water baptism (Acts 16:31–33); or believing, water baptism, laying on of hands, reception of the Spirit, and speaking in tongues (Acts 19:1–6; see also 9:17–18; 22:16)? But when we recognize that becoming a Christian is a process, a journey, that is conversion-initiation, such questions lose their relevance, as the sovereign activity of the Spirit of God is recognized in the various ways the Spirit works in bringing people to new life in Christ.

For an increasing number of Baptists, Christian initiation is expressed in the liturgy of baptism, acceptance into membership of the local church, and the eucharist. This pattern can take place in a single service, or in a morning then evening service on the same Sunday or over two Sundays. However, expressing a pattern of initiation is not possible when baptism has been separated from conversion by a period that can extend from several months to decades, or when believers participate in the Lord's supper before they have been baptized. This is most clearly seen in open membership churches, but is not uncommon in closed membership churches, not least because the majority of Baptists have separated baptism from conversion both in time and liturgically. Also, while Christian initiation in paedobaptist churches begins with infant baptism, Baptists have a service for the blessing/presentation/dedication of their children in which thanks is given to God for the life of the child, prayers are offered for the child, their growth into Christian faith, and for their parents, and promises are made by the parents and the local church to continue to pray for and nurture the child in the Christian faith.

Many Baptist churches have baptismal candidates wear white robes, the symbolism of which is linked to baptism as the cleansing/washing from sin, while others have them wear their ordinary, day-to-day clothes symbolizing that they are committing the whole of their day-to-day lives to Christ. But the change of clothing for baptism reminds us that the Christian's new life is to be lived according to God's ways. We recall that in baptism we "clothe ourselves with Christ" (Gal 3:27; Col 2:11–12), but, when linked to Christ's death and resurrection and our death to our old lives and resurrection to new life in Christ, it also reminds us that, as baptized believers, we have "put away [our] former way of life, [our] old self" and are to "clothe [ourselves] with the new self" (Eph 4:22, 24), because "in Christ," we are "a new creation," the old has gone and the new has come (2 Cor 5:17; cf. Col 3:5–11 with verses 12–17). Baptism, then, has ethical implications: those in Christ are to live the baptized Christian life (cf. Rom 6:1–11).

Building on this, the church as the baptized community is a witness to the gospel of Christ in that it shows that here, in contrast to the world, is an image of the way the world was intended to be and can be when Christ is Lord, for here there are no worldly divisions between race, social class, or sex, for all are "one in Christ" (Gal 3:26–28; cf. 1 Cor 12:12–13), the new community of brothers and sisters, and here a new, counter-cultural way of life is lived (cf. Matt 5–7).

Eph 4:4–6 sets out seven essential onenesses for the people of God, and baptism's inclusion here shows how important it is, more important than is often recognized by Baptists. So often, Baptists focus simply on the subjects of baptism (believers) and the mode of baptism (immersion) so that they fail to do justice to the richness of New Testament baptism. Often Paul's statement in 1 Cor 1:17 is taken to justify this position and is interpreted to mean that preaching the gospel is more important. But this fails to do justice to what Paul is saying here and what the rest of the

New Testament says about baptism. In 1 Cor 1 and 3 Paul is opposing the disunity of the Corinthian church in which different key figures (Paul, Apollos, Cephas, and Christ) and baptism by them were being used as an excuse and justification for the divisions in the church. But, as Paul shows later in 1 Cor 12:13 and Eph 4:5, a proper theology of baptism is integral to Christian life and witness. Its importance is nowhere more clearly seen than in the fact that Jesus commands it as one of the two aspects of making disciples (Matt 28:19), and in the New Testament church it was an essential part of the preaching of the gospel (e.g., Acts 2:38, 41).

Bibliography

Beasley-Murray, George R. *Baptism in the New Testament*. London: Macmillan, 1962.

Colwell, John E. *Promise and Presence: An Exploration of Sacramental Theology*. Milton Keynes: Paternoster, 2005.

Cross, Anthony R. *Baptism and the Baptists: Theology and Practice in Twentieth-Century Britain*. Carlisle: Paternoster, 2000.

———. *Recovering the Evangelical Sacrament: Baptisma Semper Reformandum*. Eugene, OR: Pickwick, 2013.

Fowler, Stanley K. *More Than a Symbol: The British Baptist Recovery of Baptismal Sacramentalism*. Carlisle: Paternoster, 2002.

Schreiner, Thomas R., and Shawn D. Wright, eds., *Believer's Baptism: Sign of the New Covenant in Christ*. Nashville, TN: Broadman & Holman, 2006.

5

Eucharist

Steven R. Harmon

Baptists regard the Eucharist, or "Lord's Supper," as one of the two central sacraments or "ordinances" of the church. While the term Eucharist (from the Greek word for "thanksgiving") is not unknown among Baptists, they most commonly refer to it as the "Lord's Supper," taking the use of that designation in 1 Cor 11:20 as their biblical precedent. They have called this act both a "sacrament" and an "ordinance." In their early confessions of faith Baptists referred to both the supper and baptism as "sacraments" in the sense that they represent not merely human actions, but acts in which God graciously transforms human lives. When later in their history many Baptists have expressed a preference for "ordinance," it has been to underscore the status of these acts as instituted by Christ himself and sometimes to differentiate their perspective on these acts from what they may perceive as understandings of the sacraments in terms of the mechanistic dispensing of divine grace. This more recent preference for "ordinance" has its origins in British Baptist reactions against the mid-nineteenth-century Oxford Movement within the Church of England, reactions that influenced Baptists in North America and elsewhere. Nevertheless, many Baptists in Great Britain, North America, and beyond have since the last half of the twentieth century advocated for the recovery of "sacrament" as term for the Lord's Supper and as a theological category for understanding its significance.

The typical Baptist rite of the Lord's Supper itself is strongly scriptural, emphasizing the reading of the biblical words of institution. This places the supper within a narrative framework that highlights its anamnetic character: by means of the supper worshipers who share in it not only remember events from the salvific history of the work of Christ but also participate in those events as present realities, made present in the celebration of the supper. While the pastor normally presides at Baptist celebrations of the supper, Baptists do not link their encounter with the risen Christ in the supper with a sacramental office of ministry that makes the celebration of the supper a valid Eucharist. Rather, they view the table as the Lord's table and the gathered congregation as the celebrants. In many Baptist churches the elements are distributed by deacons to the members of the congregation, who then pass the paten and chalice (or sometimes individual communion cups) to each other, serving the bread and wine to one another. Baptists will sometimes point to this practice as an embodiment of their theological account of the connections between church, ministry, sacrament, and the presence of Christ that associates the representative role of the minister presiding at the supper with the whole gathered congregation that makes the risen Christ present as his body under his rule.

Baptists thus affirm that Christ is really present in the celebration of the Lord's Supper, but they do not explain this presence in terms of a transformation of the underlying substance of the elements of bread and wine. They maintain that Christ is present with, in, and as the body of Christ in the form of the gathered congregation celebrating the supper, and they also generally acknowledge that the celebration of the supper draws the members of the church into a deepened awareness of the presence of Christ. Baptists have tended to embrace the Zwinglian option among the main Eucharistic theologies that stem from the Protestant Reformation: that is, the supper functions as a memorial meal recalling Christ's saving acts, and the bread and the wine function as symbols of the body and blood of Christ. The table used for the service of the Lord's Supper in many Baptist worship spaces will underscore this understanding of the supper's significance with words engraved on the congregation-facing side of the table from the Lukan institution narrative: "Do this in remembrance of me" (Luke 22:19).

Yet for Baptists the remembering function of the supper is not merely a matter of cognition, for it makes present the drama of Christ's saving work and draws worshipers to participate in this drama, and the symbolic nature of the elements does not mean that they are devoid of real connections with the realities they signify. Nor is the Lord's Supper merely a human action undertaken in obedience to Jesus's instructions to observe it. Baptists who believe that the proclamation of the word in the form of a sermon or homily is not merely a human action but one through which God acts transformatively in the lives of those hear and heed it, and thus have an appreciation for the sacramentality of the word, are able to recognize that through the Lord's Supper as well God acts through the Holy Spirit to transform the lives of those who share in it and from it receive spiritual nourishment. In summary, Baptists define Christ's presence in the supper (1) as an *ecclesial* presence, through the church as the gathered body of Christ; (2) as an *anamnetic* presence, through the narrative re-presentation of Christ's saving work; and (3) as a *pneumatic* presence, through the Holy Spirit's presence with and transformation of the members of the church who celebrate the supper together. Because the bread and wine have acquired new significance through these ecclesial, anamnetic, and pneumatic associations with divine presence, Baptists will dispose of the bread and wine that remains after the celebration of the supper with reverence, but they do not hold it theologically necessary to consume the remaining wine or reserve the remaining bread.

In addition to "Lord's Supper," Baptists frequently refer to the Eucharist as "communion." This designation has theological significance for them in light of 1 Cor 10:16, which refers to the cup and bread as "sharing" or "participation" in the blood and body of Christ. The celebration of the supper draws the members of the church into closer communion with Christ and with one another. Thus the supper also is an expression of and motivation toward the unity of the body of Christ, and even a means by which ecclesial unity may be strengthened: the unity of the elements of the supper and the unity of the church are interrelated, for those who partake of "one bread" constitute "one body" (1 Cor 10:17). This connection between the Eucharist and the unity of the church is embodied in the practice of most (but by no means all) Baptist congregations worldwide of "open communion" in which all believers in Christ, whether Baptists or members of other Christian churches, are invited to share in the Lord's table. According to this understanding of the relation between Eucharist and unity, the already-present spiritual unity of the body of Christ is the precondition for unity at the table. In the minority of Baptist churches that still practice "closed communion" in which only members of Baptist churches are invited to share in the supper, a concern for the unity of the church is still maintained, though differently: for these churches, church-dividing doctrinal differences must be overcome as a precondition for full Eucharistic communion. Thus within the larger fellowship of Baptists there exist the same basic differences over the proper extent of the practice of Eucharistic hospitality that currently mark the whole church, but in this divergence is a Baptist consensus that there must be a connection between ecclesial unity and Eucharistic unity.

Bibliography

Anglican Consultative Council and Baptist World Alliance. *Conversations Around the World 2000–2005: The Report of the International Conversations between the Anglican Communion and the Baptist World Alliance.* London: Anglican Communion Office, 2005.

Baptist Union of Great Britain and Ireland. "The Baptist Doctrine of the Church." In *The Baptist Union: A Short History,* by Ernest A. Payne, 283–89. London: Carey Kingsgate, 1958.

Baptist World Alliance and Catholic Church. "The Word of God in the Life of the Church: A Report of International Conversations between the Catholic Church and the Baptist World Alliance 2006–2010." *American Baptist Quarterly* 31 (2012) 28–122.

Baptist World Alliance and Lutheran World Federation. "A Message to Our Churches." In *Growth in Agreement II: Reports and Agreed Statements of Ecumenical Conversations on a World Level, 1982–1998,* edited by Jeffrey Gros et al., 155–75. Faith and Order Paper no. 187. Geneva: WCC, 2000.

Baptist World Alliance and Mennonite World Conference. "Theological Conversations, 1989–1992." In *Growth in Agreement II: Reports and Agreed Statements of Ecumenical Conversations on a World Level, 1982–1998,* edited by Gros, Jeffrey et al., 426–48. Faith and Order Paper no. 187. Geneva: WCC Publications, 2000.

Swarat, Uwe. "Die baptistische Lehre im Spiegel der ökumenischen Dialoge auf Weltebene." *Freikirchen Forschung* 24 (2015) 18–59.

Thurian, Max, ed. *Churches Respond to Baptism, Eucharist and Ministry.* 6 vols. Geneva: World Council of Churches, 1986–88.

6

Ministry

Steven R. Harmon

The rule of Christ in the congregation is the foundational principle upon which Baptists base their understanding of ministry in the church and of its relation to configurations of ecclesiastical and civil authority. It is rooted in the New Testament ecclesiological image of the church as the body of Christ that has Christ as its head (1 Cor 12:12–31; Col 2:19; 3:15; Eph 2:16; 4:4, 15–16; 5:29–30). Christ is the prototypical minister—the chief *episkopos* (overseer) of the church (1 Pet 2:25)—and the members of his body share in Christ's ministry, including his ministry of oversight. The church in Baptist understanding is the embodied community brought into existence by Christ that seeks to live together under the rule of Christ. As the body of Christ, the church has *koinonia* (fellowship or joint participation) with Christ, and thus with the Triune God, and with one another. Baptists have often given expression to this ecclesiology of participatory relationship under the rule of Christ through church covenants that specify their mutual obligations to God and one another as sharers of the ministry of Christ.

Though they are not alone in doing so, Baptists understand the whole membership of the church to have a participation in the *munus triplex* (threefold office) of Christ as prophet, priest, and king. Thus while God grants the church gifts of individual ministers who have distinctive roles of leadership in equipping the body of Christ to exercise its ministry (Eph 4:11–16), the whole membership of the church participates in Christ's prophetic ministry of proclaiming the word of God, his priestly ministry of reconciling people to God, and his kingly ministry of oversight (*episkopē*). While some Baptists, especially in the United States, have tended to associate their advocacy for liberty of conscience for all individuals with the concept of the priesthood of all believers that had been emphasized by the Protestant Reformers, its biblical basis in 1 Pet 2:9 suggested another connection to the early English Baptists. If according to that text the people of God constitute a "royal priesthood" or "kingdom of priests" (*basileion hierateuma*), then the church and all its members share in the kingly ministry of Christ as well. If only Christ is king in the realm of the conscience, then neither civil nor ecclesiastical authorities may coerce the conscience.

Yet the primary implication for Baptist ecclesiology of Christ's ministry as king has to do with the ministry of oversight (*episkopē*) in the church. For Baptists, this ministry is communal as well as personal, and local as well as trans-local. As an embodied community, the members of the church "watch over" one another. This ministry of mutual watch-care involves seeing to the needs of one another, spiritual as well as physical, and holding one another accountable in walking together under the rule of Christ. The ministry of communal oversight also includes the authority for the decisions the membership of the congregation must make from time to time in their quest to bring their life together under the rule of Christ, an authority that is located in the whole congregation. Baptists thus hold to what has been termed a "gathering church" ecclesiology, for which Matt 18:20 is an important biblical basis: "For where two or three are gathered in my name, I am there among them" (NRSV).

In their exercise of communal oversight, the members of Baptist congregations recognize among Christ's gifts to the church the gift of individual ministerial leaders, whom the members of the local church appoint as their pastors. These pastors exercise personal *episkopē* through preaching and teaching, leading worship, administering the sacraments (or ordinances) of baptism and the Eucharist (or Lord's Supper). This personal oversight is at the same time collegial, for the ordained pastoral ministers both offer their own convictions and insights and listen to those of other members of the congregation as they confer and make decisions about what the rule of Christ means for their life together. They also have a distinctive voice within this collegial effort to bring the life of the congregation under the rule of Christ, for by virtue of their theological education and connections with other ministers from other churches, Baptist and non-Baptist, they are able to lead the congregation to consider voices from the whole church extended through time and throughout the world today. In this way the Baptist exercise of *episkopē* fulfills one of the historic functions of the ministry of oversight: seeing to the unity of the church by relating the life of the local church to the life of the church in its ecumenicity.

While the primary location of communal and personal *episkopē* for Baptists is the local congregation, it also has a trans-local dimension. From their seventeenth-century beginnings through the present, Baptist congregations have organized themselves into associations of churches. Local Baptist churches are independent in the sense that no expression of church beyond the local church has authority over the decisions that the local church makes to bring its congregational life under the rule of Christ, but they also recognize that they are interdependent with other local churches. To paraphrase an expression from Reformed ecumenist Jean-Jacques von Allmen: a local Baptist church is wholly church, but it is not the whole church.[1] These associations of churches to which local Baptist churches belong include local or regional associations as well as national Baptist unions and the Baptist World Alliance, the world Christian communion to which the majority of national Baptist unions throughout the world belong. While these expressions of Baptist associations of churches do not exercise authority over independent local churches, the associations may also independently determine their membership and may remove from their membership a local church deemed not to be in a cooperative relationship with the association.

It should be clear from the preceding paragraphs that Baptists do not typically understand references to "bishops" (*episkopoi*) in the New Testament to imply a personal expression of the ministry of oversight beyond the local churches with authority over them. Baptists have traditionally held not to a "threefold" ministry, in which bishops or "overseers" whose ministry is trans-local are distinguished from the pastors (or elders or priests) and deacons whose ministries are in local congregations, but rather to a "twofold" ministry. The Baptist pattern of a "twofold" ministry is based on the twofold lists of qualifications for bishops and deacons in 1 Tim 3:1–13 and on the seeming equation of references to the titles and functions of bishops, elders, and pastors in Acts 20:17, 28, and 1 Pet 5:1–2. On this reading of the New Testament and the subsequent history of the early church, a trans-local role for bishops who oversee multiple

---

1. Allmen, "L'Église locale," 512.

local congregations is a development beyond New Testament Christianity. Yet Baptists throughout their history have recognized the need for some trans-local expression of personal *episkopē* to foster and serve the interdependence of local congregations. The English General Baptists of the seventeenth century appointed not only local church pastors but also ministers called "messengers" who had trans-local ministries. Contemporary Baptists in many settings have charged trans-local ministers with coordinating the ministries of associations of local churches in relation to their communities and regions, often known as "regional ministers" in the United Kingdom and "directors of missions" in the United States. Some Eastern European unions of Baptists, notably in Estonia, Latvia, and Georgia, have even accorded the designation "bishop" to such trans-local ministers. These Eastern European Baptist adaptations of the three-fold ministry are rooted in the biblicism of the Baptist tradition, for the Bible does refer to bishops, as well as a receptive ecumenical engagement with an Eastern Orthodox ecclesial and cultural context (especially in the case of the Evangelical Baptist Church of Georgia).[2] These Baptist bishops, however, exercise oversight in ways that emphasize its collegial and communal dimensions and foster the interdependence of independent congregations rather than exerting authority over them.

Ordination to pastoral ministry in the Baptist tradition is primarily authorized by the local congregation, which discerns that one of its members has been given gifts for the exercise of ministry and has been called by God to do so. But the interdependence of Baptist congregations is reflected in the practice of inviting representatives of other congregations with which the local church has associational relationships to participate in the questioning of candidates for ordination and in the service of ordination itself. Some Baptist unions have a role in recognizing at the denominational level ordinations performed by local churches and may have educational and other requirements for those so recognized by the national union.

Like many other Christian communions, Baptists have varying perspectives on the relation of gender to ordained ministry. Those who restrict the role of pastor to men appeal to passages of Scripture that seem, according to certain interpretations of them, either to restrict the role of women in the leadership of the church and its worship or to assume that pastors will be men (for example, 1 Cor 11:2–16; 14:34–35;

2. See the article by Ilia Osephashvili, "The Evangelical Baptist Church of Georgia," printed as chapter 21 of this volume.

1 Tim 2:8–15). But such passages are interpreted differently by Baptist congregations and unions that ordain women as well as men to pastoral ministry; these Baptists point also to Paul's insistence in Gal 3:28 that baptism into Christ creates a new basis for community in which "male and female" is no longer the basis for the privileging or restricting certain classes of persons in their status within the community, and to New Testament texts that highlight the leadership of women in the life of the early church (for example, Rom 16:1–7; Acts 18:24–28). Baptists who ordain only men to pastoral ministry sometimes also point to the gender of Jesus and the apostles as precedent; Baptists who also ordain women to pastoral ministry sometimes explain the preponderance of men in the leadership of the early church as an accommodation to a patriarchal culture that is not binding as a timeless principle. The patterns of reasoning reflected in both Baptist perspectives on the question of women as pastors reflect the biblicism of theological authority as practiced by Baptists, and the variety of Baptist perspectives on the issue illustrates the freedom of local congregations to follow the leading of the Spirit in bringing their life together under the rule of Christ so prized by Baptists.

Bibliography

Allmen, Jean-Jacques von. "L'Église locale parmi les autres Eglises locales." *Irénikon* 43 (1970) 512–37.

Anglican Consultative Council and Baptist World Alliance. *Conversations Around the World 2000–2005: The Report of the International Conversations between the Anglican Communion and the Baptist World Alliance*. London: Anglican Communion Office, 2005.

Baptist Union of Great Britain and Ireland. "The Baptist Doctrine of the Church." In *The Baptist Union: A Short History*, by Ernest A. Payne, 283–89. London: Carey Kingsgate, 1958.

Baptist World Alliance and Catholic Church. "The Word of God in the Life of the Church: A Report of International Conversations between the Catholic Church and the Baptist World Alliance 2006–2010." *American Baptist Quarterly* 31 (2012) 28–122.

Baptist World Alliance and Lutheran World Federation. "A Message to Our Churches." In *Growth in Agreement II: Reports and Agreed Statements of Ecumenical Conversations on a World Level, 1982–1998*, edited by Jeffrey Gros et al., 155–75. Faith and Order Paper no. 187. Geneva: WCC, 2000.

Baptist World Alliance and World Alliance of Reformed Churches. "Report of Theological Conversations Sponsored by the World Alliance of Reformed Churches and the Baptist World Alliance, 1977." In *Growth in Agreement: Reports and Agreed Statements of Ecumenical Conversations on a World Level*, edited by

Meyer Harding and Lukas Vischer, 132–51. Faith and Order Paper no. 108. New York: Paulist, 1984.

Songulashvili, Malkhaz. *Evangelical Christian Baptists of Georgia: The History and Transformation of a Free Church Tradition.* Waco, TX: Baylor University Press, 2015.

Swarat, Uwe. "Die baptistische Lehre im Spiegel der ökumenischen Dialoge auf Weltebene." *Freikirchen Forschung* 24 (2015) 18–59.

Teraudkalns, Valdis. "Episcopacy in the Baptist Tradition." In *Recycling the Past or Researching History?*, edited by Philip E. Thompson and Anthony R. Cross, 279–93. Studies in Baptist History and Thought 11. Milton Keynes: Paternoster, 2005.

Thurian, Max, ed. *Churches Respond to Baptism, Eucharist and Ministry.* 6 vols. Geneva: World Council of Churches, 1986–88.

7

Freedom of Religion and Conscience

MASSIMO RUBBOLI

Every major doctrine is related to human rights,
beginning with the biblical revelation of God.
(Fourteenth Baptist World Congress, 1980, Toronto)

The Reformation: the Equal Dignity of all Believers

THE PROTESTANT REFORMATION CREATED a new historical and theological scenery in which medieval concepts of freedom, conscience, and
rights were re-evaluated in the light of new understandings of Christian
teaching, but the changes that came about in relation to religious liberty
and freedom of conscience were not the direct result of the particular
teachings of the first reformers, who accepted the conventional view of
their time that heretics should be suppressed, as did their Catholic contemporaries. Luther, Melanchthon, and Calvin still perceived liberty of
conscience essentially as obedience to the divine word.

However, some of the Reformation's principles were influential in
preparing the ground for religious liberty and freedom of conscience.
The affirmation of the "priesthood of all believers," a theological principle
that emphasized the equal dignity of all believers and their common mission in the world, was intended by Luther to demolish the hierarchical

structure of the entire medieval ecclesiastical institution.[1] It hence follows that every person had equal access to the Scriptures and had the right to interpret it,[2] under the guidance of the Holy Spirit (*testimonium spiritus sancti internum*). A modern Baptist version of this principle affirms: "no authority can force or presume to compel submission to his or her interpretation or belief by another believer."[3]

The new theological scenery created by the Reformation, combined with the wars of religion, the growth of national states, and a variety of religious beliefs gave rise to the rejection of established religious institutions by religious groups who were being persecuted and sought toleration of their own beliefs. Their pleas were not at first based on any devotion to religious liberty as such, but from the middle of the sixteenth century onward a few voices were raised in defense of true religious freedom.

Religious Liberty in Early Baptist Authors

In reconstructing the genealogy of unrestricted religious toleration, modern historiography has emphasized the direct or indirect influence of Anabaptist arguments in the debate on religious freedom and liberty of conscience.[4] The large majority of English religious tolerationists belonged to the "non-conformist" branch of Protestant Christianity, formed by the Dissenters who did not "conform" to the established Church of England and refused to use the Book of Common Prayer in church services. In seventeenth-century England, controversies were not only theoretical, but had much to do with society and politics and addressed directly the relation between individual conscience and community.

In this context, well before Locke and with exclusively theological motivations, early Baptist authors such as John Smyth (1554–1612), Thomas Helwys (ca. 1575–ca. 1614), John Murton (1585–ca. 1626), and Leonard Busher (?-?) presented their demands for religious toleration in

---

1. Luther, *An den christlichen Adel*, 407: "we are all one body, yet every member has its own work that it may serve the others, this is so because we have one baptism, one Gospel, one faith, and are equal Christians, for baptism, Gospel, and faith alone make spiritual and Christian people."

2. Luther, *An den christlichen Adel*, 412, stated that every believer has "our faithful understanding of scripture."

3. Baptist General Association of Virginia, "On These Truths We Stand," n.p.

4. Wright, *Early English Baptists*; Lee, *Theology of John Smyth*; Haefeli, *New Netherland*.

works published during the second decade of the century.[5] All of them had sought refuge in the Dutch Republic, where they had become acquainted with arguments and opinions in favor of tolerance and religious freedom. These ideas were also circulating through *Liberty of Religion*,[6] an historical compilation by the Mennonite Pieter Jansz Twisck (1565–1636) published at the beginning of the Twelve Years' Truce (1609–21). Twisck claimed not only that no civil authority had the right to interfere in religious matters but also that it was necessary to consider others' opinions with toleration and moderation.

It is well known that the progress of toleration in England was quite arduous, being partly conditioned by the politics of the reigning monarch, who was the head of the Church of England: Edward VI (1547–53) promoted the Swiss reformed model; Mary Tudor (1553–58) reintroduced Roman Catholicism, and Elizabeth I (1558–1603) reinforced royal supremacy on the Anglican Church. While under Mary many Protestants were sentenced to death or forced into exile, Elizabeth continued with the executions of heretics, including two Dutch Mennonites—Jan Pieters and Hendrick Terwoort—and three Separatists—Henry Barrow, John Greenwood, and John Penry.[7]

Thomas Helwys published an urgent plea addressed to Elizabeth's successor, James I (1603–25), who had continued the policy of repression of nonconformism, so that he would cease to persecute religious minorities, Christian and non-Christian, that dissented from the Church of England. Helwys believed that the magistrate should exercise exclusively the civil power, and that obedience to the king was due only in secular questions and not in spiritual matters:

> we do freely profess that our lord the king has no more power over their consciences. . . . For our lord the king is but an earthly king, and he has no authority as a king but in earthly causes. . . . men's religion to God is between God and themselves. Neither may the king be judge between God and man. Let them be heretics, Turks, Jews, or whatsoever, it appertains not to the earthly power to punish them in the least measure.[8]

---

5. See previous footnote.

6. Twisck, *Religions Vryheyt*. On the cultural and religious context, see Hsia and van Nierop, *Calvinism and Religious Toleration*; den Hollander et al., *Religious Minorities*.

7. Tracy, *Europe's Reformations*, 186–95.

8. Helwys, *Short Declaration*, 53.

For expressing these views, Helwys was taken to Newgate prison in London, where he died (the exact date is unknown, but documents dated 1614 make reference to his widow). Helwys could have limited himself to defending the rights of Christian minorities, as other supporters of religious liberty of the period. However, maybe because of his own suffering from religious persecution, he opted for a broader concept of toleration, with no exceptions to the refusal of every form of violent coercion of conscience.

Helwys developed his own concepts of liberty and of separation of church and state: what prevented the interference of the magistrates into religious matters was not the supposed autonomy of conscience or a demand for individual liberty, but Christ's lordship over conscience. The exercise of conscience had to be free from every human control, because conscience—in the relationship between the human being and God—represented the setting where the Spirit made God's voice heard through the Scriptures.

John Murton, another important advocate of religious toleration, submitted a "humble supplication"[9] to the king in favor of victims of persecution for religious cause, published anonymously in 1620. Murton had been arrested in England after a sojourn in Amsterdam for the publication of an apology of toleration that summarized Twisck's work.[10] Moving from the consideration of "how heinous it is in the sight of the Lord to force men and women by cruel persecution, to bring their bodies to a worship whereunto they cannot bring their spirits," Murton concluded that "the kings of the earth have not power from God, to compel by persecution any of their subjects to believe as they believe" and "that no man ought to be persecuted for his religion, be it true or false."[11]

A year before the publication of Murton's book, Leonard Busher published, probably in Amsterdam, *Religion's Peace*—most likely the first Baptist text entirely devoted to religious liberty. In this tract, Busher declared that not only *no king nor bishop can, or is able to command faith,* but *persecution for difference in religion is a monstrous and cruel beast* and, in capital letters, added:

---

9. Murton, *Most Humble Supplication*, reprinted in Underhill, *Tracts on Liberty of Conscience*, 183–231.

10. Bangs, "Dutch Contributions," 586.

11. Murton, *Persecution* (1615), cited in McBeth, *Sourcebook*, 75.

IT IS NOT ONLY UNMERCIFUL, BUT UNNATURAL AND ABOMINABLE; YEA, MONSTROUS FOR ONE CHRISTIAN TO VEX AND DESTROY ANOTHER FOR DIFFERENCE AND QUESTIONS OF RELIGION.[12]

For the first generation of English Baptists, conscience did not concern the liberty of individual choice but rather a question of judgment and responsibility: Conscience was a vehicle for recognizing God's will, not for validating one's own ideas. Conscience was not autonomous but subdued to God's authority, as revealed in the Scriptures, and "liberty of conscience" was not a natural right, as John Locke would affirm later in his *Letter Concerning Tolerance* (1689), but a religious obligation. Their thinking was influenced by a long tradition that can be traced back to Augustine, for whom conscience was not an innate personal moral sense nor an ethical awareness, but rather a means used by the eternal or natural law—to which every man must obey in every circumstance—to exercise its control on individual behavior.

In this cultural milieu, that did not include modern notions of natural human rights nor of individual liberty, Richard Overton, a Baptist who was also involved with the Levellers, provided a positive evaluation of natural human rights.[13] He based his arguments on Scripture as authoritative but also on human reason, "identified with the spirit of God working in the human soul."[14] For Overton, human rights included religious liberty as well as civil liberty for all: civil magistrates had no authority in spiritual matters, and only God could govern the spiritual lives of people. Therefore, he and three other Leveller leaders affirmed that authorities could not

> compel by penalties or otherwise any person to anything in or about matters of faith, religion, or God's worship, or to restrain any person from the profession of his faith, or exercise of religion according to his conscience—nothing having caused more distractions and heart-burnings in all ages than persecution and molestation for matters of conscience in and about religion.[15]

12. Busher, *Religion's Peace*, 17, 41, 21.

13. On Overton's association with the Levellers see Gibbons, "Richard Overton," 63–75.

14. Gibbons, "Overton, Richard (*fl.* 1640–1663)."

15. See John Lilburne, William Walwyn, Thomas Prince, and Richard Overton *Agreement,* cited in Sharp, *English Levellers,* 173.

The Principle of Religious Freedom and Liberty of Conscience in New England

Afterwards, in the *Second London Confession of Faith*, Baptists re-affirmed that liberty was a gift from God, made possible by Christ's sacrifice on the cross and his resurrection: "*God alone is Lord of the conscience, and has left it free from the doctrines and commandments of men which are in any thing contrary to his word, or not contained in it*" (art. XXI, 2). In the early seventeenth-century, "*toleration*" and "*liberty of conscience*" were equivalent and interchangeable terms, and this was true also for Roger Williams (1603–84), the Puritan pastor and theologian who co-founded with John Clarke (1609–76) the first Baptist church on American soil in the small colony of Rhode Island.[16] Being forced to escape from Massachusetts Bay Colony in 1636, Williams initially took refuge in a village of the Narragansett Indians and thereafter, with a few other dissenters, he founded Providence to be "*a shelter for persons distressed for conscience.*"[17]

Williams was the first North American to defend religious toleration and liberty of conscience in his book *The Bloudy Tenent of Persecution, for cause of Conscience* (1644).[18] The safeguard of religious liberty deeply concerned him because of his personal experience, since in Massachusetts the Congregationalist Standing Order did not consent believers "*to worship God after their consciences.*"[19] The forcing of a person's conscience was compared by Williams to physical violence, "*a spirituall and soule rape.*"[20]

Williams rejected the coercive religion, supported by the government, that allowed only members of Congregationalist churches to enter public offices, and he contended against infringements on religious liberty by adopting the arguments of the early seventeenth-century Baptists who attributed different objects and weapons to Christ's kingdom and to

16. Gaustad, *Roger Williams*, 205.

17. LaFantasie, *Correspondence*, 2526.

18. Williams, *Bloudy Tenent*. In the same year, 1644, an anonymous author published in London a pamphlet against "universall libertie of conscience," affirming that "A universal liberty of conscience is a universal liberty to sin, to maintain heresy, to practice idolatry, to vent blasphemy," from *Against Universall Libertie of Conscience*, cited in Durso, *No Armor for the Back*, 60.

19. Williams, *Bloudy Tenent*, 3:283.

20. Williams, *Bloudy Tenent*, 3:219.

civil government.[21] In explaining the limits of civil jurisdiction, Williams drew also upon the parable of the Wheat and the Tares (Matt 13:24–44),[22] claiming that only God and not an earthly government can decide about the final uprooting of the tares from the garden. Only with the imminent Second Coming the heretical Christians and the non-Christian tares would be separated from the "wheat," i.e., the faithful Christians, "Because Christ commandeth to let alone the Tares and Wheat to grow together unto the Harvest."[23] Williams believed that the civil state could apply its civil penalties to civil offenses, as these were opposed to the state, but it could not apply such punishments to consciences or worship, as these related to Christ's kingdom. Conversely, Christ's kingdom had complete jurisdiction over conscience and worship but none over civil offenses. Thus, in contrast to John Cotton (1584–1652) and the other Massachusetts Puritans who held that there, as in Israel, the magistrate possessed both civil and spiritual power, Williams was convinced that civil governments had not been given authority over spiritual matters.

Individual Liberty of Conscience and Community

The founding document of the colony of Rhode Island contained the principle of liberty of conscience. However, without an established church as a benchmark for social solidarity and moral influence, the first inhabitants of the new colony were sailing uncharted waters and Williams had to face a completely new challenge, i.e., to reconcile individual liberty of conscience with a disciplined cohabitation in a society devoid of rigid religious norms. For the authorities in Massachusetts, Rhode Island's internal conflicts were the evidence that church and state could not be two separate entities, but had to remain in a relationship of mutual support.

The "New England Way" developed by the Puritans did not allow the possibility of dividing theology from the social and political organization of the community and required that every form of religious dissent be repressed inasmuch as it endangered the commonwealth. The opposition

21. For Williams's views on these different jurisdictions, see, among others, Hall, *Separating Church and State*, 72–98.

22. The parable of the Wheat and the Tares (Matt 13:24–44) was at the center of the debates on toleration. Cf. Bainton, "Parable," 67–89.

23. Williams, *Bloudy Tenent*, 43.

of the Puritan leaders toward dissenters such as Anne Hutchinson and
Roger Williams was accounted for by the firm belief that it was necessary
to prevent the spread of doctrines that undermined the very foundation of a society submitted to God, created factions, and deflected the
attention of the community from its principal objective, i.e., living a holy
life. For the magistrates, Hutchinson's revelations divided families and
churches, whereas Williams's ideas threatened the legitimacy of the religious, social, and political project that the Puritans were realizing.

Williams's defense of universal toleration was neither the result of
relativizing religious truth, since he was deeply convinced that Protestantism, in its Puritan/Separatist version, was the "true" faith, nor simply
a means to deal with and solve doctrinal conflicts between Christians.
General toleration was meant to make possible the realization of a society of individuals with profound and irreconcilable religious and cultural differences. The term that best explains his concept of toleration is
"civility," a respectful and tolerant behavior towards everyone, different
from "civilization," a combination of social patterns and cultural norms
of behavior. Martha Nussbaum has observed that Williams's concept of
toleration as respect for diversity and liberty of individual conscience
went well beyond an understanding of "toleration as concession."[24] "If
Men keep but the Bond of Civility," wrote Williams, "notwithstanding
these spiritual oppositions in point of worship and religion," there would
be "not the least noise . . . of any civil breach, or breach of civil amongst
them."[25]

Williams's idea of religious toleration was shared by John Clarke,
pastor of the Baptist church of Newport, but it was very much opposed
by Puritan divines like John Norton (1606–63). Clarke personally experienced this opposition when, in 1651, he and two other members of
the Newport church, Obadiah Holmes and John Crandall, were arrested
in Lynn, Massachusetts, for preaching in a private home. Clarke and
Crandall were released after their fines were paid by local friends, but
Holmes refused to accept the offer and was publicly whipped on Boston
Common.[26] In a detailed exposé of religious persecution in New England, published in London a year later, Clarke repeated that spiritual sins
like apostasy or blasphemy did not concern the civil order and that the

24. Nussbaum, *Liberty of Conscience*, 52.
25. Williams, *Bloudy Tenent*, 74.
26. On Obadiah Holmes see Gaustad, *Baptist Piety*.

magistrate's only duty was to safeguard "the peace, liberty and prosperity of a civill State, Nation and Kingdom."[27]

As a consequence of the public beating of Holmes, Rhode Island Baptists desisted from entering into Massachusetts territory for many years. Thereafter, they concentrated on the defense of their own rights[28] even if, "in seeking Christian liberty for themselves, they helped (almost in spite of themselves) to expand the concepts of freedom and equality for everyone."[29]

After the American Revolution: Dissenters, Religious Liberty, and Disestablishment

During the Revolutionary War, religious toleration was granted to Protestant dissenters and even to Catholics living in the rebellious colonies, because it was necessary to form a united front against the British.[30] After the war, the choice had to be made between the recognition of a national church or disestablishment. On the one hand, Anglicans (now called Episcopalians) and Congregationalists strongly favored a national church, provided that it be their own; on the other hand, Dissenters, Deists, and other religious and secular groups opposed any form of national church establishment.

In the confrontation between these opposite fronts, that took place first at state and later at the federal level, Baptists stood in the forefront of the battle for separating church and state and for the recognition of the right to liberty of conscience. Isaac Backus (1724–1806), a steadfast advocate of religious liberty, accused the Massachusetts' authorities of forcing the "the Baptists to . . . support the worship which they conscientiously dissent from. . . . [M]any who are filling the nation with the cry of LIBERTY and against oppressors are at the same time themselves violating that dearest of all rights, LIBERTY of CONSCIENCE."[31] In 1779, Samuel

27. Clarke, *Ill Newes from New England*; Gaustad, "Preface." For Clarke, conscience was that "sparkling beam from the Father of lights and spirits that . . . cannot be lorded over, commanded, or forced, either by men, devils, or angels" (*Ill Newes from New England*, 6).

28. McLoughlin, *Soul Liberty*, 32–33.

29. McLoughlin, *New England Dissent, 1630–1833*, 1281–82.

30. On the expansion of religious liberty as a result of political calculation and economic advantage, see Gill, *Political Origins*, 26–113, and Hanson, *Necessary Virtue*.

31. Backus, *Seasonable Plea*, cited in Bailyn, *Ideological Origins*, 263. See also

Stillman (1737–1807), pastor of the First Baptist Church in Boston, was invited to deliver the annual Election Sermon before the Massachusetts General Court, the first time for a non-Congregationalist. Stillman used the occasion to make an ardent plea for religious equality.[32]

When in October 1791 the Connecticut's general assembly passed "An Act securing equal Rights and Privileges to Christians of every denomination in this State"[33] John Leland (1754–1841), leader of the Virginia Baptists during and after the Revolutionary War, was "one of the few dissenting leaders"[34] of the time to criticize the exemption of the Protestant dissenters from taxation for the support of the clergy and from military service; few if any clergy conscientiously objected to taxes other than the tax for the established church, and few clergy outside the historic peace churches conscientiously objected to military service. In his most famous sermon against establishments, *The Rights of Conscience Inalienable*, Leland stated that

> Ministers should share the same protection of the law that other men do, and no more. To proscribe them from seats of legislation, &c. is cruel. To indulge them with an exemption from taxes and bearing arms is a tempting emolument. The law should be silent about them; protect them as citizens (not as sacred officers) for the civil law knows no sacred religious officers.[35]

Leland attacked the exemption for not going far enough, i.e., for failing to exempt Jews, Catholics, Turks, and "heathens." He claimed that

> Government has no more to do with the religious opinions of men than it has with the principles of mathematics. Let every man speak freely without fear— maintain the principles that he believes—worship according to his own faith, either one God,

Mayhew, *Sermon Preach'd*, 32: "It may be worth considering whether we have not some laws in force, hardly reconcilable with that religious liberty which we profess." Mayhew was the pastor of the West Church in Boston who preached the "election sermon" May 29, 1754.

32. Stillman, *Sermon Preached before the Honorable Council*. For the novelty of a non-Congregationalist preacher, see Marini, *Radical Sects*, 23.

33. This law allowed Christians who had joined dissenting congregations to file certificates with the clerks of the established ecclesiastical societies in their localities and thereby gain exemption from taxation to support the established church; it also granted dissenting denominations equal power with the established societies to support their own churches financially.

34. Hamburger, *Separation of Church and State*, 84.

35. Leland, "Rights of Conscience," 188.

three Gods, no God, or twenty Gods; and let government protect him in so doing, i.e. see that he meets no personal abuse or
loss of property for his religious opinions.[36]

The belief that religious belonging was irrelevant from a social
and political perspective had been already expressed also by Thomas
Jefferson,[37] with whom Leland cooperated in the drafting of the First
amendment of the US Constitution, that prohibited the recognition of
an official religion and guaranteed religious liberty for all. The "free exercise of religion" had been deliberately substituted for a guarantee of "toleration" in drafting the Virginia Declaration of Rights,[38] and was finally
adopted in the federal Bill of Rights instead of "liberty of conscience."[39]
With Leland, the concept of toleration and "free exercise of religion" was
definitively substituted by "liberty of conscience" for all:

> The notion of a Christian commonwealth should be exploded
> forever. . . . Government should protect every man in thinking
> and speaking freely, and see that one does not abuse another.
> The liberty I contend for is more than toleration. The very idea
> of toleration is despicable; it supposes that some have a pre-
> eminence above the rest to grant indulgence, whereas all should
> be equally free, Jews, Turks, Pagans and Christians.[40]

The long march for the affirmation of the principle of religious liberty and for the denial of the state's jurisdiction over religion was not yet
finished, but it had reached an important goal. In 1834, looking back to
the struggle in which he had been so much involved, John Leland could
write "The plea for religious liberty has been long and powerful; but it
has been left for the United States to acknowledge it a right inherent, and
not a favor granted: to exclude religious opinions from the list of objects
of legislation."[41]

36. Leland, "Rights of Conscience," 184.

37. Jefferson, *Notes on Virginia*, QUERY XVII: "The rights of conscience we never
submitted, we could not submit. We are answerable for them to our God. The legitimate powers of government extend to such acts only as are injurious to others. But it
does me no injury for my neighbor to say there are twenty gods, or no god. It neither
picks my pocket nor breaks my leg." Koch and Peden, *Life and Selected Writings*, 254.

38. Curry, *First Freedoms*, 135.

39. McConnell, "Origins," 1488–1500.

40. Leland, *Writings of the Late Elder John Leland*, 118.

41. Leland, *Writings of the Late Elder John Leland*, 39.

Baptists' Renewed Concern for Religious Liberty, Freedom of Conscience and Disestablishment in the Nineteenth Century

In England, religious liberty and freedom of conscience continued to be a preeminent concern of the Baptists, who played a relevant role in the formation of Nonconformist voluntary organizations like the Evangelical Voluntary Church Association and the Religious Freedom Society, both established in 1839, the British Anti-State Church Association (founded in 1844 and renamed in 1853 as the Society for the Liberation of Religion from State Patronage and Control)—all created to pursue the aim of disestablishment the Church of England[42]—and the Evangelical Alliance (1846), that campaigned internationally for religious freedom. Edward Steane (1798–1882), one of the main promoters of the formation of the Evangelical Alliance, was also co-secretary of the Baptist Union.

The nineteenth century's missionary movement played an important role in revitalizing the British, American, and Canadian Baptist churches' concern for religious liberty, because missionaries had to deal with restrictions imposed by local government regulations and established churches. Baptist involvement in overseas missionary enterprise dates back to the formation of the Particular-Baptist Society (later renamed Baptist Missionary Society) in 1792 and William Carey's (1761–1834) mission in India and Burma from the end of the following year. Until 1813 the British East India Company did not tolerate dissenting missionaries, because it aimed at "instilling the virtuous and moral principles of the religion of the Church of England" among the natives.[43] The British Baptists' work prepared the way for the US Baptists' engagement in missionary endeavors in Burma with Adoniram (1788–1850) and Ann Hasseltine (1789–1826) Judson, and Samuel S. Day (1807–71); in Africa with Lott Cary (ca. 1780–1828) and Collin Teague (c. 1780–1839), free African Americans from Virginia, supported by the General Missionary Convention; in China with William Dean (1807–95); and in Latin America with Archibald B. Reekie (1862–1942).[44]

---

42. See, among others, Machin, "Disestablishment," 120–48.

43. Carey, *William Carey*, 56, quoted in Brackney, "Baptists, Religious Liberty," 315.

44. Pierard, *Mission and Baptist Identity*, and Brackney, *Bridging Cultures and Hemispheres*, 1997.

While continuing to affirm religious liberty and freedom of conscience, a large part of US Baptists, especially in the South, failed to connect them to a full acknowledgment of human rights and continued to support slavery. The largest Baptist body, the Southern Baptist Convention (SBC), remained hostile to desegregation even when—in the 1950s and 1960s—the civil rights movement was led by Baptist ministers like Martin Luther King Jr. and Ralph Abernathy. Only in 1995, on its 150th anniversary, did the SBC issue an apology for its earlier stance on slavery and segregation. In January 1999, an International Summit of Baptists against Racism was held in Atlanta.[45]

The Incomplete Recognition of "the Right to Freedom of Thought, Conscience, and Religion"

The final outcome of the long struggle for freedom of religion and conscience, fought by Protestant minorities in England and America, was the proclamation of religious human rights as an essential feature of the Christian faith itself, as it had been already proclaimed by seven Baptist leaders in a pamphlet of 1661: "the liberty of men's consciences . . . is also a part of the Christian religion."[46]

The violation of religious liberty was one of the main issues discussed at the creation of the Baptist World Alliance (BWA), founded in London in 1905, with the mission

> to empower and enable national Baptist leaders to effectively witness and minister in the name of Jesus Christ and to represent and support Baptists throughout the world in defense of human rights and religious freedom. Furthermore, the world must not be permitted to forget what the Baptist doctrine of soul liberty, broadening into the conception of personal liberty and finding expression in the ordinances of civil liberty, has wrought for the political emancipation of mankind.[47]

Several Baptist national bodies participated in the ecumenical Oxford Life and Work Conference of 1937 and the Madras Missionary Conference of

---

45. Lotz, *Baptists Against Racism.*

46. Monck et al., *Sion's Groans,* 379.

47. *Proceedings Baptist World Congress,* 1905, 76, cited in Brackney, *Baptists,* 103.

1938, where the issue of religious liberty was addressed as a fundamental human right.[48]

During the 1930s, Baptists became increasingly concerned about the threat posed to religious liberty by the rise of totalitarian regimes across Europe and about the Roosevelt administration's favorable policies towards Catholics, specifically with regard to the idea of establishing formal diplomatic relations with the Holy See. In response to these concerns, representatives of three Baptist denominations—the Northern Baptist Convention, the National Baptist Convention, USA, and the Southern Baptist Convention—met in 1939, and jointly issued "A Pronouncement on Religious Liberty," officially published under the title *American Baptist Bill of Rights*. The document warned that religious liberty was under threat and proclaimed that because religious liberty was "not only an inalienable human right, but indispensable to human welfare," Baptists had to protect "absolute religious liberty" for Jews, Catholics, Protestants, and "everybody else," and they should "condemn every form of compulsion in religion or restraint of the free consideration of the claims of religion. We stand for a civil state, with full liberty in religious concernments."[49]

Representatives of the three denominations formed the Associated Committees on Public Relations, that in 1942 became the Joint Conference Committee on Public Relations (JCCPR) and, in 1950, was renamed Baptist Joint Committee for Public Affairs (BJCPA). In 2005, the name was changed again to Baptist Joint Committee for Religious Liberty to reflect more accurately its mission "to defend religious freedom for all in the historic Baptist tradition."[50] In his memoirs, Joseph M. Dawson, first executive secretary of the JCCPR, recalled his participation in the organizational meeting of the United Nations, that took place from April 25, 1945 to June 26, 1945 in San Francisco: "To that meeting I carried a hundred thousand petitions from Baptists, North and South, white and Negro, asking that the Charter to be adopted would include guarantee of full religious liberty for every human being."[51]

Baptists were to be disappointed because there was no specific reference to religious freedom in the new UN Charter. Nevertheless, they can be included—together with many other religious dissenters—among

48. Koshy, "Ecumenical Understanding," 137–54.

49. *The American Baptist Bill of Rights*, 17–18. See Brackney, "American Baptist Bill of Rights," 21; also Leonard, *Baptists in America*, 167.

50. Baptist Joint Committee, *Report from the Capital*, 2; see also Parry, *On Guard*.

51. Dawson, *Thousand Months To Remember*, 161.

the forerunners of the Universal Declaration of Human Rights (UDHR), adopted in 1948 by the United Nations General Assembly. Article 2 of the UDHR stated that everyone is to be entitled to all the rights and freedoms without respect to religion. Article 18 affirmed,

> Everyone has the right to freedom of thought, conscience and religion; this right includes freedom to change his religion or belief, and freedom, either alone or in community with others and in public or private, to manifest his religion or belief in teaching, practice, worship and observance.[52]

In 1950, the eighth Baptist World Congress in Cleveland urged all nations to support the Universal Declaration of Human Rights by ratifying the agreements designed to put its requirements into international law.

However, the UN recognition of "the right to freedom of thought, conscience and religion," did not put an end to intolerance and persecution, and conspicuous violations of human rights have occurred and still take place in many areas of the planet. Without a comprehensive and universal recognition and implementation of human rights no peaceful and just world-order will be possible.

Bibliography

The American Baptist Bill of Rights: A Pronouncement Upon Religious Liberty. Washington, DC: Associated Committees on Public Relations, 1940.

Backus, Isaac. *A Seasonable Plea for Liberty of Conscience, against some later Oppressive Proceedings . . .* N.p., 1770.

Bailyn, Bernard. *The Ideological Origins of the American Revolution.* Cambridge, MA: Belknap, 1967.

Bainton, Roland H. "The Parable of the Tares as the Proof Text for Religious Liberty to the End of the Sixteenth Century." *Church History* 1 (1932) 67–89.

Bangs, Jeremy Dupertuis. "Dutch Contributions to Religious Toleration." *Church History* 79 (2010) 585–613.

Baptist General Association of Virginia. "On These Truths We Stand." http://bgav.org/wp-content/uploads/2014/01/On-These-Truths-We-Stand.pdf.

Baptist Joint Committee: Working Together in Common Cause. *Report from the Capital.* September 2011. Special Anniversary Issue.

Biagini, Eugenio F., ed. *Citizenship and Community: Liberals, Radicals and Collective Identities in the British Isles, 1865–1931.* Cambridge, MA: Cambridge University Press, 1996.

52. *The Universal Declaration of Human Rights,* http://www.un.org/en/documents/udhr/index.shtml#a18 (accessed 20 September 2015).

Brackney, William H. "American Baptist Bill of Rights." In *Dictionary of Baptists in America*, edited by Bill J. Leonard, 21. Downers Grove, IL: InterVarsity, 1994.

———. *The Baptists*. Westport, CT: Praeger, 1994.

———. "Baptists, Religious Liberty and Evangelization: Nineteenth-Century Challenges." In *Baptist Identities*, edited by Ian M. Randall et al., 311–36. Milton Kenyes: Paternoster, 2006.

———. *Bridging Cultures and Hemispheres: The Legacy of Archibald Reekie and Canadian Baptists in Bolivia*. Macon, GA: Smyth & Helwys, 1997.

Busher, Leonard. *Religion's Peace: or a Plea for Liberty of Conscience*. In *Tracts on Liberty of Conscience and Persecution 1614–1661*, edited by Edward Bean Underhill, 15–78. London: Hanserd Knollys Society, 1846.

Carey, S. Pearce. *William Carey*. New York: Doran, 1923.

Clarke, John. *Ill Newes from New England: or A Narrative of New-Englands Persecution. Wherein Is Declared That While Old England Is Becoming New, New-England Is Become Old*. N.p., 1652.

Curry, Thomas J. *The First Freedoms: Church and State in America to the Passage of the First Amendment*. New York: Oxford University Press, 1986.

Dawson, Joseph Martin. *A Thousand Months to Remember: An Autobiography*. Waco, TX: Baylor University Press, 1964.

den Hollander, August, et al., eds. *Religious Minorities and Cultural Diversity in the Dutch Republic*. Leiden: Brill, 2014.

Durso, Keith E. *No Armor for the Back: Baptist Prison Writing, 1600s–1700s*. Macon, GA: Mercer University Press, 2007.

Gaustad, Edwin S. *Baptist Piety: The Last Will and Testimony of Obadiah Holmes*. Grand Rapids, MI: Christian University Press, 1994.

———, ed. "Preface." In *Colonial Baptists: Massachusetts and Rhode Island*, n.p. The Baptist Tradition. New York: Arno, 1980.

———. *Roger Williams*. New York: Oxford University Press, 2005.

Gibbons, Brian J. "Overton, Richard (*fl.* 1640–1663)." In *Oxford Dictionary of National Biography*, n.p. Oxford: Oxford University Press, 2004. https://www.oxforddnb.com/view/article/20974.

———. "Richard Overton and the Secularism of the Interregnum Radicals." *Seventeenth Century* 10 (1995) 63–75.

Gill, Anthony. *The Political Origins of Religious Liberty*. Cambridge, MA: Cambridge University Press, 2008.

Haefeli, Evan. *New Netherland and the Dutch Origins of American Religious Liberty*. Philadelphia: University of Pennsylvania Press, 2012.

Hall, Timothy L. *Separating Church and State: Roger Williams and Religious Liberty*. Champaign, IL: University of Illinois Press, 1998.

Hamburger, Philip. *Separation of Church and State*. Cambridge, MA: Harvard University Press, 2009.

Hanson, Charles. *Necessary Virtue: The Pragmatic Origins of Religious Liberty in New England*. Charlottesville, VA: University Press of Virginia, 1998.

Helwys, Thomas. *A Short Declaration of the Mystery of Iniquity*. Macon, GA: Mercer University Press, 1998.

Hsia, Ronnie Po-Chia, and Henk van Nierop, eds. *Calvinism and Religious Toleration in the Dutch Golden Age*. Cambridge, MA: Cambridge University Press, 2002.

Jefferson, Thomas. *Notes on Virginia*. N.p.: QUERY XVII, 1781.

LaFantasie, Glenn W., ed. *The Correspondence of Roger Williams*. 2 vols. Hanover, NH: University Press of New England, 1988.

Koch, Adrienne, and William Peden, eds. *The Life and Selected Writings of Thomas Jefferson*. New York: Random House, 1944.

Koshy, Ninan. "The Ecumenical Understanding of Religious Liberty: The Contribution of the World Council of Churches." *Journal of Church and State* 38 (1996) 137–54.

Lee, Jason K. *The Theology of John Smyth: Puritan, Separatist, Baptist, Mennonite*. Macon, GA: Mercer University Press, 2003.

Leland, John. "The Rights of Conscience Inalienable, and therefore, Religious Opinions not Cognizable by Law." In *The Writings of the Late Elder John Leland Including Some Events in his Life, Written by Himself, with Additional Sketches & c. by Miss L. F. Greene*, 179–92. New York: G. W. Wood, 1845

Leonard, Bill J. *Baptists in America*. New York: Columbia University Press, 2005.

———, ed. *Dictionary of Baptists in America*. Downers Grove, IL: InterVarsity, 1994.

Lotz, Denton, ed. *Baptists Against Racism: United in Christ for Racial Reconciliation*. McLean, VA: The Baptist World Alliance, 1999.

Luther, Martin. *An den christlichen Adel deutscher Nation von des christlichen Standes Besserung*. Kritische Gesamtausgabe 6. Weimar: H. Böhlau, 1888.

Machin, Ian. "Disestablishment and Democracy, c. 1840–1930." In *Citizenship and Community: Liberals, Radicals and Collective Identities in the British Isles, 1865–1931*, edited by Eugenio F. Biagini, 120–47. Cambridge, MA: Cambridge University Press, 1996.

Marini, Stephen A. *Radical Sects in Revolutionary New England*. Cambridge, MA: Harvard University Press, 1982.

Mayhew, Jonathan. *A Sermon Preach'd in the Audience of His Excellency William Shirley, Esq.* Boston: Samuel Kneeland, 1754.

McBeth, H. Leon, ed. *A Sourcebook for Baptist Heritage*. Nashville, TN: Broadman, 1990.

McConnell, Michael W. "The Origins and Historical Understanding of Free Exercise of Religion." *Harvard Law Review* 103 (1990) 1488–1500.

McLoughlin, William. *New England Dissent, 1630–1833*. Vol. 2, *The Baptists and the Separation of Church and State*. Cambridge, MA: Harvard University Press, 2014.

———. *Soul Liberty, The Baptists' Struggle in New England, 1630–1833*. Hanover, NH: Brown University Press, 1991.

Monck, Thomas, et al. *Sion's Groans for Her Distressed, or Sober Endeavours to Prevent Innocent Blood*. In *Tracts on Liberty of Conscience and Persecution 1614–1661*, edited by Edward Bean Underhill, 343–82. London: Hanserd Knollys Society, 1846.

Murton, John. *A Most Humble Supplication of Many of the King's Majesty's Loyal Subjects, Ready to Testify All Civil Obedience, by the Oath of Allegiance, or Otherwise, and that of Conscience; Who Are Persecuted (only for Differing in Religion) Contrary to Divine and Human Testimonies*. In *Tracts on Liberty of Conscience and Persecution 1614–1661*, edited by Edward Bean Underhill, 183–231. London: Hanserd Knollys Society, 1846.

Nussbaum, Martha. *Liberty of Conscience: In Defense of America's Tradition of Religious Equality*. New York: Basic Books, 2010.

Parry, Pam. *On Guard for Religious Liberty: Six Decades of the Baptist Joint Committee*. Macon, GA: Smyth & Helwys, 1996.

Pierard, Richard V. *Mission and Baptist Identity*. Beverly, MA: Richard Henry, 2004.

Proceedings of the Baptist World Congress, 1905. London: Baptist Publications Department, 1905.

Randall, Ian M., et al., eds. *Baptist Identities*. Milton Kenyes: Paternoster, 2006.

Sharp, Andrew. *The English Levellers*. Cambridge University Press, 1998.

Stillman, Samuel. *A Sermon Preached before the Honorable Council, and the Honorable House of Representatives of the State of Massachusetts-Bay, in New-England, at Boston, May 26, 1779. Being the anniversary for the election of the Honorable Council*. Boston: N.p., 1779.

Tracy, James D. *Europe's Reformations*. Lanham, MD: Rowman & Littlefield, 1999.

Twisck, Pieter J. *Religions Vryheyt. Een korte Cronijcsche beschryvinghe van die Vryheyt der Religien, tegen die dwang der Conscientien . . . tot den Jare 1609. s.n.* N.p.: Hoorn, 1609.

Underhill, Edward Bean, ed. *Tracts on Liberty of Conscience and Persecution 1614-1661*. London: Hanserd Knollys Society, 1846.

Williams, Roger. *The Bloudy Tenent of Persecution, for Cause of Conscience, discussed in a Conference between Truth and Peace*. In *The Complete Writings of Roger Williams*, edited by Samuel L. Caldwell, 3:1-425. New York: Russell & Russell, 1963.

Wright, Stephen. *The Early English Baptists, 1603-1649*. Wodbridge, Suffolk: Boydell, 2006.

8

Baptists and Sociopolitical Involvement

David P. Gushee and Larry L. McSwain

The global Baptist movement is the story of a mixed heritage when it applies to the application of the gospel in the sociopolitical arenas of world Christianity. On the one hand, Baptists in most regions of the world are relatively small gatherings of individuals and congregations with a strong pietistic theology that emphasizes the personal relationships between believers and Jesus Christ to the exclusion of larger social concerns. Most of the ethical thought and practice in Baptist history has addressed personal behavior rather than issues of justice and peace so important in all nations. This strong "separation from the world" motif is a legacy of a theology of individual salvation that suggests moral individuals are the means for a moral society.

On the other hand, Baptists in selected global regions have been on the forefront of addressing a broad range of sociopolitical issues where they have been numerically strong enough to form conventions and educational institutions that have fostered an informed sociopolitical consciousness. Since the first formal Baptist congregation was established by English dissenters in Amsterdam in 1609, it is only natural that the early strength of the Baptist Movement was in Britain, pockets of Europe and the American Colonies. The modern missionary movement beginning in the eighteenth century spread Baptist theology, polity, and ethical concerns to mostly colonial regions of the world in which pockets of numerical strength are found to this day.

Estimates of the number of Baptists worldwide exceed 105 million, with some 35 million located in North America. The Baptist World Alliance (BWA) is the largest organization of worldwide Baptists with 238 member bodies (associations, unions, conventions, fellowships) in 124 countries with a total of 48 million members in 168,885 churches in 2017. The Southern Baptist Convention does not participate in BWA but adds 15.87 million members and 46,000 plus churches to this global total. The geographic strength of the movement is found in order of location in North America, Africa, Asia Pacific, South America, and Europe.

Baptist Principles for Sociopolitical Action

The very identity of Baptists provides a clue for understanding the complexity of our public theology and action. Baptists have no magisterium for developing an authoritative theological framework as a foundation for ethical thought. Consequently, all of the classic streams of Christian thought—Catholic, Reformation (both Calvinist and Arminian), Anabaptist, and humanist—may be adopted within some Baptist group. Neither is there any organizational structure with authority to impose a viewpoint or enforce an action on any Baptist individual, congregation, fellowship, association, denomination, or alliance. Yet the contributions of this complex collection of Christians have been significant historically and continue to be in the twenty-first century. How?

Baptists are characterized by a set of generally held principles. Those principles tend to find their way into statements of faith adopted by conventions of churches within a geographic region. Adherence to such statements can be enforced upon convention-related employees but upon no other individual or Baptist body. These principles are:

1. *Radical discipleship emphasizing the Lordship of Jesus Christ as the only authority for true faith.* Faith requires an individual decision of obedience to Christ and each person is accountable before God. Participation in the church at whatever level of its organization is rooted in this discipleship which is a decision symbolized by the act of baptism by immersion in most Baptist groups.

2. *The source of authority for belief and behavior is the Bible interpreted within the framework of obedience to Jesus Christ.* This is a universal Baptist claim. Yet differences in theological and ethical understandings are rooted in differences in how one interprets that authority. Pastors and

teachers who approach Scripture from a Fundamentalist/Conservative/
Literalist perspective often derive polar opposite viewpoints from those
with a Historical-Critical/Progressive/Symbolic interpretation of the
same texts. Consequently, one can find both proponents and antagonists
of pacifism, in dealing with war, or capital punishment in response to
violent crime, among the same groups of Baptists.

3. *Soul competency defines the role of the individual believer.* Baptists
are inherently individualistic (or, one might say, personalistic) because
of the historical understanding of the priesthood of all believers. Each
person is able to interpret Scripture for herself or himself and make decisions as an individual guided by the Spirit. Mobilizing such individuals
for social action requires achieving consensus, which is usually difficult.
The principle of soul competency is important for understanding the
freedom with which Baptist individuals have been able to address even
the most controversial issues, enabling Baptists at times to be trailblazers
on controversial topics. Consider the role played by Baptists like Clarence
Jordan (1912–69) and Martin Luther King Jr. (1929–68), when it came to
racial integration in the United States.

4. *Each Baptist congregation is autonomous, as are the associations
and fellowships formed within convention bodies.* Most of the public positions representative of Baptist groups are formulated as resolutions
which have no binding power on individuals or entities. They are useful,
however, for engaging in education on public issues, developing lobbying
efforts, and providing position statements for public decision-makers.

5. *Religious liberty and separation of church and state have united
Baptists in political action*—and set limits on such action. These commitments give Baptists a framework for addressing human rights in all
of their dimensions of equality—racial, gender, economic status, ethnicity, and increasingly sexual orientation. They also remind Baptists of the
limits of the state in coercing at least some aspects of social change. In
those regions of the world where majority economic and political status
have been achieved, such as the southern United States, maintaining this
historic commitment has proven difficult in the face of a temptation toward cultural hegemony. In most of the Baptist global context, though,
minority status keeps this commitment alive. When you are a tiny sect of
believers in a dictatorial state or state controlled religion, survival may
depend on international support for minority religious rights.

6. *Support for Baptist organizations is required to address the complexity of social and political decision-making.* The social gospel movement of

the late nineteenth and early twentieth centuries provided the impetus for creating denominational, interdenominational, and international entities that became channels for mobilizing Baptist people in social ministries such as disaster relief, hunger and economic development ministries, legislative engagement through lobbying, voter registration and mobilization, and legal action on church-related issues.

Multiple examples of these efforts can be cited. The creation of the BWA in 1905 gave Baptists an international forum that now provides through Baptist World Aid disaster relief to devastated regions, hunger projects, and economic development. Commissions on Human Rights Advocacy, Peace, Religious Freedom, and Social and Environmental Justice engage in study of critical ethical issues and provide a forum for recommending resolutions addressing critical issues. A review of the resolutions approved by BWA from 1981–2014 will identify a comprehensive list of the issues of concern to Baptists that have been addressed in staff visits, efforts to mount pressure on governments, and creation of support services for victims of injustice.[1]

A similar effort of education and support for political actions characterizes creation of ethical concern groups within denominational and fellowship groups. Leaders of the Baptist Union of Great Britain routinely participate in ecumenical communications to lawmakers on issues of peace and economic justice. The American Baptist Churches USA have a distinguished history of addressing through policy statements and resolutions a full range of ethical positions for member congregations and constituents to address.[2]

The largest Baptist body, the Southern Baptist Convention (SBC) and associated state conventions, has a mixed history of involvement. Organized in 1845 as a breakaway from American Baptists over issues of missionary policies and slavery, it has made significant strides in racial inclusion in recent decades. Formal involvement in sociopolitical issues emerged at the level of state conventions in the SBC with the organization of the first Christian Life Commission (CLC) in the Baptist General Convention of Texas in 1950. The national body followed the Texas lead and formed the SBC Christian Life Commission in 1953. A. C. Miller (1891–1984) was the first executive director of both and was followed in both by Foy Valentine (1923–2006). Valentine was a towering figure in

---

1. Cf. http://www.baptistworld.org/resolutions.
2. Cf. https://www.abc-usa.org/policy-statements-and-resolutions.

SBC life and served at the CLC from 1960 until his retirement in 1987. During his twenty-seven years he was a strong advocate of racial equality and shaped multiple convention resolutions with a moderating perspective leaning toward a progressive social gospel direction.

The divisive theological controversy in SBC life from 1979 to the mid-1990s enlarged the activism of the SBC but in decided opposition to the progressive direction it had been moving. The agenda of the religious right embodied by the Moral Majority was adopted by the new SBC leadership which focused the work of the former CLC into a renamed entity, the Ethics and Religious Liberty Commission. The convention withdrew from the Baptist Joint Committee for Religious Liberty and the Baptist World Alliance to form its own separatist approach under the leadership of Richard Land from 1987 to 2012 and Russell Moore since 2013 to 2021.

The most activist of the Baptist entities in North America have been African American Baptists, especially strong pastors who lead their congregations in active political engagement, support of people in navigating political processes, and open endorsement of political campaigns. There are four major conventions. The National Baptist Convention, USA, Inc., is the historic body from which others have emerged. The Progressive National Baptist Convention, Inc. was founded in the 1960s with leadership from Martin L. King, Jr. and is the most publicly political of the conventions. Among its four main goals is advocacy for the voiceless in the form of "full voter registration, education and participation of members in society, economic empowerment and development, and universal human rights and total human liberation for all people."[3] It coordinated recent efforts with the other black Baptist conventions including the Lott Carey Foreign Mission Convention to educate members on Ebola and raise $250,000 in funds for work in West Africa. The National Missionary Baptist Convention of America was formed in 1988, from which developed the National Baptist Convention in America International, Inc. in 1995. It has an active public emphasis on social action with commissions on Social and Community Justice, Criminal Justice, as well as Labor Relations.

While active congregations are highly visible in the political arena, there is a more conservative stance required to maintain consensus at the denominational level. A recent example was the communication to

---

3. See https://www.pnbc.org/.

the NBC USA constituency on the issue of President Barack Obama's support of gay marriage in which the convention president, Julius R. Scruggs, disagreed with the President on this issue but openly stated the areas of public support for his policies:

> Indeed, we have great appreciation for our President and for many of the stands that he has taken. For example, we appreciate his positions on health care reform, public education, student college loans, ending of the war in Iraq, leading in turning around the U. S. automobile industry, expanding Pell Grant spending, expanding health care for children, providing payment to wronged minority farmers, framing a foreign policy that has improved America's image in the global community and advocating freedom and justice for all people, regardless of race, creed, color, ethnic background or gender.[4]

A number of Baptist organizations have developed in North America to address focused issues of concern. The Baptist Joint Committee was formed in 1946 as a collection of Baptist bodies to address issues of religious liberty and separation of church and state. It maintains a lobbying presence in the US capital as well as a close observation of the Supreme Court to monitor church-state cases. Fifteen Baptist bodies fund and provide oversight of its work.

The Baptist Peace Fellowship of North America is a small but effective group of individuals and churches from Canada, the United States, Mexico, and Puerto Rico addressing issues of conflict and organizing peacemaker events. Its programs of conflict transformation training have been conducted in multiple global regions where violent conflicts are dividing local people.

The issue of attention to LGBT (Lesbian, Gay, Bisexual, and Transgender) persons is a divisive one in most Baptist bodies. Changes in the culture are forcing Baptists to a new level of conversation and study of the issue. SBC leaders recently met to attempt a civil conversation with little change in its positions. The coauthor of this chapter, David Gushee, has stimulated significant recognition for the acceptance of LGBT persons in his writings with a book.[5] The Association of Welcoming and Affirming Baptists was formed as a group that began in the ABC-USA but separated in response to major opposition in the denomination's regions. The

4. Scruggs, "Statement on the Same-Sex Marriage Issue."
5. Gushee, *Changing Our Mind.*

Alliance of Baptist is publicly supportive of LGBT persons and numerous other progressive social issues.

Prophetic Individuals and Sociopolitical Action

Historically, a strong minority of Baptist individuals have been at the forefront of addressing a multitude of ethical issues that require action in the political arena. As an example, Thomas Helwys (ca. 1575–1616), founder with John Smyth (ca. 1554–1612) of the first Baptist congregation, wrote one of the most powerful challenges to political authority, directed to King James I in 1612 (*A Short Declaration of the Mistery of Iniquity*). Of course he was imprisoned, where he died.

Almost all change in the social arena has begun with individuals who stepped outside the dominant viewpoint of their environment to champion new understandings of a biblical application to critical issues. Whatever the issue—slavery, discrimination, oppression, economic injustice, or violence—it has been the prophetic minority that has often brought attention to the full range of sociopolitical concerns through denominational resolutions, formation of organizations addressing specific issues, mobilization of political action to influence governmental policies, and creation of helping agencies to serve victims of injustice. A comprehensive examination of these efforts is not possible in this brief discussion, but attention will be given in summary fashion to several key shapers of the Baptist moral consciousness and the issues they addressed.

The Social Gospel

The leaders of the social gospel movement of the late nineteenth and early twentieth century helped redefine the scope of the gospel from an individualistic understanding to a theology of public Christianity. John Clifford (1836–1923) engaged in Britain as an opponent of the Boer War and organized passive resistance among Nonconformists against the Education Act of 1902 which would fund only Anglican and Roman-Catholic denominational schools. Mahatma Gandhi considered Clifford's strategy a forerunner of his *satyagraha* methods in South Africa. Clifford became widely recognized as president of the key Baptist and Evangelical organizations of Britain and was elected the first president of the BWA. His presidential sermon at the 1911 General Meeting of the BWA was a passionate apologetic for the Alliance and for Baptist embrace of the social gospel, declaring, "we have to fight against all the encroachments of might on the rights of the weak, against commercial and social, military and ecclesiastical systems linked together for the defense of wrong."

The dominant figure of the social gospel in the United States was Walter Rauschenbusch (1861–1918). As a Baptist pastor in the Hell's Kitchen neighborhood of New York City, he became personally aware of the devastating impact of "robber baron" capitalism on the poor. Joining other Baptists in forming "The Brotherhood of the Kingdom," he began refining his theology in dialogue with the progressive era political and sociological writings of the time. When deafness limited his abilities as a pastor, he moved to Rochester Theological Seminary where he became a popular teacher, writer, and public speaker. His *Christianity and the Social Crisis* (1907) became a bestseller, and *A Theology of the Social Gospel* (1917) remains a classic for understanding the implications of Jesus for public faith.

The social gospel movement was largely embraced by Northern Baptists and mainline Protestants with little appeal in the US South until post-war efforts for racial equality took root. Fundamentalist Baptists resisted it with great controversy and Neo-Orthodox theologians critiqued it as utopian, but its influence released new energy in developing social ministries and political efforts. Among the first to embrace its implications was a cadre of women who led in reforms in education, civil rights and social justice, including gender equality. Nannie Helen Burroughs (1879–1961) was a driving force and leader of the Woman's Convention of the National Baptist Convention from 1900 until her death in 1961. From her post she founded the National Trade and Professional School for Women and Girls in Washington, DC and became a public figure at the forefront of minority education, civil rights, and gender equality.

A similar emphasis was developed in London by Muriel Lester (1883–1968) as a British pastor, social worker, and peace activist. Born into a prosperous Baptist family, she and her sisters purchased a Baptist chapel in the Bow neighborhood of East London. They renovated it into a community worship and service center called Kingsley Hall where Muriel preached and taught. She became a socialist member of the city council of Poplar, became a pacifist in 1914 joining the Fellowship of Reconciliation, and served as traveling secretary of the International Fellowship of Reconciliation in 1933. She visited, hosted, and wrote about Gandhi.

Marian Wright Edelman (b. 1939) is president of the Children's Defense Fund, the leading child advocacy organization in the United States. As founder, she has given forty years of leadership in addressing issues of national policy related to child poverty, abuse, deficient education, and the need for moral training for children.

The Quest for Racial Equality

One can hardly affirm the human dignity so important in Baptist principles of faith and not be embarrassed by the lack of Baptist practice in addressing the injustices of race-based slavery and continuing discrimination toward racial and ethnic minorities. Race is an issue that has divided denominations, congregations, and families. Yet, there are glimmers of hopefulness in the progress that has been made societally as the result of Baptist voices. The General Baptist Assembly of England went on record as early as 1787 opposing the trading of slaves. Throughout the long struggle against legal slavery in the United States, abolitionists were as likely to be Baptist as other Christians, though most were in the North. Within months of the US Supreme Court decision in 1954 against school desegregation in *Brown v. Board of Education*, the SBC passed a resolution in support of the court's decision, to the consternation of many of its members. It also approved a statement of confession in 1995 repenting of past injustices and requesting forgiveness. The New Baptist Covenant meetings led by former president Jimmy Carter since 2005 have all emphasized interracial planning and participation.

Yet it was the nurturing community of African American Baptists that birthed the most prophetic and revered Baptist prophet of the modern era, Martin Luther King Jr. (1929–68). King was a third-generation preacher who inherited the legacy of his father, M. L. King Sr., at Ebenezer Baptist Church in Atlanta. That legacy was strengthened by learning from Howard Thurman (1899–1981), author, pastor, university faculty member and chaplain, and adviser to the major leaders of the modern civil rights movement. Benjamin E. Mays (1896–1984) mentored King as president of his alma mater, Morehouse College, a leading voice for civil rights in his own right. Add an infusion of insights from studying the social gospel at Crozer Theological Seminary and a PhD from Boston University studying nonviolent social change movements, and King was ready to lead.

But he never acted alone. King was surrounded by a national community of equally concerned advocates, most of whom were Baptist pastors: R. D. Abernathy, Jesse Jackson, John Lewis, Fred Shuttlesworth, W. T. Walker, A. D. King, John Porter, A. C. Powell, and Gardner Taylor. They helped the newly formed Southern Christian Leadership Conference succeed in mobilizing the nation to support change and pressing Washington to pass the Civil Rights Act (1964) and the Voting Rights Act (1965). King went on to pursue the related issues of poverty with the Poor People's Campaign and peace with sermons opposing the Vietnam War. For all of his many efforts this prophetic preacher became the first American of the South to be given the Nobel Prize for Peace, an honor later awarded to southerners Jimmy Carter and Albert Gore, both also Baptists.

Violence and the Sacredness of Life

Certain notable Baptists have also provided substantial leadership in peacemaking, opposition to violence, and concern for the sacredness of life. The US Baptist Glen H. Stassen (1936–2014) provided significant global leadership to nuclear disarmament efforts during three decades of the Cold War. Simultaneously he developed, first on his own and eventually in interfaith coalition efforts, a new approach to peace and war which he called just peacemaking. This approach is rooted biblically in the recognition that Jesus blesses not pacifists or warriors but *peace-makers* (Matt 5:9)—those who actively take the steps necessary to make peace amid conflict. Stassen further pioneered a "transforming initiative" understanding of Jesus's teachings, especially in the Sermon on the Mount, claiming that Jesus taught concrete and practical ways to break vicious cycles of sin, including sinful conflict. For example, in teaching us to go and talk with our adversaries (Matt 5:21–26), Jesus, says Stassen, is offering not a dreamy ideal but the most important concrete step one can take to restore communication between those whose relationship is damaged and thus begin the process of peacemaking. Stassen analyzed numerous conflict situations in world history and described ten just peacemaking practices that have proven successful in lancing the boil of conflict and bringing a just peace. His approach is now integrated into most thoughtful treatments of the ethics of war and peace.

Former US President Jimmy Carter (b. 1924), a committed Baptist, was a passionate peacemaker during his time as president of the United States. Perhaps his greatest accomplishment was brokering the peace agreement between Israel and Egypt, which still stands amidst all the conflicts and regime changes of that region. President Carter has spent much of his post-presidency undertaking peacemaking efforts in many troubled regions of the world.

David Gushee, coauthor of this chapter, offered what is widely believed to be the most substantial Protestant analysis of the moral principle of the sacredness of human life. In his 2013 book on the subject, Gushee argues that belief that each and every human being is a person of immeasurable and sacred worth is Christianity's greatest moral contribution to global civilization, and underwrites critically important Christian (and other) moral efforts in peacemaking and human rights. Gushee led a US evangelical effort to apply such commitments to the issue of US-sponsored torture of suspected terrorists held in US custody after 9/11. These efforts spotlighted US abuses and eventually contributed to a roll-back of such policies and finally their elimination under Barack Obama.

Conclusion

At their best, Baptists have contributed a voice for justice, peace, and human rights to national and global sociopolitical debates of various types over many centuries. Rooted in Scripture, and above all the lordship of Christ, and emboldened by a fiercely held tradition of dissent and freedom of conscience, Baptists have sometimes "fought above their weight" in the global Christian world, making a difference for those who most desperately needed a voice of solidarity and compassion.

Bibliography

BWA Commission on Freedom, Justice and Peace. "Declaration on Human Rights," 1980.

Carter, Jimmy. *Our Endangered Values*. New York: Simon & Schuster, 2005.

Clifford, John. "The Baptist World Alliance: Its Origin and Character, Meaning and Work." In *The Life of Baptists in the Life of the World*, edited by Walter B. Shurden, 30–50. Nashville, TN: Broadman, 1985.

Gushee, David P. *Changing Our Mind*. Canton, MI: Read the Spirit, 2014.

———. *The Sacredness of Human Life*. Grand Rapids, MI: Eerdmans, 2014.

Helwys, Thomas. *A Short Declaration of the Mistery of Iniquity*. Amsterdam: N.p., 1612.

King, Martin Luther, Jr. "Letter from Birmingham Jail, April 16, 1963." In *Why We Can't Wait*, 64–84. New York: Signet Classics, 2000.

McSwain, Larry L., ed. *Twentieth Century Shapers of Baptist Social Ethics*. Macon, GA: Mercer University Press, 2008.

McSwain, Larry L., and David P. Gushee. "Baptist Ethics." In *Dictionary of Scripture and Ethics*, edited by Joel B. Green, 89–93. Grand Rapids, MI: Baker Academic, 2011.

Scruggs, Julius R. "A Statement on the Same-Sex Marriage Issue, Voting and Christian Responsibility." https://www.nationalbaptist.com/assets/uploads/2017/12/785169_SamesexMarriageVotingandChristianResponsibility.pdf.

Stassen, Glen H. *Just Peacemaking: The New Paradigm for Ethics of Peace and War*. Pilgrim, 2008.

Stassen, Glen H., and David P. Gushee. *Kingdom Ethics: Following Jesus in Contemporary Context*. Downers Grove, IL: InterVarsity, 2003.

Williams, Roger. *The Bloudy Tenet of Persecution, for Cause of Concience [sic], Discussed in a Conference between Truth and Peace*. N.p.: S. L., 1644.

D. Baptist Women

9

British Baptist Women in Ministry

Faith Bowers and Ruth Gouldbourne

At the 1984 European Baptist Federation Congress in Hamburg English eyes new to the wider Baptist world were surprised both to see German deaconesses in traditional veiled uniforms and a woman General Secretary, Birgit Karlsson of the Baptist Union of Sweden. The Baptist Union of Great Britain (BUGB) had women ministers but none in a prominent post, while British deaconesses had long abandoned the veil and the Order closed in 1975, when serving deaconesses were recognized as ministers. Most were already in pastoral charge. Not until 2013 was a woman, the Rev. Lynn Green, appointed BUGB General Secretary.

Historical Overview

Women usually accounted for over half the membership of Baptist churches but were subservient to men, as in society at large. Some old church rules specified that women might *vote* in church meetings but must ask a man to *voice* their contributions. At Dublin Street, Edinburgh, the 1850s title deeds precluded women from voting on property matters, perhaps reflecting their legal position. Women were always involved in pastoral care, and some with private means were generous donors. When in the later nineteenth century larger churches formed ancillary societies for mission, young women proved persuasive fundraisers. Work with women and children, Bible sales, care for those in need, teaching and nursing were all acceptable voluntary work for church women. The

Baptist Missionary Society (BMS) had used missionaries' wives but did not send a single woman overseas until 1871 when Miss Fryer went to India with the Baptist Zenana Mission, a separate branch for work with women.

In 1890 the London Baptist Association began to train full-time deaconesses. This idea quickly spread and was taken over by the Baptist Union as the Order of Baptist Deaconesses. Some developed a preaching ministry, although not all churches were happy with this. Deaconesses left on marriage, but many then served as ministers' or missionaries' wives.

During the 1914-18 War women took over civilian work vacated by men joining the military forces. This strengthened the movement for women's emancipation. Suffrage was extended to women over thirty in 1918, and in 1928 to all aged twenty-one, as for men. In 1919 Nancy Astor became the first woman Member of the British Parliament.

This period first saw women accredited as Baptist ministers. In 1922, accepting a church's right to choose the pastor, the Baptist Union recognized Edith Gates as minister of Little Tew and Cleveley, Oxfordshire; she took the Union's qualifying examination. Her long pastorate commanded respect and she later served as President of the local Association. Maria Living-Taylor, a university graduate working alongside her husband at Barking Tabernacle, East London, was recognized in 1924. The couple later ministered in Newport and Bradford. Violet Hedger was the first to train at a Baptist college, Regent's Park, then in London. Called to Littleover, Derby, she was ordained in 1926. That year the Deaconesses told the Baptist Union Council that "It would be contrary to Baptist belief and practice to make sex a bar to any kind of Christian service." Over the next three decades, however, only one more woman became a Baptist minister: Gwyneth Hubble, trained at Bristol Baptist College, was ordained in 1938. She was Assistant General Secretary of the Student Christian Movement 1938-45, Principal of Carey Hall, training deaconesses, 1945-60, and served the World Council of Churches' Division of World Mission and Evangelism from 1961, but was never pastor of a local church.

The role of deaconesses was changing. Some were still pastoral assistants to male ministers in large churches, but others were effectively in pastoral charge. As new housing estates were built after 1945, deaconesses were sent to plant churches. Once these were financially viable, a man would replace the deaconess—on a higher stipend.

In the early 1960s several women heard God's call to ministry. Marie Isaacs was followed by Ruth Vinson at Regent's Park College, by now in Oxford, where they found practical problems yet to be addressed. Bristol and Northern Baptist Colleges quickly followed. Thereafter a slowly growing number joined the ranks of ordained ministers serving churches in England and Wales. This second wave of pioneers still faced difficulties. Churches were reluctant to call a woman and, even when accepted and affirmed by a local congregation, women ministers were not always well received in wider church circles.

Although some conservative evangelicals and charismatics would not accept women as ministers, others were supportive. Writing for the BUGB Ministry Department in 1983, George Beasley-Murray, New Testament scholar and principal of Spurgeon's College, declared, "Man and Woman, created for partnership, have been redeemed for partnership in service. It is high time to make that partnership truly effective in the service of God in His church and His world."

Women's fruitful pastorates in small churches, usually in challenging rural or inner city contexts, gradually changed the views of many who had found it hard to believe that God called women to ministry. London examples included the work of Carol McCarthy (Upper Holloway, 1980–2001) and Sarah Parry (Shoreditch, 2001–2010), both overseeing major redevelopments, and the remarkably long ministry of Jane Thorington-Hassell (Victoria Park, Bow, 1985–2020).

In the 2012 *Baptist Directory* it is possible to identify 282 women ministers, most (181) were in pastorates (whether sole or assistant is unclear). Four had joint pastorates with their husbands. Several of the churches had had previous women ministers, suggesting good experience. BUGB and BMS each had three on their staff, eight were on regional ministry teams, five teaching in Baptist colleges; four were in community ministries, two were spiritual directors, one was a schoolteacher. Seventeen were chaplains (one military, three university, one school, five hospice, six hospital, and one prison). A few had no current appointment, the rest were retired. The first woman BUGB President (1978) was Nell Alexander, a lay woman. It was more challenging to appoint a woman minister but the Rev. Margaret Jarman, a deaconess made full minister in 1975, was President in 1987. In a 1986 article, Jarman noted that three women had chaired Union committees; others followed, including the present authors.

By 2000 BUGB's list of ministers included 155 women (below 7 percent). They were, however, beginning to appear in influential roles. Vivienne Lassetter and Anne Wilkinson-Hayes were on the BUGB staff, Ruth Matthews (née Vinson) and Ruth Bottoms chaired major executive committees. Myra Blyth was Deputy General Secretary 1999–2003. In 1998 the Rev. Dr. Pat Took was the first woman appointed as Area Superintendent, "pastor of the pastors." She served London until 2010, becoming Regional Team Leader with reorganization, and was BUGB President in 2011. Before her, the third woman President was the Rev. Dr. Kate Coleman in 2006, who was also the second black President. Coleman has since also chaired the Evangelical Alliance Council. Ruth Bottoms chaired the BUGB Council and then the new Trustees, guiding the Union through major structural change. The Rev. Dr. Anne Phillips was co-principal of the Northern Baptist Learning Community, 2009–13, sharing the role with the Rev. Dr. Richard Kidd, succeeded by co-principals, the Rev. Dr. Clara Rushbrook (formerly McBeath) and Rev. Glen Marshall.

In 2006 the Rev. Dr. Ruth Gouldbourne was called from Bristol College to Bloomsbury Central Baptist Church and the Rev. Kathryn Bracewell to New Road Baptist Church, Oxford, the deliberate choice of churches that would expect no difficulty in finding willing men. Ruth worked with Simon Woodman at Bloomsbury, modeling a new way as equal co-pastors bringing different personalities and gifts. She served on the Prague International Baptist Theological Seminary Board of Trustees from 2002, chaired this 2006–13. Since 2018 she has been minister of Grove Lane Baptist Church, Cheadle Hulme.[1]

In 2013 14 percent of BUGB's active ministers were women (230 out of 1,626), and 39 percent of those in formation for ministry (57 out of 148), considerably lower than for the Church of England, which had only ordained women as priests since 1994. Baptist growth has been slow. The January 2021 Baptist figures were 216 (18 percent) fully accredited, but of those sixty were newly accredited, with fifty-seven (47 percent) in training. By comparison, the Church of England proportion in 2012 was 38 percent in stipendiary ministry, and in 2020 was 33 percent ordained women, including 55 percent newly priested, with 54 percent of women among those beginning training.

1. Contact Ruth M. B. Gouldbourne at ruth@grovelane.org for a copy of her Whitley lecture from 1997/98 entitled "Re-Inventing the Wheel: Women and Ministry in English Baptist Life."

Paul Goodliff, then BUGB Ministry Team Leader, observed that the early years of the new century saw a remarkable period of women's leadership in BUGB: Lynn Green as General Secretary, Jenni Entrican as President for 2015-16, Sheila Martin as Council moderator, and Jenny Royal chairing the Trustees: the Union's four main governance structures (Baptist Steering Group, Trustee Board, Assembly and Council) all led by women. Such momentum is not always maintained. In 2021 there is one woman on the Core Leadership Team and team leadership at Association level is mostly male. Things have changed, but there remain unresolved issues.

How, as Dissenters, Do We Deal with Dissent?

Although it is apparent that God blesses their labors, some churches still refuse to call a woman minister, believing that Scripture bans them from preaching. Various strategies have evolved to cope with disagreement, but British Baptists have yet to work out how to deal theologically with internal dissent. Discussion of issues with those who dissent from the dominant position is almost impossible. A 2012 example was debate over whether churches openly unwilling to consider a woman pastor should be eligible for grants from the common fund.

Most attacks on women ministers still center on gender. Men ministers also get attacked but the reasons are more varied. Nevertheless, all attacks revolve around the idea that they have "got God wrong." The attackers are always sure they understand God correctly. One woman giving a lecture about women's ministry remembers a questioner begin, "Bearing in mind that God does not call women to the ministry . . ." She hopes younger women do not often face such conviction.

Women's ministry gradually won respect and acceptance among most English and Welsh Baptists, but was still problematic in Scotland. The Baptist Union of Scotland eventually agreed to accept women in October 1999. Two were ordained in 2000 and fully accredited in 2003. Marjorie McNair served as a hospital chaplain. Beth Dunlop, a former Salvation Army officer, served as Associate Minister at Dumfries. Catriona Gorton has been minister of Glasgow's Hillhead Baptist Church since October 2009, but her training and first pastorate were in England. In 1919, Annie Aiken, trained in the Glasgow college, was called to the church at Leslie in Fife.

Social Impact

Baptist ministers already serving in England and Wales noticed a marked change in their apparent social status when the Church of England priested women in 1994. When a large number were promoted at once, the media took note. Free Church women ministers felt the difference: with more public visibility their occupation no longer caused such surprise. It became possible to buy clerical shirts in women's sizes! Even the television comedy series, *The Vicar of Dibley*, helped people accept women's ministry as "normal."

Style

Wider acceptance makes it easier for women ministers to "be themselves." The pioneers had to carry the burden for them all, making it harder to develop a personal style. At first they needed to adapt to "the system," to act like men: many women would, for example, more naturally work by negotiation than confrontation, but in some contexts, especially in the wider groupings of Association and Union, they were forced to fight their corner. Within the existing system they could not allow themselves the luxury of showing vulnerability. Some were strident in their feminism, at least in those wider spheres, although the affection of their churches suggested they were not normally so aggressive (note: strident men tend to be seen as "assertive," but women as "aggressive").

A wider range of styles is now acceptable, making it easier to work in ways that suit individual personality. This may also prove liberating for those men whom the "expected" role did not really suit. As women have been called as Regional Ministers, handling the role in various ways, they have proved that different approaches can earn respect. Women called to wider leadership among British Baptists have brought a certain vulnerability, an "unprotectedness" to the role. They perhaps find it easier to admit that they cannot "do it all" alone yet affirm that that is fine, no one has to be perfect. They are not feeble but honest. They bring their gifts and dedication but invite help from others. As opportunities to share their experience increased, they found much in common and no longer felt "strange." The tone in women's groups is mainly collaborative and supportive. For some, ministry has proved so bruising that they are extremely careful how they handle others, for fear of hurting them.

Marital Stress

A number of women ministers have broken marriages. For some, that precedes calling to ministry but sadly others have broken while in ministry. Whether that is limited to Baptist women ministers is not clear: it may equally affect Baptist men ministers or women in other branches of the church. Where the woman has responded to the call in mid-life, perhaps as children grow up, this complete role change must affect the relationship and the strain may be too great. It may be a little easier where the call came early and has always been part of the marriage: one minister's husband comments that he always knew he had to share her. Marital breakup is always unfortunate but circumstances vary and BUGB does not automatically reject a man's or a woman's ministry.

The Way Forward

Baptist numbers have risen slowly and it has become easier to place women in churches. Indeed, these days it is harder to place single men, unless still young and "nubile": the specter of human sexuality issues looms large on churches' horizons.

After such efforts to gain recognition, older ministers want to see growth sustained after they retire. For Pat Took the challenge of misogyny goes way beyond feminism. She called for a wider and mutually liberating collaboration between men and women, both made in God's image. "If the church is to present to the world *the true image of God*, it will have to demonstrate in its gender relationships that self-emptying mutuality which lies at the heart of the Trinity."[2]

To mark a hundred years of women ministers, BUGB has appointed the Rev. Jane Day in 2019 as Centenary Enabler. Among new initiatives, she has launched the three-year, participatory research Project Violet, to understand more fully the theological, missional, and structural obstacles faced by Baptist women ministers and identify ways forward. Women ministers have already produced a celebratory book of liturgical and prayer resources.

2. See Patricia Took's address to the Baptist Ministers' Fellowship on May 2008, titled "In His Image." Available from pmtook@aol.com.

Bibliography

Baptist Quarterly 31.7, July 1986. This issue focused on women which contained: Edward C. Lehman, "Reactions to Women in Ministry: A Survey of English Baptist Church Members"; Shirley Dex, "The Church's Response to Feminism"; M. F. Jarman, "Attitudes to Women in Baptist Churches in the mid 1980s"; Ruth Matthews, "God, Women and Men: Language and Imagery"; Carol McCarthy, "Ordained and Female"; Paul Fiddes, "Women's Head Is Man: A Doctrinal Reflection upon a Pauline Text"; John H.Y. Briggs, "She-Preachers, Widows and Other Women: The Feminine Dimension in Baptist Life since 1600."

Baptist Quarterly 45.8, October 2014. This issue again focuses on women, with papers from Faith Bowers, "Liberating Women for Baptist Ministry"; Karen E. Smith, "The Balfours and the Burns: Baptists Battling the Power of Strong Drink"; Michael J. Collis, "Female Baptist Preachers and Ministers in Wales"; Paul Goodliff, "Women's Ministry: An Exploration at a Historic Moment."

Beasley-Murray, George R. *Man and Woman in the Church*. N.p.: BUGB Ministry Department, 1983.

Bowers, Faith. "For God and the People: Baptist Deaconesses 1901-1905." *Baptist Quarterly* 43 (2010) 473-93.

Champion, L. G. "Ministerial Service of Women." *Baptist Quarterly* 20.5 (1954) 201-5.

"Free Indeed: Discussion Material on the Role of Women and Men in the Church." BUGB Mission Department, 1980.

Gorton, Catriona, et al. *Gathering up the Crumbs: Celebrating a Century of Accredited, Ordained, Baptist Women in Ministry in the United Kingdom*. N.p.: BUGB, 2021.

Morris, Nicola. *Sisters of the People: The Order of Baptist Deaconesses, 1890-1975*. Centre for Comparative Studies on Religion and Gender Research Paper 2, University of Bristol, 2002.

Randall, Ian. *The English Baptists of the 20th Century*. Didcot: Baptist Historical Society, 2005.

Rose, Doris M. *Baptist Deaconesses*. London: Carey Kingsgate, 1954.

Smith, Karen E. "Beyond Public and Private Spheres: Another Look at Women in Baptist History and Historiography." *Baptist Quarterly* 34.2 (1991) 79-87.

———. "British Women and the Baptist World Alliance: Honoured Partners and Fellow Workers?" *Baptist Quarterly* 41.1 (2005) 25-46.

Troughton, Patricia. *Women, Baptists and Ordination*. Didcot: BUGB, 2006.

Women in Leadership among the Churches of the Baptist Union of Great Britain: A Report to Council. March 2010.

Women in the Service of the Denomination. BUGB, September 1967.

Woodman, Simon. *The Story of Women in Ministry in the Baptist Union of Great Britain*. Didcot: BUGB, 2011.

10

Baptist Women and Ordination

Pamela R. Durso

MOST PEOPLE READILY ACKNOWLEDGE that for the four hundred years that Baptists have been around, women have been central to the growth of their churches, the upkeep of their buildings, the funding of their programs, and the theological education of their children. Yet, during most of those four hundred years, women did not hold formal leadership positions in Baptist churches. They were not given official titles or paid salaries. And only in the last fifty years or so have significant numbers of Baptist women been ordained either as deacons or as ministers. Despite the lack of recognition and despite opposition, Baptist women have served and led and ministered from the earliest days of the history of the Baptist faith.

Following is a chronological timeline of the history of Baptist women's ordinations. Included is a tracing of known "first" ordinations of women both in the United States and in nine countries around the world.

"First" Ordinations of Baptist Women in the Nineteenth Century

Numerous Baptist denominations throughout the world have ordained women to the ministry. What I have collected in the past few years are the known "first" ordinations of women by six Baptist denominational bodies in the United States and by Baptist denominations in Australia, Brazil, Cuba, England, Germany, Mexico, Nicaragua, the Philippines, and

Tasmania. The ordinations cited are the earliest documented ones. Other earlier ordinations may have taken place, and as more research is done in this field, other ordinations surely will be discovered and documented.

The earliest known ordination of a Baptist woman was that of M. A. Brennan, who in 1876 was recognized as a minister by the Bellevernon Freewill Baptist Church in Pennsylvania. While specific information about her ordination has not been found, the fact that Brennan was listed on the Quarterly Meeting's annual ministerial list of newly ordained ministers indicates that she indeed had been ordained. The ordination of a second Freewill Baptist woman, Lura Maines, most likely occurred in 1877, when two Michigan churches listed her as a minister, although not the pastor, in their annual reports. In 1880, Maines was called as a pastor and served two churches.

The first ordination of a woman associated with the Northern Baptist Convention, which is now known as the American Baptist Churches, USA (ABC-USA), occurred six years after the first Freewill Baptist ordination. On July 9, 1882, May Jones was ordained at a meeting of the Baptist Association of Puget Sound in Washington. Apparently, her ordination caused quite a controversy. Opponents charged that Jones's church, First Baptist Church of Seattle, had not properly presented a request for ordination to the association or scheduled an ordination council. Instead, church delegates, while their pastor was on a European tour, had proposed to the association that on July 9, 1882 Jones be ordained that very day after the close of the official meeting. Participants at the meeting who were offended by the proposal walked out, leaving only those supporting Jones's ordination to vote on the recommendation. Not surprisingly, the recommendation was accepted, and following her ordination, Jones served briefly as interim pastor of First Baptist Church, Seattle, and beginning in 1883, she pastored six Baptist churches, sometimes serving two or three churches simultaneously.[1]

The first Seventh Day Baptist woman to be ordained was Experience Fitz Randolph Burdick, who grew up in West Virginia. As a child Burdick felt God's call to preach, but not until 1882, when she was thirty-two years old, did she publicly acknowledge her calling and begin preaching. Three years later, in 1885, Burdick was ordained by the Seventh Day Baptist Church in Hornellsville, New York. She served several churches in New York, and at the time of her death in 1906, she was pastor of a Seventh

1. Lynch, "Baptist Women," 311.

Day Baptist Church in New Auburn, Wisconsin. During her ministry, Burdick conducted fifty weddings, ninety funerals, and preached 890 sermons. Since her ordination in 1885, fourteen other Seventh Day Baptist women have been ordained.[2]

While the nineteenth century had some firsts with regard to women in ministry, the twentieth century saw more and more "firsts." Edith Gates was the first English woman to serve as a Baptist pastor, serving the British Union's Little Tew and Cleveley Church from 1918 to 1950. Gates did not enter ministry through the traditional English Baptist method, which was to graduate from a Baptist college and then be ordained and added to the list of accredited ministers. Instead, Gates qualified for the pastorate by passing the Baptist Union Examination. Most likely she was ordained in 1922, after having already served in ministry for several years.[3] For a period of forty years, from the early 1920s to the late 1950s, no other "first" ordinations of Baptist women have been discovered. In 1959 and the years that followed, however, numerous "first" ordinations began to occur.

Within Southern Baptists circles, the first woman to be ordained was Addie Davis. On August 9, 1964, Watts Street Baptist Church in Durham, North Carolina, ordained Davis. When news of her ordination became public, Davis and Watts Street Baptist Church's pastor, Warren Carr received letters of opposition from Southern Baptist all over the country. One man wrote to Davis, calling her a "child of the devil" and instructed her to renounce her ordination. After an unproductive search among Southern Baptist churches, Davis contacted the American Baptist Convention and soon was called by the First Baptist Church of Readsboro, Vermont. Davis pastored American Baptist churches for eighteen years, and then returned to her hometown of Covington, Virginia, and co-pastored an ecumenical church until her death in 2005.[4]

Five years after Addie Davis's ordination, Uvee Mdodana Arbouin became the first woman ordained by the Progressive National Baptist Convention. Her ordination service took place on October 5, 1969. Arbouin served as co-pastor of the Zion Temple Baptist church in Richmond Hill, New York.[5]

2. Bancroft, "Chosen by God," 21–22, 24–25.

3. Badham, *Religion, State, and Society*, 299.

4. Pierce, "Addie Davis."

5. Smoot, "'Hear the Call,'" 56.

Beginning in 1975, ordinations of Baptist women began to occur more frequently in other countries. The first woman ordained in the Baptist Convention of the former German Democratic Republic (East Germany) was Ursula Jöhrmann, whose 1975 ordination was followed by that of Carmen Rossol who in 1979 became the first woman ordained in the Baptist Convention of West Germany. Her congregation, Gummmersbach-Windhagen, was located in a small town near Cologne. Neither of these women were allowed to use the title "pastor," but were instead called "theological co-workers." Only in 1992 did the German Baptist convention, the *Bund Evangelisch-Freikirchlicher Gemeinden*, decide that congregations could use the title pastor for ordained women.[6]

In 1978, Marita Munro became the first woman to be ordained by a Baptist church in Australia. While a student at Whitley College, she pastored several churches. One of these churches, Collins Street Baptist Church, ordained her on October 1, 1978.[7]

Two years later, the Convention of Philippine Baptist Churches ordained Angelina Buensuceso, making her the first ordained Filipino Baptist woman. From 1938 to 1965, Buensuceso served five Baptist churches, holding the positions of associate pastor, choir director, and pastor. She then began a teaching ministry, serving on the faculty of Central Philippine University from 1967 to 1974. From 1974 until her retirement in 1983, Buensuceso was the director of the Convention Baptist Bible College. In 1980, after forty-two years of ministry, she was ordained at the age of sixty-three.[8]

In 1992, the Fraternity of Baptist Churches in Cuba ordained Ena González Garcia, Clara Rodés, and Xiomara Gutiérrez Diaz.[9] The next year, the Baptist Convention of Nicaragua made history on January 30, 1993, by ordaining Carmen Pena Garay, who was then serving as pastor of Hebron Baptist Church.[10] In 1996, Pastor June Robertson was ordained by Launceston's Memorial Baptist Church in Georgetown, making her the first female Baptist minister in Tasmania.[11]

---

6. Andrea Strübind, email to author, August 15, 2012.
7. Cronshaw, "History of Women's Ordination."
8. Romarate-Knipel, "Angelina B. Buensuceso," 8–15.
9. "Recent Events."
10. "News and Notes," 3.
11. "First Female Baptist Minister," 9.

On March 25, 2000, Rebeca Montemayor López became the first Mexican Baptist woman to be ordained. She was ordained at Shalom Baptist Church in Mexico City.[12] A few months later, on July 10, 2000, Sílvia da Silva Nogueira became the first Baptist woman to be ordained in Brazil. Following her ordination, her church was "put out of the state convention."[13]

Statistics Relating to Baptist Women Serving as Pastors

Estimating the number of Baptist women worldwide who have been ordained or who are currently serving as pastor is a difficult task. Even offering an accurate estimate of the number of Baptist women ordained within the United States is challenging. Yet, some statistics relating to Baptist women pastors are available.

The ABC-USA collect information from their affiliated congregations with regard to ministry positions and gender. As of August 7, 2012, that denominational body had 378 women serving as pastors, forty-six as interim pastors, thirty-seven as co-pastors, and twenty-four as bivocational pastors for a total of 485.[14] Among moderate Baptist bodies that grew out of or have previous connections with the Southern Baptist Convention (SBC), the numbers are harder to come by. Denominational organizations and fellowships tend not to keep good lists and statistics, and many churches are dually aligned with several state and national bodies. But in 2012, an unofficial list kept by Baptist Women in Ministry has 150 Baptist women pastors and co-pastors that affiliate with the Alliance of Baptists, the Baptist General Association of Virginia (BGAV), the Baptist General Convention of Texas (BGCT), and the Cooperative Baptist Fellowship (CBF). Of the 150 women, 106 serve as pastor and forty-four serve as co-pastor. A breakdown of the 150 by denominational affiliation is difficult given the dual alignment of some churches and also the lack formal affiliation statements by other churches, but in 2012, the best estimate is that the Alliance of Baptists has forty-three women serving as pastors or co-pastors; the BGAV had twenty-five; the BGCT had twenty-five; and the CBF had ninety.[15]

12. "Baptist Briefs."

13. Carolyn Goodman Plampin, e-mail to author, 20 June 2006.

14. ABC-USA Professional Female Summary, August 7, 2012.

15. Durso, "Baptist Women in Ministry List," 1–2; Alliance of Baptists,

In addition to these moderate Baptists, Seventh Day Baptists had three women serving as ministers. Statistical information is not available from any of the African American Baptist conventions, but in Memphis, Tennessee, alone, three women served as pastors of National Baptist Convention churches in 2020. Gina Stewart was pastor of Christ Missionary Baptist Church in South Memphis; Lynn Dandridge was pastor of Central Baptist Church; and Mary E. Moore has been pastor of New Salem Baptist Church since 1998.[16]

Despite the difficulty of gathering statistics and incompleteness of the data, what is known is that there has been a significant increase of women serving in pastoral roles in the past few years. In 2009, at least 526 Baptist women in the United States were serving as pastors and co-pastors. In 2012, that number has jumped to 638.[17] While the number of women serving has increased rather dramatically, the overall percentage of Baptist churches that have called a woman as pastor remains small. The Baptist bodies from which statistics have been collected (ABC-USA, the Alliance, BGAV, BGCT, and CBF), when taken all together, have less than 5 percent of their churches that are currently pastored by women. Only three of those denominational organizations, the Alliance of Baptists (31 percent), ABAC-USA (9.8 percent), and CBF (5 percent), have more than 5 percent of their churches pastored by women.[18]

While the overall percentage of Baptist churches that are willing to call a woman as pastor remains small, the ordination of Baptist women has increased dramatically since the early 1960s. By 1997, Sarah Frances Anders, who was then professor of sociology at Louisiana College and the keeper of statistics about Baptist women, had documented 1,225 ordinations of Southern Baptist women.[19]

In 2005, Baptist Women in Ministry began tracking ordinations and keeping records. In 2007, Eileen Campbell-Reed and Pamela R. Durso estimated that at least 2,000 ordinations had taken place.[20] Since that report, Baptist Women in Ministry has continued to collect ordination information. Documented ordinations in recent years include forty-five

"Congregations."

16. Bradley, "Dynamic Pastor Dr. Gina Stewart."

17. Durso, "Baptist Women in Ministry List."

18. Campbell-Reed, "Baptists in Tension," 64.

19. Anders, "Historical Record-Keeping," 6.

20. Campbell-Reed and Durso, "State of Women in Baptist Life, 2007," 11.

in 2011, forty-two in 2010, and fifty-five in 2009.[21] Given that not all ordination information is submitted or documented, these numbers are low. But given known information as well as an educated estimate, in 2012 the total number of women ordained since 1964 in churches affiliated with Baptist bodies located mostly in the South is upwards of 2,200. Including women ordained by churches affiliating with American Baptists, Free Will Baptists, National Baptists, Progressive National Baptists, and Seventh Day Baptists would probably double that number. Estimating ordination numbers among Baptist women worldwide is impossible but would certainly be an interesting project to undertake for a young scholar interested in researching Baptist women ministers.

The great majority of recently ordained Baptist women are serving as chaplains or on church staffs, working with children or youth, or serving as associate pastor and are part of a larger trend within Baptist life. During the latter part of the twentieth century, Baptists began to ordain ministers, women and men, who were serving in positions other than the pastorate, and this trend reflected a change in the Baptist understanding of ministry. For most of their history, when Baptists heard the word "minister," they meant pastor or preacher. Around the middle of the twentieth century, however, the understanding of the role of church staff members other than the pastor began to be redefined within the larger Christian community and within Baptist congregations as more churches began to hire new staff members to lead and plan their music programs; to work with preschoolers, children, teenagers, college students, and senior adults; and to oversee administration, education, and recreational activities. Eventually, some Baptist churches recognized and publicly identified these staff members as ministers. With these new position titles sometimes came ordination. This changing attitude toward ministers and ministry among Baptists resulted in thousands of women being given the title of minister and being ordained.

Baptist Opposition to the Ordination of Women

In the past thirty years, many Baptist denominations in the United States and around the world have begun to recognize women as ministers of the gospel and to ordain them. Yet, many Baptist groups continue to oppose women ministers. The Original Free Will Baptist denomination, which

21. Durso, "Baptist Women in Ministry List."

traces its roots back to the early New England Free Will Baptists who early on endorsed women in ministry, began to exclude women from leadership positions in the 1950s. Since then, while the denomination has not taken an official position against female pastors and women's ordination, women have rarely been offered leadership opportunities in the churches, nor have they been approved for ordination.

National Free Will Baptists also have been reluctant to allow women to serve in ordained ministry positions. In the past few decades, some National Free Will Baptist associations have ordained women to the gospel ministry, but most disagree with this practice.[22] The official policy of the National Baptist Convention of America, the second largest African American Baptist denomination, is that women should not be ordained as ministers.[23]

Southern Baptists in 1984 stated their opposition to the ordination of women in a resolution titled "On Ordination and the Role of Women in Ministry."[24] In 2000, the SBC revised its confessional statement of faith, the *Baptist Faith and Message,* to contain a clear denouncement of women's ordination and service as pastors: "While both men and women are gifted for service in the church, the office of pastor is limited to men as qualified by Scripture."[25]

Conclusion

Official and recognized ministry leadership by Baptist women is on the rise. Baptist women are slowly but steadily making progress in finding churches that affirm and celebrate their God-given gifts. Numerous cultural, theological, and denominational factors have contributed to the increasing numbers of women serving. Baptists and Baptist churches were influenced by the women's movement of the 1970s and by the increasing visibility of women in all facets of public life from politics to medicine to business. Reinterpretations of and new insight into biblical and theological teachings on gender roles have also contributed to more openness in Baptist life. Sadly, the other reality that must be acknowledged is that

22. Pinson, *Free Will Baptist Handbook,* 76.

23. Stephen John Thurston, president of the National Baptist Convention of America, telephone interview with author, June 29, 2006.

24. *Annual,* Southern Baptist Convention, 1984, 65.

25. *Baptist Faith and Message,* 13.

Baptists have lost hundreds, perhaps thousands of women, who have fled their childhood denomination and moved into Methodist, Presbyterian, Disciples of Christ, and United Church of Christ circles.

What does the future hold for Baptist women in ministry? The bad news first. The opposition to women preachers and women ministers in some circles will not end any time soon. The good news, however, is that given trends of the past fifty years, especially the last twenty, Baptists in the next ten years will move closer to mainline Protestant groups and at least 10 percent of all Baptist pastors will be women. The number of ordained Baptist women serving in all capacities of ministry—on church staff, as chaplains, with non-profit agencies, as missionaries, as professors—has surely increased dramatically since 1964 when Addie Davis was ordained, but gathering information and statistics about the full spectrum of women in ministry certainly needs more attention and research. Preserving, telling, and interpreting the stories of individual Baptist women also must be done in order to educate churches about the giftedness and readiness of women ministers and to encourage girls and young women who are discerning a call to ministry.

Bibliography

Alliance of Baptists. "Congregations, Theological Schools, and Organizations." https://web.archive.org/web/20111231022953/http://www.allianceofbaptists.org/connect/congregations.

Anders, Sarah Frances. "Historical Record-Keeping Essential for WIM." *Folio* 15.2 (1997) 6.

Badham, Paul. *Religion, State, and Society in Modern Britain.* Lewiston, NY: E. Mellen, 1989.

Bancroft, Patricia A. "Chosen by God: Women Pastors on the Frontiers of the Seventh Day Baptist Denomination." *Baptist History and Heritage* 40.3 (2005) 17–26.

"Baptist Briefs." *Baptist Standard*, April 17, 2000.

Baptist Faith and Message. Nashville, TN: LifeWay, 2000.

Bradley, Barbara. "Dynamic Pastor Dr. Gina Stewart Leads the Way as More Women Shepherd Black Protestant Flocks." *The Commerical Appeal*, July 18, 2010. https://web.archive.org/web/20110816184739/http://www.commercialappeal.com/news/2010/jul/18/spreading-the-word/.

Campbell-Reed, Eileen. "Baptists in Tension: The Status of Women in Leadership and Ministry, 2012." *Review & Expositor* 110 (2013) 49–64.

Campbell-Reed, Eileen, and Pamela Durso. "The State of Women in Baptist Life, 2007." Atlanta, GA: Baptist Women in Ministry, 2011.

Cronshaw, Darren. "A History of Women's Ordination in the Baptist Union of Victoria." MTh thesis, Whitley College, June 1998.

Durso, Pamela R. "Baptist Women in Ministry List of Women Pastors and Co-Pastors, 2012." Unpublished List, August 9, 2012.

"First Female Baptist Minister Ordained in Tasmania." *Folio* 14.4 (1997) 9.

Lynch, James R. "Baptist Women in Ministry Through 1920." *American Baptist Quarterly* 13.4 (1994) 304–18.

"News and Notes." *Folio* 10.4 (1993) 3.

Pierce, John "Addie Davis, First Woman Ordained as Southern Baptist Pastor, Dies at 88." *Baptist News Global*, December 8, 2005. https://baptistnews.com/article/addie-davis-first-woman-ordained-as-southern-baptist-pastor-dies-at-88/#.YgP2Wu5KhpQ.

Pinson, J. Matthew, ed. *A Free Will Baptist Handbook: Heritage, Beliefs, Ministries.* Nashville, TN: Randall House, 1998.

"Recent Events Signal New Hope for Women in Ministry in Cuba." February 25, 1998. https://archive.wfn.org/1998/02/msg00131.html.

Romarate-Knipel, Carla Gay A. "Angelina B. Buensuceso: Harbinger of Baptist Ordination of Women in the Philippines." *Baptist History and Heritage* 41 (2006) 8–15.

Smoot, Pamela A. "'Hear the Call': The Women's Auxiliary of the Progressive National Baptist Convention, Inc." *Baptist History and Heritage* 56 (2011) 49–59.

11

A Brief History of the Baptist Women's Union of the South West Pacific

Julie Belding

Introduction

THE BAPTIST WOMEN'S UNION of the South West Pacific (usually short-ened to BWUSWP and informally pronounced "Bizz-wup") is one of the seven regions (also known as "continental unions") of the Baptist World Alliance Women's Department and was formed in 1968. The work of Baptist women goes back much further, however. It was foreshadowed in the birth of the Baptist World Alliance in 1905. Seeds for the found-ing of the BWA had begun in the late eighteenth century, when God's world was very much on the minds of British Baptists. In 1790 the mis-sionary crusader, William Carey (1761–1834), had been insisting that Christians of all generations were under divine command to preach the gospel of redemption to all peoples. While no definite action was taken by the British Baptists at that time, the comfort of their leaders was dis-turbed. Within two years they would organize for worldwide conquest and William Carey would become the first missionary of the first foreign mission society.

By 1843 the number of Baptists had greatly increased, and their missionaries had spread geographically to Asia, Africa, Australia, and the Pacific Islands. American Baptists, too, had organized for overseas service. A visionary Baptist minister in Virginia wrote that year of his dreams for a Baptist World Fellowship. On July 30, 1896 and again in December 1900, Dr. Robert H. Pitt (1854–1937), editor of *The Religious Herald*, urged upon Baptists of the world a meeting that would look to organize a Baptist World Alliance. Another editor, Dr. John N. Prestridge (1853–1913) from Kentucky, added his support. In 1904 the British Baptist Union invited Baptists of the world to hold their first Congress in London. In 1905, when 3,000 delegates from twenty-four countries had converged in London, the *Baptist World Alliance* was born.

Difficult days lay ahead, however. Two world wars and many smaller conflicts would divide the Alliance, placing their youth in opposing battle lines. Yet "the spark of love and brotherhood, kindled in the London Congress of 1905, [would] not be extinguished."[1] Today, the BWA brings together 238 Baptist groups representing a total of 48 million baptized believers in 124 countries. The stated goals are to nurture mission and evangelism, to promote worship, fellowship and unity, to respond to people in need, to defend human rights and justice, and to advance theological reflection.[2]

Baptist Women and the BWA

At that first Congress, 219 women were registered from nations outside of Britain. Two women's organizations were formally registered—the Woman's Baptist Foreign Missionary Society of Boston, and the Woman's Baptist Home Mission Society of Chicago. In a speech to all the delegates, Mrs. Lucy Waterbury (1861–1949)[3] of Boston said, "Earth will not be a perfect garden for our Master, until with the roses and lilies of Europe and America, He shall find the cherry blossoms of Japan, the lotus of India and the precious black pansies of Africa." No effort was made at the London Congress to hold a separate women's meeting, but certain

---

1. My source of this early history is a little (undated) book called *Jesus Shall Reign: Highlights and Hopes of the Women United in the Baptist World Alliance*. It was published by the North American Baptist Women's Union, probably around 1950.

2. Cf. BWA's website bwa@bwanet.org.

3. Lucy Whitehead McGill married Baptist minister Norman W. Waterbury in 1881; he died in 1886. Twenty years later she married Henry W. Peabody who passed away in 1908. She is remembered for having worked to establish an annual day of prayer for missions, known as the World Day of Prayer.

women watched the proceedings, listened to the messages, and went home to meditate and pray.

In 1911, at the second Baptist Congress in Philadelphia, the program included an afternoon meeting for women. Mrs. A. G. Lester presided over this first women's sectional gathering, where three thousand women were present. Greetings were brought by women from many lands. Miss Fannie Heck[4] (1862–1915) of the USA, a principal speaker, said: "This meeting will mean little if we adjourn, disintegrate and that is all. But if we keep so in touch with one another by our love and sympathy that Baptist women will, in some sense, in the greater necessary sense, *be a unit around the world*, this meeting will have meant much." At this meeting, the first Women's Committee of the BWA was organized, chaired by Martha Hilliard MacLeish (1856–1947)[5] of Chicago, and a circular letter was instituted.

The third BWA Congress was held in Stockholm, Sweden, in 1923. There, ties which had been strained by the Great War were cemented in fellowship. At a meeting of the Women's Committee, three recommendations were directed to the Alliance Executive:

1. that the Women's Committee should continue;

2. that two of its members should be added to the Executive Committee of the Alliance through the Nominating Committee;

3. that no decision of the Women's Committee on major policies should be operative until it had been confirmed by the Executive.

In 1928, at the fourth BWA Congress in Toronto, a special committee was appointed "to develop and express the sentiment of Baptist women throughout the world in favor of peace and disarmament." It was also agreed, however, that "as women are to be placed on the Executive Committee of the Alliance, there seems no need for a separate organization." So, the Women's Committee, born in 1911, was dissolved just seventeen years later.

4. She was the first president of the Southern Baptist Convention Woman's Missionary Union (1895–99, 1906–15).

5. She was married to Chicago merchant Andrew MacLeish who was one of the founders of Chicago University. Martha was the driving force behind organizing the Women's American Baptist Foreign Mission Society and a close friend of Jane Addams, the first American woman to receive the Nobel Peace Prize. This friendship helped to establish Hull House for underprivileged people.

In 1934, however, at the fifth BWA Congress, held in Berlin, the constitution of the Alliance was amended to include "no fewer than five women" on its Executive Committee. A women's sectional meeting was held, planned by Dr. Rushbrook (1870–1947), the Alliance secretary. Nineteen women answered the roll call, but a restlessness was felt in the air. One paragraph of Dr. Rushbrook's observations read:

> Some service, especially for peace, has also been undertaken by the women, and it has revealed a weakness in our organization. More and better work could have been done, in the opinion of many, if there had been a standing committee to lead the women as the Youth Committee leads, and at this Congress your Executive had already given notice of a constitutional amendment to secure, in future, a sufficient number of women members to make a special committee possible. Spirit is more than organization, but we wish to make our organization capable of giving full expression to the spirit of our people!

In 1939, the sixth BWA Congress was held in Atlanta, USA, and it was recommended: "that the women on the Executive Committee be constituted a Women's Committee . . . and that they be given power to co-opt an equal number of other women, and that they report to the Executive Committee."

Dr. Rushbrook again made some observations:

> Criticism has been forthcoming that [the women] scarcely had a fair share in view of their strength in the churches. . . . I am disposed to admit, at least in part, the force of this criticism, but the newly appointed Women's Committee, under the leadership of Eva Brown,[6] will make it impossible henceforth to overlook their claims.

Thus, the Women's Committee of the BWA now became, on paper, worldwide in its membership. Within a month after its leaders returned home, however, World War II broke out. In the mayhem the Women's Committee was almost forgotten. But Mrs. Brown continued to pray, to plan and to correspond with women in the nations not cut off by hostilities.

In 1947 the seventh BWA Congress was held in Copenhagen, and Dr. Rushbrook, president of the Alliance, planned tentatively for a

---

6. She was the wife of British MP Ernest Brown (1881–1962) who also served as cabinet minister in various capacities.

women's sectional meeting, at which Mrs. Brown was asked to speak. Sadly, Dr. Rushbrook's sudden death meant the women leaders had to reorganize the program. No business session of the Women's Committee was held, and the sectional meeting closed without an election of officers. But in the hands of the three members of the Alliance Executive—Mrs. Eva Brown, Mrs. Marion Bates and Mrs. Olive Brinson Martin—lay the future of the Women's Committee. In August 1948, the Executive of the BWA met in London and once more formed a Committee on Women's Work. This time it was composed of two representatives each from the continents of Africa, Asia, Australia, Europe and South America, and four representatives from North America. Olive Martin was later appointed chairwoman of this enlarged committee.

The European Baptist Women's Union

In connection with that executive meeting of the BWA in 1948, the European Baptist Women's Union was organized as a new unit within the Women's Committee, and adopted its own constitution. An EBWU pamphlet included the words:

> Women whose husbands and sons had been fighting on different side during the war came face to face with each other—and discovered two things: on the one hand they recognized an underlying desire for an increase in fellowship and reconciliation; but on the other hand, many of the twelve or so women uncovered their feelings of anger and bitterness—the legacy of war. Could any progress towards reconciliation be made, even among this small group?

The following statement by Blanche Sydnor White (1891–1974), issued by the women who met in London in 1948, and quoted from *The Tie That Binds*, showed that fellowship with God was the prerequisite for fellowship and service among his followers:

> Facing the world . . . today, with its desperate need of faith, of hope, and of love, we turn to our heavenly Father for purification, for guidance and for strength. He has great blessings in store for us, which He is longing to give us, but which can only be given to us in answer to our prayers. . . . Let us, as European women, dedicate the first week in November as a week of prayer when we unitedly pray for each other and for all the world.

Never is the fellowship deeper, richer and stronger than when
we as one heart and soul are praying together.[7]

Baptist Women Become Global

Baptist women were moving steadily towards world organization. Unde-
terred by the apparent failures of the past, the third Women's Committee
of the BWA was launched with high hopes and global plans. Inspired
by the formation of EBWU, the BWA executive instructed the Women's
Committee to organize the women on every continent. A women's sectional meeting was planned for 1950 at the eighth BWA Congress which
was to take place in Cleveland, USA. At that meeting the Women's Committee brought a recommendation to the BWA executive that they would
contribute to the work of the Alliance by

1. Promoting closer fellowship, deeper sympathy and fuller understanding among Baptist women throughout the world;

2. Encouraging them to band themselves together for Christian
   service;

3. Exchanging information concerning activities, ideas, and literature.

In Cleveland, the roll call of nations was answered by women representatives from Great Britain, Canada, Denmark, Norway, Italy, Germany, Brazil, Nigeria, China, Finland, Hawaii, India, and the USA. Members
of the Committee discussed the formation of other continental unions.
They agreed that the secretary would circulate quarterly newsletters.
They also resolved to hold an annual World Day of Prayer, a tradition that
has remained central to the Women's Department. On the first Monday
of every November, Baptist women around the world continue to unite in
prayer for one another and for worldwide social and evangelistic needs.
They learn of one another's vision and struggles, and give and accept offerings for special projects.

The North American Baptist Women's Union

A third continental union was about to join the Australian and European Women's unions, so that the energies of Baptist women on three

7. Quoted in Pusey, *European Baptist Women's Union*, 9.

continents could be combined and directed. In April 1951, the North American Baptist Women's Union (NABWU) was constituted. A budget for 1951–52 was approved, the Baptist Day of Prayer for December 1951 was emphasized, and plans were made for this newest continental union to meet in 1953. NABWU was aware of its favored situation in comparison to the Baptist women of Europe who were leading lives of incredible hardship following the war. "Of instant and pressing concern," said Marion Bates, the chairman of NABWU, "is the promotion of our second worldwide Baptist Day of Prayer on Friday December 7. It is hoped that every constituent member group will meet this year to claim God's promises for prayer." It was suggested an offering be taken during the Day of Prayer to finance the administrative expenses of the union. This offering would also help the Latin American women who would form their own continental union in 1952.

"Very few now living," said Mrs. Bates, "had the privilege of being in attendance at the birth of the Baptist World Alliance. What a time of enthusiasm and excitement was that!" She pointed out that each of her listeners was automatically a charter member of NABWU and would have the opportunity to attend its first general meeting, in November 1953. A pioneer of the Women's Department was Miss Lois Chapple, a former secretary of the BWA Women's Committee. In 1956 she wrote: "If our Continental Unions are to do their best work and fulfill their highest function, we must never lose sight of the fact that they are part of a great whole, that they belong to a world fellowship of Baptist women. We must always keep our windows open upon the world."[8]

The Baptist Women's Union of the South West Pacific

In 1955 the Australasia Baptist Women's Union (comprising Australia and New Zealand) was set up, but according to historian Rena Smith, "it lacked the organization and impetus to do more than distribute Day of Prayer materials each year."[9] New growth came in 1964 when the president of the Women's Department, Mrs. Marion Bates of Canada, visited Australia and New Zealand with Mrs. Church. Traveling through the region, they realized the women were behind other continental unions in the wider work of Baptist women. So the Department appointed two

8. Cited in Smith, *History of Baptist Women.*
9. Smith, *History of Baptist Women.*

members-at-large, Phyllis McIntosh of Australia and Esme Denison of New Zealand. In 1965 these two women, with Mrs. Church, attended the Women's Department meetings in Florida, USA. Margaret Schroeder was there too, "and so began a triumvirate which was to be a force in the Union in the years to come."

The BWA was by now divided into five political regions—Asia, North America, South America, Europe, and Africa. The South West Pacific was considered part of Asia by the BWA administration, as there seemed to be no other place for it. Yet Asia was too big and too far away. Moreover, politically and ethnically, the South West Pacific did not seem to fit the Asian mold. Baptist women leaders in the region decided the women of the South West Pacific needed their own organization. But this was messy, from an administrative viewpoint, because the BWA would continue to recognize five regions, while the Women's Department would now have six![10]

Nevertheless, with the support of the Women's Department officers, a meeting was called in Melbourne in 1968. At this time, finally, the Baptist Women's Union of the South West Pacific was formed. Its purpose, according to its constitution, was "to provide Baptist women of the South West Pacific area with information concerning the Baptist World Alliance, and to promote a closer relationship between Baptist women of our area and Baptist women in other parts of the world," Esme Denison wrote: "In changing the name, we had a wider vision to include PNG [= Papua New Guinea] and Irian Jaya." She added that those first five years were "hard going." Each president would serve for a five-year term, and the first nine presidents alternated between Australian and New Zealand women. In 1969 the first issue of *Involved* was published. This was the BWUSWP newsletter, subtitled, "Every Baptist woman INVOLVED for Christ in the South West Pacific." It had an initial circulation of 7,000. Distribution challenges, however, along with the greater advantages and cost-effectiveness of email, meant that the newsletter was discontinued after three decades.

The early years of BWUSWP had coincided with the thrust of mission work into Papua New Guinea by Australia and New Zealand, and the attendance of women from PNG at the first General Assembly brought joy to the sending countries. The member countries of BWUSWP needed to learn about one another as much as they needed to learn about the

10. Later the Caribbean region became the Women's Department's seventh continental region.

rest of the world, and the General Assemblies gave the opportunity and impetus for that learning. Margaret Schroeder had contacted missionaries in PNG, Irian Jaya, Indonesia, and the Solomon Islands, asking if they wished to be part of BWUSWP and to share in the Baptist Women's World Day of Prayer. "The answer," she wrote, "was an overwhelming 'Yes!'"

In 1972 Margaret Schroeder visited PNG, the first time a representative of the BWA Women's Department had visited this area. She wrote in her report:

> Hearing [women] pray in unison, giving thanks as they realized that they too were now part of this wonderful family, was like a chorus of praise to our heavenly Father. I held a beautiful, warm, naked, four-day-old baby in my arms and thought, "You are my responsibility too, and what you become in the future is my concern." Yes, that little one, and hundreds like her, depended on our prayers and giving to the people in this area of the world.

Reports from the Annual Day of Prayer were exciting. Missionaries wrote of women walking many miles to come to share in prayer for the first time. Four hundred women attended the first prayer meeting in Tekin in PNG. Shy women prayed aloud for the first time. At Baiyer River it was the first time that women had met alone for prayer, and there were too many to fit into the church. In Irian Jaya 370 women were present at three separate meetings, with the program translated into the western Dani dialect.

From 1973 to 1978

In October 1973, the first ever General Assembly of BWUSWP was held in Auckland, at the Baptist Tabernacle. Three hundred and fifty women were present, from Australia, New Zealand, Irian Jaya and PNG, plus officers from the BWA Women's Department. The theme *Jesus is Lord* dominated the scene from a huge banner on the back wall. At that Assembly Phyllis McIntosh was elected President. She had been involved in the Union from the beginning and had attended the Women's Department meeting in Miami in 1965. Along with Margaret Schroeder and Esme Denison she had dreamed of a day when a Union embracing all of its women would exist in the South West Pacific. Of her contacts with the women of the Union, Phyllis wrote that a tour of the Aboriginal mission stations in 1976 was a highlight of her term. She said, "I learned that our missionary women were always in need of prayer for safekeeping and courage in danger, and comfort in loneliness." She added: "When it came to the Stockholm Congress in 1975 can you imagine my feelings when I stood on the platform and introduced women from PNG, Irian Jaya, Australia, and New Zealand, including one Maori woman? The dream our women had in Miami was almost a reality."

From 1978 to 1983

The second Assembly of BWUSWP was held in Melbourne in 1978 at Whitley College, the site of the Victorian Baptist Theological College. Mrs. Joyce Nicholson, who had been present at the inaugural meeting of the Union ten years previously, was elected BWUSWP president for the next five years. Two hundred and twenty-three women were present, coming from all the countries of the Union, plus Fiji. But there was tragedy. One of the Aboriginal women, Bindi Doris, from Northern Territory, died on the first night of the meetings. The outgoing president, Phyllis McIntosh, described what happened next:

> As the announcement was made, a group of Maori women held hands and prayed quietly. The other Aboriginal, Rosaleen, who was just a girl, showed the reality of her faith as she took part in the meetings in a wonderful way. For an Aboriginal to look on the face of a dead person meant death for them, and Rosaleen had found Doris. The Maori women supported her and we saw what the Women's Department was all about—a sisterhood in Christ. Christian love is the bond, regardless of color, race or culture.

During the term of her presidency, Joyce Nicholson visited each of the Australian states, PNG, and Irian Jaya. She reported,

> This was a precious time, experiencing the joys of Mission Aviation Fellowship transport, fellowshiping with the Australian and New Zealand missionaries and meeting and speaking to the national women in a number of places. These women walked many miles and many hours to attend the gatherings, eager to question, happy to fellowship and to share their dedicated faith with each other.

At the 1980 BWA Congress in Toronto, Joyce was chosen to carry the flag for New Zealand in the "Parade of Nations." This was on the night of the final plenary session, when more than 20,000 delegates filled the arena. "All was ready for the start of the program," she wrote.

> When Noni Ransfield, our New Zealand Maori delegate, came over to me from far away in the great meeting hall, carrying a bag, and asked me if I would wear her Maori cloak in the parade. So of course, I agreed. . . . As the line wound round the great hall in a long procession, I felt so proud to be the representative of all the women of the South West Pacific. In response to the roll call we each went to the microphone to say in our own language the theme for the Congress, "Celebrating Christ's presence through the Spirit." I wished I had been able to respond in all the languages of our Union.

From 1983 to 1988

The third General Assembly of BWUSWP took place in August 1983 in Christchurch, New Zealand. It was held on the Ilam campus of the University of Canterbury, with the theme, *Christ—His Love, His Purpose, His Glory.*

One hundred and sixty women were present—sixty-seven from Australia, ninety-one from New Zealand and two from PNG, as well as five visitors from the BWA Women's Department. At this event Mrs. Valma Manning was elected BWUSWP president for the next quinquennium. In 1968, at the time the Union was being established, Valma was a missionary in the jungles of PNG. She was there when Margaret Schroeder had visited, and had been inspired by the vision of BWUSWP, as well as being impressed by the PNG women's enthusiasm for the Day of Prayer. When she visited PNG during her presidential term, Valma was able to communicate in both a local dialect and in Pidgin. She described the experience as "like going home after nearly fifteen years." She found that the women's work in PNG was now strong and serving that country well, and asserted that what was happening among Baptist women there "should be a challenge to us all."

At the time Valma was elected BWUSWP president, the relationship between the BWA Women's Department and the various continental unions was deepening. The presidents of the continental unions were now all ex-officio vice-presidents of the Women's Department and members of the BWA General Council. This was due partly to constitutional changes and partly as a consequence of the new status of the Women's Department which now had a full-time Executive Director and a permanent office in Washington, USA.

From 1988 to 1993

The fourth BWUSWP Assembly (or "conference" as it came to be called) was held in Brisbane in 1988, and Janice Bowman of Auckland, New Zealand, was elected the new president.

During her term, she visited every Australian state plus Fiji. Twenty years on from the establishment of the Union, changes were evident in the patterns of leadership. These reflected the changing lifestyles of women, not only in the secular world but in church life as well. Of the six Continental Union presidents who took office at their Assemblies in 1987 and 1988, two were headmistresses of girls' secondary schools, two were engaged in full-time denominational work, one spent time as a psychologist and teacher of gifted children in the USA, and the new BWUSWP president, Jan Bowman, was an administrative secretary at the Auckland University School of Medicine. The 1960s patterns of well-attended, regular women's meetings had changed markedly by the 1980s, so that there was no longer an easily identifiable channel of communication to women. This was where Jan Bowman's leadership skills were particularly valuable. She had already been heavily involved in the work of the BWA Women's Department's administrative committee during the months leading up to the 1985 Congress in Los Angeles.

In summing up her presidential term, Jan wrote:

> The emphasis of my executive during our term has been on *communication*. We agreed in Brisbane that during our five years we would do all we could to keep our women informed about the activities within our own continental union. Our challenge was to highlight the profile and awareness of the ministry of the Women's Department and to excite and enthuse women to become part of a worldwide group. How to do this is not so easy! Our main source of contact is through *Involved*, and therefore as Editor I have tried to convey the varied activities within our countries to stimulate interest and prayer. . . . Because there are many women within our churches in Australia

and New Zealand who do not come from a Baptist background,
or who are not informed or not interested in Baptist women's
ministries. . . . , I firmly believe we must get our material into
the hands of our women and educate them about the excitement
and opportunity that there is in Baptist women's ministry.

A highlight of Jan's term was the formation of the Fiji Baptist Wom-
en's Fellowship, that had applied for membership of BWUSWP. Indeed,
Fiji was planning to send seventeen women to the next Assembly in
Auckland. So now the Union consisted of five Pacific nations: Australia,
New Zealand, PNG, Papua Indonesia (the new name for Irian Jaya) and
Fiji. Some people have wondered why the women of Papua were included
in BWUSWP. After all, since Papua was now part of Indonesia, its women
should have, in theory, belonged to the Asia Baptist Women's Union. It
was their choice, however, to belong to the South West Pacific, since ethnically they were closer to the women of neighboring PNG than they
were to the people of Indonesia.

From 1993 to 2003

At the fifth BWUSWP conference, held in Auckland in 1993, Jean Mc-
Callum of Australia was elected president for the next five years.

Jean and her husband traveled around Australia in their motor
home, making a point of visiting each of the Australian states. In 1997
Jean toured New Zealand, visiting women's groups in both the North and
South Island. In 1999 she traveled to PNG and attended a women's conference in Telefomin.

In October 1994 Catherine Allen, president of the BWA Women's
Department, visited the South West Pacific region, encouraging women
wherever she traveled. The following year a BWA World Congress, held
in Buenos Aires, included a good representation from BWUSWP. At the
Canberra BWUSWP conference in April 1999, which 250 women attended, Olwyn Dickson from Auckland, New Zealand, became the new
president of BWUSWP. As a pastor's wife, Olwyn had a deep denominational knowledge. She had also worked with Baptist women for most of
her life and knew their concerns and challenges. Olwyn traveled widely
throughout the region, visiting Fiji twice and PNG once. However, she
was unable to get into Papua (the new name for Irian Jaya) because of its
unstable political situation. During Olwyn's term of office there was also a

political coup in Fiji, something nobody expected to happen in the South Pacific. Nevertheless, she decided the next BWUSWP conference would be held in that island nation. It was time for the Baptist women of Fiji to gain more recognition.

Olwyn Dickson said a highlight of her presidency was getting a motion passed by the BWA General Council that the South West Pacific be recognized by the Asia Baptist Federation (ABF) as a distinct and equal partner rather than just a subsidiary. Soon afterwards, the ABF changed its name to the Asia *Pacific* Baptist Federation (APBF) and the president of BWUSWP became an ex officio member of the APBF executive. From then on, the president of BWUSWP would attend all the official meetings of ABPF as a voting member. Indeed, in February 2012 the ABF held its annual executive meeting in Auckland, hosted by BWUSWP.

From 2004 to 2014 and Beyond

In 2004, at the end of the conference in Fiji, Lorraine Walker, from Queensland, Australia (another pastor's wife, as well as a trained nurse) was elected president of BWUSWP.

Walker had been president of the Baptist Union of Queensland. She, too, traveled widely, including a visit to New Zealand, and communicated regularly through email newsletters. In 2009, a conference in Cairns, Queensland, saw Julie Belding of Auckland succeed Lorraine as president. Julie was a writer and editor, and wrote a regular column for women in the monthly *New Zealand Baptist* newspaper as well as producing an occasional newsletter called *Pacifica* which was emailed around the region. She traveled to all five member countries of BWUSWP at least once, as well as attending the annual executive meetings of the Asia Pacific Baptist Federation. With the BWUSWP treasurer, Judith Searle of Queensland, she traveled to the highlands of PNG to speak at a national Baptist women's conference. In 2011 she traveled to Sorong, in Papua, to speak at the Fifth Congress of the Indonesia Baptist Alliance.

The annual Day of Prayer was still the biggest item on the calendar, and in Auckland the event took place variously in conjunction with a breakfast, a dinner, a lunch or an afternoon tea. A team of Baptist women from Fiji, led by Amelia Gavidi, visited New Zealand in May 2011, presenting a program in various churches. In 2014, the quinquennial BWUSWP conference was held in Auckland, again at the Baptist

Tabernacle just as the first one had been, four decades earlier. Special guests were Raquel Contreras, the Women's Department president, and Patsy Davis, its executive director. The leadership mantle of BWUSWP was passed to Amelia Gavidi of Suva, Fiji who had been president of the Fiji Baptist Women's Fellowship. She would continue in this role until the next conference, which was held in Fiji in August 2019. At that event the women from Vanuatu, another island nation in the Pacific, attended for the first time. The tent was being enlarged!

Where to From Here?

In July 2016, Amelia Gavidi attended the executive meeting of the BWA Women's Department in Vancouver. She said the board had discussed further, "Why a Women's Department?" and all had affirmed that when Baptist Women came together in Christ, God created *shalom* for all. "Amen!" added Amelia. Rena Smith had written a quarter century earlier: The women of each new generation need to see themselves not simply in the setting of their local Baptist church, but as members of that wider group of women who are their sisters in Christ worldwide, women from different cultures, with different challenges and opportunities, but all looking to serving the same Lord Jesus Christ. This continuing education process is the task to which the Baptist Women's Union of the South West Pacific has been called.

In the September 2016 issue of *Pacific Waves*, the new e-newsletter of BWUSWP, edited by secretary Anne MacCarthy of Auckland, the annual Day of Prayer, which continues to be the cornerstone of the Baptist Women's movement worldwide, was highlighted. The 2016 program, used by every continental union in the world, had been prepared by the Baptist women of North America and continued the theme of "Arise and Shine." "They are challenging us to see needs in the community," wrote Anne, "and with Christ's help to . . . shine the light of God's love to those in need. Remember that you may be the only Jesus some people will ever see. Ksenija Magda [the current world president] invites us to start in a small way, one person at a time."

Reading List

Jesus Shall Reign: Highlights and Hopes of the Women United in the Baptist World Alliance.

Pusey, Yona. *The European Baptist Women's Union: Our Story 1948–1998.* London: EBWU, 1998.

Smith, Rena. *A History of Baptist Women in the South West Pacific, 1968–1993.*

E. Baptists on All Continents

12

The Baptist World Alliance (BWA)

Erich Geldbach

1. The Beginning

BETWEEN JULY 11 AND 17, 1905 about three thousand delegates from twenty-six countries met in London's Exeter Hall for the purpose of bringing the BWA into existence. On July 18 a final celebratory meeting was convened in the Royal Albert Hall before the delegates disbursed with the overwhelming impression that a new chapter had been opened in the nearly three-hundred-year history of the Baptist movement. Why was the BWA founded? The first president of the Alliance, British pastor Dr. John Clifford (1836–1923), observed in his presidential address in 1911 at the Second Congress in Philadelphia that the organizing of the BWA was so much more remarkable as Baptists were a people totally delivered to individualism, "and in mortal terror of the slightest invasion of their personal and ecclesiastical independence." Did individualism and independence give way to inter-dependence through the new worldwide organization of Baptists? Even though Clifford's assessment may have been too harsh, there can, nevertheless, be no doubt that individualism and independence at both the personal and ecclesiastical level were so deeply ingrained in Baptist thinking and practice that the new organization had somehow been structured in such a way as to reflect these characteristics.

Before this can be further examined, it needs to be pointed out that the formation of the BWA followed the "spirit of the time" among Christians of various denominational backgrounds. They all began to see that their denominations had been established in different countries around the globe. Some Christians had followed the mandate of Jesus Christ to go into all the world and "make disciples of all nations, baptizing them in the name of the Father and of the Son and of the Holy Spirit" (Matt 28:19), commonly referred to as the Great Commission in the English language. Baptists can claim that one of theirs, William Carey (1761–1834), is today remembered as the "father of the modern missionary movement" among Protestants. When in 1806, Carey proposed a meeting of all Christian denominations and missionary societies at The Cape of Good Hope in 1810, not only the name of the place carried a highly symbolic meaning, but this "most startling missionary proposal of all time"[1] foreshadowed the idea that Christian mission and the quest for Christian unity go hand in glove. This could be observed, when in 1910 the World Missionary Conference in Edinburgh under the energetic leadership of Methodist layperson John Mott (1865–1955) took important steps that helped fulfill one of Carey's "pleasing dreams" exactly a hundred years later: Both the International Missionary Council (1921) and the World Council of Churches (1948) came into being as a result of the Edinburgh meeting.

Carey was a missionary forerunner of inter-Baptist and inter-church cooperation. The success of the missionary efforts that followed Carey's initiative must be considered a leading reason why converts in Africa, Asia, the Caribbean, and Latin America wanted to unite in their respective countries and to link with other Baptists around the world. A number of Protestant Churches moved also in this direction, among them Adventists (1863), Anglicans (1867), Reformed and Presbyterians (1877), Methodists (1881) and Congregationalists (1891). Others would follow later. British Baptist leader John Clifford had been invited to the meetings when the International Congregational Council was founded. There, the hope was expressed that the "other great branch of the Congregational family," i.e., the Baptists, would join the Council.[2] This never happened, but it clearly shows the urge to come together which must have impressed Clifford.

---

1. Rouse, "William Carey's 'Pleasing Dream,'" 181.
2. Russell, "Early Moves," 7. For the following details see 13–17.

In the USA, Baptist Congresses were convened from 1882 until 1914 "for the Discussion of Current Questions." Participants were mostly from the North, but there were also some Southerners, Canadians, a few from Britain and from the Afro-American Baptist community. Of equal importance were individuals with a wide-ranging appeal such as Baptist pastor William W. Landrum who in some of his sermons recommended a "Pan-Baptist Conference." This idea was picked up by Robert Healy Pitt (1853–1937) who was the editor of the Virginia Baptist newspaper *Religious Herald*. Even though his advocacy was unsuccessful, there was another editor, John Newton Prestridge (1853–1913) who edited the paper *The Baptist Argus* (since 1908 named *Baptist World*) in which Archibald T. Robertson (1863–1934), professor of Greek at Southern Seminary, published an editorial in mid-January 1904 that called for a conference on Baptist world problems in London later in 1904. Prestridge immediately seized upon this idea and contacted various Baptist organizations in America to enlist their support. Most importantly, he was able to win the backing of the British Union so that on October 4, 1904 a resolution was adopted to invite representatives from Baptist bodies worldwide to gather in London the following July. Thus, the idea of a pan-Baptist congress took shape.

In North America, a committee representing the Southern Baptists and various other Baptist agencies was set up to work closely with the British planning committee which was headed by the British Union's general secretary John Howard Shakespeare (1857–1928) and pastor William T. Whitley (1861–1947).[3] The pastor of Union Chapel in Manchester, Alexander Maclaren (1826–1910), was named as president of the Congress with John Clifford[4] of Westbourne Park Chapel in London as vice chair. Clifford, an outspoken critic of both the House of Lords and the Tories, was a social activist for religious liberty, free church causes, and the betterment of the lower classes. When the Congress was in session, Maclaren was assisted by ten vice presidents of whom seven were laypersons.[5] A very important step was taken at the opening session by Maclaren when he asked all attendees to recite the Apostles' Creed. Thus, Baptists made sure that they came together not only to seek closer ties

3. Whitley had served from 1891 to 1902 as head of the Baptist College of Victoria in Melbourne which is today named after him. For a short description see Sellers, "W. T. Whitley," 159–73.

4. Geldbach, "John Clifford," 62–83.

5. Briggs, "From 1905 to the End," 21.

with each other, but also that they are part of the Universal Church and not a fringe sectarian movement.[6] This move had far-reaching ecumenical implications as the Baptist movement was not detached from the ongoing quests for Christian unity.

A number of other issues that were addressed at the first Congress in 1905 would in subsequent Congresses re-surface. One precedent was the debate over how biblical scholarship would tie in with current problems. Professor Milton Evans from Crozer Seminary in Upland, Pennsylvania, praised modern scholarship as a tool to have rendered "a better appreciation of early Christianity" and, therefore, it presents the truly "human nature of the incarnate Word of God, without shaking confidence in the true Deity." Consequently, the written word of God is "truly human literature, without destroying its inspirational character." Not everyone was confidant with this assessment, but there was no fight.[7] It may have been that the address given by Southern Seminary's president Edgar Young Mullins (1860–1928) helped to avoid misunderstandings. He critiqued both the old and the new methods as questionable and submitted six axioms which he felt were Scripture-based, were conversant with Christian experience and universal as well as self-evident forms of religious life:

1. The theological axiom: The holy and loving God has a right to be Sovereign;

2. The religious axiom: All men have an equal right to direct access to God;

3. The ecclestical axiom: All believers have equal privileges in the Church;

4. The moral axiom: To be responsible man must be free;

5. The social axiom: Love your neighbor as yourself;

6. The religio-civic axiom: A free church in a free state.[8]

In accordance with Baptist history and forthcoming Congresses, another precedent is evident, i.e., the emphasis on social issues and, in particular, the concern for religious liberty. This topic was picked up by every Congress in the history of the BWA. Even in Britain, the question was high on the agenda as the Education Act of 1902 favored

6. Briggs, "From 1905 to the End," 24.
7. Briggs, "From 1905 to the End," 26.
8. Briggs, "From 1905 to the End," 27.

Anglican and Roman Catholic schools by directing public funding for their operation. Besides, non-Anglicans could not be headmasters in the 11.731 state schools as John Clifford had written. People of free-church background were thus lured into the Anglican Church, "and I, as a Free Churchman, am asked to share in this act of bribery. It is putting a premium on hypocrisy, and I, as an honest man, am to join in the creation of hypocrites"?[9] As a way out of this dilemma, George White, an MP and in 1903 the president of the Baptist Union, together with Clifford as the driving force, organized the Passive Resistance Movement and appealed to free church people to withhold the tax with which the Anglican and Catholic schools were funded. At the Congress, Baptists were asked to stand up who had been imprisoned for being "passive resisters." Quite a number of people stood up and demonstrated that persecutions were not only a thing of Eastern Europe, especially Russia and Romania, but occurred in the West as well.[10] Besides religious liberty, other social issues were also addressed so as not to "divorce the gospel from social reform" as E. Y. Mullins emphasized.

Another recurring theme was mission and evangelism. That mission, education, and ecumenical endeavors for a united Protestant action in mission would best go together was highlighted in some papers.

On the first day of the Congress President Maclaren was unanimously authorized to appoint a Committee on Future Congresses with J. N. Prestridge and Shakespeare as conveners. The committee's task was to draft a constitution and by-laws for a new organization by July 17. When the report was presented, it was carried and a nominating committee was charged with choosing the officers and an Executive Committee. The preamble of the constitution[11] expressed the need to manifest "the essential oneness in the Lord Jesus Christ as their God and Savior of the Churches of the Baptist order and faith throughout the service and cooperation among them." The Alliance, however, while "extending to every part of the world," was not a confederation. The independence of every member church was recognized, and the Alliance would not assume any functions

---

9. Marchant, *Dr. John Clifford*, 126.

10. The Passive Resistance Movement had widespread repercussions as through one of "Clifford's boys," Rev. J. J. Doke, the idea was transmitted to Mahatma Gandhi who did not like the word "passive" because he felt that resisting was a very active behavior. He as well as Martin Luther King later would call it non-violent. See Jonsson, *Gandhi Alive*, and Geldbach, "Von Gandhi zu Martin Luther King," 60–101.

11. For the following see Briggs, "From 1905 to the End," 31.

of existing churches. Individual persons or congregations could not apply for membership, but only unions, conventions, or associations of Baptist churches. The officers would be a President (John Clifford[12]), a Vice President from each country represented in the Alliance, a Treasurer (Henry Porter of Pittsburgh, PA), an Eastern Hemisphere (British) Secretary (Shakespeare) and a Western Hemisphere (American) Secretary (Prestridge). The Executive Committee would be made up of the president, the treasurer, two secretaries, and twenty-one members according to a geographical quota. The Alliance would meet in general assembly every five years at which time the Executive Committee would also be elected. After the Congress an office for the BWA was made available in the Baptist House in London from where the new organization was organized until German bombs destroyed the Baptist House and made it necessary for the BWA to move the headquarters to Washington, DC.

The language of the preamble uses familiar "ecumenical" terms: Jesus Christ as "God and Savior" is taken from the "Paris Basis" of the Young Men's Christian Association of 1855, and "order and faith" was later used in reverse by the Faith and Order movement and the Faith and Order Commission of the World Council of Churches. The new organization of the Baptists was structured in such a way that the independence of each Church and congregation was left untouched. At the same time it was open to reflect what Baptist "order and faith" could mean in various countries around the world. Essentially the BWA was constructed so as to offer "a forum for fellowship, an agency of compassion, a voice for liberty, an instrument for evangelism and a channel of communication."[13]

2. The Achievements of the BWA throughout Its History: A Systematic Approach

What follows is the attempt to list the concerns and problems which the BWA faced in the ensuing years. The intention is not to present the different Congresses in the timely order they occurred,[14] but rather to present

12. The officers were presented by the nominating committee the following morning and accepted by acclamation.

13. Briggs, referring to Shurden, *Life of the Baptists*, 13–14.

14. The reader who looks for this narrative is referred to the book *Baptists Together in Christ 1905–2005*. At the end of this essay a summary is given by former General Secretary Neville Callam that covers his term of office from 2007 through 2017. For a short summary of BWA's history see Pierard, "Baptist World Alliance," 707–32.

systematically the questions, the issues, and the possible answers as they are mostly found in the non-binding resolutions for which special committees were installed. Before this is taken up, a list of Baptist Congresses is now presented:

Date	Place	Theme
1905	London, England	
1911	Philadelphia, PA, USA	The Christianization of the World
1923	Stockholm, Sweden	
1928	Toronto, Canada Baptist	Life in the World's Life
1934	Berlin, Germany	One Lord, One Faith, One Baptism: One God and Father of All
1939	Atlanta, GA, USA	
1947	Copenhagen, Denmark	Unity in Christ
1950	Cleveland, Ohio, USA	And the Light Shineth in the Darkness
1955	London, England	Jesus Christ, the Same Yesterday, and Today, and Forever
1960	Rio de Janeiro, Brazil	Jesus is Lord
1965	Miami Beach, FL, USA	Jesus Christ in a Changing World
1970	Tokyo, Japan	Reconciliation Through Christ
1975	Stockholm, Sweden	New People for a New World— Through Christianity
1980	Toronto, Canada	Celebrating Christ's Presence through the Spirit
1985	Los Angeles, CA, USA	Out of Darkness into the Light of Christ
1990	Seoul, Korea	Together in Christ
1995	Buenos Aires, Argentina	Celebrate Christ: The Hope of the World
2000	Melbourne, Australia	Jesus Christ, Forever: Yes!
2005	Birmingham, England	Jesus Christ Living Water
2010	Honolulu, Hawai'i, USA	Hear the Spirit
2015	Durban, South Africa	Jesus Christ, the Door

Because of the COVID pandemic, the 2020 Congress scheduled for Rio de Janeiro was rescheduled as a virtual gathering from July 7 through 10, 2021 under the original title "Together."

It is obvious that the overwhelming themes had to do with Christological items and the place of Christ in the world today. When in 2010 delegates to the Congress were asked to hear the Holy Spirit, a slightly different emphasis was introduced, possibly because General Secretary Neville Callam had been exposed to ecumenical experiences and was aware that a trinitarian approach was needed.

2.1 Ecumenism

John Clifford saw the central ideas of Baptists as a coherent whole and therefore the BWA had for him the function of a universal Council. The "Pentecostal fellowship" of Baptists was "catholic," but represented a wider catholicism than that of Rome, and "orthodox," but more spiritual and biblical than the Eastern Church.[15] When the Church of England in its 1920 Lambeth Appeal invited various British free churches to engage in closer ties, British Secretary Shakespeare of the Baptist Union had responded favorably whereas Rushbrooke cautioned. He wrote to Shakespeare that in North America all friends of the BWA were "most resolutely opposed to the lines of union." The SBC was concerned about this issue, discussed it in 1922 at their convention and sent a letter of disapproval to the BU. Archbishop Nathan Söderblom, a Lutheran pioneer of the early ecumenical movement, invited Shakespeare to preach in the Uppsala Cathedral during the 1923 Congress in Stockholm.[16]

The issue of ecumenism was hotly debated, particularly after the Baptists had been invited to participate in the Lausanne Faith & Order Conference to take place in 1927. Mullins and Rushbrooke coauthored a document which stated that the BWA is a voluntary and fraternal organization to promote fellowship and cooperation among Baptists. The BWA is not an administrative, legislative, judicial or authoritative body. Its authority extends only to its own activities. The aims of the BWA are moral and spiritual. It seeks to express and promote unity and fellowship among the world-wide Baptist community; to secure and defend religious freedom; and to proclaim the great principles of our common faith.[17] At the Toronto Congress in 1928, Rushbrooke reassured delegates who might be anxious about ecumenical involvement that "ecclesiastical

15. BWA, Congress 1911, 56–57, 62.
16. Pierard, *Baptists Together in Christ*, 56.
17. For the text see: Lord, *Baptist World Fellowship*, 57–58.

machinery, by papacy, episcopacy, or synod could not hold Christians together." The Alliance demonstrated that it was "liberty in Christ" which led to "full and joyous oneness in Him."[18] In Atlanta 1939 the issue was addressed what distinctive contributions Baptists could make to Christian unity and the ecumenical movement.

British Baptists had from the beginning of the World Council of Churches (WCC) in 1948 been active in that organization. One year before the WCC was founded, the BWA Congress in Kopenhagen heard from British pastor Henry Cook an urgent appeal for Baptists to participate in this quest for unity: "If only all Christians in all denominations and in all lands would act together and put themselves at the disposal of the one Spirit, what tremendous things might we not see!"[19] At the fourth General Assembly of the WCC in 1968 in Uppsala, Sweden, Ernest Payne of the British Union was elected one of the six presidents, much to the joy of Martin Niemöller.[20]

The BWA began to embark actively in the movement for Christian unity by joining in ecumenical efforts through bilateral conversations.[21] So far the following talks with other Christian World Communions were held:

- From 1973 to 1977 with the World Alliance of Reformed Churches;

- from 1984 to 1988 with the Vatican Secretariat for Promoting Christian Unity;

- from 1986 to 1989 with the Lutheran World Federation;

- from 1989 to 1992 with the Mennonite World Conference;

- from 2000 to 2005 with Anglican Consultative Council; these conversations did not aim to overcome theological differences, but rather to explore the way in which Christian faith and witness is

18. Green, *Tomorrow's Man*, 109.

19. Pierard, *Baptists Together in Christ*, 108.

20. The present author heard a remark by Niemöller to this effect, very likely in the summer semester of 1962 at Marburg University. Niemöller had been a leader of the Confessing Church and had been imprisoned in the Sachsenhausen and Dachau concentration camps from 1938 to 1945. After the war he served as President of the regional church of Hessen-Nassau. He refused to accept the title "bishop" as he wanted the church to be more democratic and thought a "President" as head of the church was a step in that direction.

21. Ken Manley gives an overview of the dialogs: "Baptist World Alliance and Inter-Church Relationships."

shared by Anglicans and Baptists in different regions of the world. The Report "Conversations around the World 2000 to 2005" was published in 2005. The first part explores themes of theological convergence and difference, while the second part sets out some of the creative ways in which Anglicans and Baptists have engaged in co-operation in life and mission across the globe. A new procedural approach was tried: A core committee of three persons from each denomination and one from each headquarters met in 2000 in Norwich Cathedral, and the following years in Yangon (Myanmar), Nairobi (Kenya), Santiago de Chile, in the Bahamas, and in Wolfville, Nova Scotia. On each continent, the kernel group was joined by local scholars to take part in the conversation. Oxford professor Paul Fiddes led the Baptist delegations;

- from 2006 to 2010 a second phase with the Vatican;

- from 2014 to 2018 with the World Methodist Council; a special feature of this conversation is that the final report "Faith working through Love" is accompanied by a study guide for congregations, edited by French Baptist scholar Valerie Duval-Poujol and German Methodist professor of church history Ulrike Schuler on behalf of the BWA/WMC dialogue team 2018;

- from 2017–ongoing a third phase with the Vatican.

The attempt to begin a dialog with the Ecumenical Patriarchate and representatives of Orthodox Churches never succeeded, but ended in preconversations. As there exist tensions in a number of majority Orthodox countries which sometimes give rise to discriminatory actions, the bilateral talks, it was hoped, would result in better relations, but the Orthodox discontinued the contacts. Recently, however, it seems that talks will begin, probably in May 2022 at the University of Bucharest with professor Otniel Bunaciu as leader of the Baptist delegation.

Why are such talks organized? The usual answer is that the quest for unity is to fulfill Christ's prayer that "all may be one" (John 17:11). However, the unity that Christ prayed for is not for its own sake, but according to John 17:21 the aim of unity is "that the world may believe." The question is so much more urgent how this unity must look like. Several models such as "organic" or "federated" or "unity in progress"[22] are being discussed in ecumenical debates, and some churches argue that certain

22. An example is the difference between "united" and "uniting" churches.

requirements, such as the recognition of the "historic episcopate" or the "papacy" or the "first seven ecumenical councils" must be met before unity can be achieved. Baptists with their emphasis on congregational polity and the "autonomy of the local church" must further face the difficulty of who may with some kind of authority speak for them. This is a very important issue when it comes to the "reception" of the achievements of inter-church conversations. From a Baptist point of view it may be said that the very fact of ongoing dialogues is a sign of unity "in the making." Other churches or denominations are recognized from the outset of conversations as entities that worship the same God, follow the same Lord and listen to the same Spirit. The dialogs are initiated to explore avenues of closer cooperation in fellowship, service and theological teachings. The presupposition of talks with other traditions is an awareness of one's own identity which can be further elaborated by exposing one's own position to a critical appraisal by others. Thus, inter-church conversations are advantageous for all participants, and they are also a witness to the world of how Christians can peacefully talk to one another, overcome exclusive claims, yet face differences, but still recognize each other as sisters and brothers in the faith.

The next phase of talks is with non-Christian religious traditions. These are very important in areas where other religions constitute a majority or even run the state. A BWA response was made by a special commission under the leadership of Oxford professor Paul Fiddes to a document that 138 Muslim scholars published on October 13, 2007 "A Common Word between Us and You." This "Common Word" assumes that there exists a "common ground" which consists of three principles— the unity of God, love of God, and love of neighbor. The Baptist response is more cautious:

> We do not even need to assume at the beginning of our dialogue that we mean exactly the same thing by "love of God" and "love of neighbour." Rather, we understand "common ground" to mean that this double command to love opens up a space or area ("ground") in which we can live together, talk with each other, share our experiences, work together to enable the flourishing of human life and explore the eternal truths to which our respective faiths bear witness.[23]

---

23. *Common Word Between Us and You*, 53–54, 214–15.

2.2 Social Issues

2.2.1. Religious Liberty

The situation in Russia and Romania was especially difficult for the Baptist communities as the Orthodox Churches tried to maintain religious control through the governments and suppress not only Baptists, but other communities as well. In Toronto 1928 Rushbrooke told the delegates that he had repeatedly visited Romania and told one Minister of State that Baptists should not be treated as "anarchists and pariahs." He continued that the suffering may concern only a few, but "the insult touches millions the world over, who will not rest until their brethren are free." He assured the delegates what the Alliance was all about: it means "the message of Roger Williams uttered to the ends of the earth."[24] When Stalin's program to persecute all religions meant for Baptist preachers to be imprisoned and for houses of worship to be closed, the BWA urged President Roosevelt to use his influence to secure mitigation of the persecution. At a reception in 1937 Rushbrooke remarked: "When the Alliance acts in the interests of liberty of conscience, of worship, of preaching, it acts not for Baptists only but for all."[25]

When after the First World War a Conference was convened in London in 1920, a manifesto on religious liberty was made public. It emphasized "the inalienable and God-given right of every human being to the free exercise of his mind and conscience in all matters of religion" and went on to state: "Religious liberty places all men on exactly the same basis before God and in relation to human governments. We therefore call on the governments of the world to delay no longer in enacting into law this priceless human right."[26]

Baptists were of the opinion that religious freedom mattered in international relations which is why Baptist leaders were involved when in May 1945 the United Nations was being organized. Then BWA General Secretary Walter Oliver Lewis (1877–1965) together with Joseph Martin Dawson (1879–1973) rushed to the scene in San Francisco to make sure "that the Charter to be adopted would include a guarantee of full religious liberty for every human being." To support this end, Dawson

---

24. BWA, Congress 1928, 66–67.

25. Green, *Tomorrow's Man*, 125.

26. Green, *Tomorrow's Man*, 149.

"carried a hundred thousand petitions from Baptists, North and South, white and Negro."[27]

During the Copenhagen Congress in 1947 the Executive Committee charged a Commission on Religious Freedom to prepare a "Manifesto on Religious Freedom." The foundation of all freedoms is the dignity of the human person which, for Baptists, is grounded in the *imago Dei*. Therefore, it is the duty of every Christian "to extend the rights of conscience to all people, irrespective of their race, color, sex, or religion (or lack of religion)." The Baptist concept of separation of church and state is affirmed and religious establishments rejected. The Manifesto concluded with a "Charter of Freedom" which demanded for all people:

Freedom to determine their own faith and creed;

Freedom of public and private worship, preaching and teaching;

Freedom from opposition by the State to religious ceremonies;

Freedom to determine their own ecclesiastical government and the qualifications of ministers and members, including the right of the individual to join a church of one's own choice, and the right to associate for corporate action;

Freedom to control the education of ministers, the religious instruction of their youth;

Freedom of Christian service, relief work, and missionary activities at home and abroad;

Freedom to own and use facilities and properties as will make possible the

accomplishment of these ends.[28]

The "Golden Jubilee Congress" in London 1955 adopted a "Golden Jubilee Declaration on Religious Liberty." Its five points affirm (1) the right to be free in religious matters; (2) one's right to choose or change one's faith; (3) mere toleration is not enough, all churches must be accepted as equals; (4) liberty includes the right to preach, teach, publish, and advocate openly and without hindrance the gospel of Christ or other

27. Dawson, *Thousand Months*, 16. Dawson was the founder of the Baptist Joint Committee on Public Affairs.

28. Quoted in: *Baptists Together in Christ*, 107–08.

convictions; (5) churches are willing to cooperate with the state, but must be free from its interference.[29]

In his presidential address at the 1960 Congress in Rio de Janeiro Theodore F. Adams called for freedom *for*, freedom *from*, freedom *through*, freedom *in* and freedom *of* religion.[30] In 1974 the BWA was recognized as a Non-Governmental Organization (NGO) by the UN which was an important step for the Alliance in its work for human rights and especially religious liberty world-wide. During his term as General Secretary, Denton Lotz (1939–2019) was especially active as an ambassador for religious liberty when he traveled extensively throughout the world to confer with governments, activist groups, church leaders and others to advance the cause of human rights in general and religious liberty in particular. Sometimes Baptists would emphasize that religious liberty is the cornerstone of all liberties and rights,[31] at other times they would refer to religious freedom as an important or highly important human right.

2.2.2 War and Peace

At the Second European Congress in Stockholm 1913 peace was very much an issue as had been the case two years earlier at the second BWA Congress. US steel industrialist Andrew Carnegie (1835–1919) had endowed the Church Peace Movement to promote peace efforts by the churches. The first meeting was scheduled August 1–3, 1914 in Constance, Germany, but the outbreak of the Great War made it impossible to complete the conference. Participants who had already entered Germany were escorted to Aachen to cross the border. When the train stopped in Cologne, a few people organized the World Alliance for Promoting International Friendship through the Churches under the leadership of German minister Friedrich Siegmund-Schulze (1865–1969), a pioneer of the ecumenical movement. The War brought this Alliance and the BWA activities to a standstill.

The topic of war and peace was taken up again at the Berlin Congress in 1934. Before this can be reviewed, a few sentences are in order

---

29. *Baptists Together in Christ*, 120.

30. *Baptists Together in Christ*, 129.

31. George W. Truett in his presidential address in Atlanta called religious liberty "the nursing mother of all liberty." BWA, Atlanta Report, 27.

to understand the circumstances.[32] When at the Congress in 1928 the decision was made to hold the next Congress in Berlin in 1933, a new methodology was used. Five topics were chosen for plenary sessions, and 155 Baptists from different countries had been appointed to five study commissions that would engage in inquiries by sending out questionnaires and draft their reports on nationalism, racialism, family morality, temperance and economics. Because of the political and economic conditions in 1933, the Congress came together one year later. In view of the tense political climate that prevailed in Nazi Germany, these reports were remarkably candid and powerful. In fact, some of the findings of the commissions have not lost their convincing power over the decades and are worth quoting to some extent.[33]

In addition to these reports, newly-elected BWA president George W. Truett (1867–1944) introduced a strong resolution opposing war and advocating peace which was one of the highlights of the Congress. The first sentence gives the theological basis: "This Congress affirms its profound conviction that war is contrary to the mind of Christ." It goes on to identify that international misunderstandings, jealousies, rivalries, and in particular special interest groups for which the development and production of munitions of war is a commercial value[34] are the causes that made every effort impossible to secure general disarmament. There needs to be an international agency which can effectively deal with international injustice.

The practical step to establish such an agency is the most far-reaching idea of the resolution. The proposal was to modify the doctrine of national sovereignty substantially so that certain rights are taken from national governments and invested into the authority to be created.[35] To make this happen all churches and Christians are urged to put utmost pressure on their governments in order to establish an international authority for the maintenance of peace in the world "on the basis of

32. Cf. my essay "Gerechtigkeit in Berlin 1934?" 87–105.

33. For the Atlanta Congress in 1939 three commissions (on war and peace, Baptists and Christian unity, and the ecumenical conferences of 1937 in Oxford and Edinburgh) had been charged to prepare reports.

34. The Atlanta Report 1939 was very outspoken: "we express our disgust at the immoral view which allows profiteering on war [..]."

35. Apparently this idea was one of Rushbrooke's insights. He proudly emphasizes that the Oxford Conference in 1937 took it up and that the British ambassador in Washington, Lord Lothian, emphatically and repeatedly insisted on the importance of this idea. BWA, Atlanta Report, 38.

equity and right." The Congress further recommended strongly that "all Christian men and women constantly to bear their personal testimony against the inhumanity and anti-Christian character of war." The BWA realized that its own strength was not enough. It therefore appealed to all churches: "The Congress would welcome the calling if practicable of an international Conference of the Christian Churches to avert war and establish peace, and it would urge its constituent bodies to join in such a movement."[36]

This ecumenical proposal is so much more outstanding as it had no precedent. German martyr Dietrich Bonhoeffer (1906–1945) who, at an ecumenical gathering in Farö, Denmark a few weeks after the BWA Congress, pleaded with the churches to convene a "Council of Peace." The time had come, Bonhoeffer said, that the Church Universal must come together in a Council, as the Church of the first centuries had done, to discern the signs of the time. The Baptists, being more democratic in orientation, called for a conference rather than a Council, but both pleas indicate the urgency of the task at the time when nationalism was in the process of showing its ugly face.

At the next Congress in Atlanta 1939, a few weeks before German troops invaded Poland which marked the beginning of the Second World War, the question was addressed what Baptists can do to avert war and promote peace.[37] The Study Commission firmly rejected the fatalistic notion of the inescapability of war and first reflected upon the function of the state. The state must insure justice, law and order and is therefore "the most important expression to promote human community-life." Justice, law and order must also prevail in international relations. In keeping with the Berlin resolution, the Commission asserts that the individual states must be willing to settle their disputes in a legal way before an international Court of Justice. The report describes in very strong terms the nature of war. War is "enforced enmity," "diabolic violation of human personality," "distortion of truth," "disregard of law and right," "hatred," "systematic brutality" and "one of the most appalling expressions of human sin." As such war is "incompatible with the ideal of Jesus for human community-life" and is "something from which Christ wants to save us."[38]

36. BWA, Report Berlin 1934, 14.
37. BWA, Atlanta Report, 1939, 96–110.
38. BWA, Atlanta Report, 1939, 101.

Despite these statements the report admits that among Christians there are differences of opinion. The pacifist position calls for definite abstention from any participation in military actions. Others think that the State may exercise power of which war is a "last resort" or a "necessary evil." There are still others who hold a middle-of-the-road standpoint: War is sinful and Christians must counteract war and its causes, but it may be ethically justified for the purpose of maintaining law, order, and liberty.[39] Under the prevailing conditions of the time the Commission prefers the third position although it also believes that God may call people to pacifism as to awaken the conscience of the public "to the awful evil of war." Later, when the world was in fear of nuclear annihilation, the General Council in 1981 condemned reliance on nuclear weapons "as abhorrent as bacteriological or chemical warfare."

In his Christmas letter of 1940 to the BWA Executive Committee members, Rushbrooke looked beyond the war and wrote: "The safety of each finally depends on justice for all—not excluding Germany or Russia, Italy or Japan. Isolation must give way to co-operation, and the question 'Am I my brother's keeper?' cease to be asked [...] This is but another way of saying that the Golden Rule must govern the relations of societies, including States, no less than individuals."[40] When the Conference on Security and Cooperation in Europe adopted the "Helsinki Accords" in 1975 to recognize the national borders as drawn after the Second World War and also to respect human rights, the BWA at its Stockholm Congress applauded this development. Even after the cold war was not over, the BWA continued to work for world peace and human rights as former US President Jimmy Carter did in his address to the Congress in Los Angeles. An International Baptist Peace Conference was held in Sjövik, Sweden in August 1988[41] and references were made to the Helsinki Accords in papers by Glen Stassen (USA), A. M. Bichkov (USSR) and Michael J. Cleaves (UK). Others invoked Anabaptist and Baptist history (H. Wayne Pipkin, Heather M. Vose and Paul R. Dekar). When the Soviet

---

39. It is fascinating to note that the report appealed to individuals to ask themselves "whether it can be considered a higher way and more in harmony with the ethical claims of Christianity to refuse under all conditions [...]." This was the stand which the churches in the former German Democratic Republic under heavy political pressure took in the 1980's and concluded that objection to military service was the "*eindeutigeres Zeichen*" = the clearer sign.

40. B. Green, *Tomorrow's Man*, 183

41. Pipkin, *Seek Peace and Pursue It*, 1989.

Union fell apart and the Warsaw pact countries were freed from Soviet control, there was talk about a "peace dividend," and new opportunities for religious freedom and mission work ensued.

The General Council which met in Kuala Lumpur, Malaysia in July 2011 endorsed ten practices of "just peacemaking" which had been developed by scholars led by Baptist Professor Glen Stassen;

1. support nonviolent direct action,

2. take independent initiatives,

3. use cooperative conflict resolution,

4. acknowledge responsibility for conflict and injustice,

5. seek repentance and forgiveness,

6. promote human rights, religious liberty, and democracy,

7. foster economic development that is just and sustainable,

8. work with cooperative networks in the international system,

9. strengthen the United Nations and international organizations,

10. reduce offensive weapons and weapons trade,

11. and support grassroots peacemaking groups and voluntary associations.

2.2.3 Nationalism

The Berlin Congress established the close tie between war and nationalism. The report of the study commission on nationalism[42] undoubtedly caused the Nazi authorities considerable discomfort. It declared that nationalism constitutes one of the greatest obstacles to peace and understanding between nations. The Church must determine what is legitimate patriotism and what is illegitimate chauvinism. If the state demands action that would outrage the Christian conscience, a Christian has no choice: "Loyalty to Christ must be placed before every other loyalty." Nationalistic states are based upon the "absolute and unlimited sovereignty of the state" so that every citizen is required to submit *unconditionally* to its authority. In the case of Nazi Germany the state authority was additionally strengthened by a crude form of social Darwinism and

42. BWA, Report Berlin 1934, 30–38.

the notion of superiority of the Germanic race through "blood and soil." When this chauvinistic nationalism is not only applied internally to all citizens, but also to international relations, the citizens "lose their liberty, and separations, hatred and enmity between the nations are created." One people furthers its own interests by means that involve the "violation of the rights of others."[43] In contrast to this nationalism, it is the Christian obligation to display universal love[44] and "sacrificial service" to all fellow-beings and to promote the welfare of all, irrespective of race, nationality, religion or social standing. The fundamental principle of moral action, both in private and public life, is the serving and sacrificing love that goes together with a new mind and a new relationship.

The report finds nationalism to be counterproductive to Christian mission and most dangerous "in league with militarism." If these forces "continue to exercise their destructive influence among the peoples, humanity will certainly face a very dark future." National isolation must be overcome by international friendship and cooperation. All churches must "proclaim the incompatibility of selfish nationalism and warfare with the Christian spirit" and, in contrast, promote the principles of justice, peace, and reconciliation. This can only be achieved if the church labors untiringly for an international standard of justice so that international disputes may be settled by an international court of arbitration. In this connection the work of the League of Nations is emphasized, and churches are called upon to provide the moral conditions for the League to attain success. One of the means the churches can use is the education of the new generation. The youth must not be taught "to look upon other nations as enemies to their own." Instead, it is urgent to create "a new mentality in youth in regard to international peace."

In May 2001 Berlin was again the site of a conference on Baptist Identity and National Culture. This conference confirmed what had been said in 1934 that nationalism which exalts one's own nation over others is a "form of idolatry" and not compatible with Christian faith.

43. As an example the report cites the offensive and exclusive sentence "my country - right or wrong."

44. This love must not be identified with "altruism or feelings of sympathy."

2.2.4 Racism / Racialism

The report on "racialism" must have been equally threatening to the Nazi government as the one on nationalism. Again, the two issues are closely related and in conjunction with war are expressions of human distortions. Not only do people ask *"whether the world could survive another great war, but whether any civilization can live that tolerate the survival of cruelty and injustice of race toward race."* Nothing could be further from the truth than such a statement in the German capital in 1934 when Nazi propaganda and brutal actions against the country's Jewish citizens were making life ever more miserable for them. The report charges the Baptists as a world-wide fellowship with the task to destroy what is wrong in racial relationships. To be sure, the biological fact of different races is divinely ordained and should be viewed positively, but racial antipathies are an ethical matter and are based on fear arising from "pride, sordid greed and economic rivalry."

It is astounding that an article in the German secular press can be found in which the reporter wrote very favorably about the gathering in Berlin. He marveled that delegates from sixty nations could sit peacefully side by side

> the negro next to the Chinese, the Englishman next to the Argentine, the Swede next to a Capelander, the New Zealander next to the Laplander: A truly colorful mix of peoples, a picture which the German capital has never seen before. And all the thousands were one in the search for truth.[45]

The Baptist report noticed that the antagonistic tendencies in the world—the mingling of races on the one hand and the attempt to enforce absolute separation on the other—should not divert Baptists to declare "without any uncertainty" and "in every land" "that race differences are no justification or excuse for any exploitation or selfish racial domination." The report applied this principle to specific situations:

1. A racial bar to worship and fellowship in the church "is a monstrous denial of the Lord."

---

45. Cited by Flügge, *Die Botschaft der Baptisten*, 39 emphasis in the original. Flügge refers to the newspaper Berliner Lokal-Anzeiger, 11 Aug. 1934. His booklet was spread by the thousands, but had to be taken off the market in 1936.

2. The caste system in India is classified as "one of the most insidious of civilized sins."

3. The rivalry between Jews and Arabs in the British mandate of Palestine is not really racial in nature, but economic and cultural. It can only be dealt with "under free and fair conditions of intercourse."

4. The report labeled the exploitation of "defenseless subject peoples of any race or color" and the "appropriation of native lands" by powerful commercial interests for the benefit of a favored race as "shameless greed" and "robbery."

A litmus test for race relations came at the Congress in Atlanta where segregation laws made common worship of different races virtually impossible (see the previous paragraph number 4.). The organizing committee was made up of white and black Baptists, and for the duration of the Congress the segregation laws in Georgia were suspended, but not done away with. Instead, powerful addresses were delivered, condemning racialism and segregation, and the Congress was deemed a success. Much later, the General Council in 1986 condemned racism and especially the Apartheid system in South Africa. After race riots in Southern California, the BWA organized a Special Commission of Baptists Against Racism under the chair of John O. Peterson of the Progressive National Baptists and Jimmy Carter acting as honorary chair.

The Commission formulated the Harare Declaration which challenged Baptists to expose the sin of racism through evangelism, worship, education, fellowship and prophetic action and to engage in a ministry of reconciliation. At the 1998 General Council meeting in Durban, South Africa, Archbishop Desmond Tutu presented the Truth and Reconciliation Commission which he had chaired as a convincing model for achieving reconciled community relations after a conflict such as apartheid. In January 1999 an International Summit of Baptists Against Racism and Ethnic Conflict came together at the historic Ebenezer Baptist Church in Atlanta, Georgia where both father and son Martin Luther King had served as pastors. The Summit published the "Atlanta Covenant" which called upon all Baptist unions and conventions to promote racial justice by: "a.) efforts to eradicate racism wherever it emerges, b.) engaging in the struggle against ethnic conflict."[46]

46. Lotz, *Baptists Against Racism*, 176.

2.2.5 Antisemitism[47]

An especially ugly form of de-humanizing a people is the contempt of
Jews which over centuries has been like a cancer in the Body of Christ. In
1873, a German journalist first used the term Antisemitism as a negative
characterization of Jews based upon a biological construct of superior
and inferior races. Much of what the report on "racialism" had asserted
was directly applied to the question of "antisemitism." "The spirit of
suspicion and animosity known as Anti-Semitism which exhibits itself
in racial persecution is quite unassociated with questions of color and
has but slight connection with religion." With these words, the report
on racialism begins with its fourth application.[48] Antisemitism, the commission writes, is "fundamentally a matter of political and economic
competition." If it were a question of religion, then Baptists as followers
of Jesus Christ "*would have to declare that among all the other faiths in the
world, there is none for which we have more reverent honor than for that of
the Jew.*" The report unequivocally deplored "*the long record of ill-usage
of Jews on the part of professedly Christian nations*" as "*a violation of the
teaching and the spirit of Christ*" and expressed "*to the Jews by word and
act the spirit of Jesus Christ our Lord, their Saviour and ours.*" Even though
the last sentence seems to imply that the church of the gentiles had an
obligation to evangelize the Jews so that they would recognize "their Saviour," the report is, nevertheless, a strong rejection of Antisemitism.

Of equal importance is the resolution on racialism that was unanimously adopted by the Congress:

> "This Congress representing the world-wide, inter-racial fellow-
> ship of Baptists, rejoices to know that despite all differences of
> race, there is in Christ an all-embracing unity. . . ."
>
> This Congress deplores and condemns as a violation of the
> law of God the Heavenly Father, all racial animosity, and every
> form of oppression or unfair discrimination toward the Jews,
> toward coloured people, or toward subject races in any part of
> the world.
>
> This Congress urges the promotion of Christian teaching
> concerning respect for human personality regardless of race,
> and as the surest means of advancing the true brotherhood of

47. An excellent summary on this topic is given by Lee B. Spitzer, The BWA and
Antisemitism, 177–200.

48. The others are listed in the previous section.

all people, urges the active propagation of the Gospel of Christ throughout the World."

The resolution begins on a positive note by affirming the "interracial" nature of the Baptist movement and rejoices because of its Christ-centered unity. The second paragraph uses very strong expressions which are additionally underscored by "all" and "every form" to denote what is being condemned. It is the way majorities in societies everywhere in the world treat their minorities, be they Jews, "colored" people or subject races. The resolution invokes the highest norm, "the law of God the Heavenly Father," which is being violated by the deplorable behavior of the majorities. The last section combines two Baptist principles which were upheld throughout history: (1) every human being is created in the image of God and therefore deserves equal respect by everybody else as all taken together make up the "true brotherhood of all people." The report knows that this goal has not yet been achieved because of ideologies, notably National Socialism, which do not promote the equality of every race, but distinguish between superior and inferior races. (2) To advance the equality of all, the "brother"- and sisterhood of all, the Good News needs to be propagated as the best way to reach a humanity without oppression and discrimination on the basis of race.

Given the place and the time this resolution was adopted, one must agree with Lee Spitzer who writes: "This was the first such protest against German anti-Semitism by an international Christian organization on German soil, and as such, it deserves an important place in the history of the church and the Holocaust."[49] He is also correct by pointing out that the Atlanta Congress in 1939 merely reiterated verbatim the Berlin resolution "as if nothing had happened in the interim period," whereas, in fact, the systematic and bureaucratic persecution of Jews, their elimination, the burning and looting of Jewish businesses and properties, the burning and demolition of synagogues throughout the Reich,[50] the constant

49. Spitzer, *Baptists, Jews, and the Holocaust*, 405. To my knowledge this resolution was the only protest against the treatment of Jews by an international Christian organization during the time of the Nazi regime in Germany.

50. Propaganda minister Goebbels called what happened during the night November 9/10, 1938 a "spontaneous eruption" of the German people and referred to it euphemistically and cynically as "Kristallnacht." It was a centrally orchestrated pogrom which sent the message to the Jewish people who had so far remained in Germany that the Nazis had nor respect whatsoever for them, not even for their houses of worship. Today, the event is referred to as *Reichspogromnacht*.

threat of being deported to concentration camps and many other actions by German authorities would have justified a "strengthening of the earlier statement of concern."[51] In Atlanta it was evident, perhaps more so than in Berlin, that the German Baptist leadership defended Hitlerism and did not understand the Baptist emphasis of the principle of separating the secular government from the church and the latter's obligation in a time of severe crisis to speak prophetically to the powers that be.

The first Congress after the devastating war was held in Copenhagen in 1947. The "Resolution Concerning the Jews" referred to "*the unprecedented sufferings through which the people of Israel have passed*" and noted that millions of Jews were "*exterminated by the most inhuman means*." The Congress expressed its "*sense of sorrow and shame*" that the "*poisonous propaganda and destructive designs of anti-Semitism*" were still alive and urged Baptists "*to manifest the Spirit of Jesus Christ, Himself a Child of Israel, and to do everything in their power to alleviate the sufferings of the Jews*." The nations are called upon to open their doors to the homeless refugees. The resolution then appeals to the Jews "*everywhere to refrain from provocative acts and to restrain those among them who would resort to violence*." Considering that the Jews had been the victims of the Holocaust only two years before and had experienced what Martin Buber called the "eclipse of civilization," the question must be addressed whether Baptists were in a position to advice Jews how to behave. Worse yet, the Congress stated that the Great Commission of Christ "*was intended to include the people of Israel*." Baptists were called upon "*to do their part in supporting missionary work among the Jews. We believe that only when Christ is accepted as Lord will the Jews or any other people find salvation, peace, and freedom*."[52] This language can only be described as insensitive toward the Jews as a people of the First Testament.

2.2.6 Economic Issues

Ever since Baptist theologian Walter Rauschenbusch (1861–1918) emphatically called for the Christianizing of the social order has the concern with economic matters been on the agenda of Baptists. Shailer Mathews (1863–1941) maintained that evangelization was more than preaching an escape from punishment to come. It is rather "such a transfusion of the

51. Spitzer, *Baptists, Jews, and the Holocaust*, 422.

52. BWA Report Copenhagen, 99.

forces of civilization with the ideals of the gospel as to bring justice into the economic order." In Berlin a Commission raised the question "how the spirit and attitude of Jesus [...] is related to the economic conditions of the present" and "how the spiritual resources in our common Christian faith can contribute to a just and equitable economic arrangement."[53] The Commission lists as three basic assumptions that Jesus "taught the absolute worth of the individual" as well as "the social principle of co-operation and mutuality" and that his "most frequently used social conception was the Kingdom of God, or the Family of God." From these follows the challenging task for Baptists to extend democracy "to industry and economic life." This involves the rejection of the philosophy of *laissez-faire* and uncontrolled competition as not only unethical and unscientific, but also as anti-Christian. In a society "where the strong and clever and selfish have a distinct advantage," Christians must try to reconstruct the economic order which calls for immediate action in three areas: (1) A living wage must be paid; (2) a planned economy must be insisted upon to utilize properly the resources in capital and labor; (3) unemployment must be overcome.

Christians and churches should become involved in combating economic problems, the ministers as prophets of the church must inform and direct the social conscience as to evils and injustices in the system, Christians must support legislation that curbs anti-social practices, and all should engage in a new form of "social evangelism" that seeks "to convert the strong to the principles of Jesus." This would "supplement the older individualistic evangelism" and make Christian capacity available for economic reconstruction. As this Commission favored head-on "a planned economy" which for many meant socialism or even communism, the topic of economic justice was never discussed again. Instead a Commission on Social and Economic Justice was created for that purpose.

Other social concerns which were targeted by the BWA included:

Climate Change: 2008–9;[54]

Climate Change: 2009–4;

Climate Change and our Responsibility: 2012–5;

Paris Agreement and Climate Change: 2016–3

53. BWA Report Berlin, 57–62.

54. The year and number refer to *Baptist World. A Magazine of the Baptist World Alliance.*

Human Rights: A Call to Action Against Torture: 1984–7

Human Slavery and Trafficking: 2017 1

The Humanitarian Crisis in Venezuela: 2017–5

Humanitarian Crisis of the Mass Migration of Unaccompanied Minors in the Americas: 2014–6

Opposing Violence and Abuse of Women and Girls: 2018–2

Poverty and the Nations: 1993–4

2.3 Mission and Evangelism

At the European Congress in Berlin 1908, John Clifford remarked: "With one hand on the cross, we reach out with the other to the circumference of the human race. We are therefore missionary."[55] In Philadelphia 1911 British pastor J. E. Roberts of Union Chapel, Manchester argued that the evangelization of the cities was impossible as long as the churches were aloof from one another: "The divided state of Christendom is one chief cause of our lost influence over the masses."[56] In Stockholm 1923 it was argued that responsibility for mission work must be turned over to indigenous people without the missionary societies keeping control. The Tokyo Congress, the first to be held in Asia, called on all member bodies to embrace a mission program in such a way that each region or country should define the way the gospel was to be contextualized and communicated. The urgent call was "for reconciliation of social, racial, economic and political structures" by spiritual renewal, an activated laity, a cooperative and diversified witness and positive expressions of God's love through ministries of reconciliation.

Mission, evangelization, and education would normally be addressed in BWA resolutions and other pronouncements. In fact, the BWA has a Division for Evangelism and Education. From it a "Vision 2000" was presented to and endorsed by the General Council in 1989, and General Secretary Denton Lotz proposed at the Seoul Congress that 1990–2000 be declared a "Decade of Evangelism." New opportunities for mission work ensued after the Soviet Union fell apart and the Warsaw pact countries were freed from Soviet control. Social concerns,

55. BWA, First European Baptist Congress, 59.
56. BWA, Report Philadelphia Congress, 198.

especially peace and reconciliation, were part of the mission and evangelism agenda. Evangelism and contextualization of the gospel (resolution in 2008–4) were to lead to a "holistic approach."

Under the leadership of Australian Tony Cupit the Division of Evangelism and Education held conferences on church planting in Berlin, Moscow, Bratislava, Culcutta, Pokhara (Nepal), and Toulouse. Additional meetings were called "Conferences on Unevangelized People" and held in Larnaca (Cyprus), Madras, Tura (Northeast India) and North Thailand. Earlier, education and evangelization conferences were convened in Singapore, Cuba, Ukraine and Poland.

In May 2003 Secretary Lotz convened a "Summit on Baptist Mission in the Twenty-first Century" in Swanwick, England. An interesting aspect was the new way mission was conducted in the West by a "reverse mission," i.e. a new missionary thrust from the Two-thirds World to the countries from where missionaries had once come. Many small conferences throughout the world followed. From 2005–2010 Tony Cupit conducted "Living Water" seminars and conferences to equip Baptists for evangelism and leadership.

2.4 Aid and Relief Work

Aid and relief work was high on the agenda after both World Wars. Individual and small groups were sent to areas to review the situation and submit reports. Then attention was given to immediate help to ease the situations of hunger, housing, chapel building, but also to long-range planning. Relief was offered to all who suffered regardless of religious or other differences. The long-range planning included the need for pastoral training.

During the Second World War a relief committee was set up so that the Alliance was prepared to assist countries devastated by the war on a large scale, often in cooperation with other churches and CARE[57] as well as other such programs. The problem of world hunger began to be studied in the 1960's. The HIV/AIDS crisis also elicited a positive response despite the fact that some separate Baptists, not part of the BWA, were spreading ugly interpretations of the epidemic. The Micah Challenge (cf. Micah 6:8) and the UN Millennium Development Goals to cut the level

57. CARE = Cooperative for American Remittances to Europe.

of world poverty in half were commended to all member bodies and their churches.

General Secretary Gerhard Claas (1928–1988) emphasized in his inaugural address to the 1980 Congress that "Christian pro-existence manifests itself in financial support and aid." Claas had been active in the German inter-denominational organization "Bread for the World" which worked for long-range global change, and, therefore, Claas challenged his listeners that too often Christians give only "crumbs for the world." He opted for an "alternative life-style" and gave some details: We are called to set signs in our personal life-style—by renunciation of consumerism, by working for peace and social justice, by struggling against exploitation of natural resources and pollution, by supporting the underprivileged and minority groups, and most of all "by serving the poorest and lowest brothers of Jesus."[58] In the aftermath of Mikhail Gorbachev's attempts of glasnost and perestroika (openness and change), Eastern European countries experienced a massive wave of material assistance which Paul Montacute (1946–2020), who assumed the directorship of BWA in 1990, compared to the efforts of the BWA after both World Wars.

A critical appraisal must ask the question why this was the case. It would be a worthwhile project to compare these undoubtedly impressive achievements with the amount of financial and other assistance by the BWA to so-called "two-thirds world" countries after civil wars, famines, natural catastrophes, or other calamities in those regions. Is there a balance in the supply of relief work to different parts of the world or do figures show a preference? If the latter were the case, would this reflect a lack of internationalization of the BWA and a dominance of North American and European leadership? Could one go so far as to suggest that there exists a racial bias, albeit unconscious, in favor of "whites"? Or would it be because natural disasters and hardships occur mostly in Africa and Asia and do not cause so many headlines in Western media? Or is it, perhaps, a combination of these factors and some more?

It seems, in any case, remarkable that in 2019 a Forum for Aid and Development (BFAD) was created with the goal to coordinate response efforts, create greater impact, and strengthen partnerships on the ground.

It seems that a "response" is not enough, but that greater emphasis must be placed on development projects and their sustainability. This would require a larger budget, but so far the BWA's financial resources do

58. BWA Congress 1980, 99–100.

not allow for more expenditures. Secretary Denton Lotz once remarked that in North America a rather large number of congregations have a much higher budget than the BWA. The question is whether Baptist aid and development projects should not be carried out on a larger scale as a cooperative effort between experts from the countries concerned in close co-action with BWA officials and congregations with high budgets which would be asked to give voluntarily 10 percent of their funds to the BWA, Gerhard Claas's dream of Baptist pro-existence would come true not only on an individual basis, but a form of pro-existence of congregations and the BWA as well. This would require a slight deviation from the cherished heritage of congregational independence and a shift to a new phase of inter-continental, interdependent, and authentic sharing of resources.

2.5 Baptist Distinctives and Summary

Edgar Y. Mullins drafted a document which was addressed to the "Baptist Brotherhood, to Other Christian Brethren, and to the World" during the Congress in 1923. The intention was for readers to see who Baptists are, what they stand for, and that they are not "dangerous citizens." He also wanted his comprehensive document to create an atmosphere for Baptists of diverse theological opinions to work together in the cause of mission and evangelism.[59] At the 1939 Congress in Atlanta, a commission explored the relationship between Baptist "distinctives" and Christian unity. The Anglican insistence on the "historic episcopate" was not seen as essential to Christian unity; neither were "organic" union with or a "federal" relationship to other denominations necessary. Through the BWA, Baptists should rather cooperate with others in Christian service. The commission that investigated the ecumenical conferences of 1937 in Oxford and Edinburgh urged to rethink Baptist exclusiveness.[60]

Even though the commission was reluctant to lend support to the creation of a World Council of Churches because most churches would be "state churches" or would advocate hierarchical structures or "sacramentalism," yet the commission felt a "yearning for the ecumenical spirit on the part of Baptists." Organic union carried the danger of impairing

---

59. See *Baptists Together in Christ*, 60.

60. Baptist exclusiveness had in the past been partially the result of persecution by other churches.

important Baptist distinctives, yet "sectarianism" and "provincialism" among Christ's followers constitute a "deep disloyalty" to him.[61]

The BWA's Heritage Commission was enlarged to include Baptist Identity. In 1999 the Study and Research Division published a booklet *We Baptists* which was edited by eminent Baptist scholar James Leo Garrett (1925–2020).[62] What does it mean to be a Baptist in a world that considers distinctions between churches increasingly less important? Are we moving in the direction of non- or post-denominationalism? What do Baptists teach about the church, about its structures and changes, about its autonomy or inter-relatedness with neighboring churches, about the role of pastors and the laity, about women in leadership positions and being ordained? What difference is there, if any, between ordained persons and others? What does "priesthood of all believers" mean? Perhaps all these questions and what the BWA may stand for can be answered by taking a close look at the Baptist distinctives and use the name "Baptist" as an acronym:

1a. The letter "B" stands for the Bible as the prime authority for life and work. However, there needs to be a warning sign so as not to fall into the trap of fundamentalism based on non-biblical terms that the Bible is "inerrant" or "infallible" and that history unfolds in "dispensations."

1b. The letter "B" also stands for baptism which, as a sacrament or ordinance, is administered only to believers who can consciously make a public confession. This act of baptism also determines the church as a "believers' church."

2. The letter "A" stands for the autonomy of the local church. Only it decides about its finances, its pastor, its officers, its programs; no other church authority may intervene in its affairs. However, in today's world the autonomy must be supplemented by an inter-relatedness of congregations. Even very early in Baptist history the churches of certain regions organized "associations." Today this pattern goes beyond to embrace national and continental unions or conventions and eventually the BWA. The principle of "autonomy" and "associationalism" needs to go beyond the denomination and relate to Christians of other traditions.

3a. The letter "P" stands for the priesthood of all believers, women and men of all ethnic backgrounds alike. Every believer has direct access to God, every believer has one vote when decisions need to be made,

---

61. See the entire report in: BWA Atlanta Congress 1939, 126–38.

62. Garrett, *We Baptists*.

every believer may exercise "priestly" functions, i.e., talk to people who need pastoral help, pray with people who ask for it, and other functions. There is also no ontological difference between ordained and laity; the difference is merely functional. The "priesthood of all believers" reflect the egalitarian principle of Baptist life.

3b. The "priests" may also, if occasions call for it, exercise their "prophethood" and raise their "prophetic" voice in society.

4. The letter "T" stands for trinity. God is the creator of all who acts like a father and consoles all her children like a mother. In the power of the Holy Spirit we encounter Jesus Christ as redeemer of the world and of every individual believer. God sent Jesus Christ into this world to bring the good news, and Jesus Christ sends his people. God and Christ are "sending," thus making the church part of the *missio Dei*. Baptists seem to have a tendency not to talk or preach much about the trinity, but it is essential and life-sustaining to Christian and therefore also to Baptist theology. Baptists baptize in the name of the trinity so that at every baptism service the trinitarian God is invoked and the "missional" church reactivated to her task.

5a. The letter "I" stands for individualism in the sense that God calls each person to trust in the redeeming love that God displays in Jesus Christ. Christian individualism is not crude egotism or driven by self-interest or hunger for power, but is integrated into the fellowship of believers.

5b. The letter "I" may also stand for internationalism. In the nineteenth century, e.g., Baptists in Germany were accused of "internationalism" because they were considered "religious intruders" of Anglo-Saxon (and not German) origin. Today, Baptists can proudly proclaim to have overcome provincialism and narrow nationalism through the worldwide organization which is called a World Alliance.

6a. The letter "S" stands for the separation of the Spirit-filled church from the state or government. The principle of separation prevents the state from using the church as its instrument or that the church imposes its particular views on society by manipulating the government. The church is free from government control just as the government is free from church control. The relationship between the two should be one of critical cooperation and mutual non-intervention. Thus Baptists hold that there are certain limits that governments must respect and that, likewise, there are boundaries that churches must accept in order to secure true religious liberty. A free church in a free society is the Baptist ideal which also implies that democracy as practiced in congregational meet-ings is the best way to run a state in order to keep society free. The secular state may also not sponsor secular ideologies to replace the church, but be neutral toward all religions and worldviews which necessarily elimi-nates all forms of persecutions.

6b. The letter "S" can also stand for a wide range of social concerns and social activities in which Baptists have been involved throughout their history. The struggle for religious liberty, freedom of worship, and freedom of conscience is part of the principle of separation and has had a large social impact on societies which implemented these freedoms in their constitutions or legal systems. Educational and medical institutions as well as a wide range of social services such as hospitals, homes for se-niors, visitation programs to prisoners and shut-ins, soup kitchens, etc., make up for Christian "*diakonia*."

6c. The letter "S" can also stand for separation and division. In their pursuit of freedom, Baptists have often overdone it and split over minor things. For a long time the Baptist World Alliance was the one institution that could hold different groups together. This changed significantly in 2004, when the world's largest Baptist body, the Southern Baptist Con-vention, left the BWA under the influence of separatist fundamental-ism. The fundamentalists had managed to align this convention totally by their standards on the basis of biblical inerrancy. The six theological seminaries were purged from so-called "liberal" or "leftist" "elements," and a mandatory creed was introduced which all professors have to sign, stating that the husband is the "servant leader" of the family and that the wife is to be "gracefully submissive" to his leadership in the home and in the church. This functional superiority of men was broadened by denying women the ordination for the ministry. The executive committee of this church is almost exclusively male and white. Pastors have by now been trained in the fundamentalist system for decades at the seminaries. The convention has more and more abandoned the Baptist characteristics set forth here, making it a fundamentalist organization with little regard for historic Baptist principles and references. Male superiority is thinly veiled by what supporters call "complementarianism," i.e., the notion that male and female are equal in value, but in their different functions and roles they complement, enhance, or enrich each other.

7. The second "T" stands for transformation. Not only individual people must be transformed or undergo a conversion experience, but societies as well. One can think of South Africa to overturn the inhuman

apartheid system or the deadly racism in Nazi Germany when Baptists instead of being bystanders should have put their lives on the line to challenge the Nazi ideology or the system of segregation of US society in the Southern states. Prophetic utterances and actions are part of the transformational process.

2.6 The BWA: 2007–17

Neville Callam

During the 2007–17 period, BWA focused on a theological interpretation of its life. Just prior to the period, the Twentieth Century Committee had concentrated its efforts on clarifying the major features of the ministry the organization seeks to fulfill. For its part, the Implementation Task Force developed a proposed structure for BWA's effective operation in pursuance of its ministry. BWA understands its mission in terms of several priorities: promoting worship, fellowship and unity; nurturing the passion for mission and evangelism; defending religious liberty and justice; fostering holistic community development; and advancing theological reflection. These were affirmed on the basis of an understanding of what participants in the global Baptist movement believed about the organization's purpose.

During 2007–17, the organization concentrated primarily on the following:

1. Beyond the concern for BWA's purpose, the organization considered how it understood its nature. BWA secured convergence around its ecclesial nature and significance. It followed up with a celebration of the Lord's Supper at the Durban Congress in 2015 with the BWA President and General Secretary presiding. This was achieved without a claim that BWA is "a church."

2. If BWA is an ecclesial movement, what are the norms that apply among people associated together in the movement relate to each other? In answer to this, BWA developed and affirmed *Principles and Guidelines for Intra-Baptist Relationships*, which appeared in many languages.[63] Within this context, BWA made strenuous effort

---

63. https://web.archive.org/web/20200203181750/http://bwanet.org/about-us2/intra-baptist-relations.

to find consensus around a theological understanding of the role of the regional organization within BWA as a global movement.

3. Because BWA is an authentic worldwide organization, and not an organization comprising Baptist groups in the Western World together with the "younger organizations" they formed overseas, BWA changed the way committees, commissions, and study groups were constituted. In addition, BWA intensified the use of multiple languages during our Gatherings and Congresses. Varied cultural forms were included in the services of corporate worship organized by BWA.

4. What is the relationship between BWA and the other Christian World Communions? Much time was devoted to laying the foundation for Baptist churches associated with BWA understanding themselves as one authentic expression of the church that claims no wholeness for itself apart from our relationship with other churches and church groups. The 2007–17 period was one of exciting and committed international bilateral dialogues. An effort was made to foster the reception of the fruit of these dialogues. When the period (2007–17) ended, BWA was ready to embark on the process of agreeing a document comparable to the *Directory for the Application of Principles and Norms of Ecumenism*, approved by Catholics in 1993. The hope was for BWA to achieve clarity and specificity regarding a theological rationale for its involvement in bilateral dialogues that could commend itself to many BWA member bodies. It would also help BWA members to agree on the legitimacy of the dialogical process and so, hopefully, play a fuller role in the reception of the fruits of the dialogues in which BWA participates. In addition, it would help inexperienced persons appointed to dialogue teams fully understand the purpose that these dialogues serve.

3. The Organizational Structures of the BWA

Erich Geldbach

3.1 Regional Fellowships

The regional fellowships are to reflect the objectives of the Alliance in six geographical regions (in alphabetical order):

All Africa Baptist Fellowship (AABF)
21, Obafemi Awolowo Way, Oke Bola PMB 5113 Ibadan, Oyo NIGERIA[64]
Email: aabfgs@gmail.com
Website: www.aabfellowship.org.

Asia Pacific Baptist Federation (APBF)
APBF Okinawa 3-22-5 Goya Okinawa City, Okinawa 904-0021 JAPAN
Email: info@apbf.info
Website: www.apbf.info

Caribbean Baptist Fellowship (CBF)
27 Balmoral Avenue, Kingston 10 JAMAICA
Email: caribbaptistfell@gmail.com
Website: www.caribbeanbaptistfellowship.com

European Baptist Federation (EBF)
Baptist House Postjesweg 150, 1061 AX Amsterdam, THE
NETHERLANDS
Email: office@ebf.org
Website: www.ebf.org

North American Baptist Fellowship (NABF)
6015 Walter Gage Road, University Endowment Lands, British Columbia
V6T 1Z1 CANADA
Email: jeremy@jeremyrbell.com
Website: www.nabfellowship.org

Union of Baptists in Latin America (UBLA)
822 e Higueras Urdesa Central Guayaquil, ECUADOR
Email: pjacomeh@hotmail.com
Website: www.ubla.net

---

64. The address will most likely change in 2022 as a new general secretary was elected in November 2021. It is Rev. Elias Guinos Amatepeh Apetogbo from Togo. See his acceptance speech https://link.medium.com/tIF7KS567kb. His ministry was summed up by the word "minutes": mission, impact, network, unity, togetherness, evangelism, service.

3.2 *The Internal Structures of the BWA*

1. BWA Executive Committee
Committees of the Executive Committee:
Audit Committee
Baptist World Aid (BWAid)
BWA Awards
Budget and Finance Committee
Congress Committee
Constitution and Bylaws Committee
Human Resources Committee
Membership Committee

2. Advisory Committees:
Communications Advisory Committee
Mission, Evangelism, and Justice (MEJ) Advisory Committee
Promotion and Development Advisory Committee

3. Commissions:
Commission on Creation Care
Commission on Human Rights Advocacy
Commission on Interfaith Relations
Commission on Peace and Reconciliation
Commission on Racial and Gender Justice
Commission on Religious Liberty
Commission on Social and Economic Justice
Commission on Baptist Heritage and Identity
Commission on Baptist Worship and Spirituality
Commission on Christian Education/Nurture
Commission on Christian Ethics
Commission on Baptist Doctrine and Christian Unity
Commission on Evangelism
Commission on Ministry
Commission on Mission
Commission on Theological Education

4. Committees of the General Council
Nominations Committee
Resolutions Committee

3.3 Statistics:

Churches Members

Totals for Africa	43.857	18.929,416
Totals for Asia Pacific	34.530	5.070,578
Totals for the Caribbean	2.854	367.367
Totals for Central America	3.349	232,714
Totals for Europe	13.132	732.038
Totals for Middle East	106	6,440
Totals for North America	55.649	19.766,653
Totals for South America	15.014	2.395,118

Total Countries and Territories: 126
Total Member Bodies: 241
Totals as of December 31, 2017: 168.491 churches and 47.500.324 members
Totals as as December 31, 2016: 168.885 churches and 47.976.960 members.
Address: N. Washington Street
Falls Church, VA 22046, USA
Tel.+ 1 (703) 790–8980
Website:info@baptistworld.org

3.4. Excerpts from the Constitution of the Baptist World Alliance as Amended by the General Council Zürich, Switzerland, July 2018

Preamble:
The Baptist World Alliance, extending over every part of the world, exists as an expression of the essential oneness of Baptist people in the Lord Jesus Christ, to impart inspiration to the fellowship, and to provide channels for sharing concerns and skills in witness and ministry. This Alliance recognizes the traditional autonomy and interdependence of Baptist churches and member bodies.

II. Objectives

Under the guidance of the Holy Spirit, the objectives of the Alliance shall be:

1. To promote Christian fellowship and cooperation among Baptists throughout the world.

2. To bear witness to the gospel of Jesus Christ and assist member bodies in their divine task of bringing all people to God through Jesus Christ as Savior and Lord.

3. To promote understanding and cooperation among Baptist bodies and with other Christian groups, in keeping with our unity in Christ.

4. To act as an agency for the expression of Biblical faith and historically distinctive Baptist principles and practices.

5. To act as an agency of reconciliation seeking peace for all persons, and uphold the claims of fundamental human rights, including full religious liberty.

6. To serve as a channel for expressing Christian social concern and alleviating human need.

7. To serve in cooperation with member bodies as a resource for the development of plans for evangelism, education, church growth, and other forms of mission.

8. To provide channels of communication dealing with work related to these objectives through all possible media.

V. Baptist World Congress

1. The Alliance shall normally assemble in a Baptist World Congress once in five years for the purpose of fellowship, inspiration, information, enrichment, encouragement, and required business

3.5 The Presidents of the BWA:

John Clifford, United Kingdom	1905–11
Robert Stuart MacArthur, USA	1911–23
Edgar Young Mullins, USA	1923–28

John McNeill, Canada	1928–34
George Washington Truett, USA	1934–39
James Henry Rushbrooke, United Kingdom	1939–47

After his death in February 1947, the Executive Committee appointed two Vice Presidents (Elmer A Fridell and C. J. Tinsley) as interim Presidents to serve until after the Congress that summer over which Tinsley presided.

C. Oscar Johnson, USA	1947–50
F. Townley Lord, United Kingdom	1950–55
Theodore F. Adams, USA	1955–60
Joao Filson Soren, Brazil	1960–65
William R. Tolbert, Liberia	1965–70
V. Carney Hargroves, USA	1970–75
David Y. K. Wong, China / Hong Kong	1975–80
Duke K. McCall, USA	1980–85
G. Noel Vose, Australia	1985–90
Knud Wümpelmann, Denmark	1990–95
Nilson do Amaral Fanini, Brazil	1995–2000
Billy Jang Hwan Kim, Korea	2000–2005
David Coffey, United Kingdom	2005–10
John Upton, USA	2010–15
Paul Msiza, South Africa	2015–20
Tomas Mackey	2020–

3.6 The General Secretaries of the BWA

James Henry Rushbrooke, United Kingdom	1928–39
Walter O. Lewis, USA	1939–48
Arnold T. Ohrn, Norway	1948–60
Josef Nordenhaug, Norway	1960–69
Robert S. Denny, USA	1969–80
Gerhard Claas, Germany	1980–88
Denton Lotz, USA	1988–2007
Neville Callam, Jamaica	2007–17
Elijah Brown, USA	2017–

Bibliography

Briggs, John H. Y. "From 1905 to the End of the First World War." In *Baptists Together in Christ, 1905–2005. A Hundred-Year History of the Baptist World Alliance*, edited by Richard V. Pierard, 20–46. Birmingham, AL: Samford University Press, 2005.

Common Word Between Us and You. 5-Year Anniversary Edition. Amman: MABDA, 2012.

Dawson, Joseph Martin. *A Thousand Months to Remember. An Autobiography*. Waco, TX: Baylor University Press, 1964.

Flügge, Carl A. *Die Botschaft der Baptisten im Echo der Presse. Erklärungen führender Männer über religiöse Duldsamkeit im Neuen Deutschland*. Kassel: Christliche Traktatgesellschaft, 1935.

Garrett, James Leo, ed. *We Baptists*. Franklin, TN: Providence House, 1999.

Geldbach, Erich. "Gerechtigkeit in Berlin 1934? Ethische Fragen auf dem Fünften Kongress des Baptistischen Weltbundes." In *Kriterien der Gerechtigkeit. Festschrift für Christofer Frey*, edited by Peter Dabrock et al., 87–105. Gütersloher Verlagshaus, 2003.

———. "John Clifford: Sein Konzept eines 'individuellen Sozialismus.'" *Zeitschrift für Theologie und Gemeinde* 17 (2012) 62–83.

———. "Von Gandhi zu Martin Luther King. Ein vergessenes Kapitel transkontinentaler baptistischer Geschichte." *Zeitschrift für Theologie und Gemeinde* 6 (2001) 60–101.

Green, Bernard. *Tomorrow's Man. A Biography of James Henry Rushbrooke*. Didcot: The Baptist Historical Society, 1997.

Jonsson, John N. *Gandhi Alive: Reflections on the Gandhi File in South Africa*. N.p., 1995.

Lord, Fred Townley. *Baptist World Fellowship: A Short History of the Baptist World Alliance*. London: Carey Kingsgate, 1955.

Lotz, Denton, ed. *Baptists Against Racism: Addresses and Papers Delivered at the International Summit of Baptists Against Racism and Ethnic Conflict*. McLean, VA: BWA, 1999.

Manley, Ken. *The Baptist World Alliance and Inter-Church Relationships*. Baptist Heritage and Identity Booklet No. 1. Falls Church, VA: BWA, 2003.

Marchant, James. *Dr. John Clifford, C.H. Life, Letters and Reminiscenses*. London: Cassell, 1924.

Pierard, Richard V. "The Baptist World Alliance: An Overview of Its History." *Review and Expositor* 103 (2006) 707–32.

———, ed. *Baptists Together in Christ, 1905–2005: A Hundred-Year History of the Baptist World Alliance*. Birmingham, AL: Samford University Press, 2005.

Pipkin, H. Wayne, ed. *Seek Peace and Pursue It (Psalm 34:14)*. Proceedings from the 1988 International Baptist Peace Conference Sjövik, Sweden, August 3–7, 1988. Memphis, TN: Baptist Peace Fellowship of North America and Rüschlikon, Switzerland: Institute for Baptist and Anabaptist Studies, 1989.

Rouse, Ruth. "William Carey's 'Pleasing Dream.'" *International Review of Mission* 38 (1949) 181–92.

Russell, Horace O. "Early Moves in the Direction of Greater Cooperation." In *Baptists Together in Christ, 1905–2005: A Hundred-Year History of the Baptist World Alliance*, edited by Richard V. Pierard, 1–19. Birmingham, AL: Samford University Press, 2005.

Sellers, Ian. "W. T. Whitley. A Commemorative Essay." *The Baptist Quarterly* 37 (1997) 159–73.

Shurden, Walter B. *The Life of the Baptists in the Life of the World: 80 Years of the BWA.* Nashville, TN: Broadman, 1981.

Spitzer, Lee B. "The Baptist World Alliance and Antisemitism: An Historical Overview." *Journal of European Baptist Studies* 21 (2021) 177–200.

———. *Baptists, Jews, and the Holocaust. The Hand of Sincere Friendship.* Valley Forge: Judson, 2017.

i. North American Baptists

13

Baptists in the United States and Canada

WILLIAM H. BRACKNEY

How Baptists Came to Be in North America

BAPTIST ORIGINS IN NORTH America (what is now the United States and Canada) exhibit a variety of circumstances, sometimes related and sometimes unique in their circumstances. Only a polygenetic explanation does justice to early Baptist history in North America. According to this thesis, there is no one explanation and lineage of Baptist origins in the United States and Canada. Rather, the movement grew from a multiplicity of circumstances, including General Atonement Baptists in New England and Carolina, Calvinistic Baptists in New England, the Middle Colonies, and the South, sabbatarian Baptists, Black Baptists, Separate Baptists, and eventually varieties of ethnic and racial Baptists that had unique origins, and finally independent Baptists that arose congregation by congregation.

The first appearances of Baptists in North America are to be found in obscure references in the Jamestown colony record and in the Plimouth Plantation and Massachusetts Bay colonies. In these instances, persons described as holding "Anabaptist"[1] sentiments are said to be present among Anglican and Congregationalist establishments. By

1. A generally pejorative term for the "re-baptizers" of the Reformation era and later for Baptists as well.

mid-seventeenth century, clearly identifiable Baptists were found in Massachusetts and Rhode Island and by the 1680s in Pennsylvania, New York, the Jerseys, and Carolinas. These were very diverse evidences of Baptist principles.

Roger Williams (ca. 1603–84), a Baptist for a brief time, with Ezekiel Holliman (fl. 1640) helped to establish the Baptist congregation at Providence, Rhode Island, in 1638/39. During much of its seventeenth- and early eighteenth-century history it was a General Atonement-oriented congregation. Williams is also remembered for laying the foundation for the first statement on religious liberty in North America. To the south of Williams's colony, at Newport on Aquidneck Island, John Clarke (1609–76) established a Baptist congregation in 1649. From the 1660s scattered evidences of Baptists were found in various Massachusetts townships, notably Rehoboth and Swansea in Plimouth Colony and Beverly, Mendon, and Taunton in the Bay Colony. For instance, John Myles (1621–84), previously of Ilston, Wales, settled a new town in western Plimouth that included one congregation, on open or "mixt" communion[2] bases in 1663. Myles accepted persons of baptizing and anti-paedobaptist sentiments in the congregation. In the Middle Colonies, Baptists from Ireland via Long Island settled a congregation at Cold Spring, Pennsylvania, and fanned out on both sides of the Delaware River in East Jersey and Pennsylvania. In 1681 a theologically-mixed Baptist congregation was founded at Charleston, South Carolina, an offshoot of an anti-paedobaptist work in Kittery, Maine, and the Baptist Church in Boston in Massachusetts Bay. At the end of the seventeenth century, Baptist presence was known and felt along the east coast colonies, most notably in the creation of associations of churches in the eastern Massachusetts region (General Six Principle[3]) and the Delaware River Valley (Calvinistic, Five Principle[4]).

Other types of Baptists found in the American colonies included those General [Atonement] Baptists who settled in the Albemarle Sound region on the North Carolina coast as early as 1700. Extant correspondence with their English brethren indicates the need for books and financial assistance for those in Carolina. Later, their influence was seen in the

2. The congregation included paedo-baptists and adult baptizing believers.

3. By "general" is meant advocates of a general atonement theory of the work of Christ. The six principles are drawn from Hebrews 6:1–2: repentance, faith, baptism, laying on of hands, resurrection of the dead, and eternal judgment.

4. The five principles of the Calvinistic Baptists were: total depravity, unconditional election, limited atonement, irresistible grace, and perseverance of the saints = TULIP.

Virginia and Maryland colonies. Sabbath-keepers settled in Rhode Island and through controversy, they started a separate church at Newport. Later their influence was seen in West and East Jersey colonies as well. A third group of Baptists from Wales were noticed in all three regions of the seaboard colonies: the Swansea congregation in Massachusetts, plus individual scattered colonists in Massachusetts; those in the Delaware Valley; and a group that settled at Welsh Neck in southern Carolina. Welsh Baptists were uniformly of the Calvinistic bent theologically. Finally, in 1719 the first group of German Baptists, the Dunkards or Tunkers, arrived in Philadelphia, Pennsylvania, and began a community at Germantown. From them emerged a distinct Sabbath-keeping branch under Conrad Beissel (1690–1768) who built a cloister at Ephrata in 1721/28.

Establishing a Base in the Colonial Era

The colonial Baptist population grew according to two factors. First there was scattered but effective evangelization conducted at the edges of the western frontier. This accounted for Calvinistic congregations being established in Maine, New Hampshire, central Pennsylvania, and Virginia. Second there was the evolution of scores of "Separate" Congregationalist churches from paedobaptist identity to Baptist principles. This was driven by the Great Awakening and Baptist emphases on believers' churches as articulated by preachers whose conversion occurred directly or indirectly related to George Whitefield's itinerancy. Among the Baptist converts to the Awakening were men like Isaac Backus (1724–1806), Ebenezer Moulton (1709–83), Thomas Greene (1699–1773), James Manning (1738–91), and Hezekiah Smith (1737–1805). As numerous Separate churches transitioned to Baptist principles, Congregationalists renewed their legal opposition to Baptist avoidance of paying taxes to support the official parish and town churches. Baptists were frequently accused of going down to the rivers for baptisms, to "wash away their taxes." But, they continued to grow in significant numbers.

At the conclusion of the French and Indian or Seven Years' War (1754–63), the first Baptist congregations were established in what is now Canada. In 1761–63 two congregations were established by New Englanders. A breakoff group from Swansea, Massachusetts, under the leadership of Nathan Mason (1726–1804) and Charles Seamans (fl. 1760), emigrated to Sackville, New Brunswick, where they set up a community and organized a church. After a nine-year sojourn, the entire community moved back to Cheshire, Massachusetts. About the same time, a New Light pastor from South Brimfield, Massachusetts, Ebenezer Moulton (1709–83), fled his creditors and settled in Nova Scotia. Serving as a surveyor, he started several preaching stations, notably in 1763 at Mud Creek (Wolfville) in Kings County. It is the oldest continuous Baptist congregation in Canada. Moulton later returned to pastoral ministry in his native Massachusetts.

As Baptists started new congregations and conducted preaching tours, they drew the strong opposition of existing Protestant denominations, especially the Church of England, the Congregationalist Standing Order, and to a lesser extent, the Presbyterians. In the early years in New England, Congregationalists opposed the practice of believer's baptism because it negated their entire sacramental system as well as their town-church amalgam of governance. Massachusetts Bay authorities frequently tried to control Baptist evangelical efforts. For example, in 1651 Obadiah Holmes (1607–82) of Newport, Rhode Island, was incarcerated and whipped for engaging in a visitation to an ailing man in Lynn, Massachusetts. Henry Dunster (1612–59), the first president of Harvard College and an anti-paedobaptist, was denied his position as well as his home and banished to Plimoth Colony. A prosperous merchant operating out of Kittery, Maine, William Screven (1629–1713), was harried out of his community for not adhering to the laws requiring children to be baptized.

Religious freedom was an important element in the emerging Baptist character. What Baptists wanted was freedom to worship, educate their children and seek converts to the Christian faith. They also wanted to be exempt from local taxes that supported the Congregationalist churches and ministers. Isaac Backus of Middleborough, Massachusetts, was a leader in fighting the eighteenth century colonial establishment to release Baptists from the burdens of taxes in support of the established church in Massachusetts Bay. In 1777 Backus was a delegate from Massachusetts to the Continental Congress, and his correspondence prompted many to join the cause of religious liberty. Closely akin to Backus was John Leland (1754–1841) who moved from Connecticut to Virginia where he became a major advocate of religious liberty. Backus heavily influenced the Adams family in New England and Leland was a major opinion upon which James Madison drew.

During the era of the American Revolution, Baptists were on both sides of the cause. Morgan Edwards (1722–95), an immigrant from Bristol Baptist College, settled in Philadelphia and was supportive of British colonial sovereignty. Among Americans, he was accused of being a Tory. Others like David Jones (1736–1820), Hezekiah Smith, and John Gano (1727–1804) joined the colonial army and fought for the Patriotic cause. Still others like Richard Furman (1755–1825), Oliver Hart (1723–95) and Samuel Stillman (1737–1807), called the "Patriot orator," rallied support for the cause in the Baptist communities. John Hart (ca. 1706–79), associated with the Hopewell Church and a resistance leader in New Jersey, was a signer of the Declaration of Independence.

With the close of military hostilities, Baptist evangelists and church planters looked west. In the 1790s Elkanah Holmes (1744–1832) conducted missions among the Tuscarora Indians on the Niagara frontier. John Gano of New York went to Ohio Country and helped establish the first Baptist congregation west of the Appalachian Mountains at what would become Cincinnati, Ohio. Others like the family of Daniel Boone traversed the Cumberland Gap to settle lands in Kentucky. From Georgia and Virginia Baptist preachers settled in Alabama, Mississippi, and Texas. On the northern frontier, hundreds of Baptists from the eastern colonies moved to New Brunswick and Nova Scotia as United Empire Loyalists, accounting for the significant presence of Baptists in the developing Maritime Provinces of Canada.

A major achievement of Baptists in the eighteenth century was the founding of a college in Rhode Island. James Manning, a New Light[5] graduate of the Presbyterian "Log College" at Princeton, was the choice to organize efforts toward founding the college and securing a charter. Manning encountered stiff opposition from Congregationalists like Ezra Stiles (1727–95) to their plan to be the controlling interest in the institution. The fledgling school closed during the Revolution due to military occupation of the premises, but Manning valiantly protected its interests. He first worked from a pastoral base in Warren, Rhode Island, and later moved the college to the provincial capital, Providence. Eventually, the College of Rhode Island set the standard for a classical model of undergraduate education for Baptists, and without a religious test for faculty and students. Baptists made a major statement about their support for a learned ministry and their desire to be part of a denominational tradition

---

5. New Lights were advocates of the Great Awakening who propounded a vivid conversion experience and were supposedly influenced by a "new light."

in America. The College of Rhode Island served the needs of the Canadian Maritime Baptists as well.

Building on a Strong Base

The nineteenth century exhibited important Baptist tendencies. The mainstream group engaged energetically in various kinds of missions. A second characteristic that came to the fore was the diversification of the Baptist movement in the USA and Canada.

In 1800 only a few Baptist congregations were unaffiliated with mainstream Baptist associational life.[6] The principle associations were located in New England, New York, Pennsylvania, Virginia, and Charleston. Being part of an association meant mutual support and accountability. The domestic missionary effort contributed greatly to associational cooperation, in a threefold organizational program where churches were planted, then gathered into near-region associations of congregations, and finally organized by public statute into state conventions.

The congregations created a grassroots base, according to Baptist polity, and were always the center of authority. The associations blended the interests and needs of ministerial validation, mutual support, and conflict resolution among the churches. State conventions were political/geographical units that championed the identities of religious groups according to states, rallying interest in and financial support for missions. One student of this history referred to the conventions as "the kingdom within the states." A great cultural achievement of the state conventions was the establishment of at least one Baptist academy, college, or university in each state that trained not only Baptist ministers, but also educated good citizens for the Republic.

The diversification of Baptist life followed patterns or types. Some new Baptist groups were born over theological emphases, like the Freewill and Free Communion Baptists. The Freewill Baptists were followers of Benjamin Randal (1749–1808) of New Durham, New Hampshire, whose experience with his Calvinistic Baptist brethren was largely negative. The Free Communion Baptists, born in the 1840s, were a frontier New York version of the same emphases. They both underscored a

---

6. The associational principle involved cooperation among churches in a circumscribed region, not more than one day's ride from each other. It had its origins among English Baptists and imitated the Congregationalist system of consociations.

common opposition to Calvinism and closed communion at the Lord's Table. The Free Baptists occupied Canadian territories in Upper Canada and the Maritimes.

Other congregations and leaders left the Baptist mainstream over the question of the legitimacy of missionary endeavor. Historic churches in Hopewell, New Jersey, and Southhampton, Pennsylvania, developed "Old School" hyper-Calvinistic identities and slid from the roster of the Philadelphia Association. In the Ohio Valley, anti-missionary Baptists equaled those who supported domestic and foreign missions. Close to the anti-missionary type was the collection of churches that engaged in local church protectionism. Some of these were in the New England region where fierce independence of congregations overcame the associational principle. Others were found in the eastern New York State and New Jersey regions where they called themselves "Hardshell," or Primitive Baptists, still others in Maryland who followed the Black Rock Resolutions of 1832, and many in the South who heard the voice of men like James R. Graves (1820–93), pioneer of the Landmarkist movement.[7]

Another important reason for the diversification of the Baptist family in North America was racial-ethnic in character. Early language diversity could be seen in Welsh-speaking congregations in Delaware, Pennsylvania, and South Carolina. In the 1830s and 1840s a significant number of immigrants entered the United States and Upper Canada from northern Europe, principally Germans, Swedes, Danes, and Norwegians. The American Baptist Home Mission Society and the Ontario and Quebec Mission Board sent domestic missionaries into these communities and enabled churches to be started within the Old World languages. German congregations commenced in Philadelphia, New York, Rochester, and Chicago. Swedish churches began in Chicago, and the Upper Midwest. Danish and Norwegian Baptists found roots in Illinois, Iowa, and Nebraska. In 1845 a German Baptist Conference was formed, and in 1851 a Swedish Baptist conference held its first meeting. Danes and Norwegians followed suit in 1884. Each of these ethnically defined Baptist communities reinforced their culture through hymnals, newspapers, and magazines and established institutions to train their clergy. Typically, their worship services were conducted in the original language. The Germans centered their efforts as a department of Rochester Seminary, the Swedes as a part of Morgan Park Seminary in Chicago, and

7. The Landmarkers understood the terminology literally interpreting Prov 22:28.

the Danes and Norwegians combined their efforts in several schools in Iowa. In the 1880s work among Italian immigrants in Philadelphia and New York began, supported by a training program relating to Colgate University initiated in 1907. The Home Mission Society did not neglect smaller immigrant groups like Spanish, Hungarians, Polish, Czechs, and Portugese, tying them to a multi-ethnic seminary that was started in East Orange, New Jersey, in 1919, the International Baptist Seminary. A parallel school, the Seminario Bautista Hispano-Americano was opened in Los Angeles in 1922 meeting the needs of Mexicans, Cubans, and Puerto Ricans.

A similar ethnicity factor was evident in later generations among Chinese immigrants in California and the Pacific Northwest. In the Canadian West, communities of Baptists grew up in Saskatchewan, Alberta, and among the Chinese in British Columbia. The later ethnic churches did not develop institutions until the twentieth century. The Canadian Baptist family imitated ethnic mission work, tied to the "His Dominion Movement," a plan to make all of Canada a Christian country. Their work included efforts among Ukrainians, Germans, Swedes, Russians, Ruthenians, the French in Quebec, and the Chinese in British Columbia and eventually Toronto. As the ethnic groups separated from the mainstream in the United States in the early twentieth century, the same pattern of separation occurred in Canada, the resulting smaller denominations tilting toward relations with more definitively Evangelical groups, like the Fellowship of Evangelical Baptist Churches and the Evangelical Fellowship of Canada.

The Home Mission Society favored a policy of "Americanization" by which they meant to replace the European orientation of the immigrant churches with an English-speaking pastorate and full integration into the existing English-speaking associations and conventions. This effort largely failed because the first generations remained loyal to their languages and differentiated language associations, plus the relative success of their educational institutions. There was also a significant resistance to modernist theological trends in the English-speaking communities. By the 1920s, the Germans and Swedes had graciously separated from the Northern Baptist Convention to form their own "denominations," respectively the North American and Baptist General Conferences. The Danish Norwegian Conference was formally integrated into the Convention in 1957, and the Italian Baptist Association continued as a distinct entity in the Northern (American) Baptist family.

Geography also played a role in the settlement of Baptists in North America. As we have seen, in the mid-1700s, congregations were established in the Canadian Maritime provinces, the outreach of American missionary-pastors. By 1800 sufficient congregations existed in Nova Scotia to create the Nova Scotia and New Brunswick Association. It was patterned after New England Baptist experience. In the 1790s mission work from New York State started churches on the northern shore of Lake Ontario, commencing Baptist life in Upper Canada. Montreal was the epicenter of English Baptist influence in the 1830s. There a Baptist college was opened in 1838, first of its kind north of the American border. A final beginning was made in the Ottawa Valley where Scotch Baptists settled, bringing their unique ethos to the burgeoning Baptist cause. They were much influenced by Glasites from Scotland.[8] The early culmination of Canadian Baptist organization occurred in 1846 with the establishment of a regional convention in the Maritimes and missionary organizations in Upper Canada (Ontario) and Lower Canada (Quebec). Acadia University, chartered in 1838 in Nova Scotia, became a strong permanent influence for Baptists in the Maritimes.

Voluntary Societies and Missions Create a Denomination

What held mainstream Baptists together for three decades in the United States and Canadian contexts was their commitment to missions. Pastors on local and distant evangelistic missions were sent from the Philadelphia Baptist Association in the 1770s. This extended to the Appalachian Country and Virginia and the Carolinas. Likewise, the New York Baptist Association sent missionaries to the Indians on the Niagara frontier in the 1790s. Starting in the first decade of the nineteenth century Massachusetts Baptists organized a missionary society that commissioned short and long term appointees to Canada, Maine, and the western New York frontier. The society model would be employed quickly and strategically to meet common needs in variegated contexts.

William Carey's (1761–1834) work for the English Baptist missionary society from 1792, plus the establishment of the London Missionary Society and the Church Missionary Society drew attention to India and

---

8. Glasites were the following of John Glas (1695–1773) of Scotland, an independent thinker who was a precursor to the Disciples of Christ movement in North America.

contiguous countries and kingdoms. Carey followed a pattern of voluntary societies first used by Danish missionaries to push beyond the English regional associations. Baptists in New England learned about the society idea from the *Periodical Accounts* that the Baptists in England distributed among the American churches.

In 1812 an even larger vision came to the fore of the scattered Baptist churches. Adoniram (1788–1850) and Ann Hasseltine Judson (1789–1826) of Massachusetts offered themselves as the first Protestant candidates from America to missionary work in faraway India. En route they were converted from allegiance to the American Board of Commissioners for Foreign Missions (supported by Congregationalists and Presbyterians) to Baptist principles from their reading of William Carey's work. When they arrived in India they were baptized and subsequently began work in Burma as the first Baptist missionaries from North America.

Back home in the United States, in 1814 a major step was taken in forming the General Baptist Missionary Convention for Foreign Missions in the United States of America (GMC), coordinating domestic and foreign missions and higher education. It was the collaboration of Luther Rice (1783–1836) of Massachusetts with William Staughton (1770–1829) of Philadelphia and Richard Furman (1755–1825) of Charleston, SC. Rice was the organizational genius who had spent a short time in India, and Staughton and Furman lent their considerable pastoral reputations to the project. The convention, popularly known as the 'Triennial Convention,' because it met every three years, became the rallying point for all mainstream Baptists in America, plus some churches in Canada. Only the difficult issue of slavery would lead to the breakup of the Convention in 1844/45. The meetings of the Triennial Convention were held in cities along the east coast, facilitated by passenger boat service, and the major meetings in the larger urban centers, Philadelphia, New York, Baltimore, and Richmond.

In the 1830s united American Baptist missionary efforts extended from Europe to Asia, Africa to Latin America, and the Caribbean across the century. The first footholds were established in Burma and Madagascar. Extending from Burma were missions in Siam, Hong Kong, and mainland China. Next, American Baptist missionaries were appointed to Greece, Germany, and Russia. The great heroic figure of missions in Germany was Johann Gerhard Oncken (1800–1884), for many years an appointee of the American Baptist Foreign Mission Society. Gradually, the

Board appointed personnel to Africa and Haiti, like Lott Carey (1780–1829) and Thomas Paul (1773–1831), respectively.

When the Southern Baptist Foreign Mission Board was established in 1845, new separate fields were started in China, Africa, and Latin America. J. Lewis Shuck (1812–63) and his wife Henrietta Hall (1817–44) were pioneer missionaries to China with the Board, having begun with the Triennial Convention. Mexico became a major field for Southern Baptists. Later both Southern Baptists and American Baptists worked in Japan and the Philippines and geographically separated their territories. Many of the smaller Baptist groups sent out missionaries: the American German Conference in Cameroun; the Seventh Day Baptists in India; the American Swedish Baptists in Africa and India; and the Freewill Baptists in Bengal/Orissa/Bihar. Once organized separately in the 1890s, American Black Baptists supported missions in the Caribbean and Africa. Canadian Baptists cooperated at first with American Baptists in India, then formed their own works in Bolivia, India, and Korea.

American and Canadian Baptist missions comprised several objectives. First was translation of the Scriptures: learning the language, creating linguistic aids like dictionaries and thesauri, and translation itself. Next came evangelism and church planting. Then, institutions followed as colleges, theological schools, hospitals, and associations of churches were built. Print media produced locally, told the exciting stories of Baptist missions, accompanied by journals and magazines published by the sending organizations.

The split between the Southern and Northern delegates in 1845 was deliberate and irreparable. Although harmony existed on the surface for three decades, the Baptist Board of the Convention that met annually, continually debated two issues: the morality of slaveholding and the all-inclusive nature of the Convention. Numerous churches supporting the national Convention included slaveholding members. Behind growing antislavery, then abolitionist,[9] interests led by men like Francis Wayland, president of Brown University, the northern representatives made their feelings about slavery known. In 1843 an abolitionist society for missions was formed: the American Baptist Free Mission Society. By 1843/44, the majority of the Baptist Board for Foreign Missions from northern states refused to appoint a slaveholder as a missionary and the Southern delegates took offense. Their argument was that political issues had no

---

9. These terms refer to varying degrees of advocacy of ending slavery: antislavery was gradual, abolition was immediate.

connection with missions. Southern delegates also advocated a comprehensive organization that brought missions, foreign and domestic,
publications, and education under one umbrella. The die was cast at the
Providence, Rhode Island, meetings of the Triennial Convention, as the
southern delegates walked out of the sessions forever.

Change was in order. At Augusta, Georgia, in May 1845, the Southern Baptist Convention was formally organized. It was a centralized national body with a regional name. Its work was to be conducted through
boards of foreign and domestic mission, publication, and an executive
committee that nominated persons for all convention agencies. The
Convention struggled for identity in the years before the War Between
the States, managing to establish foreign missions in Europe, China, and
Latin America. In a parallel organization, the Baptists in the northern
states reorganized their foreign mission efforts as the American Baptist
Missionary Union, and continued in the United States and its territories
as the American Baptist Home Mission Society. Thus the work of Baptists
in the United States was now a two-pronged effort.

The Black Baptist saga of coalescing Baptist presences is a remarkable result of Reconstruction America. In the last decade of the nineteenth century, Black Baptists coalesced in the United States. The earliest
black churches were slave congregations, like the one on the William
Byrd Plantation in James City County in Virginia that was recorded in the
1750s. White preachers are known to have visited plantations in South
Carolina in the 1740s. This led to the later establishment of a Black congregation at Silver Bluff, near Augusta, Georgia. An important figure in
the South Carolina and Georgia coastal regions in the 1770s was George
Liele (c.1750-1800). Liele was a convert under New Light preaching in
the 1770s, and he itinerated in the Savannah River area. Later he started
the first slave churches in Jamaica, creating an historic connection with
the mainland.

The African American Baptist movement was negatively affected by
harsh slave laws in the southern states in the antebellum era. Thus, the
future lay in escaping to the north and eventually to Canada. African free
congregations were started in southern Ohio, Illinois, and western New
York. In key centers of freedmen populations, major Black churches were
supported by the white congregations of those cities, like Abyssinian in
New York, Union in Philadelphia, and First African in St. Louis, Missouri. As clusters of free Black churches emerged, the first Black Baptist
associations were formed in Meigs County, Ohio, Wood River in Illinois,

and Amherstburg in Upper Canada. The latter association claimed a membership of over a thousand by 1861.

Following established Baptist organizational lines, the first African conventions were begun in the West in 1853, with a similar effort in the Chicago area. During the War Between the States, the American Baptist Home Mission Society greatly aided the cause of planting churches, schools and organizations across the border regions and eventually in every southern state. Black leaders like W. J. Simmons (1849–90) in Kentucky and E. C. Morris (1855–1922) in Arkansas led in the formation of the American Baptist Missionary Convention and American National Baptist Convention. These regional efforts combined in 1895 as the National Baptist Convention, USA, the historic capstone achievement of Black Baptist life. The Convention was truly a body of Black Baptists under the auspices of Black leaders.

Unfortunately, the unity of the National Baptist Convention USA was not to last long. In 1897 a new Black Baptist missionary convention was formed in Washington, DC: the Lott Carey Baptist Foreign Mission Convention. It concentrated its efforts in West Africa and Haiti. An ongoing debate between Lott Carey leaders and National Baptists ensued over the nature of cooperation with other Baptist organizations. A second major rift ensued in 1915 when Richard H. Boyd (1843–1922) of Texas formed the National Baptist Convention of America. Boyd lost an attempt to take control of the National Baptist Publishing Board and broke away from the National Baptist Convention USA. Much later in the 1960s, driven by the civil rights movement, Martin Luther King Jr. (1929–68) and Gardner C. Taylor (1918–2015) left the National Baptist Convention USA with scores of congregations, to form the Progressive National Baptist Convention.

New Century, New Configurations

A singularly important international step was taken by Baptists in 1905 that involved most major groups in North America. That year the Baptist World Alliance (BWA) was formed, the result of two decades of planning in Britain, Canada, and the United States, In the United States three sectors of Baptist life took the lead: Northern (American) Baptists, Southern Baptists, and Black Baptists. The Northern Baptists were the collective expression of the Baptist societies, Southern Baptists were led by

Southern Seminary alumni and a prominent Kentucky newspaper editor, and Black Baptists included the National Baptist Convention, USA, and the Lott Carey Baptist Foreign Mission Convention. From Canada, the regional conventions, Maritimes, Ontario/Quebec, and congregations from the West all sent delegates to the first BWA meeting in London. Behind the founding of the BWA were several streams of growth and development among Baptists in North America.

As the twentieth century dawned, Baptists in the United States and Canada were strongly established in every state and province and focused on missions. Their duplicative efforts in a given field lead to discussions of cooperation, and ultimately to an interest in an international organization.

Northern Baptists in the United States followed a unifying theme toward a national organization. Starting in the 1890s there was energetic discussion among the leaders of the national societies, accompanied by annual scholarly exchanges at the Baptist Congress, and informal conversations with the Free Baptists and the Disciples of Christ. Specific steps were taken in 1896 with a Commission on Systematic Beneficence and toward greater cooperation in 1901. Sensing an important cooperative tendency afoot, Dean Shailer Mathews (1863–1941) of the University of Chicago and J. Spencer Dickerson (fl. 1900) of the Chicago Baptist Association, spearheaded a provisional organizational meeting at Calvary Baptist Church in Washington, DC in 1907. The affirmations at this meeting included the independence of local churches and the advisory nature of local, state, and national organizations.

The new Northern Baptist Convention swiftly created a unique Baptist witness. Two national boards were created: the Ministers and Missionaries Benefit Board and the Board of Education. The M&M Board[10] responded to a need to care for retired clergy and the Education Board assumed tasks of coordinating relations with colleges and universities and overall denominational education. Within three years, the Northern Baptist Convention became the first Baptist organization to join the newly-chartered Federal Council of Churches of Christ in the United States. With this move, Baptists in the United States officially joined the ecumenical movement. Northern Baptists were charter members of the BWA in 1905. Further, in 1911 the Northern Baptists officially merged with the Free Baptist General Conference in America, thus putting to rest

10. See the essay by Everett C. Goodwin, "Ministers and Missionaries Benefit Board (MMBB)," printed as chapter 16 of this volume.

the old theological distinctions between Calvinistic and Arminian bodies of Baptists. The driving impulse among Northern Baptists were a group of theologically moderate to liberal leaders including Shailer Mathews, Samuel Zane Batten (1855–1925), Harry Pratt Judson (1849–1927), and Walter Rauschenbusch (1861–1918). The leading intellectual centers were the University of Chicago, Newton Theological Institution, Crozer Theological Seminary, and Rochester Theological Seminary.

The Southern Baptist Convention, dating from 1845, gained in unity and territory served. Through a series of comity agreements with the American Baptist societies, Southern Baptists expanded west into New Mexico, Arizona, and southern California. Northward Southern Baptists started churches in Kansas and southern Illinois, and Missouri gradually moved to a relationship solely with Southern Baptists. Southern Baptists also assumed administration of missions in Mexico, Latin America, and Cuba.

In 1914 Southern Baptists debated whether to join in the emerging ecumenical movement or continue their separate identity. Under the influence of Landmarkism, Southern Baptists resolved to devote themselves "with singleness of heart" to fostering their own denominational agencies and schools and they embarked upon a program to unify their strength in the southern states and redouble their overseas missionary work. Turning aside participation in the Interchurch World Movement, they launched the 75 Million Campaign on the seventy-fifth anniversary of the Convention. A series of Convention recommendations undergirded their efforts in 1914 and the result was the retirement of a considerable portion of Convention debt and the creation of a new theological confessionalism based upon regional solidarity: in 1925 Southern Baptists adopted the "Baptist Faith and Message" and a permanent structure for coordinated fundraising and distribution, the Cooperative Program. Another important initiative in this era was the strengthening of the executive committee of the SBC that coordinated all boards and agencies and expenditure of funds and a new geographic home for both the executive committee and the Sunday School Board, in Nashville, Tennessee. From its new self-understanding, the SBC grew from 2 percent of the US population in 1925 to 5 percent by 1950, becoming a major element of American Protestantism.

Against this background of growth and consolidation, a major redefining set of events occurred within American Protestantism in general and which had profound impact upon Baptists across the continent.

Collectively labeled "fundamentalism," the phenomenon was at its core a grassroots pushback to theological modernism, ecumenism, diversification of leadership, and general cultural change. Baptist roots of fundamentalism can be found in the schismatic career of Charles Haddon Spurgeon (1834–92), the English "prince of preachers." Spurgeon, self-educated, built a showplace of ministry in nineteenth-century Britain, always critical of the Baptist Union establishment. He was a formative leader in the creation of the Evangelical Alliance in 1846, which reached beyond his own denomination. When faced with mounting liberal tendencies in the Baptist Union in the 1860s that Spurgeon thought was causing the Union to "downgrade at breakneck speed," Spurgeon took his Metropolitan Tabernacle out of the Union to an independent status. The entire saga of C. H. Spurgeon was recounted in monthly installments in his magazine, *The Sword and Trowel*, circulated on both sides of the Atlantic. With Spurgeon's example, Baptists in North America considered the real option of schism from their convention relationships, if similar conditions ensued.

The immediate catalyst for concern in North America was the publication of *The Finality of the Christian Religion* in 1905. The author was Professor George Burman Foster (1857–1918) at the University of Chicago, also a Baptist minister. Foster's thesis was that Christianity was an evolved religion and that due consideration should be given to the value of other religions. Christianity's "finality," therefore, was subject to debate. Baptists and others responded volcanically to the Chicago professor and vowed to restore and affirm the time-honored essentials of the Christian faith. Two Presbyterian brothers on the West Coast, Lyman (1840–1923) and Milton (1838–1923) Stewart, sponsored a series of pamphlets entitled "The Fundamentals" which covered a series of topics considered to be definitive and non-negotiable to true Christians. They were sent to every Protestant church in the United States. The battle for the "Fundamentals" was thus joined fully by 1920.

Baptists were a major participant group in the defense of the faith. On the one hand there were leading champions like William Bell Riley (1861–1947), Jasper C. Massee (1871–1965), and John Roach Straton (1875–1929), who formed a Baptist phalanx among Northern Baptists, joined by J. Frank Norris (1877–1952) in the American South, and Thomas Todhunter Shields in Canada. In 1925 in an editorial, a Philadelphia Baptist, Curtis Lee Laws (1868–1946), coined the term, "fundamentalist," that he applied to those who held to the historic fundamentals of the faith. Not to be outdone by their anti-modernist adversaries, anti-fundamentalist Baptists joined the fray around the theme, "Shall the Fundamentalists Win," to cite an important sermon by Harry Emerson Fosdick (1878–1969) of Riverside Church in New York City. Joining Fosdick were Shailer Mathews of Chicago, Henry C. Vedder (1853–1935) in Philadelphia, and Cornelius Woelfkin (1859–1928) of New York City, in alliance with William L. Poteat (1856–1938) of North Carolina and L. H. Marshall (1882–1953) of Toronto, Ontario. A World's Christian Fundamentals Association was formed in 1919 in which Baptists played a prominent role, and in 1920 the Baptist Bible Union was founded as an action group to propel the delegates at the annual meetings of the major conventions toward a fundamentalist agenda. At this high water mark, the fundamentalists were defeated in their attempt to pass a binding confession of faith, by a majority of Northern Baptists who believed the sole rule of faith and practice should be the New Testament. Presiding over the debates was the first woman elected to the presidency of any American denomination, Mrs. Helen Barrett Montgomery (1861–1934) of Rochester, New York, in herself a troubling presence for the fundamentalists.

Fundamentalism, as developed and realized among Baptists, had several leading characteristics about itself.[11] In general, it was a way of looking backwards toward a romanticized view of a rural Christian society. To conserve the evangelical accomplishment of the eighteenth and nineteenth centuries was a major objective. Fundamentalist response to existential questions did not include non-theistic ideas of the origins of the earth, nor ambivalence about the end of the world. Fundamentalists held to a literal seven-day creation week and a premillennial return of Jesus Christ. Fundamentalists dealt with the realities of the present by maintaining a negative worldview that ends in judgment and destruction, then a new world order. Progressivism and projects like the Social Gospel were anathema to fundamentalists. Science was incompatible with religion, and associations with other groups and ideas were discouraged-to-banned. The Bible was a literal textbook on history, geography, theology, and prophecy. Miracles were affirmed as they occurred, not to be explained as naturalistic or coincidental phenomena. Soul salvation was the true meaning of the gospel, not the transformation of social and economic structures. War and militarism were quietly allowable, if in

11. On "fundamentalism" see the essay by Barry Hankins, "Fundamentalist Controversy Among Baptists in Twentieth-Century America," printed as chapter 15 of this volume.

defense of gospel truths. Gradually by the 1960s, other social positions and attitudes often combined with the classic fundamentalist agenda, including a defense of male leadership in society, racial superiority of certain groups, and heterosexual relationships and marriages as biblical models of Christian ethics.

In the Baptist family in North America, the first impact of fundamentalism was felt among Northern Baptists. With the loss of the attempt to create a creed for the Northern Baptist Convention, some churches and pastors went into a quiet phase, supported by new conservative evangelical seminaries, like Northern Baptist in Chicago, Eastern Baptist in Philadelphia, California Baptist in Los Angeles, and Gordon Divinity School in Massachusetts. The more strident groups left the Convention and formed new groups. The Baptist Bible Union evolved by 1932 to be the General Association of Regular Baptist Churches, adopting the creed of fundamentalists. Within the next decade, a second come-outer group emerged over issues of appointing liberal missionaries in the American Baptist Foreign Mission Society. This resulted in the formation of the Conservative Baptist Association. In its orbit were three new seminaries, in Denver, Minneapolis, and Portland, Oregon. Quietly noticed in the 1920s were the disaffiliations of the old ethnic groups, the Germans and Swedes, to form theologically conservative new Baptist denominations, supported by seminaries in Sioux Falls, South Dakota, and St. Paul, Minnesota, respectively. Finally, in the 1950s across the Northern Baptist denomination, independent Baptist churches cropped up, both as new church plant in the northern states, and as older churches left the denomination remaining independent of any larger association. Their educational identity has been sustained among several Baptist bible colleges.

The remaining core of Northern Baptist life went through two more major changes in the post-war era. In 1950, seeking to recover their diminished influence, Northern Baptists voted to change their name to the "American Baptist Convention." In the late 1940s rumors abounded of Southern Baptist interest in taking a more inclusive name than the regional identity of "southern" Baptists. Northern Baptists took the initiative, hoping for a reconciliation of all major Baptist groups in the United States under the name "American Baptists." In fact, the earliest examples of the Baptist societies continued to carry that nomenclature. While the Northern/American Baptists claimed to hold the new name in trust, anticipating further amalgamations, the only group that responded was the Danish-Norwegian Baptist Conference that formally merged with

American Baptists in 1957. A second, even more consequential name change occurred in 1973 when the American Baptist Convention became the American Baptist Churches in the USA, emphasizing the importance of local congregations and underscoring the ongoing tension between autonomy and interdependence in that family.

Three decades after the immediate impact of fundamentalism in the Northern Baptist family, the impact upon Southern Baptists was noticeable. We have previously noted the creation of a confessional statement by Southern Baptists in 1925. The *Baptist Faith and Message* (1925) was actually a recension of the New Hampshire Baptist Confession of Faith (1832) that President E. Y. Mullins (1860–1928) of Southern Seminary and a Convention committee concocted in the midst of the fundamentalist outbreak in the North. Ironically, the New Hampshire Confession of Faith was an example of local church protectionism in New England, which found much affirmation among Landmarkers in the South. Mullins was able to ward off both Landmarkers and fundamentalists by this move.

The consensus reflected by E. Y. Mullins did not last long. In the greater Southern Baptist orbit, beginning in the 1880s major defections occurred over clashes with convention authority, biblical literalism, racism, and regional leadership. The fallout became the Landmarkist Movement, the Baptist Bible Fellowship, the World (Premillennial) Baptist Fellowship, the Southwide Baptist Fellowship, and later the Alliance of Baptists, and the Cooperative Baptist Fellowship. The Landmarkist movement, led by James R. Graves (1820–93), Amos C. Dayton (1811–65), and J. M. Pendleton (1811–91), was concentrated in western Kentucky, Tennessee, Arkansas, and Texas. Stridently anti-convention, it focused on local congregations who held to a set of landmark principles. Gradually major coalitions of Landmarkers formed the American Baptist Association (1924) and later the North American Baptist Association (1950).

Alongside the Landmarkers after the 1920s was the Premillennial Baptist movement headed by leaders J. Frank Norris (1877–1952) and G. Beauchamp Vick (1901–75) from Texas and Ohio who were equally critical of the Convention. In the Southeast, Lee Roberson (1909–2007) of Chattanooga, Tennessee, led a loosely-organized revolt against the Convention that called itself the Southwide Baptist Fellowship. Finally, the Rev. Jerry Falwell (1933–2007) in Lynchburg, Virginia, founded the Liberty Baptist Fellowship in 1978 that emphasized biblical inerrancy, anti-abortion, and formation of a "Moral Majority" as its major objectives. The divisions among Baptists North, South, and Canadian, that occurred from the 1920s through the 1970s were all conservative in theological orientation.

In contrast to the early SBC offshoots were two major come-outer groups with a progressive to liberal outlook. During the later 1960s a theological debate arose in the Southern Baptist Convention over biblical authority and confessionalism. Churches in Texas, Arkansas, Georgia, Louisiana, and Florida joined in a call for biblical literalism. Their champion was W. Amos Criswell (1909–2002) of First Baptist, Dallas, Texas, author of *Why I Believe the Bible Is Literally True* (1970). Sharp differences of opinion were expressed in Southern Baptist state newspapers. Seminary degree programs at New Orleans and Southwestern Baptist in Ft. Worth, Texas, were urged on conservative candidates, as were several bible colleges across the convention. Southern and Southeastern seminaries were considered the epicenters of Neo-Orthodoxy.

In 1963 the progressives among the seminaries plus other prominent pastors across the Convention, like Herschel H. Hobbs (1907–95) of Oklahoma City, won a victory in revising the *Baptist Faith and Message* to reflect more Barthian understandings of the Bible and Christology. In response, a long-term grassroots resurgence of conservative evangelicals emerged to contend for the control of the convention. A strong, small collection of congregations in the middle Atlantic and upper South formed the Alliance of Baptists to articulate a progressive to liberal understanding of Baptist principles. Utmost in their concern were religious liberty, Christological hermeneutics, women in ministry, and strict separation of church and state. Later their platform included acceptance of same sex marriages and ordination of gay persons. The Alliance established a liberal margin in Southern Baptist life.

When election of a moderate candidate to the SBC presidency seemed beyond the grasp of any of the traditional coalitions, a large contingency of progressives formed the Cooperative Baptist Fellowship (CBF) in 1991. It was composed of theologically moderate pastors and congregations among the Southern (Louisville) and Southeastern (Wake Forest) Seminary alumni, plus religious studies faculty in many of the colleges and universities across the South. The CBF affirmed progressive ideas of a Christological biblical interpretation, ecumenical cooperation with other Christians, women in ministry, and greater cooperation across racial lines. It formed new seminaries, largely out of cooperating universities, notably Baylor, Mercer, and several schools in Carolina and Virginia.

What remained loyal to the Southern Baptist Convention was a collection of new conservative evangelical leaders, plus many congregations uncertain of their identity. In Texas, for instance, scores of congregations leaned toward the theological center, following the lead of Baylor University, but refused to defund the SBC Cooperative Program. This led to establishment of parallel Baptist bodies in Texas: the older Baptist General Convention of Texas, and a new Southern Baptist Convention of Texas. This duality was replicated in states across the Baptist South. At the national level, new hard-line leaders supplanted the older progressive heads of boards and agencies. The outstanding "Resurgents" included Judge Paul Pressler (*1930) of Houston, Texas, Richard Land (*1946) and Paige Patterson (*1942) of Dallas, Texas, R. Albert Mohler (*1959) of Louisville, Kentucky, Bailey Smith (1939–2019) and Richard Mellick (*1950) of Arkansas, Jerry Vines (*1937) of Florida, and Charles Stanley (*1932) of Georgia. They assumed positions of elected leadership in the Convention and related institutions, plus appointing positions over Convention boards and the six seminaries. The capstone achievement of the Resurgency was the third iteration of the *Baptist Faith and Message*, adopted by the Convention in 2000. Virtually a creedal statement because it was a litmus test of orthodoxy and fidelity to the SBC, it affirmed an inerrant understanding of the Scriptures, male headship in Christian homes, and an exclusively male pastoral ministry. Relationally, the SBC withdrew from the BWA and the Baptist Joint Committee on Public Affairs, both of which Southern Baptists had helped to found and sustain. In place of these two multiple-Baptist agencies, Southern Baptists organized their own international mission network, the Great Commission Churches, and the Ethics and Religious Liberty Commission, the latter to deal with church-state concerns in the United States. Southern Baptists also withdrew support from the International Baptist Seminary in Rüschlikon, Switzerland, crippling a center of Baptist life in Europe. Increasingly after 1970, two independent institutions had profound influence upon Southern Baptist leadership: Liberty University, founded by independent Baptist pastor and evangelist, Jerry Falwell, and Dallas Theological Seminary that is defined by an independent fundamentalist, dispensationalist theology.

Baptists in Canada found opportunities for growth and consolidation similar to their US neighbors. Following a cooperative surge among

Canadian Protestants in general at the turn of the twentieth century, Maritime Baptists led the way in 1905 by combining efforts with the Free Christian Baptists, forming a United Baptist Convention. The same year a Baptist Union of Western Canada was established by combining organizations in the Prairie Provinces and British Columbia. It was heavily influenced by the Mission Board of the Baptist Convention of Ontario, and McMaster University's theological program. A fourth small body of mainstream churches were formed in Quebec as *L'Union d'Eglises Baptistes Françaises au Canada*. For a time Canadian overseas interests were channeled through the American Baptist Missionary Union until a separate mission board was established with work in India, Bolivia, and Indonesia. The collection of four regional conventions and unions in Canada, plus the mission board, combined in 1944 to become the Baptist Federation of Canada, later known as Canadian Baptist Ministries. The term "Convention Baptists" is applied to this evolved family.

The fundamentalist impulse had its effect in Canada as well as the United States. Influenced by Spurgeonic trends in Britain, Toronto Baptists divided over educational appointments at McMaster University in the first two decades of the twentieth century. The leader of the arch-conservatives was T. T. Shields (1873–1955), pastor of the influential Jarvis Street Baptist Church in the heart of Toronto. In 1925 Shields took his congregation and a hundred other churches out of the Convention of Ontario and Quebec and formed a new movement called the Union of Regular Baptist Churches. Eventually by mid-century, it joined forces with a similar fundamentalist movement in British Columbia to create the Fellowship of Evangelical Baptist Churches in Canada. The strength of Fellowship Baptists was in central Canada and to a lesser degree in the Far West and Quebec.

Fundamentalism as a broad phenomenon was slow to take root among the Maritimes churches, in that region being the result of small clusters of churches which reacted against liberal teachings at Acadia University and the isolationism of central and northern New Brunswick. Outside influences from schools in the United States prompted a home-grown form of dispensationalist cross-confessionalism centered in the New Brunswick Bible Institute. A smaller but regionally significant rift occurred among mainstream Free Christian/Calvinistic Baptists in the last decades of the nineteenth century over holiness theology. Following the lead of pastor-advocates of entire sanctification (also called perfectionism), a small denomination of "Reformed Baptists" arose around a series of camp meetings and fundamentalist positions. This group eventually joined the Wesleyan Methodists and accounted for a departure of congregations in the coastal areas of the provinces from the Convention.

In the new millennium, Baptists in North America pursued a fragmented course. American Baptists, suffering from internal controversies of national versus regional control and same-sex and charismatic issues, declined dramatically. Southern Baptists likewise stagnated in their attempt to become the premier Baptist body in the United States. Smaller Baptist bodies turned toward greater cooperation with evangelical organizations like the National Association of Evangelicals and emerging church projects, while reducing their central services and national presences. This could be seen among the Conservative Baptist Association, the North American Baptist Conference, the Baptist General Conference, and the Seventh Day Baptist General Conference. Canadian Baptists reflected a similar pattern to their American counterparts.

Into a New Era

Baptists in North America were permanently reconfigured in the latter half of the twentieth century. Unlike Methodists, Lutherans, Presbyterians, and Congregationalists, Baptists could not find their way back to a unified witness. Instead, theological differences permanently delineated Baptist witness.

One major stream of Baptists has coalesced around historic libertarian, ecumenical principles. This tradition recognizes its rootage in English Puritan Separatism of the seventeenth century. It recognizes commonality with other mainstream Protestants, notably the Anglicans, Presbyterians, and Congregationalists. Stress is placed upon a denominational ecclesiology, in conversation and cooperation with other Christians, recently even with Roman Catholics and Orthodox. This irenic vision affirms complete liberty of conscience and full religious liberty for all people. It has nurtured a strong social activist interest ranging from antislavery to women's recognition and rights and liberation of oppressed peoples worldwide. Baptists of this orientation have sometimes been open to persons of same-sex relationships and they cross lines of color and ethnicity. When national councils of churches, and later the World Council of Churches, were formed, these Baptists became charter members. The BWA was founded from among these Baptists, and continuing conversations with other Christian groups and other religions are part of this Baptist family's experience. Included here specifically are American Baptists, Cooperative Baptists, the Alliance of Baptists, National Baptists USA, and Canadian Convention-related Baptists.

A second group of Baptists have gravitated to an experiential conservative evangelicalism, held in common with other denominations. From the earliest years, also rooted in the seventeenth century, these Baptists have underscored the need for a deep religious experience in believers' baptism and faithful discipleship. They value Scripture as a treasury of revealed truth, using words like "infallible" and "inerrant" to describe the Bible. These folk are strongly confessional in nature throughout their history, defining their identity by doctrinal statements and covenants that explicate personal and social ethics. Positions affirming male leadership and opposition to same-sex relations are not uncommon. The associational principle is usually restricted to "congregations of like faith and order." Participation in interdenominational bodies or interfaith conversations is rare. Educational attainment is secondary to Christian discipleship and fidelity to landmark principles. Finally, reaching back to an Anabaptist sect model, these Baptists are not comfortable conforming to modernist ideas and patterns, preferring a stance described by H. Richard Niebuhr (1894–1962) as "Christ Against Culture." Ethnic denominations, sabbatarians, come-outer associations, National Baptists of America and Black Missionary Baptists, Charismatic Baptist groups, Primitive Baptists, and Southern Baptists are found in this category. There is a noticeable tendency for these groups to be seen amongst historically Evangelical traditions, regardless of Baptist principles.

A third collection of Baptists in North America may be described as independent or non-aligned. This hard-to-define category may include evangelicals and liberals alike. What they have in common is their self-understanding of being unattached to associations, conventions, unions, or alliances. They are usually the result of an entrepreneurial pastor who weaves the fabric of their life. Among these Baptists, the true church is the solitary local congregation. It may be Baptist because it practices believers' baptism and congregational governance, but "Baptist" may not appear in its name. Education may be frowned upon as secondary to community involvement or relationships. On biblical principles, their independence is their moniker and their social homogeneity is clear. Baptistic community churches and fundamentalist congregations belong in this category. Some of these congregations may have distant links to independent fundamentalist groups or coalitions for fellowship purposes. "King James Version Only" Baptist churches, as well as the Riverside Church in New York City and the Church of All Nations in Los Angeles, plus federated congregations exemplify this type.

Baptists in North America have flourished as a religious group in an unusual way. This is part due to the freedom of local communities to propagate their faith and draw strength from grassroots constituency. The adoption of democratic principles in the political culture interfaces with basic Baptist principles. Baptist missionary organizations have been unusually successful in domestic efforts. Baptist advocacy of separation of church and state and religious liberty has resonated with important leaders like Thomas Jefferson (1743–1826) and James Madison (1751–1836). Great preachers have challenged the consciences of the public, like George W. Truett (1867–1944) and Billy Graham (1918–2018). Tommy Douglas (1904–86), a Baptist preacher-become-political leader, and author of national health care, has been acclaimed as the most significant leader in Canadian history. Finally Baptists have aligned themselves with American and Canadian democratic ideals and energetically defended those ideals beyond North America.

Bibliography

Backus, Isaac. *An Abridgement of the Church History of New England, from 1602 to 1804...with a Concise Account of the Baptists in the Southern Parts of America.* Boston: E. Lincoln, 1804.

Bentall, Shirley. *From Sea to Sea: The Canadian Baptist Federation 1944-1994.* Mississauga, ON: Canadian Baptist Federation, 1994.

Bill, I. E. *Fifty Years with the Baptists of the Maritime Baptists.* Saint John: Barnes, 1880.

Brackney, William H. *Baptists in North America: An Historical Survey.* Oxford: Blackwell, 2006.

———, ed. *Baptist Life and Thought.* Rev. ed. Valley Forge, PA: Judson, 1998.

———. *Congregation and Campus: North American Baptists in Higher Education.* Macon, AL: Mercer University Press, 2008.

———. *A Genetic History of Baptist Thought.* Macon, AL: Mercer University Press, 2004.

———. *Historical Dictionary of the Baptists.* 3rd ed. Lanham, MD: Rowman & Littlefield, 2021.

Byrd, James P. *Religious Liberty, Violent Persecution, and the Bible: The Challenge of Roger Williams.* Macon, GA: Mercer University Press, 2002.

Fletcher, Jesse C. *The Southern Baptist Convention: A Sesquicentennial History.* Nashville, TN: Broadman & Holman, 1994.

Ford, Murray J. S., ed. *Canadian Baptist History and Polity.* Hamilton, ON: McMaster Divinity College, 1982.

Gaustad, Edwin S. *Baptist Piety: The Last Will and Testimony of Obadiah Holmes.* Grand Rapids, MI: Eerdmans, 1978.

———. *Historical Atlas of Religion in America.* New York: Harper & Row, 1962.

Gibson, Theo T. *Robert Alexander Fyfe: His Contemporaries and Influence.* Burlington, ON: G. R. Welch, 1988.

Grant, John Webster. *The Church in the Canadian Era.* Toronto: McGraw-Hill, 1998.

———. *A Profusion of Spires: Religion in Nineteenth Century Ontario.* Toronto: University of Toronto, 1998.

Handy, Robert T. *A History of the Churches in the United States and Canada.* New York: Oxford University Press, 1976.

Hudson, Winthrop Still. *Baptist Concepts of the Church.* Philadelphia: Judson, 1959.

———. *Religion in America: An Historical Account of the Development of American Religious Life.* New York: Scribner's, 1973.

Ivison, Stuart, and Fred Rosser. *The Baptists in Upper and Lower Canada Before 1820.* Toronto: University of Toronto, 1956.

Lemons, J. Stanley, ed. *Baptists in Early North America.* Vol. 2, *First Baptist Church, Providence, Rhode Island.* Macon, GA: Mercer University Press, 2013.

Leonard, Bill J. *Baptists in America.* New York: Columbia University Press, 2005.

———. *Baptist Ways: A History.* Valley Forge, PA: Judson, 2003.

McBeth, H. Leon. *The Baptist Heritage: Four Centuries of Baptist Witness.* Nashville, TN: Broadman, 1987.

McKibbens, Thomas R., ed. *Baptists in Early North America.* Vol. 4, *First Baptist Church of Boston, Massachusetts.* Macon, GA: Mercer University Press, 2017.

McLoughlin, William G. *New England Dissent, 1630-1883.* 2 vols. Cambridge: Harvard University Press, 1971.

Moir, John S., ed. *The Cross in Canada*. Toronto: Ryerson, 1966.

Murphy, Terrance, and Roberto Perin. *A Concise History of Christianity in Canada*. New York: Oxford University Press, 1996.

Newman, Albert H. *A Century of Baptist Achievement*. Philadelphia: American Baptist Publication Society, 1901.

Noll, Mark A. *A History of Christianity in the United States and Canada*. Grand Rapids, MI: Eerdmans, 1992.

Prentice, Roger H. "The Impact of Walter Rauschenbusch in Canada." In *In the Shadow of a Prophet: The Legacy of Walter Rauschenbusch*, edited by William H. Brackney and David Gushee, 93–124. Macon, GA: Mercer University Press, 2020.

———. "Wolfville Baptist Church." In *Baptists in Early North America*, 10:n.p. Macon, GA: Mercer University Press, forthcoming.

Rawlyk, George, ed. *Henry Alline: Selected Writings*. Marynoll, NY: Paulist, 1987.

———. *The Canadian Protestant Experience*. Kingston/Montreal, PQ: McGill-Queens University Press, 1990.

Renfree, Harry A. *Heritage and Horizon: The Baptist Story in Canada*. Mississauga, ON: Canadian Baptist Federation, 1988.

Sanford, Don A. *A Choosing People: The History of Seventh Day Baptists*. Nashville, TN: Broadman, 1992.

Saunders, Edward M. *History of the Baptists of the Maritime Provinces*. St. John, NB: Burgoyne, 1902.

Shreve, Dorothy Shadd. *The Afri-Canadian Church: A Stabilizer*. Jordan Station, ON: Paideia, 1983.

Sobel, Mechal. *Trabelin' On: The Slave Journey to an Afro-Baptist Faith*. Princeton, NJ: Princeton University Press, 1988.

Torbet, Robert G. *History of the Baptists*. Valley Forge, PA: Judson, 1963.

Van Broekhoven, Deborah Bingham, ed. *Baptists in Early North America*. Vol. 7, *First Baptist Church, Philadelphia, PA*. Macon, GA: Mercer University Press, 2021.

Washington, James Melvin. *Frustrated Fellowship: The Black Baptist Quest for Social Power*. Macon, GA: Mercer University Press, 1986.

List of Baptist Churches in the USA and Canada[12]

USA

Alliance of Baptists (1987)

American Baptist Association (1924)

American Baptist Churches in the USA (1972, formerly American Baptist Convention)

American Baptist Convention (1950, formerly Northern Baptist Convention)

American Baptist Evangelicals (1992)

Antimissionary Baptists, also called Hardshell or Primitive Baptists

Baptist Bible Fellowship (1950)

Baptist Bible Union (1923)

Baptist Church of Christ (1825, also called Duck River and Kindred Baptists)

Baptist General Conference (1856, also known as Swedish Baptists)

Baptist Missionary Association of America (1969)

Bible Baptists (1944)

Caucus Nacional Bautista Hispano (1970)

Conservative Baptist Association (1947)

Conservative Baptist Fellowship (1965)

Cooperative Baptist Fellowship (1991)

Czecholovak Baptist Convention (1909)

Danish Baptist General Conference (1910)

Finnish Baptist Union (1901)

Free Communion Baptists (1840)

Freewill Baptists (1781, later known as Free Baptists)

French-Speaking Baptist Conference of New England (1895)

Fundamental Baptist Fellowship (1974)

12. The list is in: William H. Brackney, *Baptists in North America: An Historical Perspective* (Oxford: Blackwell, 2006), 270–72.

Fundamental Baptist Missionary Fellowship (1939)

General Association of General Baptists (1870)

General Association of Regular Baptist Churches (1932)

General Six Principle Baptists (1670)

Great Commission Baptists (2005)

Hampton (University) Ministers Conference (1914)

Hardshell Baptists (1820, also known as Primitive Baptists)

Hungarian Baptist Union (1908)

Independent Baptist Fellowship International (1984)

Independent Baptists (1756)

Italian Baptist Association of America (1898)

King James Only Baptists (1950)

Liberty Baptist Fellowship (1977)

Lott Carey Baptist Foreign Mission Convention (1897)

Mainstream Baptists (2001)

Mexican Baptist Convention of Northern North America (1910)

Missionary Baptists (1901)

Moderate Baptists (2000)

National Association of Freewill Baptists (1935)

National Baptist Convention of America (1915)

National Baptist Convention USA, Inc. (1895)

National Baptist Missionary Convention (1988)

New Testament Association of Independent Baptist Churches (1974)

Norwegian Baptist Conference of America (1864)

North American Baptist Association (1950)

North American Baptist Conference (1851, also known as German Baptists)

Northern Baptist Convention (1907; later American Baptist Convention, 1950; today American Baptist Churches, USA, 1972)

Old Regular Baptists (1892)

Old School Baptists (1832)

Pentecostal Freewill Baptist Church (1959)

Polish Baptist Conference (1912)

Portuguese Baptist Conference (1919)

Premillennial Baptist Missionary Fellowship (1933)

Primitive Baptists (South 1829, North 1832)

Progressive National Baptist Convention (1961)

Regular Baptists (1707)

Rogerenes (1674)

Romanian Baptist Association of America (1913)

Russian and Ukrainian Evangelical Baptist Union (1919)

Separate Baptists (1754)

Southern Baptist Convention (1845)

Southwide Baptist Fellowship (1956)

Two Seed in the Spirit Double Predestinarian Baptists (1817)

Welcoming and Affirming Baptists (1993)

World Baptist Fellowship (1950, formerly the Premillennial Baptist Missionary Fellowship

Canada

AfriCanadian Baptists (1782)

Amherstburg Association (1841)

Association of Regular Baptist Churches (1957)

Atlantic Baptist Fellowship (1970)

Baptist Convention of Ontario and Quebec (1888)

Baptist Federation of Canada (1944, later called Canadian Baptist Ministries)

Baptist General Conference of Canada (1906, originally Swedish Baptists)

Baptist Union of Western Canada (1905)

Canadian Convention of Southern Baptists (1985)

Convention of Baptists in Atlantic Canada (1846)

Fellowship of Evangelical Baptist Churches (1953)

Free Baptists (1832, also known as Freewill Baptists)

Gathering of Baptists (1994)

North American Conference Baptists (1902, originally German Baptists)

Primitive Baptists (1875)

Reformed Baptists (1886, later joined the Wesleyan Church)

Regular Baptists (1925)

Scotch Baptists (1816)

L'Union d'Eglises Baptistes Françaises au Canada (1966)

14

The African American Baptist Journey

"Salvation, Hope and Liberation: A Journey of Faith"

Edward L. Wheeler and Mary S. Wheeler

Introduction

From its earliest beginnings in England and the Netherlands, Baptist history has been a story of struggle and sacrifice. While that is true for Baptists in general, there is arguably no community of Baptists for which that struggle has been more profound or prolonged than within the community we now know as Black or African American Baptists.

Born in the crucible of an inhumane slavery, racial oppression, and often violent discrimination, African Americans had the daunting task of hearing a gospel that did not affirm their humanity and translating that message into a gospel of hope for the oppressed. Black Baptists in America had to reframe the gospel that was often used to justify their oppression into a transforming, liberating word that enabled them to build communities of faith that served as buffers and shields from the forces of degradation and destruction that surrounded them in both the so-called free North and the slave South.

The fact that Black Baptists came to exist in the cultural milieu of North American racism and slavery must not blind us to the reality that the African slave did not arrive on the shores of North America devoid of a religious history and heritage. While an argument can be made as to how much that history and heritage impacted the ways the slaves heard the gospel, West African traditional religions and the exposure to Christian understandings of God provided fertile soil for Baptist themes of freedom in Christ to be planted and then take root.[1] This chapter will attempt to provide insights into the history of Black Baptists in America. It is a difficult task to tell such a rich history in a chapter, but it is a story that deserves to be told even in a shortened version.

Black Baptist Beginnings

Despite the myth that religious freedom as expressed through the Christian faith was the primary factor in the founding of the English colonies in North America, most colonists had no strong religious sentiments until the mid-eighteenth century. The major exception to that truth would be the early settlements in what was known as the New England Colonies. Other colonies, especially in the South, were prized for their commercial potential. That perspective fueled the slave trade and the oppression of millions of Africans. Contrary to much of the propaganda used to justify slavery, Africans were civilized and religious. While they were only able to bring their collective memories with them to the new world, those memories included their religious practices and beliefs. In West Africa, from whence most slaves in North America originated, God was in everything and so the concept of an all-powerful God was not foreign.[2]

Christianity's belief that Jesus came among people, living as a human and as God, and being concerned with each person's everyday life fit well with African theology. West Africans also had a practice of adjusting their religious experience to their existential reality. Therefore, God was still God wherever they might be. God might be called by a different name in this new place, but that did not change who God is.[3]

Despite some early limited attempts to Christianize slaves, it was not until the outbreak of religious fervor known as the First Great Awakening (1730–75) that African slaves in North America had their first widespread exposure to the Christian faith. The Great Awakening exhibited

1. Imasogie, "African Traditional Religion," 283–93.
2. Raboteau, *Slave Religion,* 15–16.
3. Raboteau, *Slave Religion,* 22.

elements that were similar to African worship practices—ecstatic dancing, shouting, spirit possession, and singing. African Americans readily
responded and participated at every level of the worship experience. The
First Great Awakening campground preachers made the gospel plain and
clear. They were for the most part illiterates speaking to illiterates. These
preachers were predominantly Baptists or Methodists.

A pioneering group of African American church leaders emerged
from the Awakening who would take the gospel to the African American
community on their own terms. Though often under the watchful eye
of white slave owners, these leaders preached the gospel as a liberating
force and not as a control mechanism as white preachers often did. Jesus
was a liberator whose love and concern extended to each individual. Everyone converted and baptized was new in Jesus and a person of worth.
The stories of the Old Testament confirmed that African slaves would
someday be delivered from bondage just as they had been set free from
sin because the weak always triumphed over the strong with God's help.
African Americans identified with the children of Israel and their attainment of freedom from bondage.[4] It was in this context that the Black
Baptist church was born.

Although some scholars believe that the first Black Baptist church
was founded in Virginia,[5] the vast majority of scholars who study the
Black church follow in the footsteps of Carter G. Woodson and identify
the Silver Bluff Baptist Church as the first formally established African
American Baptist congregation in North America.[6] That church was
formed on the property of George Galphin, a prominent trader and en-
trepreneur, along the Savannah River at Silver Bluff, South Carolina near
Augusta, Georgia sometime between 1773 and 1775. Galphin permitted
his slaves to gather to hear the itinerant preacher, Wait Palmer. In his
absence another itinerant, George Liele, a Black man who had been given
his freedom so that he could proclaim the gospel in the Baptist tradition,
also preached to the Silver Bluff congregation. A member of the church,
David George, soon became the resident pastor when the outbreak of the
Revolutionary War made it more difficult for itinerant preachers to travel
freely.

4. See Rawick, *From Sundown to Sunup*, 30–51 and Wilmore, *Black Religion and
Black Radicalism*, 1–28.

5. Sobel, *Trabelin' On*, 83.

6. Woodson, *History of the Negro Church*, 35–36.

In 1778, the British captured Savannah and the American revolutionaries found themselves under pressure from both the British and those Americans who were loyal to England. Apparently responding to British offers to free slaves who came under their protection, sometime in 1779 David George led the Silver Bluff congregation to Savannah. George Liele was already in Savannah serving as a servant to the Commanding Officer of the British forces in Savannah, Colonel Kirkland. Liele had established a Black Baptist church in the city. Two other African American Baptist congregations would be formed in Savannah within a decade. However, when the British evacuated Savannah in 1782 both Liele and David George left Savannah and became the first Baptist missionaries to establish churches outside of what became the United States. Liele went to Jamaica where he established the Baptist church in that country.[7] David George went to Nova Scotia in 1782 where he established a Black Baptist congregation but facing religious and racial opposition, he departed for Sierra Leone, West Africa in 1792 where he founded another Baptist congregation.[8] At least two other former slave members of the Silver Bluff congregation became preachers and pastors. Andrew Bryan stayed in Savannah. Jesse Peter, with several former Silver Bluff members, founded the First African Baptist Church in Augusta.

About the same time as Silver Bluff was making its mark in history other Black Baptist churches were being formed in Virginia. However, in the South most slaves who were Baptist worshiped with whites though often restricted to the rear or the balcony of churches. Independent Black Baptist worship in the southern context would later be seriously curtailed after the slave revolts of 1822 and 1831.[9]

In the North, where there was a smaller African American presence prior to the Civil War, Black congregants often worshiped in White churches. However, as the nineteenth century arrived, there were some notable exceptions to the general situation. The First African Church of Philadelphia, the Joy Street Church of Boston and the Abyssinian Baptist Church of New York City were among the Baptist Churches established by Blacks in the first decade of the 1800s. As the states of Ohio and Illinois were settled, Black Baptists formed churches in those areas. As a result of the numerical growth of Black Baptists in Ohio, the first Black Baptist

7. Shannon, *George Liele's Life and Legacy.*
8. Gordon, *From Slavery to Freedom.*
9. Wilmore, *Black Religion,* 57–73.

Association was formed in 1836, the Providence Baptist Association. Two years later twelve Black Baptist congregations in Illinois formed the Wood River Baptist Association. These two associations merged in 1853 to form the Western Colored Baptist Convention. It is very likely that the merger resulted from the passage of the oppressive Fugitive Slave Law in 1850 that led many runaway slaves and other African Americans who recognized the tentative nature of their freedom to flee to Canada.[10] Once again the desire to be free impacted the development of Black Baptist life in the United States.

Black Baptist Foreign Mission Efforts and Denominational Structures

Even as African American Baptists struggled with slavery in the South and prejudice in the North, the earliest efforts to initiate an intentional mission outreach to the African continent was taking shape. In 1815 Lott Carey helped to found the Richmond African Baptist Missionary Society. Carey was an exhorter at the First African Baptist Church of Richmond, Virginia and he brought together members of First African Baptist and Blacks from white churches in the area to form the Society. By 1821, enough support had been garnered to send Carey, his wife and several other missionaries to Liberia to begin their missionary efforts. Unfortunately those early ambassadors of the faith died soon after they began their work. Despite the founding of the American Baptist Missionary Convention by African American Baptists in the New England and Middle States region in 1840, there would not be another Black Baptist Missionary sent to the African continent by Black Baptists until after the Civil War.

After the Civil War, slavery was ended and in the aftermath, Black Baptists flourished. The freedom of conscience, the independence of the local congregation and the opportunity to worship God in their own way no doubt contributed to the rapid growth of Black Baptist churches after 1865. The growth in the number of local churches also led to the creation of Black Baptist denominational structures such as state conventions and national conventions. North Carolina's Black Baptist state convention was started in 1866 and was followed by Arkansas, Kentucky, and eventually all the other southern states.

10. Wheeler, "Beyond One Man," 314–15.

Among the first national conventions formed by Black Baptists was the Foreign Missions Convention of the United States of America. The Reverend W. W. Colley was the person most responsible for this effort that focused on missionary efforts to West Africa. Colley had served as a missionary for the Southern Baptist Convention and believed that African Americans should lead in taking the gospel to the African continent. The headquarters for the new convention was in Richmond, Virginia even though the 151 delegates who founded the organization had met in 1880 in Montgomery, Alabama. Richmond was where Lott Carey had launched his missionary endeavor and that area had a passion for missions.

Six years later Black Baptists met in St. Louis, Missouri to respond to the identified need for missionary efforts among the freedman in the United States. The Rev. William J. Simmons, a noted leader, preacher, educator, and author, was the guiding force that brought six hundred delegates together to form the American National Baptist Convention in 1886. Simmons was elected President and served until his death in 1890.

The need to have a national organization to help train African American church leaders led to the formation of the Baptist National Education Convention in 1893. However, one year later, Dr. Albert W. Pegues, a pastor and educator from North Carolina, introduced a resolution at the fourteenth annual meeting of the Foreign Mission Convention that the three existing national conventions merge. This idea gained traction in part because of the lack of opportunities Black Baptists had to publish their written work through the American Baptist Publishing Society. Black Baptists believed that by combining their organizations and resources they could create their own publishing house while strengthening their other ministries. Their efforts resulted in the creation of the National Baptist Convention, USA in 1895 in Atlanta, Georgia. The Reverend E. C. Morris was elected as the first president. This convention would send delegates to the 1905 Baptist World Alliance meeting in London.

Despite the cooperation and unity that had led to the formation of the National Baptist Convention USA, tensions soon rose over the role foreign missions would play in the new structure. The election of Dr. Lewis Jordan as the Corresponding Secretary of the Foreign Mission Board of the Convention was not universally celebrated, but his relocation of the headquarters from Richmond to Louisville alienated many persons who had been affiliated with previous foreign mission efforts.

Therefore, in 1897 a small group, primarily from Virginia, withdrew from the NBCUSA and formed the Lott Carey Missionary Convention. Since its creation the convention has focused on foreign missions. Ironically, the establishment of the publishing house, the cause that had initially been a major factor in uniting African American Baptists, became the primary cause of an even greater and more consequential split in the NBCUSA. The Reverend R. H. Boyd assumed major leadership roles in the NBCUSA as the Corresponding Secretary of both the Home Missionary Board and the Publishing Board. He successfully guided the effort to establish a publishing house for the NBCUSA in Nashville, Tennessee where the publishing house was incorporated as an independent enterprise. The publishing house was built on property owned by Boyd without any convention funding. From 1905 until 1915, Boyd ran the publishing house as a separate, independent entity and when an attempt was made to subordinate the publishing house to the control of the Convention, a split occurred. Boyd's legal claim was clear and led to the establishment of the National Baptist Convention of America, unincorporated with the publishing house as the center piece of the new entity. The NBCUSA was without a publishing house but incorporated to avoid a duplication of the Boyd split in the future.

The Women's Movement among Black Baptists

While male dominance in Black Baptist pulpits was taken for granted in the years following the end of the Civil War and the early years of the twentieth century, African American women were vital to local church life. They also worked for causes designed to improve the lives of African Americans who despite their recent emancipation were severely impacted by discrimination, second-class citizenship and an overt and at times violent racism. The movement that led to the formation of the Woman's Convention of the National Baptist Convention, USA in 1900 had started at the state level soon after Black Baptist state conventions were formed. Under the leadership of William J. Simmons, the American National Baptist Convention took the unprecedented position of integrating women into the leadership ranks of the Convention. However, Simmons had opposed the establishment of a separate organization for women. Despite the failure of early attempts to form their own convention, the goal of establishing a woman's convention was achieved in 1900 with the strong support of Lewis G. Jordon and Charles Parrish who had leadership roles in the Foreign Mission Board. However, it was the leadership of women such as Mary V. Cook, Lucy Wilmot Smith, Sarah W. Layten, and Nannie Helen Burroughs that made it possible for the Woman's Convention to be established and to maintain its own budget and independence in establishing its agenda.[11]

The Woman's Convention worked with the NBCUSA in many areas, including home and foreign missions. It also worked with white women in the promotion of such causes as temperance and suffrage. The Women's Convention spoke out against lynching and gender related discrimination, often calling the leadership of the NBCUSA to task. Nevertheless, the major focus was on education at every level. In the wake of legal segregation and the systematic disenfranchisement of Blacks, especially in the South, African American Baptist women saw education as the way to uplift the race and open the door to expanded opportunities. Their service in this area proved to be essential to Black progress.

Black Baptists, Migration and the Civil Rights Movement

Black Baptist growth after emancipation was phenomenal and by 1915 Black Baptists outnumbered all other religious groups in the African American community by a large margin. However, up through the first two decades of the twentieth century the overwhelming majority of Blacks lived in the rural South. That was about to change. Several factors led to what is called the Great Migration as Blacks left the rural South in historic numbers and moved to the North and West. Among the most prominent factors were the oppressive share cropper system that kept share croppers in debt, the devastation of cotton crops by the infestation of the boll weevil, the lack of educational opportunities for Black children, the opportunity in the North for employment with salaries, and the overt violent racism found in the South. The population shift was so profound that by 1950, the majority of Blacks were to be found in Northern cities like New York, Detroit, and Chicago. With this change Black Baptists also changed.

Under the leadership of pastors like Adam Clayton Powell Sr. and Lacy Kirk Williams, older established northern churches such as Abyssinian Baptist Church in New York and Mount Olivet in Chicago developed

11. See Higginbotham, *Righteous Discontent.*

programs that sought to meet the social, economic, and spiritual needs of the new migrants from the South. When the existing churches did not adapt to the migrants, new Baptist churches with worship styles more comfortable to the southern newcomers began to emerge. To be sure, other options presented themselves to those recently arriving from the South, but the vast majority sought out or established a Black Baptist church for their spiritual nurturing.

Even as Blacks moved north and west to find greater freedom and more opportunities in less overtly racist situations, those who remained in the South became less accepting of the status quo and less tolerant of the Jim Crow laws that codified second-class treatment and injustice leveled at Black people. Baptists were certainly not alone in this struggle, but the most notable leader in the crusade for equality was the Black Baptist preacher/prophet Martin Luther King Jr. The "foot soldiers" in what is now often known as the modern Civil Rights Movement were thousands of unknown and unnamed men, women, and children. Among the leadership ranks were such Baptist preacher/pastors as Fred Shuttlesworth, William Holmes Borders, Ralph David Abernathy, Thomas Kilgore, Adam Clayton Powell Jr., Wyatt Tee Walker, and Gardner C. Taylor to name only a few. Younger, courageous Black Baptist leaders included Otis Moss Jr., Prathia Hall Wynn, Jesse L. Jackson, and Albert Brinson. Black Baptist leadership in this movement for justice and equality, however, was not universally celebrated. Many white Baptists decried Black defiance of legalized segregation. Even many Black Baptists refused to join in the struggle because of reasons ranging from a reluctance to be involved with political issues to a fear of white retaliation. It was opposition to the methodology of nonviolent civil disobedience that was perhaps the major factor in the 1961 split within the National Baptist Convention, USA, the largest of the Black Baptist conventions.

It should be recognized that a growing discontent with an ineffective system of tenure for the President of the NBCUSA, Inc. had been growing for many years. However, it was the opposition to the nonviolent civil disobedience strategy for social change that the then-President, Dr. Joseph H. Jackson, forcefully articulated that alienated many of those who supported the leadership of Martin Luther King Jr. To be sure, it is very possible that Jackson and the old guard saw Dr. King as a threat to their power and authority. Nevertheless, the dissatisfaction with the policies of the NBCUSA and several contentious conventions led Reverend L. Venchael Booth to issue a call for persons interested in the formation of a new convention to meet at Zion Baptist Church in Cincinnati where he served as pastor. From that call the Progressive National Baptist Convention was formed on November 14, 1961. The first President was Reverend T. M. Chambers. The PNBC adopted a tenure policy that clearly limited the length of service for the officers and it adopted a strong stance in support of the King-led Civil Rights Movement.[12]

Black Baptists in the Post-Civil Rights Era

In some important ways, the Civil Rights Movement was among the finest hours in the history of Black Baptists in the United States. That movement helped unify African American Baptists in an effort that eventually transcended convention loyalty and merged with the ideals of freedom and self-determination, congregational independence, and a spiritually based concern for justice. However, that unity has not been maintained. African American Baptists are still the largest faith community within the Black community in the United States. However there have been additional splits and there are additional challenges that Black Baptists face in the twenty-first century. Even as many African Americans have benefited from the increase in opportunities to enter into mainstream American culture and society, large numbers of African Americans have not benefited from that progress. While many Black Baptist congregations have continued to find ways to minister to the "least of these" some churches have directed their ministry to the "up and out." Black Baptists have always been a varied lot, but the prospect that African American Baptists could be stratified along socioeconomic lines is a matter for concern.

Black Baptists have been part of white churches for over two centuries. Even as Black Baptists formed their own denominational structures, it was not uncommon for Black churches to be dually aligned with predominantly white Baptist conventions. Over the past four or five decades, however, there has been a growing number of Black Baptist churches who are solely aligned with predominantly white Baptist conventions. There are some important reasons behind this reality that include retirement and health benefits as well as programs and services that are beneficial to church development. Some Black Baptist churches were also started as church plants by white denominations. This is not necessarily a negative

12. Wheeler, "Beyond One Man," 316–18.

development, but it does raise questions about how well Black churches in white denominational structures are able to freely address those issues that relate directly to Black life.

The relationship of social issues to Black Baptist biblical hermeneutics is also a challenge in the twenty-first century. The most significant of those include the role of women in ministerial leadership, abortion, and gay rights. The growth of nondenominational churches has also impacted Black Baptists. However, in 1992 a new entity was founded, that while not claiming to be a denomination, has had an impact on Black Baptist traditions, theology and polity. The Full Gospel Baptist Fellowship International was founded in 1992 by Paul S. Morton. At the time of its founding, Morton was the pastor of the Greater St. Stephen's Baptist Church in New Orleans. He perceived that the Holy Spirit was working among his congregants in a new way. This empowering force indicated to him that there was a need for a more Pentecostal style of worship to augment traditional Baptist beliefs and worship practices. Morton described the void he had observed as Baptists failing to utilize all the "fruits of the Spirit" available to the church. This meant that worshipers in Baptist churches should be free to include glossolalia (speaking in unknown tongues) as part of their worship and that spirit-filled praise should become intentional. In addition to this ecclesiological/theological position that most traditional Baptists would question, the FGBFI has instituted an episcopal hierarchy that is foreign to Baptist polity and could be perceived as counter to the Fellowship's stated support for each church's local autonomy.

Whether the FGBFI is the wave of the future or a short-term aberration, only time will tell. However, two things are clear. The first is that since its inception, the FGBFI has grown to over two million members, who despite the claim that they are not a separate denomination, has a structure that at best requires a dual loyalty. The second thing that is clear is that in true Baptist fashion the FGBFI underwent its first major split over the election of Bishop Morton's successor in 2014.

Black Baptists in America have contributed much to the worldwide Baptist witness. Black Baptists in the United States have modeled an amazing faithfulness to God in the face of oppression, dehumanization, and discrimination. They have relied upon God for deliverance even as they saw in the word of God hope in the face of hopeless situations. Black Baptists built houses of worship where they could praise God freely. They built schools for the education of their people. Black Baptists were the first Baptists in America to send missionaries to foreign countries and have produced great preachers whose powerful proclamation has helped change their communities and the world. Black Baptists also helped lead the fight to break the legal strangle hold of racist injustice in America that still resounds around the world. The story of Black Baptists in the United States is therefore an essential part of the worldwide Baptist story.

Bibliography

Gayle, Clement. *George Liele: Pioneer Missionary to Jamaica.* Nashville, TN: Bethlehem, 2002.

Gordon, Grant. *From Slavery to Freedom: The Life of David George, Pioneer Black Baptist Minister.* Hantsport, NS: Lancelot, 1992.

Higginbotham, Evelyn Brooks. *Righteous Discontent: The Women's Movement in the Black Baptist Church, 1888–1920.* Cambridge: Harvard University Press, 1993.

Imasogie, Isadolor. "African Traditional Religion and Christian Faith." *Review and Expositor* 70 (1973) 283–93.

Pace, Courtney. *Freedom Faith: The Womanist Vision of Prathia Hall.* Macon, GA: University of Georgia Press, 2019.

Raboteau, Albert J. *Slave Religion: The "Invisible Institution" in the Antebellum South.* New York: Oxford University Press, 2004.

Rawick, George P. *From Sundown to Sunup: The Making of the Black Community.* Westport, CT: Greenwood, 1972.

Shannon, David, et al. *George Liele's Life and Legacy: An Unsung Hero.* Macon, GA: Mercer University Press. 2012.

Sobel, Mechal. *Trabelin' On: The Slave Journey to An Afro-Baptist Faith.* Westport, CT: Greenwood, 1979.

Wheeler, Edward. "Beyond One Man: A General Survey of Black Baptist Church History." *Review and Expositor* 70 (1973) 309–19.

———. *Uplifting the Race: The Black Minister in the New South 1865–1902.* Latham, MD: University Press of America. 1986.

Wilmore, Gayraud. *Black Religion and Black Radicalism.* Maryknoll, NY: Orbis, 1983.

Woodson, Carter Godwin. *The History of the Negro Church.* Washington, DC: The Associated Publishers, 1985.

15

Fundamentalist Controversy among Baptists in Twentieth-Century America

Barry Hankins

In the United States it is often said that if you encounter two Baptists, you will find three opinions. This and other jokes refer to the Baptist penchant for theological wrangling, dissent, and schism. While nearly every Baptist denomination has a history of contentious battles over all manner of social and theological issues, the two most significant Baptist controversies in America took place a half century apart—in the North in the 1920s, and in the South in the 1980s.[1]

Northern Baptists

Northern Baptists experienced rumblings of controversy between conservatives and modernists from 1890 forward. In 1918 a new round of warfare erupted that peaked in the fundamentalist-modernist controversy of the twenties. Following World War I, Protestant denominations in the United States were flush with the optimism that comes with victory. From the American perspective the war had been an idealistic crusade for democracy that prepared the way for worldwide evangelization. In December more than one hundred Protestant leaders met in New York City to launch the Interchurch World Movement (IWM). Spearheaded

---

1. Much of what is discussed in this essay has been distilled from Kidd and Hankins, *Baptists in America: A History.*

by Presbyterians, Northern Baptist leaders joined enthusiastically. One participant exulted that the IWM would bring about "nothing less than a complete evangelization of all of life," while the unofficial motto became "the giving of the whole gospel to the whole world by the whole church." Momentum built over the next year, and in January 1920 more than eighteen hundred representatives from forty-two denominations attended the IWM meeting. Curtis Lee Laws (1868–1946), conservative editor of the Baptist *Watchman Examiner,* wrote, "As a thorough-going Baptist I heard not one word in the conference to which I take exception."

But other conservatives in the Northern Baptist Convention found much that offended them. John Roach Straton (1875–1929) of Calvary Baptist, New York City and Isaac Massey Haldeman (1845–1933) of First Baptist, New York City took an immediate stand against the IWM. Firebrand Baptist organizer William Bell Riley (1861–1947) of Minneapolis, MN quickly joined the opposition. It took them less than six months to turn Laws against the IWM, and eventually they persuaded the Northern Baptist Convention to withdraw. Some Baptists detected a threat to congregational autonomy in the collective effort of the IWM. Haldeman, for example, called the movement "ecclesiastical autocracy and church sovietism," a stinging charge given the victory of the Bolshevik "Soviets" of the Russian Revolution that began in 1917. The conservatives also believed the IWM was a mushy Social Gospel that served as little more than social work. It diluted real evangelism aimed at the new birth in Christ. This Social Gospel was the product of modernist theology, the conservatives believed, and herein lay its most destructive feature.

Modernist theology entered American religious life from Germany in the late nineteenth century. It led to major controversies in the northern Presbyterian and Northern Baptist denominations and to a lesser extent among Methodists and Episcopalians. As its name suggests, modernism sought to bring Protestant theology into harmony with modern ways of thinking. As in other disciplines, modernist theologians not only believed in Darwinism but also applied the evolutionary model to theology. They argued essentially that the form of Christianity found in the Bible was a rudimentary religion that developed over the next nineteen centuries. As Congregationalist preacher Henry Ward Beecher put it in 1871, "The kingdom of God and of truth, as it is laid down in the New Testament, is a kingdom of seeds. They have been sown abroad, and have been growing and developing in the world."

The Bible, in other words, was not a timeless source of authority but rather the ancient expression of a faith in need of development and constant revision, especially in the wake of modern science. Religious experience trumped the Bible as the ultimate source of authority. Modernists also applied the techniques of literary criticism to Scripture, calling into question the historicity of many Old Testament stories and the veracity of many miracles in the Old and New Testaments. Behind all this stood a modern, scientific, nearly naturalistic worldview, which jettisoned many of the orthodox doctrines of the Christian faith. Baptist modernist Harry Emerson Fosdick (1878–1969) called the virgin birth "a biological miracle our modern minds cannot use" and the second coming of Christ merely "an old phrasing of expectancy." The new birth in Christ became less a supernatural transformation of one's sinful nature than natural growth as children of God. All of this, of course, rankled conservatives who responded in both Baptist and Presbyterian circles by drawing up various versions of "the fundamentals of the faith" that one had to believe to remain Christian.

By 1920 modernists came to be called liberals, and that year conservatives took the name "fundamentalists," a term coined by Laws. He defined a fundamentalist as a theological conservative ready "to do battle royal" for the fundamentals of the faith. At the Northern Baptist Convention meeting in Buffalo the two sides debated the IWM for three hours and the fundamentalists won. Northern Baptists withdrew, one month after the northern Presbyterians did the same. The IWM collapsed, and Riley gloated, "Let not the liberals forget that the greatest single endeavor ever attempted by them went down to signal if not disgraceful defeat."

The fight over the IWM ended but it served as a prelude to an even more intense fundamentalist-modernist controversy that heated up over the next two years. In May 1922 Fosdick preached a sermon entitled, "Shall the Fundamentalists Win?" A Baptist, Fosdick was the most famous liberal preacher in America. Ironically, he served as pastor of the First Presbyterian Church (Old First) in New York. Clarence E. Macartney (1879–1957) answered Fosdick for Presbyterians with a sermon titled, "Shall Unbelief Win?," while the firebrand Straton responded for Baptist fundamentalists with "Shall the Funnymonkeyists Win?," a facetious reference to liberals' belief in evolution. The more moderate Laws wrote editorials in the *Watchman Examiner* arguing that the liberals exhibited greater intolerance than the fundamentalists.

Still riding high from their victory over the IWM, the conservatives formed a Fundamentalist Fellowship. The 1922 Northern Baptist Convention meeting served as the theater of the next battle. Convinced the denomination had slipped its orthodox moorings, the fundamentalists sought to elect conservatives to positions of leadership in the convention. As fundamentalist Jasper Cortenus Massee (1871–1965) put it, "[I]n my judgment every man of modernistic theological tendencies, though he may at heart hold the faith of Christ, should be discontinued from any office in the Northern Baptist Convention for the simple reason that his tendency is wrong." Fundamentalists also believed the denomination needed to adopt a confession of faith. "We deplore the drift away from a sound doctrine," Massee wrote in a letter sent to fundamentalists across the denomination. "We reject the leadership of men of liberal theological views. We repudiate the over-emphasis of a social gospel."

Meanwhile, in the pages of the *Watchman Examiner*, Laws urged fundamentalists to stop the modernist "warfare against supernaturalism." Modernism, he wrote,

> scorns the miracles of the Old Testament, sets aside the virgin birth of our Lord, . . . laughs at the credulity of those who accept many of the New Testament miracles, reduces the resurrection of our Lord to the fact that death did not end his existence, and sweeps away the promises of his second coming as an idle dream of men under the influence of Jewish apocalypticism."

Liberals responded that any drive to adopt a confession amounted to creedalism that violated the tenets of the Baptist faith. As convention president Helen Montgomery Barrett (1861–1934) said in her opening address, "For us Baptists to have an official confession of faith would come perilously near to abandoning one of our fundamental principles. . . . We Baptists are the recognized democrats of the Protestant world."

On the first day of the convention fundamentalist Frank Goodchild of New York offered a resolution to form a committee that would write a "declaration of faith." Delegates debated this over the course of the next two days before William Bell Riley grew impatient. On June 16, he threw the meeting into an uproar when he moved that the convention formally adopt the New Hampshire Confession of Faith as its official creed. The New Hampshire Confession had been written by Baptist leaders in 1833 when they joined together for missions in the Triennial Convention. Following Riley's motions, liberal leader Cornelius Woelfkin (1859–1928) of Park Avenue Baptist Church, New York, strode to the podium and offered an alternative: "That the Northern Baptist Convention affirm that the New Testament is the all-sufficient ground of faith and practice, and that we need no other." As the *New York Times* reported, "From that moment on it was the New Hampshire Confession against the New Testament." A brief debate ensued before someone called the question and Woelfkin's motion passed by a 2 to 1 margin.

This was the turning point in the fundamentalist-modernist controversy in the Northern Baptist Convention. Liberals had outmaneuvered the fundamentalists and won. From that point on the NBC tolerated liberal or fundamentalist churches. But the leadership and missions programs remained decidedly moderate to liberal, which put the fundamentalists in the awkward and untenable position of financially supporting what they believed was a false gospel. Over the next decade tension developed between the more moderate and denominationally oriented fundamentalists who followed Laws, and the separatists who followed Riley. The separatists adopted a strong anti-evolutionist plank and moved increasingly into interdenominational fundamentalism. While Riley stayed in the Northern Baptist Convention until his death in 1947, he encouraged Baptist churches to leave the NBC and form fundamentalist churches and denominations. For a time in the 1940s he and pastors trained in his Bible college dominated the state convention of Minnesota and encouraged Baptist churches in other states to align with them.

The Southern Baptist Convention

Like their Northern Baptist brethren, Southern Baptists experienced controversy starting in the 1890s, but not over modernism. Rather, the issue was Landmarkism, the belief that only Baptist congregations were true churches. Landmarkers believed a succession of Baptist churches practicing immersion could be traced back to apostolic times. The Landmark party grew strong enough to force the resignation of William Heth Whitsitt (1841–1911) as president of Southern Baptist Seminary in 1899. He had authored a book showing conclusively that even the first English Baptists churches practiced effusion, or pouring, as their mode of Baptism. But this Landmark victory was fleeting. Whitsitt's successor, Edgar

Young Mullins (1860–1928), was not a Landmarker, and the movement took its place as a significant minority within a non-Landmark denomination.

In the 1920s, as Northern Baptists experienced their fundamentalist-modernist controversy, Southern Baptist moderates beat back fundamentalist efforts led by, among others, J. Frank Norris (1877–1952) of First Baptist, Fort Worth, Texas and Clarence P. Stealey (1868–1937), editor of the Oklahoma *Baptist Messenger.* There were many reasons the moderate party won in the SBC, some having to do with Norris's own irascible personality. In July 1926, he shot and killed a man in his own church office but was acquitted on self defense.[2] More importantly, fundamentalism was predicated on a defense of the orthodox tenets of the faith against modernist revision.

The militant nature of the Fundamentalist Fellowship in the Northern Baptist Convention, captured quite nicely in Laws's definition of fundamentalism, emerged from the sense that modernists threatened the theological moorings of the faith. In other words, there was a lot at stake. In the Southern Baptist Convention, by contrast, moderates were evangelical, even if not fundamentalist. E. Y. Mullins, the leader of the moderates, often sounded more like Laws than Fosdick in his critique of the naturalistic presuppositions of liberal theology. "Modernism soft pedals or denies the resurrection" he wrote in a book that appeared shortly after his death in 1928. "You cannot leave out the supernatural and keep the Christian religion."[3] Even though he shared with liberal Baptists an emphasis on the centrality of Christian experience, he warned in his systematic theology, *The Christian Religion in Its Doctrinal Expression,* "It is not implied . . . that the data of experience are sufficient apart from the New Testament."[4] Mullins insisted that the supernatural elements of the faith—the deity of Christ, the incarnation, and the resurrection—remained essential to Christianity.

With little modernism in the Southern Baptist Convention, militant fundamentalists like Norris and Stealy found it difficult to rally people to a defense of orthodoxy. But they still advocated for a confession that would include an anti-evolution statement. Mullins and the moderates met the challenge by writing the Baptist Faith and Message Statement,

2. Hankins, *God's Rascal.*
3. Mullins, *Faith in the Modern World,* 31.
4. Mullins, *Christian Religion,* 68.

the first confession in Southern Baptist history, and adopting it at the 1925 SBC meeting. The statement said nothing explicitly about evolution but was so evangelical in its doctrinal positions that it satisfied most and quelled the brewing controversy before it reached anything like the heights the Northern Baptists experienced. Norris's church remained nominally Southern Baptist even as he founded a separatist denomination called the World Fundamental Baptist Missionary Fellowship. Norris also helped Riley and Canadian fundamentalist Thomas Todhunter Shields (1873–1955) form the Baptist Bible Union. A split in the BBU in the 1930s resulted in the formation of the General Association of Regular Baptist Churches, which remains a conservative evangelical, some would say fundamentalist, Baptist denomination to this day. Another split in Norris's World Fundamental Baptist Missionary Fellowship in 1950 produced the Baptist Bible Fellowship, an important fundamentalist denomination that produced preacher and Christian Right leader Jerry Falwell Sr. (1933–2007).

After the twenties a number of skirmishes took place within the Southern Baptist Convention, but none approached the level of the Northern Baptists' fundamentalist-modernist controversy. The most severe of these took place in 1962 when Midwestern Baptist Seminary professor Ralph Elliott lost his position over his non-literal interpretation of the first eleven chapters of Genesis. This so-called Elliot Controversy led to a revision of the Baptist Faith and Message. The revised confession of 1963 included a statement on the limits of academic freedom in Christian education. The confessional revisions of 1963, like the first confession of 1925, satisfied most Southern Baptists. But in the wake of the Elliott controversy a minority grew increasingly concerned about liberalism in the denomination. In hopes of starting a movement, a few activists launched a conservative newspaper dedicated to exposing liberalism in SBC seminaries and colleges. The election of stalwart conservative Wallie Amos Criswell (1909–2002) of First Baptist Dallas to the SBC presidency in 1968 did little to mollify conservative activists.

By the 1970s, American evangelicals found themselves embroiled in what a recent historian has called "their great matter," the battle over the inerrancy of Scripture. Chief among the defenders of inerrancy was Baptist theologian Harold Lindsell (1913–98). He wrote *The Battle for the Bible*, which appeared in 1976. The book included chapters on several institutions and denominations that allegedly had rejected the inerrancy of scripture and were drifting inexorably toward liberalism. One of his chapters covered Southern Baptists. Lindsell's book encouraged some SBC conservatives, alerted others to the inerrancy problem, and gave all conservatives ammunition that could be used in a movement. In 1979 the conservative resurgence began in earnest.

Texas state court judge Paul Pressler (b. 1930) figured out that if conservatives could hold the SBC presidency for a decade, they could remake all the convention boards, most importantly the boards of the SBC's six seminaries. He recruited theologian Paige Patterson (b. 1942) and popular preacher Adrian Rogers (1931–2005), and in 1979 Rogers became president. Moderates were slow to respond, believing that Rogers's election, like Criswell's a decade earlier, amounted to nothing more than the occasional conservative blip on an otherwise moderate screen. After all, SBC presidents usually served for only two years. The moderates were wrong. The conservatives held the presidency for the requisite decade and completely remade the denomination. By 1995, moderates had quit contesting presidential elections altogether.

Rallying around the inerrancy of Scripture, Southern Baptist conservatives succeeded where their Northern Baptists forerunners of the 1920s had failed. Like other evangelicals, Southern Baptist conservatives defined inerrancy as the belief that the Bible was without error in any area of reality, not only theology and Christian practice, but history and science as well. While scholars have devised several theories and definitions of inerrancy, in the popular realm and in the denominational political arena it amounts to the plain, common-sense reading of Scripture that developed in nineteenth-century American Protestantism and continues to have unparalleled influence in American evangelicalism. The plain, common-sense approach stems from the influence of Scottish Common Sense Realism and Baconian Science. It posits that passages of Scripture should be read in a straightforward manner, that the Bible is accessible and understandable even to the theologically untrained, and that one can move fairly easily from biblical teaching to social application.[5]

During the "Southern Baptist Controversy," as the battle came to be called, conservatives focused on the inerrancy of Scripture. But other theological issues were implicated as well. Most importantly, perhaps, was the proper role of women in families and ministry. Among moderates, there was a growing consensus that ordination of women was biblical. Conservatives disagreed, believing this issue was merely a matter of

5. Noll, *America's God.*

inerrancy—i.e., a plain, common-sense reading of Scripture. Reading the Bible this way, they argued that 1 Cor 14, Eph 5, and 1 Tim 2, among other passages, teach that wives should be submissive to husbands and that women are not permitted to exercise authority over men in the family or church. Conservatives pushed through a resolution in 1984 advocating against the ordination of women. Fifteen years later they revised the Baptist Faith and Message adding a "Submission Statement," that reads in part, "A wife is to submit herself graciously to the servant leadership of her husband even as the church willingly submits to the headship of Christ." The Submission Statement also said a husband "should love his wife as Christ loved the church," as well as provide for, protect, and lead his family. Two years later the SBC revised its confession again to include a statement that only men should serve as pastors of churches, thus raising the resolution of 1984 to the status of doctrine.[6]

For conservatives, inerrancy also meant a rejection of evolution. Some evangelical theologians have devised theories of inerrancy that allow for theistic evolution or progressive creation. Even Presbyterian Benjamin Breckinridge Warfield (1851–1921), a stalwart early twentieth-century defender of inerrancy among Presbyterians, seemed to allow for the possibility of evolution. But in a popular political setting, where inerrancy cashed out as the plain, commonsense reading of Scripture, Southern Baptist conservatives argued that orthodoxy demands adherence to a literal Adam and Eve, even if not a literal seven-day creation. Moreover, they argued that the apostle Paul identified Adam as the one through whom sin entered the world and Christ as the second Adam through whom the world is redeemed. This means that the New Testament itself attests to a literal Adam and that the plan of salvation falls to pieces if Adam and Eve are interpreted metaphorically.

In addition to the inerrancy of the Bible and issues related to it, religious liberty and the separation of church and state also played prominent roles in the Southern Baptist controversy. Both sides claimed these age-old Baptist distinctives, but they interpreted and applied them in different ways. Moderates believed that full religious liberty required a robust separation of church and state, often called "strict separation." Conservatives argued that strict separation had gone too far, resulting in hostility toward religion, not neutrality. Conservatives became church-state "accomodationists," a name applied to those who believe the state

---

6. The entire Baptist Faith and Message can be found at https://bfm.sbcnet.

should accommodate religion and that to do so is not a violation of the separation of church and state.

The two sides in the Southern Baptist controversy read their history differently. Moderates viewed colonial-era Baptists like Isaac Backus (1724–1806) and John Leland (1754–1841) as both supporting strict separation in order to accomplish religious liberty. Conservatives believed that Leland and Backus differed once tax-supported churches came to an end in the early national period of US history (1787–1828). Backus, they argue, supported a broadly Christianized republic with state accommodation of religion. Finally, even the issues of America's so-called culture wars came into play in the SBC controversy. At Southern Baptist Theological Seminary, for example, beginning in 1994 candidates for faculty positions were required to espouse not only inerrancy and the rejection of ordination for women, but also opposition to homosexuality and abortion. While neither issue has yet found its way into the Baptist Faith and Message, both serve as unofficial tests for denominational employment.

Southern Baptist conservative success has resulted in the denomination becoming the largest and most influential bloc within American evangelicalism. In turn, Southern Baptist leadership in the American culture wars has aided the development of evangelicals as the most reliable voting bloc within the Republican Party. This has manifested itself most recently in the election of Donald Trump to the US presidency with nearly 82 percent of the white evangelical vote. This is the case despite the fact that as a thrice-married philanderer who seems to espouse a form of white ethno-nationalism Trump has spent a lifetime flouting the norms promoted by the evangelicals. In 2004, as but one example, there emerged within the Christian Right an "I Vote Values" movement, which was led in part by Richard Land (b. 1946) then head of the SBC's Ethics and Religious Liberty Commission. Among Trump's most visible and vocal evangelical supporters are Southern Baptist megachurch preacher Robert Jeffress (b. 1955) of First Baptist Dallas, Billy Graham's son Franklin Graham (b. 1952), and now disgraced Liberty University President Jerry Falwell Jr. (b. 1962). Like many white evangelicals in America they view Trump as a staunch defender of religious liberty for evangelicals who will appoint, and has appointed, conservative justices to the US Supreme Court. The hope is that these justices will overturn *Roe v. Wade* (1973), the decision that legalized abortion across the country. By contrast, Land's successor at the ERLC, Russell Moore (b. 1971), has spoken out consistently against Trump.[7] The same is true for Beth Moore (no relation, b. 1957) an extremely popular Bible teacher who in March 2021 left the Southern Baptists and apologized for having supported "complementarianism" and for having called homosexuality a sin. But among white SBC leaders the two represented a minority; before the Moores left the SBC, their voices were often drowned out by Trump's evangelical defenders.

Also of controversy recently has been the ousting of SBC conservative movement architect Paige Patterson from his post as president of Southwestern Baptist Theological Seminary in Fort Worth, TX. Patterson's demise came in the wake of the #MeToo movement, which, of course, resulted in the sacking of all manner of male media moguls as well as film and television personalities for either sexual harassment or sexual assault. While accused of neither himself, Patterson's troubles have resulted from accusations of insensitivity to women when they reported to him that they had been victims of sexual assault at the two seminaries he has led. Also at issue was a widely circulated video of Patterson making insensitive sexist comments in a sermon he preached. Nevertheless, Patterson has at the 2021 annual Convention tried again to push the SBC further to the right. Meanwhile, Patterson's conservative coleader Paul Pressler has for years fended off charges of sexual harassment or assault of young males he has mentored or been associated with in law practice.

Conclusion

The fundamentalist-modernist controversy in the Northern Baptist Convention and the Southern Baptist controversy roughly a half century later had much in common. In both cases combatants weighed the authority of the Bible over against the need for a Baptist confession. Conservatives argued that a confession was necessary to ensure adherence to the Bible and orthodox doctrine. Liberals in the North and moderates in the South, by contrast, argued for a conception of soul competency or the priesthood of the believer, which allowed Baptists to interpret Scripture individually. Another similarity is that in the conservative camps of both controversies there were militant fundamentalists as well as more

---

7. Moore left his position at ERLC, and as of June 2021 he serves as director of the Public Theology Project of the evangelical magazine *Christianity Today*, which had been founded by Billy Graham. The first issue appeared in October 1956.

moderate evangelicals. All conservatives in both controversies supported a vigorous defense of orthodox doctrine, but on both sides there were those who eschewed the sort of separatism that William Bell Riley and J. Frank Norris exhibited.

But the differences in the two controversies are perhaps more pronounced. First, there were more thoroughgoing modernists in the Northern Baptist Convention of the twenties. Southern Baptists had seminary professors who pushed, and in some cases crossed, the boundaries of historic orthodoxy, but there were few in leadership on the SBC moderate side comparable to Harry Emerson Fosdick. That is why in the United States the former leaders of the SBC are called moderate instead of liberal. Most of the moderates, especially those most visible in the fight, remained broadly evangelical.

Second, cultural issues played a less overt role in the fundamentalist-modernist controversy in the North. Prohibition was the leading religio-cultural issue of the Roaring Twenties, as the decade is usually called. Both liberals and fundamentalists supported it. A half century would elapse before abortion and homosexuality began to roil American culture, so those issues were not in play in the twenties, but they were in the SBC controversy.

Finally, and most obviously, the liberals won the fundamentalist-modernist controversy in the Northern Baptist Convention, while conservatives won the SBC controversy. As historians and theologians debate why this was so, cultural issues should not be ignored. Like many other evangelicals in America, Baptists believe that American life should reflect a broadly Christian worldview. In the face of secularization, they instinctively attempt to shore up the theological parameters of their denominations. They must maintain the truth against the onslaught of liberal culture. These views have always been stronger in the South, where secularization came about a half century later than in the North. In short, southern culture stayed intact until the last quarter of the twentieth century. Southern Baptist conservatives drew on the experience of Northern Baptists and determined that things would turn out differently in the SBC.

Bibliography

Hankins, Barry. *God's Rascal. J. Frank Norris & the Beginnings of Southern Fundamentalism*. Lexington: University Press of Kentucky, 1996.

Kidd, Thomas, and Barry Hankins. *Baptists in America: A History*. New York: Oxford University Press, 2015.

Mullins, Edgar Young. *The Christian Religion in Its Doctrinal Expression*. Philadelphia: Roger Williams, 1917.

———. *Faith in the Modern World*. Nashville: Sunday School Board of the Southern Baptist Convention, 1930.

Noll, Mark. *America's God: From Jonathan Edwards to Abraham Lincoln*. New York: Oxford University Press, 2002.

16

Ministers and Missionaries Benefit Board (MMBB)

A Critical Resource for Baptists in the USA

Everett C. Goodwin

The Necessity of a Benefit Board

THE MINISTERS AND MISSIONARIES Benefit Board of the American Baptist Churches, USA, has performed a critical mission in its over a hundred years of service. By providing the security of financial support for its members in retirement it allows retired or disabled ministers to live in dignity. For younger, still active ministers it provides a significant measure of security to encourage them in their work. It was achieved by equal measures of creative vision, generous support, dedicated and effective leadership by its professional and Board leadership, successful program strategy, and dedication to sound business principles focused equally on spiritual purposes and significant autonomy to adjust to changing cultural and economic realities. Its story is one of inspiration, compassion, practicality, and persistent dedication.

Baptist ministers everywhere have often served for little monetary reward and have frequently experienced poverty because they have little opportunity to plan financially for older years. This was especially true in the United States in the late nineteenth and early twentieth centuries. Low salaries in small churches with limited financial resources were a universal problem. Also, it was the common practice of churches to provide residential accommodations as a major part of a minister's compensation. This often prevented an accumulation of home equity and thus often left ministers without a place to live in old age. In stable rural communities, ministers often could depend on congregation members to supply them with firewood, food, and other requirements for life. But these practices usually ended when a minister died or ended active ministry. This practice ceased as people moved from small communities to non-agricultural work in cities.

Therefore poverty, or at least severe financial insecurity, was common for Baptist ministers: widows and families frequently were impoverished when the minister died. Aged or ill ministers endured long-term suffering. In addition, churches were often forced to continue a minister in service beyond his ability to function, to provide for him or his family beyond his service of ministry, or else to callously dismiss him to an uncertain fate or community charity. Facing disabling illness or advancing years, ministers or their widows or families often were dependent upon community charity or were forced to resort to begging.

"For the Better Maintenance of the Ministry"

Henry Lyman Morehouse (1834–1917), a pastor and later Corresponding Secretary for the American Baptist Home Mission Society, surveyed the economic plight of ministers as early as 1882 and began regularly bringing it to the attention of Baptist churches and organizations for over twenty five years. Ultimately, his persistence was successful: at the first meeting of the newly formed Northern Baptist Convention in 1908 a denominational commission was appointed to investigate his concerns. In 1911 the Ministers and Missionaries Benefit Board (MMBB) was organized for the purpose of collecting and disbursing funds. It was initiated in response to the challenge of a $50,000 pledge from an anonymous wealthy layman, later revealed to be Milo C. Treat (1841–1925) in Washington, Pennsylvania.

The required matching funds of $200,000 to be raised by the Christmas, 1911 deadline established by the challenge donor was achieved and legal incorporation was completed by 1913. Included in its charter's statement of purpose was the phrase "for the better maintenance of the ministry" which is still used as MMBB's short form of mission statement. In the same year, the first grants to retired ministers were awarded, usually in the modest amount of $50 or $100 per year. The funding was accomplished by the combined efforts of Morehouse and Everett C. Tomlinson (1859–1931), a talented and able pastor, educator, and author whom Morehouse engaged to raise the funds. Soon after the campaign to raise funds, Tomlinson was persuaded to become the first chief executive of the new organization. Soon thereafter, Tomlinson and the Board acquired the resources of several other organizations that had been previously established to provide residential facilities, pensions or other forms of relief for elderly ministers. By this means and others, in 1916 MMBB reported assets of $777,400 (USD) and soon thereafter achieved a total of $2,000,000 as a result of additional, notable gifts from Treat and several other generous givers.

After the death of Henry Morehouse in 1917, a financial campaign for "The Morehouse Million" as a memorial was highly successful in further generating and inspiring financial support, including one of $2,000,000 from John D. Rockefeller (1839–1937), the American and Baptist oil magnate. By 1920 MMBB's annual report stated $12,000,000 in assets. Over the next decade a number of gifts from generous donors continued. The Rockefeller contributions cumulatively totaled $7,119,293 and guaranteed the long-term financial viability of MMBB.

MMBB's first decade therefore was marked by vision and strong financial support. But annual grants of $100 to $300 were insufficient. And MMBB leadership soon recognized that even at that low level it would be impossible to raise funds large enough to provide meaningful support for the number of ministers in need. The second ten years, therefore, were guided by a strategy for long-term monetary growth.

Retiring Pension Fund

Instead of the practice of relying on "grants" or "gifts," the Retiring Pension Fund was created. The purpose of the Fund was to create resources contributed by ministers and the churches they served. This program followed the principles developed by a few universities and early labor unions. The Retirement Plan required an annual contribution based on 6 percent of the minister's salary, contributed on his behalf by the church or the minister or in combination. Over the years of a minister's career, the funds invested in a Permanent Fund would then provide a worthy retirement income beginning at age sixty-five. To enable a transition to this program, the contributions were originally discounted with supplementation by income from undesignated funds under MMBB control.

During its second decade, MMBB continued to develop its administrative ability: by adding staff, successfully engaging in leadership succession and identifying important procedural principals. As an example, one early, pioneering practice was to adhere strictly to actuarial principles in establishing and projecting pension benefits and contributions. It also benefited from a New York State law that prevented their investment in anything other than bonds. A member of the MMBB Board, Arthur M. Harris, was a highly regarded bond investment specialist. Thus, by law and effective leadership the Board was kept from involvement in the super-heated stock market of the 1920s and was positioned to survive the Depression. During that same time MMBB began publication of materials to support its members in their ministries and which consistently educated churches and ministers in the importance of salary support and financial planning for both ministers and churches.

The decade of the Depression and the outbreak of World War II challenged the MMBB in many ways. The Board effectively lost money by each new member's enrollment because of their heavy "discounting" of contributions. Therefore, they were forced to suspend acceptance of new members for several years. At the same time, they reaffirmed their core purpose by resisting appeals to use their fund assets for broader charitable purposes. This engendered significant criticism because there were many acute needs created: churches that closed, or were unable to pay ministers salaries, for example. But in so doing, they affirmed that the MMBB was not a charity, but a program to support its members in retirement.

"Worry Free by '43"

As a result of the financial devastation of the Depression and MMBB's decision to temporarily close membership, membership declined by nearly 25 percent from 1935 to 1940. The Board realized that MMBB was not fulfilling its purpose and in 1939 began to process new applications made possible by an infusion of funds from a denomination-wide campaign and a transfer of reserve funds. In addition, a new emphasis on churches' obligation to pay the contribution for pastor's participation led to a membership expansion drive with the slogan "Worry Free by '43" that resulted in the addition of 1201 new members. By the end of the war in 1945 72 percent of eligible pastors belonged to the Retiring Pension Fund.

This achievement signaled an era during which MMBB's purpose expanded significantly as it benefited from the American economic expansion resulting in the period from 1945 to 1965. The early years of that period reflected new vision of service and optimism at MMBB: its assets grew and therefore its capabilities did also. It participated in the development of the Interchurch Center in New York, where it located its offices, expanded its staff, and enlarged its vision to serve ministry more broadly. It joined with other denominational leadership to make it possible for ministers to belong to Social Security and labored to encourage ministers to join it. It also encouraged more adequate levels of compensation for ministers and created a Minimum Salary program to assist churches in meeting minimal standards.

It also provided support to the Civil Rights movement in the USA. MMBB sensitized church leaders on the importance of the civil rights struggle, provided crisis support for ministers who suffered loss of position because of their stand against racism, and reached out to African American leaders and pastors to provide life insurance and long term pension resources. Notably, they convinced Martin Luther King to become a member of MMBB and underwrote his insurance and pension obligation from discretionary sources. Their foresight produced lifetime income for his family after his assassination. One result was an increasing participation of African American churches, leaders, and pastors in MMBB membership and leadership.

Expansion of benefits was the norm throughout the history of MMBB: special grants for widows and families of deceased members, grants for member's children for education began early. Later, salary supplement programs for inadequately compensated ministers, and expanded categories for membership to include denominational workers, institutional chaplains, ministers in non-church special ministries such as evangelists, community development, and consultants in everything from church organization to worship and music and many more further developed its expansion. MMBB's support of the civil rights quest served to inspire additional attention on marginalized persons in ministry: the role of women in ministry, the unique needs of pastors serving congregations of immigrants and others. Optimism was evident and made such expansion possible. But with such expansion there were also new challenges.

New Challenges

One challenge was that during this period funds to provide pensions continued to grow and expand more rapidly than they could be disbursed. This was generally the fortunate result of a growing economy. Specifically, however, it was a result of an expansion of laws that had previously greatly restricted the kinds of investments a pension organization could use; changes in the law now allowed more aggressive investment. Post war expansion was also accompanied by increasing inflation which annually reduced the value of defined-benefit pension payments. MMBB began annual distribution of supplement "cost of living adjustments" made possible by increased funds from investment experience.

In 1965 the Board shifted its previous investment approach to a "variable annuity" basis, by which funds contributed on a member's behalf were invested in stock market funds and the resulting pension would then benefit from the investment result, with guarantees to prevent precipitous declines during periods of a falling market. The decade of the 1970s, with its stagnant financial returns, tested this decision, but over time, the variable annuity strategy has greatly enhanced the value of pensions. In the 1950s and 1960s MMBB also confronted the earliest stages of the continuing health care challenge and offered health and then later added dental insurance. For the long term, the Board decided to subcontract health care plans for active members, and to likewise contract supplemental plans for ministers in retirement with Medicare. The ripple effects of President Obama's Affordable Care Act and the political forces surrounding it make MMBB's long term response to health care again a challenge.

From 1970 to 1990 MMBB actively participated in confronting cultural change and transition that created many challenges for ministers. Its advocacy for women advanced the presence of women in the ranks of ministry. Its educational role at the onset of HIV/AIDS in the 1980s provided both a pastoral care direction for ministers and a mediating force in congregations to view it as an illness, not a unique "curse of God." Its continuing role to educate ministers in matters of personal financial management and planning has improved the competency of ministers regarding their own futures and careers. In quiet but persistent ways, it also has equipped ministers to deal with the tensions many congregations have faced over homosexuality and related gender and sexuality matters.

In 1990 MMBB's longest serving Executive Director, Dean R. Wright, retired after thirty-six years in the position. His lengthy tenure had been guided his sensitivity to stability, response to needs for change, and effective relationships with ministers and denominational leaders. In the subsequent twenty-five years his successors have continued the stability of MMBB, but have also responded to the turbulence of changing times: the need to redefine MMBB's core mission; turbulence created by financial market volatility, the need for organizational growth and management expertise, the changing circumstances of American religious practices, and the impact created by successive national and international crises affecting markets as well as public opinion.

In the 1990s MMBB redirected its energies and resources toward management and provision of its core service of benefits for ministers, including insurance, pension, and financial education. Advocacy for women in ministry was transferred to denominational responsibility, for example. Also, greater energy was focused on creating staff competence that assured effective and responsive service of member's needs, including use of new technology, staff organization, training, and evaluation.

Market declines including the "tech bust" of the late 1990s, the market collapse that followed the "9/11" terrorist attacks, and the recession that followed the banking and mortgage crisis of 2007–8 all seriously affected the priorities and energies of MMBB. The recession forced a decline in pension payment amounts which, though the lowered values were moderated by "guarantees" against precipitous drop, was nonetheless a serious challenge to confidence. By the end of 2010 MMBB's assets under management had regained its values and had reached $2.38 billion. Since then, financial markets have continued to improve and with it, pension values are being restored.

Regulatory changes have also allowed MMBB to expand its service base. Originally only American Baptist ministers and later churches and organizations were qualified to be members. More recently MMBB is able to include a greater variety of Baptist and other "like-minded religious organizations and affiliates" to participate. This has allowed membership to increase significantly as well as its "assets under management," amount to increase. That is a critical factor in the highly competitive investment marketplace.

Perhaps the challenge of most uncertain scope and intensity is the one presented by changing religious practices in the United States. Denominational identity is declining, as is church attendance in many instances. One result is that more ministers are "bi-vocational" or part-time in service. In many cases, fewer churches with full-time ministers are able or willing to contribute the 16 percent of salary premium that MMBB's standard retirement and insurance plan requires. That means greater financial insecurity for ministers and their families in the present, and a less promising security in retirement in the future. This is a challenge to MMBB's core service. As its most recently retired Executive Director, Sumner Grant stated, it is time for MMBB "to be nimble."

With an inspired beginning, a history more than a hundred years in the making, with a remarkable history of excellent leadership, including both Board and Executives, with a persistent dedication to its original purpose "for the better maintenance of the Ministry," and with a record that included adaptation and openness to change, it would seem well-qualified to meet the challenge.[1]

---

1. This article is drawn from the book MMBB—Everett C. Goodwin, *Pioneer in Employee Benefits: The First 100 Years* (Mercer University Press, 2012), 328p.

ii. From the Continent of Africa

17

All Africa Baptist Fellowship

Isaac Duro Ayanrinola

Origin of Baptists

The history of the Baptist movement is complex and diverse, and even its origin is disputed. Whereas modern scholarship assumes that the Baptist movement started in 1609, when John Smyth baptized himself and his followers, including his prominent friend Thomas Helwys, a nineteenth-century theory insists on Baptist "successionism" beginning with the "First Baptist Church of Jerusalem." From there this theory traces the path of the faithful witness to the truth of Christ through the early church, the various dissenting or "heretical" sects in the Middle Ages, the Anabaptists of the Reformation, and finally the emergence of the clearly defined Baptist congregation in seventeenth-century England.[1]

Notwithstanding the complexity of their origin and history, Baptists have a number of distinctives which they did not invent; rather, they discovered and articulated them afresh for their time. Richard Pierard, the general editor of the Hundred-Year History of the Baptist World Alliance quotes historian, Walter Shurden who singled out four such essential "freedoms" that Baptists believe in:

---

1. Pierard, *Baptists Together in Christ*, xv. It should be noted that some people have suggested the name Baptist is not from John the Baptist, but rather from the practice of baptism by immersion.

247

1. *Bible freedom*: the freedom and obligation of Christians to study and obey the Scriptures, which are central in the life of the individual and the church;

2. *Soul freedom*: the responsibility of every person to deal with God without the imposition of creeds, interference of clergy, or intervention of civil government;

3. *Church freedom*: the autonomy of local churches, which are free to determine their membership and leadership, order of their worship, ordain those whom they perceive as gifted for ministry, and participate in the life of the larger body of Christ;

4. *Religious freedom*: the freedom of the individual to hold and practice his or her religious beliefs without government interference.[2]

The Baptist World Alliance

The Baptist World Alliance (BWA) was established in 1905, when representatives of Baptists from twenty-six countries around the world gathered in London. Three thousand delegates registered and met at Exeter Hall July 11–19, 1905. The first president of the BWA was John Clifford from London. The issue who can claim credit for the idea of organizing a world body was a matter of debate. Did it belong to the English or did the initiative arose in the United States?[3] Today, the BWA "is a fellowship of 238 conventions and unions in 124 countries and territories comprising forty-five million members in 177,000 churches. Its priorities are nurturing the passion for mission and evangelism; promoting worship, fellowship, and unity; responding to people in need; defending human rights and justice; and advancing relevant theological reflection."

All Africa Baptist Fellowship

The All Africa Baptist Fellowship (AABF) is one of the six and the last regional fellowships to be created by the BWA. The five regional fellowships organized earlier are the European Baptist Federation (EBF), formed on October 8, 1949; the North American Baptist Fellowship (NABF),

2. Pierard, *Baptists Together in Christ*, x.
3. For details cf. chapter 12 of this volume on the BWA above.

established on March 28, 1966; the Caribbean Baptist Fellowship (CBF), set up July 1–3, 1969; the Asia Pacific Baptist Federation (APBF), founded in 1972; and The Baptist Union of Latin America (UBLA), created September 4–7, 1975. The All Africa Baptist Fellowship (AABF) was established on Saturday July 10, 1982, at Brackenhurst, Nairobi, Kenya.

African Baptists' Involvement in BWA before 1982

Africans have been involved in the BWA from its inception even though the AABF was inaugurated not earlier than 1982. An African served as President, William R. Tolbert Jr. of Liberia, 1960–1965. Many Africans served as Vice Presidents, for instance, A. H. King from South Africa, 1928–1934; J. T. Ayorinde of Nigeria who was elected Vice President two times, 1955–60 and 1970–75; Advertus A. Hoff of Liberia, 1970–75; and Arthur Kinyanjui of Kenya, 1970–75.[4] Ngwedla Paul Msiza, an African from South Africa, was inaugurated President July 25, 2015 in Durban. Some Africans served as Congress speakers, elected executive BWA staff, departmental presidents (Men's, Women's and Youth's Departments). Also, many served as members of the BWA Executive Committee, Advisory Committee and BWA Commissions, and they faithfully contributed their best to the progress and growth of the Alliance.

Inauguration of AABF

Samuel Ola Akande from Nigeria, the first AABF General Secretary/ Treasurer, described the birth of AABF as a "miracle of God." It was a miracle sparked by the awareness of African Baptist leaders of the continent-wide need for cooperation in evangelism and training of leaders.[5] Previous attempts to establish the Fellowship, including the efforts of Tolbert and Ayorinde, had failed. In 1979 at the BWA General Council that was held in Brighton, England, Advertus Hoff, one of the BWA Vice Presidents, notified the Council about the Liberia Centenary Celebration coming up in 1980. He also expressed his concern and disappointment that the various efforts made to convene a "foundation" meeting in May

---

4. Pierard, *Baptists Together in Christ*, 321–23.

5. *The Minutes, Reports and Messages of the First Assembly of the All Africa Baptist Fellowship*, 1984, 5.

of 1979 did not come to fruition. No wonder S. T. Ola Akande described it a "miracle" when it was finally formed in 1982.

It was at the BWA General Council meeting, held in Puerto Rico in 1981, that the African leaders met and set policies for the establishment of the African Baptist Fellowship. When the new development was reported to the BWA Council, S. T. Ola Akande advised the meeting on the "conclusions and recommendations" already agreed by the African group. The General Council decided that copies of the proposed constitution of the African Baptist Fellowship should be circulated to all conventions and unions in Africa. It was agreed that the formation of the African Baptist Fellowship should be done the following year, 1982, during the meeting of the BWA Evangelism and Education Division and the International Mission Secretaries (IMS) scheduled to take place in Nairobi, Kenya, July, 1982.[6]

The First All Africa Baptist Fellowship's Assembly

The first assembly of the AABF was held in the city of Harare, Zimbabwe, January 17–22, 1984. The venue of the meeting was the University of Zimbabwe, Harare; Zimbabwe had obtained political independence from Britain in 1980. The President of the country was an ordained minister. According to S. T. Ola Akande the meeting was devoted to spiritual emphasis, the establishment of various committees that would function regularly between the first assembly and the next one, and to fellowship among African Baptists. The experience of fellowship was unique and rewarding. The theme of the assembly was "Jesus Christ, for the Healing of all Peoples."[7] The number of registered delegates and observers at the assembly was 136. Nine countries, Angola, Cameroon, Kenya, Malawi, Nigeria, Rwanda, South Africa, Zambia and Zimbabwe, were represented. Three observers, led by Dr. Pearl McNeil of the Union Theological Seminary in Richmond, Virginia, came from the United States. The BWA Headquarters in Washington was represented by Dr. Archie Goldie and Mr. Samson Mathangani. Two choirs from Lusaka, Zambia (eighty-two choristers), from Matero and Chawama Baptist Churches provided inspirational singing during the conference.

6. Callam, *Pursuing Unity, Defending Right*, 53.
7. *The Minutes, Reports and Messages*, 1984, 1–2.

A major achievement of the assembly was the establishment and the inaugural meetings of the following committees:

1. The AABF Central Relief and Aid Committee;

2. The AABF Men's Fellowship Committee;

3. The AABF Communication Committee;

4. The AABF Evangelism and Christian Education Committee (established in Nairobi in July, 1982);

5. The AABF Theological Education committee (established in Nairobi in July, 1982);

6. The All Africa Baptist Youth Fellowship.[8]

The members of the Executive Committee so elected are as follows:

1. General Secretary/Treasurer: The Rev. Dr. Samuel T. Ola Akande of Nigeria

2. President: The Rev. Joao Makondekwa of Angola

3. First Vice President: The Rev. Dr. Derek Mpinga of Zimbabwe

4. Second Vice President: The Rev. Dr. Douglas Waruta of Tanzania

5. First Associate Secretary: The Rev. Wellington Selebano of Southern Africa

6. Second Associate Secretary: The Rev. Kikama Kividi of Zaire

7. Executive members at large:

8. The Rev. Dr. Osadolor Imasogie of Nigeria

9. The Rev. Ziherambere O. Eleazar of Rwanda.[9]

It was reported that the following amounts were given to the new Fellowship:

- Baptist Mission of Norway—$100

- North American Baptist Missionary Society—$500

- Baptist Union of Denmark—$700

- Nigerian Baptist Convention—$4,500 (1982); $2,025 (1983).[10]

8. *The Minutes, Reports and Messages*, 1984, 2.

9. *The Minutes, Reports and Messages*, 1984, 4.

10. *The Minutes, Reports and Messages*, 1984, 24.

All Africa Baptist Fellowship Today

The AABF continues to be the Regional Office of BWA in Africa. It is the home for sixty-one Baptist conventions and unions in thirty-two countries, with the total membership of 16,625,608 from 42,533 churches on the continent. The amended constitution states the vision, mission statements, and objectives of the Fellowship.

The vision of AABF is to network, partner, and strengthen fellowship among conventions, unions, associations and Centralized Baptist Churches in Africa to fulfill the Great Commission and engage in cooperative social action.

The mission of the AABF shall include the following:

- To network and partner with cooperating conventions, unions , associations, and Centralized Baptist Churches in Africa;

- To promote missions and evangelism of the peoples of Africa and beyond;

- To facilitate the planting of Baptist Churches in every city, town, and village in Africa;

- To promote and facilitate the social wellbeing of all peoples of Africa.

In order to fulfill the purposes defined in this Constitution, the AABF shall:

- Promote African Baptist participation in the work of the BWA;

- Promote Evangelism and Christian education;

- Promote the ministries of men, women, youth and children;

- Organize continental and sub-regional programs relevant to the needs of the AABF periodically, in conjunction with the BWA and other Baptist bodies;

- Organize programs at sub-regional level in conjunction with the leaders of the sub-regions;

- Work in cooperation with recognized ecumenical Christian bodies as needed

- Engage in investment opportunities and promote the establishment of institutions that will stimulate the growth of the organization.[11]

Regional Fellowships

Following the pattern of the BWA, AABF divides the continent into five regions, four of which are active now. The four regions are West Africa, East Africa, Central Africa and Southern Africa.

West Africa subregion: Baptists are at work in each of the countries in West Africa. A total of 80 percent of the Baptists in West Africa live in Nigeria. Baptist expansion before 1950 was slow for two major reasons:

1. Black Colonists from the USA established old Baptist work in Sierra Leone in 1722 and Liberia in 1852. Unfortunately, they did not evangelize the indigenous people.

2. Major Baptist missions started their work among English-speaking countries. The French-speaking countries were initially neglected.

Today, in West Africa, there is Baptist work in the following countries: Baptist Convention of Benin, Baptist Convention of Burkina Faso, Baptist Union in the Gambia, Ghana Baptist Convention, Liberia Baptist Missionary and Educational Convention, Inc., Nigerian Baptist Convention, Baptist Convention of Sierra-Leone, Togo Baptist Convention, Association Des Eglises Baptistes Evangeliques Du Tchad, Mambilla Baptist Convention, and Meridional Evangelical Churches in Ivory Coast.[12]

East Africa subregion: In comparison with other missions, Baptists entered East Africa late. Danish Baptist began work in Rwanda/Burundi after World War I, and other Baptist missions did not arrive until World War II. Today, the Baptists are spreading rapidly. The greatest growth has been primarily among sedentary agriculturists in Kenya, Tanzania, Uganda, Burundi and Rwanda. The following are parts of East Africa sub-region: Free Baptist Churches in Burundi, Union of Baptist Churches in Burundi, Emmanuel Baptist Church of Ethiopia, Ethiopian Addis Kidan Baptist Church, Baptist Convention of Kenya, Association of Baptist Churches in Rwanda (AEBR), Community of Christian

---

11. *All Africa Baptist Fellowship Constitution*, 2013, 2–4.

12. Wardin, *Baptists Around the World*, 67.

Churches in Africa, Reformed Baptist Churches in Rwanda, Union of Baptist Churches in Rwanda, Baptist Convention of Tanzania, Uganda Baptist Convention, Baptist Union of Uganda.[13]

Central Africa subregion: Credit for the pioneering work in Central Africa must be given to British, German, Swedish, and American Baptists who worked through the Baptists' Missionary Society, the American Baptist Union, the Mission Society of German Baptists, Mid-Mission and Orabro Society of Sweden. The Baptist conventions/unions in central Africa are: Baptist Evangelical Church in Angola, Free Baptist Church in Angola, Baptist Churches Union, Baptist Evangelical Community in Central Africa (CEBAC), Baptist Church of Congo, Baptist Community in Central Africa, Baptist Community of the Congo River (CBFC), Baptist Community of the Faithful in Africa, Baptist Evangelical Convention of Congo (CBECO), Community of Autonomous Baptist Churches Wamba-Bakali, Community of Baptist Churches Union of Congo (CUEBC), Community of United Baptist Churches (CEBU), Union of Baptist Churches of Congo (UEBCO), Baptist Convention of Angola, Native Baptist Church of Cameroon, Union of Baptist Churches in Cameroon, Association of Baptist Churches of Central African Republic, Evangelical Baptist Church of the Central African Republic, Fraternal Union of Baptist Churches, Baptist Community of Western Congo (CBCO), Community of Baptist Churches of Eastern Congo (CEBCE), Community of Baptist Churches in North Congo (CBCN).[14]

South Africa subregion: In comparison to other denominations, Baptists had a very weak start in South Africa and made little impact in the region until after World War II. Until that time, the major Baptist work agencies which had interest in Africa were forced to work for themselves with the exception of the Foreign Mission Board (FMB) of the National Baptist Convention as a result of Baptists in the territory, which later became the Republic of South Africa.

The conventions in South Africa are Baptist Convention of Malawi, Baptist Association of South Africa, Baptist Convention of South Africa, Baptist Mission of South Africa, Baptist Union of Southern Africa, Baptist Convention of Zambia, Baptist Fellowship of Zambia, Baptist Convention of Zimbabwe, National Baptist Convention of Zimbabwe, Baptist Convention of Botswana, Association of Bible Baptist Churches in

13. Wardin, *Baptists Around the World*, 13.
14. Wardin, *Baptists Around the World*, 27.

Madagascar, African Baptist Assembly, Malawi, Inc., Evangelical Baptist Church of Malawi, Baptist Convention of Mozambique, Baptist Convention of Namibia, Baptist Union of Zambia, Baptist Union of Zimbabwe, United Baptist Church of Zimbabwe.[15]

The Structure of the AABF

The AABF comprise:

- The General Assembly meets once in five years;
- The General Council meets once in two years and during the General Assembly;
- The Executive Committee meets once a year;
- The General Secretary is the Chief Executive Officer (CEO) of the AABF.

The present Executive consists of a President, two Vice Presidents, the General Secretary, the Associate General Secretary, the Regional Chairpersons for West Africa, Central Africa, East Africa, and Southern Africa. In addition there are three Auxiliary Presidents for the Baptist Women Union of Africa, the All Baptist Men Fellowship, and the All Africa Baptist Youth Fellowship. Three Members at Large, the General Secretary of BWA or his representative as an ex officio nonvoting member as well as a Vice-President of the Baptist World Alliance representative in Africa, also a non-voting member.

Additional Ministry Opportunities

Traditionally, the AABF operates through its structure, holds General Assembly and General Council meetings and meets annually for Executive Committee meetings. Two assemblies were held in July 2017 in Ghana with the theme "Jesus the Open Door" and in February 2018 in Blantyre, Malawi. The auxiliary groups (Men, Women, and Youth) hold meetings continentally and regionally.

---

15. Wardin, *Baptists Around the World*, 43.

Children's Ministry

In the last three years, the AABF Executive has approved Children's Ministry. There is a growing population of children all over Africa. It is our Christian responsibility to teach these children while they are young. They are not the future church; they are the church today. Materials have been produced and seminars, training, and workshops have been conducted in each of the regions on the continent.

Baptist Student Fellowship

Even though the AABF has a department for Youth Ministry, it is the conviction of the Fellowship to reach out to students in the universities and colleges. Today, tertiary institutions have become fertile for all kinds of philosophies. Baptists must try to reach students on their campuses, to mobilize them for missions and encourage them to serve God with the strength of their youth. The AABF is working with established Baptist Student Ministries in Africa, especially in Nigeria and Ghana, to spread the ministry in other regions in Africa as well. In 2016, the AABF organized a Students Ablaze meeting in Nairobi, Kenya and also visited Uganda and Tanzania for the same purpose.

Sunday School Literature and Writers' Conference

There is famine in Africa not caused by drought or lack of food but by lack of God's word. Many conventions and unions do not have Sunday School literature to teach God's word. Therefore, nominalism is growing. In order to combat it, AABF conducts writers' conferences to teach potential writers how to write their own literature in their indigenous cultural settings. Such training has been conducted in Nairobi, Kenya, Zambia, Burkina Faso, and Abidjan. Thank God, it is yielding fruits.

Responding to People in Need

The AABF is not doing well in this area simply because it is difficult to generate funds. Nevertheless, the AABF partners with Baptist Churches of Germany to provide relief materials for people in the horns of Africa.

Fostering Unity

The AABF is concerned about unity both within its member bodies and the continental body at large. The Lord has granted us victory over some internal crises in some conventions: Baptist Convention of Kenya, Baptist Convention of Zambia and Liberia Baptist Missionary and Educational Convention, Inc.

Conclusion

There are still many challenges facing Africans and Christianity on the continent: Islamic fundamentalism, corruption, disasters, political instability, and even nominalism among Christians. AABF is stepping up to these challenges, using its little human and financial resources as well as collaborating with other allied organizations to mitigate these problems. Efforts are also being made to reach out to North Africa which has about a 99 percent Muslim population. As we continue to network for continental peace, AABF is open to kingdom-minded collaborations to meet human needs, preach the gospel, fight nominalism, and disciple the next generation through the teaching of the authentic word of God.

Bibliography

Callam, Neville. *Pursuing Unity, Defending Right: The Baptist World Alliance at Work.* Falls Church, VA: Baptist World Alliance, 2010.

Pierard, Richard V., ed. *Baptists Together in Christ 1905–2005: A Hundred-Year History of the Baptist World Alliance.* Birmingham, AL: Samford University Press, 2005.

Wardin, Albert W., ed. *Baptists Around the World: A Comprehensive Handbook.* Nashville, TN: Broadman & Holman, 1995.

18

The Story of the Nigerian Baptist Convention

Solomon Ademola Ishola

Introduction

THIS IS A NARRATIVE history of the Nigerian Baptist Convention, the second largest Baptist denomination outside the United States of America. Nigeria is also the second oldest mission field started by the Southern Baptist Convention after China. The biblical mandate of the Lord Jesus Christ to engage and fulfill the Great Commission as found in Matt 28:16–20, and the influence of the missionary fervor of people like William Carey, "father of modern missions," and Adoniram Judson motivated the move to engage in foreign mission to other nations. The people of God called Nigerian Baptist Convention (NBC) is located in Nigeria, the largest country in Africa, located in the West of the continent. Prior to what is now known as Nigeria, the territory was a conglomeration of so many tribal kingdoms made up of around one thousand language groups. The dominant language groups are the Hausas in the North, the Yorubas in the West and the Igbos in the East, while other prominent tribal groups interspersed the three main groups. The reconfigurations of the modern geographical world spearheaded by the European powerful nations, and Britain in particular in the eighteenth century brought the present-day Nigeria into being in 1914, the same year the NBC was organized.

What we call denomination, big or small, begins without much fanfare, and sometimes could be born through internal crisis. The story of the Protestant churches of all shades started in the midst of persecution. Martin Luther from Germany never thought he was going to start a movement, but just wanted to challenge the leaders of the then-Roman Catholic Church over his understanding of what the Bible teaches on salvation, and that it must be by grace alone through faith and based mainly on the teachings of the word of God, rather than by church tradition. It was through various events that others felt Luther's protest was not thorough enough for them, and as such, various dissenters such as the Anabaptists, the Puritans and the Separatists, both in Germany and Britain gave birth to the Baptists in the Americas—the New World where most of the Separatists fled in the face of intense persecution.

The Beginning of the Baptist Witness in Nigeria

The Nigerian Baptist Convention was not born as a result of crisis, but as a direct obedience to the Great Commission. The precursor was the Southern Baptist Convention (SBC) from the USA that came into being on May 10, 1845. The mission agency of the SBC formed to send missionaries to other parts of the world was called the Foreign Mission Board (now known as the International Mission Board [IMB]). It was this Board that sent the first missionary to Nigeria in 1850. His name was Thomas Jefferson Bowen, who arrived in Nigeria on August 5, 1850. He spent the first eighteen months to learn the Yoruba language, and later authored a book on Yoruba grammar. Three years later (August 1853), two other missionaries joined Bowen. These men came back with Bowen after he went to the USA with a request for additional missionaries. Since he was single at the time he arrived in Nigeria, this time around, he returned with a wife. By 1854, the missionaries settled in Ijaye-Orile, a town close to Ibadan, and in January, Mrs. Laurenna Bowen started the *Sabbath School*, the precursor of our Sunday School, and by July 1854, the very first Baptist Church building was erected in Ijaye-Orile. This first church did not survive the tribal warfare that sacked the town in 1862, and the dispersal of the refugees led to the establishment of few other churches, especially in Abeokuta, another strategic Yoruba town. The first among them was First Baptist Church, Ijaye-Abeokuta.

Baptist Story during Missions Enterprise

The significant moment in the Baptist story started with the sending of Thomas Bowen as the first missionary to Nigeria in 1850 by the SBC. The painful irony is the fact that the SBC that started as a result of their avowed support for slavery set the pace in sending missionaries to the relatives of the slaves they were still keeping and treating as lacking "souls" to receive the gospel. Those who were taken to church were only allowed to stay at the basement of the churches where slave owners were "worshiping!"

One of the early major moments for Baptists occurred during the Civil War of the United States between 1861 and 1865. The missionaries left their posts to return home to the USA. The absence of the missionaries gave opportunity to national leaders to assume ministerial leadership. The Civil War in America helped to facilitate the freedom of majority of slaves, some of whom returned through Sierra Leone to settle in Nigeria and engaged in missionary work. The absence of Southern Baptist missionaries nurtured self-reliance among the national pastors who ably led the new churches. By the time of the return of the missionaries, there was a paradigm shift as most of the members of the churches were showing greater admiration and respect to their national pastors. The situation provided the seed of discord that finally led to the March 11, 1888 schism between the missionaries and the national leaders. The missiological implications are firstly, that the nationals are best equipped to reach their people with the gospel, and that secondly paternalism poses serious danger to the progress of any mission enterprise. The "Native Baptist Church," now Ebenezer Baptist Church that seceded from the First Baptist Church, Lagos, is still very active within the NBC. The split helped to multiply the Baptist churches within few years as national pastors intensified efforts to spread the gospel.

All the churches planted so far were independent of each other, as the so-called autonomy of the local Baptist church syndrome in the United States was imposed on the people without necessary contextualization. The reunion of the churches planted by the national leaders and that of the Mission took place in Ibadan, March 11–12, 1914 where the "Yoruba Baptist Association" was formed. These churches were mostly within the Southwestern part of Nigeria at that period, where the Yoruba people group live. The statistics of the participating churches numbered fourteen from the "Native" Baptist churches with 1,646 members, while the "Mission" churches were seventeen with 1,234 members. The formation of the Association removed the dichotomy between the "Native" and "Mission" churches, and the synergy led to the rapid growth of the Baptist witness in Nigeria, with the nationals playing active roles. While there was one Association, yet, the missionaries had their own structure separately from the national body. In other words, the leadership of the fledgling Convention was mostly in the hands of the missionaries, while the nationals served as pastors of the churches. The parallel structures remained until very recently. This Association evolved three years later to become the Nigerian Baptist Convention with about 13,000 churches today in every thirty-six states of Nigeria, and playing active role in the sociopolitical life of Nigeria.

The Fruitful Baptist Mission Stations

In April 1855, Bowen left Ijaye-Orile for Ogbomoso for the purpose of expanding the work. His intention was to stay in Ilorin, which he thought would be the gateway to entering the north of Africa. The Islamic Caliphate there did not accord him warm welcome so that he had to turn back to Ogbomoso where he was warmly accommodated. In about six months, his evangelistic efforts yielded result with the establishment of Okelerin Baptist Church in September 1855. The Ogbomoso station became one of the fruitful evangelistic works as the indigenous who were mostly traders and artisans, went to other Yoruba towns and villages to spread the Baptist faith. Some of them went to the Northern part of Nigeria where Islam predominated, yet, they were able to start churches among other tribes.

The other station that bore fruit was that of Lagos. Other missionaries' efforts yielded fruits with the planting of First Baptist Church in Lagos in July 1855, notably by Rev. J. M. Harden, an African American who joined the Baptist Mission from Liberia. It was through this Lagos end that the spread to other parts of the country took place. The First Baptist Church took the gospel through Baptist persuasion to the eastern part of the country, thus spreading beyond the Yoruba-speaking areas.

The Spread of the Work in Nigeria and Beyond

The growth and spread of the Baptist work in Nigeria came out of some challenges. The first was the Civil War going on in the United States from 1861 until 1865. The missionaries had to leave Nigeria during that period, and with them their money as well. In their absence, the nationals took over the fledgling work left by them. The work, however, experienced growth and expansion in the absence of the American missionaries who had to withdraw back home due to the devastating effects of the Civil War on the southern states of America from where the bulk of the support for the mission thrust came. Coupled with the American Civil War, there were internal tribal wars ravaging the areas of southwestern areas of Nigeria where churches were already planted. However, by providence, the nationals took the challenge of nurturing the young churches, while new ones were springing up. Again, it was during the absence of the missionaries that more churches were planted, particularly from Lagos and Ogbomoso stations.

Expansion to Ghana

Our Baptist story in Ghana is closely connected to the NBC. The earlier attempt by one Ghanaian, Mark C. Hayford, who returned home from Nigeria to introduce Baptist ways of life, bore some fruits, but his work did not survive after his death in 1935. There is a church named after him today, but its members are mostly Yoruba people who are mainly petty traders. The main thrust of Baptist presence came from Nigeria with the same Yoruba traders from Ogbomoso, an ancient town that is 80 percent Baptist. The town was simply a fertile soil for the Baptist witness as the majority of the people received the gospel, and today, the main "industries" in the ancient city are the Baptist churches. It was through the efforts of the natives of Ogbomoso who took their Bibles and copies of Yoruba Baptist Hymnal along with their petty trading that Baptist churches started to take root in Ghana from the 1920s. Of course, the churches were mainly ministering to the Yoruba people. The Southern Baptist missionaries started arriving from Nigeria in February 1947 and that was when Ghanaians started to join what they used to refer to as *Alata Asori*, literally, "Yoruba churches."

The Baptist story got more exciting with more Ghanaians coming to know the Lord when what could be considered an unpleasant experience happened to the majority of the Yoruba people from Nigeria. The Ghana government decided to effect the *Aliens Compliance Order* that forced illegal aliens to return to their countries. This was late 1969, and close to 80 percent of the Baptist folks from Nigeria had to return home abruptly. The result was the "death" of most of the Yoruba Baptist churches, leaving younger people, such as the present writer, to carry on the church activities. The 1970s saw the tremendous evangelistic thrust by the missionaries, and fortunately, investment in university students in Accra and Kumasi saw the influx of dynamic young men and women who are the key leaders of the Ghana Baptist Convention today.

Significant Events of the NBC

Possibly one of the major events in the history of the NBC was the schism that took place within the First Baptist Church in 1888. When the American missionaries were away during the American Civil War, the nationals, notably Rev. Moses Ladejo Stone who was serving as the interpreter to American missionary-pastor, felt short-changed in terms of salary being paid to him by Rev. William J. David. There was, of course, the nationalistic fervor circulating among the nationals who felt the Africans could perform as much as their American counterpart. The dispute over the non-increment of salary payment led to the unilateral dismissal of Stone by David. Rev. David felt there was no need to inform the members of the church who had admiration for Ladejo Stone, one of them who was considered to be doing better than the American missionary. When the congregation did not see Ladejo Stone the following Sunday, Rev. David was confronted and when he could not satisfy them, a majority of the members withdrew their membership to start their *Native Baptist Church* moving a block away from the former church. The development was quite unique among the Mission-related churches planted. It was a wakeup call for other groups, such as the Anglicans and the Methodists who engaged in a paradigm shift in regard to treating their native assistants with respect.

One major positive outcome of the schism was the reconciliation that took place sooner to enable the separated church and the former fellowship to engage in working relationship for the expansion of the Gospel. These churches started to plant new fellowships within the towns and beyond, particularly to those non-Yoruba tribes towards the east and the northern parts of Nigeria.

NBC's Organizational Structure

At the apex of the NBC leadership is the President, who serves as the Chief Executive Officer and Chief accounting officer for the Convention. He facilitates and coordinates the ministries of the NBC. He is assisted by three vice presidents, namely, Ministerial that handles pastoral and church ministries; administration and personnel; and then finance and investment. There is also a Chairman of the Convention who presides over the various meetings of the Executive Committee of the Convention. There are thirty-three conferences across the country. Each Conference must have at least seven associations of churches while each Association must have at least ten organized churches. The ministries of the NBC include Christian Education, Global Missions Board, Youth & Students Ministries, Publications, Medical, and Social Ministries departments which are headed by directors. All the departments have advisory committees or supervisory boards for accountability purposes. There is also the Baptist Press that handles all the printing of the educational and discipleship materials and books by the various ministries of the NBC.

Contributions of the NBC to the Socioeconomic Development of Nigeria

One of the strategies of the early missionaries was education—the training of workers to assist them in their evangelistic work. It was the earnest desire of the first missionary, Thomas Bowen, to provide the best education to some of the converts just like the Anglicans and Wesleyans were doing at the initial stage. He was the first to publish a Yoruba dictionary, but due to poor health and eventual return to the United States, his dream could not be turned into reality. Another missionary that felt the need to start training some elites was W. J. David who considered the idea as necessary to accelerate the spread of the gospel by educated Africans. Of course, at the time, none of the missionaries considered the need to sponsor the Africans to the United States for higher training. The challenges posed by the Anglicans and the Wesleyans became an impetus for the American missionaries to begin post-primary education.

As earlier listed, the first *Sabbath School* was started by the wife of the first missionary, Mrs. Bowen. A formal school was opened in Ogbomoso by Rev Smith where some of the first converts and their children were given opportunity of education. In every town where churches were planted, at least a primary school was started to provide education for the young people who served as choir members on Sundays.

The first formal training school was multidimensional as both pastoral and teacher training was put together. The idea was to provide necessary education for church planters and developers, while those in teaching would be assisting the pastors to minister to the converts. These teachers served as musicians and teachers in the primary schools started by the local churches. Of course, they also assisted the pastors to teach the Sunday School classes while helping with men and women ministries during the weekdays. The first of the formal training school was *Baptist Training School* that was started in 1896 by Rev. Charles Smith with one student who was Nathaniel Oyerinde (later Professor N. D. Oyerinde). The goal was to train young men in particular as teachers and pastors. The pastors' training started in May 3, 1898, alongside the teacher training with the name, *Baptist College and Seminary* in Ogbomoso. It was in 1939 when the teacher training became separated from the pastor's training to become *Baptist College* and was moved to Iwo, about one-hour drive away from Ogbomoso. This teacher training college turned out so many trained teachers that empowered young people who became civil servants, bankers, medical workers, lawyers, etc.

One of the missionaries, Dr. E. G. McLean, started a vocational school named *Industrial Training School* in 1908 in another Yoruba town called Saki. The school moved to places where the missionaries moved and this school later moved to Iwo where the teachers were being trained. However, the school was phased out in 1953 as some of the courses were subsumed in the curriculum of the teacher training. The school turned out so many artisans such as carpenters, masons, electricians, and the like that trained many apprentices to strengthen the building industry and infrastructural ventures across the nation. This possibly was the precursor of the technical colleges and polytechnics that emerged apart from the mainline universities.

One other major contribution was the establishment of secondary schools. Earlier, most of the churches planted in urban centers established primary schools as earlier alluded to. The first secondary school was the Baptist Academy, Lagos, in 1886 while another came up in 1923,

that is, Baptist Boys High School, Abeokuta. These two schools in particular produced several national leaders such as Governors of States and
one President in person of Chief Olusegun Obasanjo. Several Muslims
were trained in these schools who contributed immensely to Nigeria in
terms of active participation in politics and management of the economy,
and in the legal system. Today, there are uncountable numbers of such
secondary schools established by some of our churches. In the 1970s,
the military government enacted a decree that forcefully took over most
of the mission/church-owned primary and secondary schools. Some of
the secondary schools have been returned by a few states, but none were
returned to us by the northern states where their leaders are mostly Muslims. As a result, the NBC and some of the churches have started to establish privately-owned primary and secondary schools with government
license. The goal is mainly to add spiritual flavor to education which the
government literally proscribed due to fear of using it to proselyte or
evangelize the Muslim children in particular.

Contributions of Distinguished Nigerian Baptists

There are so many American missionaries who distinguished themselves
for the development of the NBC. The highlights of their contributions
have been documented elsewhere. The nationals who played significant
roles are too numerous for this short discourse. However, it is essential
that few of them should be listed.

The leading figure is definitely Dr. Mojola Agbebi who served as the
first president of the fledgling *Yoruba Baptist Association* that was formed
in 1914. That a Nigerian would be nominated by an American to lead the
foundation of the NBC speaks volumes. There are of course others like
him who stood tall among their peers, such as Moses Ladejo Stone who
became the first ordained Nigerian pastor and who led the first secession
from the American-led First Baptist Church, Lagos in 1888. Professor N.
D. Oyerinde became the first student of the missionaries and sponsored
himself to the USA for further studies and came back to serve alongside
the missionaries who literally made attempts to discourage him from
such a venture. Dr. J. T. Ayorinde became the first indigenous leader to
assume the role of the then General Secretary, the Chief Executive Officer
of the NBC in 1964. Dr. Emmanuel Ajayi Dahunsi became the second
indigenous General Secretary who was a distinguished New Testament

scholar. He assisted the Bible Society of Nigeria to translate the New Testament from the original Greek to Yoruba language. Dr. S. T. Ola Akande also distinguished himself as both the President and later as General Secretary of the NBC. He was the first General Secretary of the All-Africa Baptist Fellowship, a position presently occupied by Dr. DurosinJesu Ayanrinola. An Old Testament scholar, Dr. Samuel Ola Fadeji succeeded Dr. S. T. Ola Akande. Dr. S. Ademola Ishola also served as last CEO to bear the title of General Secretary from 2001 to 2011. He was succeeded by Dr. Samson Olasupo Ayokunle who started bearing the title of President. The first indigenous theological educator to assume the leadership of the Nigerian Baptist Theological Seminary since its establishment in 1898 was Professor Osadolor Imasogie in 1977. Others who led this oldest Seminary in Africa are: Professor Yusufu Obaje, Professor. J. A. Ilori, Professor Deji Ayegboyin, and currently, Professor Emiola Nihinlola. There are other numerous Nigerians who served the Lord with distinction as educators, medical personnel, lawyers, politicians, bankers, and merchants, just to mention a few among many areas.

Bowen University

For many years, the NBC envisioned to start a university, but was prevented by the government until early 2000s when the ban was lifted to allow private or faith-based institutions to establish their own universities. The main reason was the inability of the government-owned universities and post-secondary schools to provide enough space for the teeming youths yearning for advanced education. In a situation where over a million young people want to enter the universities, the available space can only admit about 10 percent of the applicants. Besides, more and more parents were making attempts to send their wards to foreign countries, where tuition cost is beyond the reach of the majority of parents.

When the government granted the NBC the license to establish its own university, the Bowen University was floated with the first students admitted by November 2002. The University is located in a predominantly Muslim ancient town called Iwo, in Osun State of Nigeria. The motto of the University is: *Excellence and Godliness,* and the goal is avowed commitment to adding a distinctly moral dimension and Godly values to tertiary education in Nigeria. The institution is full boarding, and students are required to participate in chapel services where biblical principles are taught. The current enrollment is about 5,500 students comprising of undergraduate and post-graduate programs.

Baptist Student Fellowship

One of the most effective agents of the NBC evangelization is the forma-tion of the Baptist Students Fellowship (BSF). As a result of the campus revivals in Europe and the USA, groups such as the Scripture Union from the United Kingdom, The Navigators, and the Campus Crusade for Christ from the USA sent their missionaries from the late 1960s throughout the 1970s to major campuses of our tertiary institutions to spread their dis-cipleship training for the students. They also flooded the campuses with their literature, which positively affected many students, many of whom came from Baptist churches across the nation.

Some of them came back to their home churches with the inten-tion to influence their conservative parents and family members with the revival fire. The attempt was rebuffed by the pastors who had never been exposed to the kind of strange firebrand Christianity, and of course, by the parents and others who could not stand the fervency with which the young men and women were exhibiting their faith. The resultant ef-fect was the expulsion of some of the young men and women from the churches, some of whom left to join churches that would accommodate them. The major issue that turned the young people against their parents and their church tradition was the Pentecostal/Charismatic movement, particularly their practices exhibiting their spiritual gifts, such as speak-ing in tongues, prophesying, extensive prayer meetings, night vigils, among other tendencies. This coincided with the deep teachings of the Scripture Union and others that were led by some lecturers who had no Seminary training. Of course, such practice was not the norm within the then-traditional Baptist churches, nor were the pastors and deacons exposed to such tendencies. Consequently, the NBC was losing many of its vibrant and promising young people to other churches that saw the potentials in them.

One of the courageous missionaries then, Miss Mary Frank Kirk-patrick, decided to engage some of the students to begin what became the Baptist Students Fellowship in 1965. Others who joined her were Marie (Polly) Van Lear and Bettye Ann McQueen among others, mostly single ladies, who started to bring the young people together to stay within the churches. They were joined by some of the Nigerian teachers in some of the tertiary institutions who understood these young people. Some of the leaders of the NBC at the time felt uncomfortable with the women's ministries with the students, due to some excesses of some young people. In 1977, Miss Mary Frank Kirkpatrick was deported from Nigeria with the connivance of some of the leaders who worked underground with the government agents to accuse her of subversive activities. Those who took over from where she stopped built on her vision to turn these young people into foot soldiers for Christ across the nation. The aftermath of the efforts made on the emerging leaders are the fruitful ministries of some of the current pastors leading most of our vibrant churches across the nation. Some of these young people are now leaders in various higher institutions, banking industries, political arenas, and in various fields of endeavor. They are today contributing immensely to the development of the NBC and the nation at large.

Empowerment of Women

The NBC at its sixth Annual Session approved the establishment of the Women Missionary Union, March 16, 1919 and inaugurated it with the name, "Baptist Women's Missionary League." The organization has been involved in the training of children, young girls, and married women to be responsible church members, and particularly to engage in carrying out the Great Commission. Prior to this development, the training of girls literally started with a young girl living with Mrs. Bowen while they were in Ijaye which metamorphosed into regular Sunday School. The first formal training school for girls was inaugurated in 1909 called, *Idi-Aba Baptist Girls School* located in Abeokuta. Most of the products of this school turned out to become medical doctors, diplomats, educationists, bankers, and other professions. Of course, most of them got married to trained pastors, teachers, civil servants, and merchants who considered the girls highly trained in Christian ideals with high sense of responsibility. Several other schools followed as a result of the success of this pioneer school for the training of female children. Notable among them are: Elam Memorial Girls' High School, Saki (1934); Reagan Memorial Baptist Girls' High School, Yaba-Lagos, (1941), and another in Agbor in the Niger Delta region (1946). Of course there are numerous mixed high schools that are established for the purpose of training young people for further training leading to great careers with added value to the nation. The NBC also provides a platform for women pastors and deaconesses who are working alongside fellow-pastors with equal competence.

There is also Men's Missionary Union, the counterpart of the women's ministry. The men's ministry oversees the Royal Ambassadors who are the young boys until they are married when they will join the men's group in the various churches.

Medical Ministry

One other major evangelizing agency for the NBC is medical ministry. As early as the arrival of Thomas Bowen to Ijaye, he made attempts to provide improvised medical care for the people in the town. However, with the arrival of one medical personnel in person of Dr. George Green, a Baptist Medical Center was established in 1907. The NBC was fortunate to have the American missionary doctors, nurses, and other medical professionals who worked in this medical center for many years until the restructuring of the International Mission Board that relocated virtually all the missionaries from their primary duty posts. The IMB embarked on a "New Direction," and the NBC was given ten years' notice from 1990 to 2000, that all the missionary personnel in the theological and medical ministries and others would be reassigned to unreached people-groups. Of course, this was what the China Inland Missions was doing all along or that of the then-known Sudan Interior Missions (SIM).

By 1998, most of the medical personnel and theological educators either resigned or were reassigned as "emergency evangelists," though most of them were still living in major cities. Along the way, several Nigerian medical doctors and nurses and other medical workers started to take over the management of this hospital and others across the nation. Apart from the one in Ogbomoso, the NBC also has two other big hospitals in Saki, Oyo State, and Eku in the Niger Delta area. These Nigerian doctors, nurses, and para-medical workers became more committed to managing and sourcing for funding through the poor patronage of the local communities. These workers endured poor salaries and of course, suffered unpaid salaries for months. The reason was the withdrawal of both personnel and money from the American partner. However, the medical ministry has survived and is trying to pay competitive salaries today. All along, these hospitals became the training ground for locally-trained medical personnel from our government medical schools across the nation.

The old Baptist Medical Center, Ogbomoso, has now become the Bowen University Teaching Hospital (BUTH) where medical doctors are being trained. The first set of students prepared to graduate by the end of 2015. With matching major funding from the Bowen University and the NBC, the hospital is moving on and satisfying the standards set by the National accrediting agency, the National Universities Commission. Part of the Hospital is the School of Nursing that was started in 1927, and later the School of Midwifery.

Apart from the main hospital, there are the Leprosarium (Leprosy Settlement Center in Ogbomoso, 1930) and Kersey Home Motherless Children Home, Ogbomoso (1926). Other medical ministries are spread across the nation. Among them are: Baptist Hospital, Iwo (1922) now Bowen University Medical Clinic; Baptist Hospital, Joinkrama, Niger Delta (1943), taken over by the government; Baptist Hospital, Eku (1947), taken over by the Delta State government in 2010; Baptist Welfare Center, Iree (1946); Baptist Hospital, Saki (1952); Baptist Dental Center, Enugu in the East (1959); and Baptist Hospital, Kontagora in the North (1960), taken over by the government. There are several new ones while plans are afoot to build more facilities as funds flow in.

Other Social Ministries

Social ministries are not left out of the NBC's missionary strategy. One of the areas of social ministry is the introduction of adult education that afforded many illiterate members of the local churches, Muslims, and local people to learn how to read and write. Of course, the goal is to help members to be able to read the Bible, particularly the indigenous dialects. However, some people have been taking advantage of this adult education to improve their lives by sitting for primary school Leaving Certificate, while some went further to complete their high school diplomas. The NBC has earned several awards from the government for this great contribution to national development.

There is also ministry to the prisoners through the supply of "prison chaplains" who visit and provide rehabilitation to prisoners who have completed their sentences. During their stay, opportunities are provided for some of them to learn how to read and write, while some are assisted in learning a trade. The main assistance comes after their prison life in forms of counseling and linking them with some local churches that may help to get them reintroduced into the society.

Orphanage ministry is under the Social Ministry Department while Home Care caters for senior adults who are assisted through recreational activities and linking them with welfare centers where they can get cheaper medical treatment. One unit under the home care caters to widows and widowers. Programs are designed for them periodically where some are assisted with food items and vocational training. In some areas of Nigeria, family members may be a source of agony to some widows when they are driven out of their matrimonial homes. In this case, some form of advocacy ministry is offered to defend their rights and speak to family members to desist from harassing the poor widows and their children.

For some years now, the *Boko Haram* insurgency has dislocated and displaced so many Nigerians and particularly when they first started targeting Christians. The Christian refugees are being assisted with food items, and temporary shelters are provided when the assistance by Red Cross and other similar organizations have spill-over. Some orphans and displaced adults are assisted to link up with relatives around the country. It is important to note that most of the churches engage in social ministries in their various localities.

Funding the Convention Ministries

The financing of the mission work for many years was borne by the missionaries through their home office which is the Foreign Mission Board based in Richmond, Virginia. During the Civil War in the USA, funding was cut short as the Southern areas where most of the missionaries came from became devastated by the war. However, when the missionaries returned, funding resumed purposefully for the missionaries to cover the expenses of their mission outreaches. As the churches multiplied, every local church was saddled with the responsibility of paying the salaries of their pastors, while most of the pastors initially had to supplement their meager pay with subsistence farming, particularly in the villages and small towns. Later there was the Cooperative Program for the purpose of financing the various ministries of the Convention. The Cooperative Program is the means by which churches pool their financial resources together for the collective responsibilities under God that one or few churches may not be able to do alone. This challenge to be "self-financing" and "self-governing" became a reality when during the Golden Jubilee celebration of the Convention in 1964 the first Nigerian as the General Secretary was elected in the person of Dr. J. T. Ayorinde. This move formed the beginning of the transfer of leadership of the Convention from the missionaries to the nationals, though most of the institutions at this period were being managed by the former. The Nigerian Baptist Theological Seminary was the first to be led by a Nigerian in 1977.

To finance the work of the Convention, churches were giving whatever they could afford. However, in 1924, a resolution was passed "that all churches having above twenty members be requested to pay the minimum sum of one pound (£1.00) to the Convention fund per annum." In 1938, the Convention took a decision to apply apportionment when the Convention's Budget was distributed on Associational basis, and it worked as the Budget was oversubscribed by fourpence. That year the Apportionment was £350 and the Receipts were £350.4. In 1949, at the annual meeting in Benin City, there was the challenge for churches to give 10 percent of their annual income. The amount apportioned to the churches was increased to 15 percent of their tithes and offerings, and at this time it increased to 20 percent. All resolutions were passed at various annual meetings of the Convention. It is from this that our annual Budget operates and covers expenses for ten theological institutions, subventions to some hospitals, social ministry, ecumenical expenses, scholarships, and of course, salaries of Convention workers. The Global Mission Board that facilitates our home and foreign mission thrust receives 20 percent of the 20 percent that comes from the churches. However, about 25 percent of the churches (about 13,000 churches in all) do not contribute regularly due to lack of commitment and largely due to lack of economic strength. The urban churches are mostly responsible for the 90 percent of the fund that come to the Convention office to cater for the various ministries listed above.

NBC and International Mission

Our Baptist story in Ghana is closely connected to the NBC to which we have referred above. Several attempts were made to engage in direct missionary thrust to other tribes with the gospel. The starting point was the Northern Nigeria in Kaduna and Kwara states. Today we have missionaries and church planters in most of the thirty-six Nigerian states. Beyond Nigeria in 1961, the NBC opened its first foreign mission field in Magburaka in Northern Sierra Leone. Later, work started in the Republic of Cote d'Ivoire (Ivory Coast), Benin Republic, Burkina Faso, Mali, Tanzania, Mozambique, and South Sudan. Efforts have been made to begin mission outreach to the United Kingdom with four churches in Liverpool and London. Funding the home and foreign mission efforts comes from the designated 20 percent of the 20 percent of the money that comes from the faithful churches which give regularly. There are other individual donors who give substantially periodically while some few individuals have given endowment and others have donated landed properties for the use of the Global Mission Board. The Board is coordinated by a Director and a Board that oversees the management of the mission enterprise

The early missionary strategy was focused on rural areas and fringe tribal groups that gulped enough resources with less results after many years. Part of the strategy then was to wean the mission field off after ten years, yet, most of the fields remain unable to be self-supporting. A major factor for the poor results is the harsh terrains in terms of poor economy, leading the younger people to migrate to urban areas where they may secure jobs and acquire training. The current strategy is to follow a Pauline missionary plan of focusing on major cities from which the gospel will then beam out to other adjacent villages or smaller towns. This strategy appears to be yielding better results than before. The case in point was our choice of Magburaka in Northern Sierra Leone when even the capital city, Freetown, lacked a robust Baptist witness at that time in the early 1960s. When the civil war came, the entire work of many years was wiped out, and we have just begun new work in Freetown with appreciable result, while helping to train young people who are identified as emerging leaders. This is the same strategy being used for other foreign mission fields in Mozambique, Burkina Faso, Mali, etc.

A paradigm shift towards biblical pattern of mission thrust focusing on urban centers with rural ministry at the background appears to be strengthening our mission strategy today. The recruitment and training of missionaries and church planters have also been restructured. The idea of recruiting just about any seminary-trained pastor, particularly at the lower level of training, has changed by extending calls to those who are well-trained with additional orientation. Cultural and language training have been added to the curriculum while the Nigerian Baptist Theological

Seminary now offers missiology degrees at both bachelor and master's levels. The graduates now make up the core of our missionary force.

In 2013, NBC started a cable television outfit known as New Frontier Cable Television that broadcast sermons and various Christian programs to reach millions of people across the world. The programs are streamed live through the internet which makes them accessible to all wherever there is internet service. The address is www.nftv.info and http://www.fb.com/nftv1. The use of electronic media for evangelistic and discipleship purposes has become necessary in order to reach difficult places where traditional missionaries and church planters may not be approved.

Concluding Remarks

The Nigerian Baptist Convention has come of age and with great potential in joining God to keep expanding his kingdom on earth. As one of the oldest denominations in the country, the NBC is involved in ecumenical relationship with other church traditions that form the Christian Association of Nigeria, and also is a member of the Christian Council of Nigeria, the National Association of Protestant Churches, an affiliate of the World Council of Churches (WCC). The NBC plays active roles in these bodies as well as in the Baptist World Alliance. As the leading Baptist Convention in Africa, the NBC has been assisting some of the weaker conventions by granting scholarship for capacity building and partnering with them in missions. The history of the NBC is still unfolding as it keeps its resolve to join others to fulfill the Great Commission to spreading the gospel and making disciples in all people groups. Overall, the social impact of the ministries of the NBC is felt across the nation and beyond.

19

Baptists in South Africa

Louise Kretzschmar and Ngwedla Paul Msiza

Introduction

THE AIM OF THIS chapter is to outline the establishment and development of the Baptists in South Africa within the wider context of the country's history. Also discussed are the many groups that make up this denomination, their contribution to the church and society, their relationship with Baptists elsewhere, and the challenges they face today.

Historical Roots

The Baptist story in South Africa starts in 1820, when a handful of Baptists arrived in the Eastern Cape as part of a group of British settlers. Following the economic hardships experienced during the long war between Britain and France, they hoped to be able to build a better life for themselves, and extend their Baptist witness in South Africa. Between 1857 and 1859, the British government also settled in this area a number of German soldiers who had fought for Britain in the Crimean War of 1854, as well as German civilians, some of whom were Baptists. Prior to their arrival, these settlers did not know that they were being used by the British government to form a human buffer between the white farmers and town dwellers already settled in the Eastern Cape, and the African

Xhosa nation to the north. It was a border region characterized by military campaigns, violent incursions, conflict over land, and cattle theft on both sides. In 1894, the whole area between the Kei River and the then Natal was annexed by Britain. As a consequence of this, the Xhosa people became extremely reluctant to respond positively to the later evangelistic efforts of the white Baptists.

These Baptists were not missionaries, and they received little support from Baptists in England and Germany. Many white settlers disliked the earlier missionaries of the London Missionary Society (LMS), such as the Revs. Johannes van der Kemp, James Read, and John Philip. The settlers saw the missionaries' attempts to secure the rights of the black indigenous inhabitants as British subjects as undermining their interests and security. The British Baptist Missionary Society (BMS) and the LMS had agreed that the BMS would focus its attention north of the Limpopo River (i.e., the modern Congo, Zambia, and Zimbabwe), while the LMS would work in southern Africa (modern South Africa, Botswana, eSwatini [formerly Swaziland], Lesotho and Namibia). The effect of this agreement was that no BMS missionaries worked in the Eastern Cape region, and little support was forthcoming from Baptist churches elsewhere. Also, Baptists in South Africa were minimally influenced by the growing social involvement of Baptists and other evangelicals in nineteenth-century Britain.[1] By contrast, the work of Methodist missionaries in establishing churches and schools led to a chain of Methodist mission stations being built between the Eastern Cape and Durban. Today, Methodists in South Africa number about 3.3 million people, whereas Baptists number approximately 100,000 baptized church members.

The main features of early Baptist work were evangelism and church planting among the white communities. Baptists had started churches in Salem and then Grahamstown (1823), but the work of church planting was interrupted by several Frontier wars (which commenced in 1834). Later Baptist churches were also started in Port Elizabeth (1854), Durban (1864), Alice (1874), and Cape Town (1876).[2] Between 1876 and 1892, as a result of the work of the German Baptists such as Carsten Langhein (1809–82), Carl Hugo Gutsche (1843–1926) and his wife, Mary (1841–1925), twenty-five churches were established. They also offered help to the poor, widows, and orphans in their communities. In 1867, an

1. Kretzschmar, *Privatization*, 186–223.
2. Hudson-Reed, *By Taking Heed*, 15–76.

Afrikaans (Dutch) farmer by the name of J. D. Odendaal was baptized by Gutsche. In 1876, Odendaal founded the first Afrikaans-speaking Baptist church, the Ebenhaezer Baptistegemeente van Cornelia, in the Orange Free State province. By 1889, this church had a mixed congregation of sixty-three white and seventy-three black members.[3] In 1877, the Baptist Union of South Africa (BUSA) was formed. Some work among the "coloreds" (people of mixed race) was also done in Port Elizabeth and Cape Town. In 1888, the Coloured Baptist Association was founded. Initially, white and "colored" Baptists worshiped together, but later white members moved away and built their own churches.[4]

In 1865, an Indian Baptist by the name of Ingham Mausvales arrived in South Africa from Bengal (where William Carey had served as a missionary). In 1860 and 1900, other Indian indentured laborers and immigrants arrived in South Africa. Many of them worked in the sugar and tea plantations. These groups included some Telugu-speaking Baptists. A lay leader, Mr. B. Benjamin, ministered to their needs. In 1903, the Telugu Baptist Home Mission Society sent Rev. and Mrs. John Rangiah to work among the Indian Baptists in Natal. However, differences arose among this group, and Rev. Rangiah resigned from the Telugu Baptist Home Mission Society in September 1914. In December 1914, a group under Rangiah formed the Natal Indian Baptist Association, which later became known as the Baptist Association of South Africa (BASA). In 1915, Rev. V. C. Jacob was sent by the Society to continue its work with the remaining Indian Baptists in Natal. They became known as the Indian Baptist Mission (IBM), now called the Baptist Mission in South Africa (BMSA).

The German Baptists were the first to do mission work among the Xhosa people. They established a missionary committee in 1868, and founded the Tschabo/Tshabo Mission Station in 1870. In 1874, Carl Pape began to work as an evangelist among the Mfengu (Fingo) people living in the vicinity of Qonce (formerly King William's Town). During the late-nineteenth century, several Baptist churches were started among the Xhosa people as a result of the work of the American National Baptists, the Lott Carey Baptist Foreign Mission Convention, and BUSA. In 1892, the latter formed the South African Baptist Missionary Society (SABMS).

---

3. Hudson-Reed, *By Taking Heed*, 207–34.

4. Hudson-Reed, *Together*, 9–27.

Following the discovery of diamonds in the 1860s, and gold on the Witwatersrand in 1886, many more immigrants arrived in South Africa. Evangelistic work was done among them, and additional Baptist churches were established outside the Eastern Cape. The Anglo-Boer Wars of 1880 to 1881 and 1899 to 1902 caused huge devastation, and led to tensions between English and Afrikaans-speaking Baptists, especially when English soldiers burnt down the Baptist church in Cornelia. Later, relations were restored, and the Afrikaanse Baptiste Kerke (ABK) were established in 1944, working mainly among Afrikaans communities.

Baptists in the Twentieth Century

The declaration of the Union of South Africa in 1910 excluded black South Africans from having equal political and economic rights with white inhabitants, and exacerbated existing racial conflict. Following the Second World War, the Nationalist Party came to power in 1948. Its policy of *apartheid* legislated and enforced the long-standing separation between black and white inhabitants, and further discriminated against and exploited the black majority. During this time, some Baptists spoke out against *apartheid* and/or more actively resisted its injustices. However, many more acquiesced with the government of the day.

Since the first democratic elections of 1994, some have attempted to unite the different Baptist groups, the largest being the Baptist Union and the Baptist Convention. The establishment of the South African Baptist Alliance in 2001 has facilitated contact and cooperation between Baptist leaders. However, Baptist groups in South Africa remain structurally divided, and local congregations have little contact with each other.

The Formation of the Baptist Convention of South Africa (BCSA)

Several churches were established among the Xhosa people as result of mission work done in the Eastern Cape. The churches were not organized into an association, but remained fragmented as mission stations or preaching sites that operated independently. The organizing of the black Baptist churches can be traced to the work of the American National Baptists in the Eastern Cape. One of their first converts, William Mashologu, was taught to do mission work among the African people, and became one of the first trained South African black Baptist pastors. He was a school teacher, who used the opportunities offered by his teaching career to plant churches. It was Rev. Mashologu who challenged the black Baptist churches in the Eastern Cape to come together. As a result, the Bantu Baptist Church came into being in February 1927. Previously, black South Africans had been called "Natives," but at that time the term "Bantu" had come into use.

The history of the Baptists in South Africa, as in other parts of the world, was influenced by the politics of the country. The Baptist churches were established on a segregated basis, and their mission work was influenced by the laws of the country. This resulted in a church that was divided along racial lines. Black churches in the rural areas and townships (segregated urban areas) were generally poor and under-resourced. These churches were strictly controlled by the SABMS, especially through the missionary superintendents. White South African missionaries were generally critical of African culture, and the movements of political resistance among blacks.

In the early 1960s, the growing struggle for political liberation in the country influenced black Baptist churches. A group of younger ministers emerged, and their transformative ministry was especially felt in two areas. The first was a spiritual revival, based on evangelistic preaching. The Bantu Baptist Church moved away from a focus on membership, church uniforms, and baptism to a focus on transformed lives. The second aspect of transformation was that of greater political awareness. As a result, the name of this group of churches was changed to the Baptist Convention of South Africa. Also, the Baptist Union was challenged to form one Baptist body in South Africa. Tragically, in 1967, the Baptist Union responded by passing a resolution to establish special associations for the "non-white" Baptist groups. The South African Baptist Alliance of "Colored" churches was formed in the early 1960s, but disbanded by 1977, after which these churches became members of the Baptist Union. The Baptist Convention was an association of the Baptist Union from 1967 to 1987. This associational status meant, for example, that only two delegates from the Convention could represent the many thousands of black Baptists at the annual Baptist Union Assembly, whereas each white church was represented by one or two delegates. Successive, but fruitless, "merger" talks were held with the Baptist Convention leaders contending that one church, with a single constitution, system of ordination, ministerial roll and theological college ought to be established.[5] In 1987, the Convention withdrew its status as an association of the Baptist Union and became an autonomous Baptist body.[6]

Formal Theological Education

Until the mid-twentieth century, informal education, part-time theological study, and mentoring were the main means of ministerial training. In 1951, the Baptist Theological College was established by the Baptist Union in Parktown, Johannesburg, mainly for white students, who could meet the educational requirements of twelve years of primary and secondary schooling. Later, this college was moved to Randburg, Johannesburg. In 1961, the Teologiese Seminarium of the ABK was established for Afrikaans-speaking students. In 1972, the Baptist Union established a satellite college in Cape Town to train ministers, especially for the colored churches. By 1974, it also admitted white and African students.[7]

Earlier, in 1940, the Millard Bible Institute had been established in Soweto to train ministers for black Baptist churches. This institution operated at a much lower educational level than the other colleges, admitting students with only primary or initial secondary school education. In 1959, in conformity with the government's Group Areas Act No. 41 of 1950, which created race-based residential areas and forcibly removed black communities deemed to be living in "white" areas, the Baptist Union moved this Bible college to the Eastern Cape. The premises of the Ennals Bible Institute in Debe Nek, near Qonce, were used and this became the Baptist Bible Institute (BBI).[8] Here, ministers for the BCSA were trained from 1961 until 1987, when the Baptist Convention became independent from the Baptist Union. In 1989, the Baptist Union sold the BBI to the Southern Baptist Mission Board, and the name was changed to the Baptist International Theological Seminary (BITS). In 1995, the Baptist Convention established its own theological college, and this led to the closing down of BITS. None of the buildings or assets of BITS, except the library and its furniture, were transferred to the Baptist Convention.

---

5. Hoffmeister and Gurney, *Barkly West*, 33–41.

6. Kanyangoga et al., *Journeying with God*, 12–14, 55–56.

7. Kretzschmar, *Privatisation*, 252–53.

8. Mogashoa, "Millard Training Institute," 134–47.

Following the meeting in Johannesburg in 1993 of the Baptist International Conference of Theological Educators (BICTE), the ABK, Baptist Convention and Baptist Union committed themselves to moving towards a "united, relevant and credible" theological education in South Africa. Until 2003, several leaders and theological educators from these groups made strenuous attempts to unite the three theological colleges situated in or near Johannesburg in a federal structure. Their efforts were not successful, and the reasons for this are disputed. What is clear is that the Convention leaders were pursuing an earlier conviction that one Baptist body needed to be formed. This goal could only be realized if Baptist ministers were trained together. Within the Baptist Union, which held significant financial and other resources, certain leaders were not willing to support this joint venture, and were also suspicious of the theology of the Convention. Hence, a vital opportunity for bridge-building was missed. Currently, there are four theological institutions run by Baptists in South Africa. The Baptist Union owns the Baptist Theological College in Randburg, Johannesburg and the Cape Town Baptist Theological Seminary. The Seminarium of the ABK in Kempton Park works with the college in Randburg. The Baptist Convention's college is situated in Soweto, Johannesburg, and is working with the Baptist Theological College in Randburg.

The Contribution of South Africa Baptists to Evangelism and Congregational Development

From the earliest days of the Baptist witness, there has been a strong emphasis on evangelism and church planting. This remains true of all the Baptist groups in South Africa. Personal evangelism, preaching, and evangelistic campaigns led to the growth of churches and the formation of new churches. Within these churches, the main areas of focus include preaching, personal Bible study, Christian education, Sunday worship, prayer, pastoral ministry, caring for the sick and troubled, and the provision of buildings and administration. All the Baptist groups in South Africa also emphasize the importance of ministries to youth, women, and men in their churches. Women's groups, in particular, meet regularly, pray, raise funds to support projects, and care for families in and around the church.

Over the past decade, the Baptist Union has established 150 new churches in different parts of the country. It issues the *Baptists Today* magazine and its Publishing Committee provides a range of materials for churches. The Cape Town Baptist Seminary publishes the academic journal, the *South African Baptist Journal of Theology*.

In the Baptist Convention, most of the evangelism and church planting is done by local churches and pastors, assisted by the Missions department that provides financial support and training to individuals and churches. From 1998 to 2014, the Baptist Convention grew from ninety-five to 198 churches. This means that each year about six churches were planted nationally by churches and pastors. Most of these churches were established in the black townships and villages, and only a few are located in the suburbs, where previously only whites resided. At present, the Baptist Convention membership comprises 23,000 baptized members and 198 churches.

Today, the Baptist Union has 50,000 baptized members and 650 churches. Between 1889 and 2014, the ABK grew from 136 members (and one church) to 1,700 members in thirty-one churches. BASA presently has 3,500 members within twenty-six churches, predominately in the KwaZulu-Natal region. The BMSA now has a membership of 2,500 within thirteen churches, also in the KwaZulu-Natal region.

Mission Work and Social Concern

In 1955, Jubilee Mission Hospital opened its doors in the poverty-stricken area of Hammanskraal, situated about forty kilometers north of Pretoria, and later home to hundreds of thousands of black people. This hospital was founded, and for many years significantly financed and supported, by churches and medical staff from the Baptist Union. Black and white Baptists also supported the work of evangelism and care for families who came to the hospital for treatment. After 1994, it was progressively taken over by the government of the North West region.

Within the Baptist Union, mission has largely been understood as evangelism and the planting of churches. Many Baptist Union churches could be described as either moderate or conservative Evangelicals, with a small but active group of Reformed Baptists that stress the link between Baptist and Calvinist theology. Today, Baptist Union missionaries are working in countries such as Kenya, Morocco, and Mozambique. The

Baptist Union encourages both short- and long-term mission work, and now has partnerships with Baptist churches in ten African countries. The ABK also engages in mission work, but to a lesser extent than the larger Baptist Union.

Mission work outside South Africa has been done on a very small scale by the Baptist Convention. Between 2002 and 2009, through the partnership with the European Baptist Mission International, the Baptist Convention was able to send short-term missionaries to Europe. Through this mission effort, a church (the Krummgasse Baptist Church) was planted in Vienna, Austria. A few churches and pastors are doing mission work in other countries, such as England, eSwatini, Lesotho, Uganda, Zambia and Zimbabwe.

Both BASA and the BMSA have engaged in mission work in India, and the neighboring countries of Eswatini and Mozambique. The BMSA has established a partnership with fifteen churches in these countries. In KwaZulu-Natal, it continues with evangelistic work and has a children's ministry program that reaches 5,000 children each year. It works with local schools and communities to improve educational levels, and to provide healthcare, help for senior citizens, and HIV screening and counseling. BASA also engages in evangelistic and a range of community work in the KwaZulu-Natal region, and provides feeding schemes for the poor.

Over the years, there have been those in the Baptist Union, who have spoken out against a range of social injustices and have worked, for example, among communities suffering as a result of poverty and drug abuse. Nevertheless, the conservative evangelical approach of many of their members has made these churches less responsive to social issues. However, the Christian Citizenship Network continues to engage with current civic and political issues.

Many leaders from the Baptist Convention drew on their own experience of oppression and the more radical elements of their Baptist theological heritage. These include elements of the sixteenth-century Anabaptist tradition, the radical English Baptists of the seventeenth century, and the socially aware Baptists in nineteenth-century England. They have also drawn on twentieth-century contextual theologies. As a result, the importance of social justice and ministry has become an integral part of the mission work of the Baptist Convention. Three areas have been stressed: education, economic empowerment, and social care.

As a result, a number of churches and individuals now offer day care for children, and some of these centers have become important community centers. In 1997, the Convention took over a skills training center at Thusong (near Soweto) from the International Mission Board of the Southern Baptist Convention of North America. Here skills training programs are offered, including computer literacy, sewing, baking, catering, and motor mechanics. The Baptist Convention also has a ministry to deal with the HIV/Aids epidemic. It offers education about the virus and how to prevent opportunistic infections, support for projects, and provides help to orphans, and those who are terminally ill. In a few areas of the country, the BCSA became the first church organization to establish HIV/Aids ministries, and assisted other churches to begin their own ministries.

Involvement with Local Ecumenical Groups and the Global Baptist Community

Unfortunately, many local Baptist churches do not have a strong consciousness of regional and national cooperation, and still less of cooperation across ecumenical groups. They tend rather to focus on their own local activities. However, this is less true of their denominational leaders. Both the Baptist Union and the Baptist Convention are members of The Evangelical Alliance of South Africa (TEASA). Between 2001 and 2007, the Baptist Convention and the Baptist Union were active members of the Interreligious Leaders Forum. Only the Convention is a member of the ecumenical South Africa Council of Churches (SACC). BASA, the BMSA, the Baptist Union, and the Baptist Convention are members of the Baptist World Alliance. The Baptist Union and the Baptist Convention are also active in the All Africa Baptist Fellowship.

Challenges Facing Baptists in South Africa Today—Unity across the Racial Divide

As can be seen from the above account, much needs to be done to promote unity among Baptists in South Africa. South African Baptists do work together on particular projects, such as preparing for the meeting of the Baptist World Alliance Congress in Durban in July 2015. But additional efforts are necessary to counteract ignorance, suspicion, and hurt at the local church, regional, and national levels within the different Baptist groupings.[9]

Growth

Despite having been in South Africa for nearly two hundred years, the membership of the Baptist churches is relatively small. In order to grow in both numbers and maturity, Baptists need to heal the hurts of the past, train their ministers together, and offer a compelling vision of the gospel of Jesus Christ to their young people. For this to happen, leadership and discipleship need to be given renewed attention. Discipleship, a holistic understanding of the gospel, and committed Christian ministry on the part of all members of Baptist churches need to be combined with the identification, development, and support of dedicated and credible leaders.

A serious challenge for many churches in South Africa is the growth of the "prosperity" gospel that originated in America. The false focus on "health and wealth" is enticing especially younger ministers to their ranks, resulting in the formation of independent ministries. Also, the new wave of "healing and prophetic" ministries, originating in Nigeria, is drawing members from established Baptist churches. These churches undermine the mission focus of the members of churches, because ministry is focused instead on the work of the so-called prophet or healer. Such churches emphasize the prosperity of the individual rather than the discipleship and ministry of all believers, and often ignore the many political and economic challenges facing the country.

The Role of Women and Women's Ordination

As is the case with other churches, women's groups are very active in all the Baptist churches. Women engage in a variety of ministries, also through the Baptist women's associations or departments. Different approaches have been adopted with regard to the ordination of women. Rather than taking an official position on the matter, the Baptist Union has allowed local congregations to decide whether or not they wish to ordain women to the ministry. This stance is influenced by the conservative theology of many of the members of the Baptist Union.

9. Ntombana and Perry, "Exploring," 1–8.

Within the Baptist Convention, many churches encourage women to preach on Sundays, teach in cell groups, be active in the various ministries of the church, and play a leading role on church boards. It also welcomes women to their theological college. The resolution to ordain women for ministry was taken in 1997, and today there are thirty-one women of 190 ministers on the Baptist Convention ministerial list. Currently, fourteen women are serving as senior pastors, seventeen are associate pastors, and some women pastors have chosen to serve with their ordained spouses.

Contemporary Social Problems

Post-1994, South Africa faces many socio-political and economic challenges. These include inequality, unemployment, especially among young people, poverty, a lack of service delivery on the part of the government, corruption, crime, family breakdown, a high incidence of HIV/Aids, and many more. Baptists and other churches have an important role to play as the conscience of the country, at a local and national level. However, contemporary Baptists need to learn from the past, and avoid the extremes of withdrawing from social involvement or being co-opted by powerful social groups. In order to be true to their Baptist witness, they need to remain institutionally separate from the state, but still engage actively with both the State and civil society, based on their theological-ethical convictions. Baptist churches need to rise to the challenge of engaging in a prophetic witness in relation to the state, and also operating a range of community projects.

We believe that this chapter provides an opportunity for Baptists in South Africa to give thanks to God for what has been achieved, and to engage in introspection. We need to repent of our many failures to honor God, to be united, and to love our neighbors. We can also celebrate the fact that Baptists have faithfully served their churches and communities over many years. We hope this chapter will inspire and inform our local and international readers, and encourage them to pray for, and participate in, the Baptist witness in South Africa and other countries.

We hereby acknowledge with gratitude the information we received from our fellow Baptists from the ABK, BASA, BCSA, BMSA, and BUSA. The authors of this chapter, Rev. Msiza and Prof. Kretzschmar, are members of the Baptist Convention of South Africa.

Bibliography

Dutta, H. J. *The Story of a One Hundred Years: Being the History of the Baptist Church in South Africa*. Cape Town: Maskew Miller, 1920.

Hoffmeister, Des, and Brian J. Gurney, eds. *The Barkly West National Awareness Workshop*. Johannesburg: Awareness Campaign Committee of the BCSA, 1990.

Hudson-Reed, Sydney, ed. *By Taking Heed: The History of the Baptists in Southern Africa 1820–1977*. Roodepoort: Baptist Publishing House, 1983.

———. *Together for a Century: The History of the Baptist Union, 1877–1977*. Pietermaritzburg: SA Baptist Historical Society, 1977.

Kanyangoga, Gabriel H., et al., eds. *Journeying with God: The History of the Baptist Convention of South Africa*. Johannesburg: BCSA, 2007.

Kretzschmar, Louise. *Privatization of the Christian Faith: Mission, Social Ethics and the South African Baptists*. Accra, Ghana: Legon & Asempa, 1998.

———. "The Implications of New Developments in Christian Ethics and Spirituality for Curricula and Staff Development at Baptist Colleges in Southern Africa." In *Southern African Baptist Educators' Conference, 2003*, edited by by Louise Kretzschmar, 80–105. Johannesburg: Baptist Convention College, 2003.

Kretzschmar, Louise, et al., eds. *Being a Baptist in South Africa Today*. Johannesburg: BCSA, 1997.

Mogashoa, M. H. "The Millard Training Institute: The Black Perspective." *South African Baptist Journal of Theology* 12 (2003) 134–47.

Nicolson, Gisella. *God Brought Me Here: The Story of Jubilee Mission Hospital, 1955–2005*, Doornpoort: Friends of Jubilee Hospital, 2005.

Ntombana, Luvuyo, and Adam Perry. "Exploring the Critical Moments When the Baptist Denomination Divided: Does Revisiting These Moments Give Hope to Reconciliation Between the 'Union' and 'Convention'?" *HTS Teologiese Studies / Theological Studies* 68.1 (2012) #Art. 1029, 8 pages.

iii. From the European Baptist Federation

20

The European Baptist Federation

Ian M. Randall and Keith G. Jones

The European Baptist Federation (EBF) consists of over fifty member Baptist unions and conventions across Europe and the Middle East. There are also a small number of affiliated Baptist churches. The purpose of the EBF, as stated in 1950 when it was founded, was:

- To promote fellowship among Baptists in Europe;
- To stimulate and coordinate evangelism in Europe;
- To provide a board of consultation and planning for Baptist mission work in Europe;
- To stimulate and coordinate where desirable foreign missionary work of European Baptists who have no field of their own;
- To promote such Baptist relief work as may be needed in Europe.

The roots of Baptist cooperation across Europe go back to the nineteenth century. The development of Baptist life in continental Europe in the early nineteenth century was initially on a very small scale, with a few pockets of indigenous growth and missionary impetus, for example in France. A hugely important step forward was taken following the adoption of Baptist beliefs and a Baptist form of church life by Johann Gerhard Oncken (1800–1884), who was baptized by an American Baptist in the Elbe near Hamburg on 22 April 1834. The vigorous church that Oncken developed in Hamburg, though persecuted, made contact with many German merchants and tradesmen from all over Europe who were working in the city, and a whole network of German-speaking Baptist churches was established in several countries throughout Europe in the succeeding years.

In 1849, fifty-six Baptist representatives met in Hamburg and organized what was called the Union of Associated Churches of Baptized Christians in Germany and Denmark. The reason given by Oncken for the creation of the Union was a theological and missiological one. He stated: "Every apostolic Christian church must be a Mission Society . . . but the mission work must be furthered by the joining together of more churches." Many churches which were to become very important in the establishment of national Baptist groupings came out of the work of Oncken and his colleagues. One example of a strategic center was what became the very large Baptist congregation in Memel (modern-day Klaipeda), Lithuania. Oncken and his missionaries had a hand in the formation of many Baptist leaders, such as Gottfried F. Alf, in Poland. There was an emphasis on training significant church-planting missionaries. A number of these were recently converted: for example, Oncken baptized several carpenters working in Hamburg, and they went back to German-speaking communities elsewhere in Europe. In this way the connectedness of Baptists engaged in church planting existed like a web across the continent. All remained interconnected in the development of Baptist life and witness.

Throughout this development of continental Baptist communities there was an emphasis on interdependency and on *koinonia*, not only in practice but also in such statements of belief as the Confession of Faith drawn up in 1913 by Johann Kargel, who had trained in Oncken's Baptist Seminary in Hamburg. Kargel became a leading and highly influential figure in the Russian Baptist community. His Confession was used as a statement of faith by Russian Baptists through to the 1980s. This is what is said about the church. It reflects a sense of the importance of unity between churches, a view which was to contribute to the formation of the EBF some decades later:

> The universal Church of Christ is built upon the foundation of the apostles and prophets, Christ Jesus himself being the cornerstone. She consists of those who are saved, who believe, who are called to be saints, who are in this world, as well as the saved ones who have gone to be with the Lord. Those and these constitute one body whose head is Christ. And although the members

of this church are from different nations, different situations and have different gifts, they all are one in Christ and individually members one with another.

The single local churches [gathering communities] are only part of one universal church; they are built by the Lord in different countries, cities and local places for the uniting of the saved children of God on earth, for the unified praising of God, for the growth of the members in the knowledge of God and Christ, for upbuilding in the life of faith after the image of Christ, for the mutual participation in all this and for the spreading of the Kingdom of God on earth.

Although the German and then the Russian Baptists offer the clearest example of Baptist fellowship across national boundaries, this experience was also to be found in other parts of Europe. By the 1930s there were other such fellowships, such as a Latin group (Belgium, France, Spain, Portugal, and Italy) which met together and which also incorporated delegates from the Anglo-Saxon world.

Organizationally, however, the world family of Baptists came into being before the EBF, through the formation in 1905 of the Baptist World Alliance (BWA). Speaking at the inaugural meetings in 1905 in London of the BWA, Joseph Lehmann of the Baptist Seminary in Hamburg talked about how difficult it was to imagine "the state of things on the Continent seventy or eighty years ago," when Johann Oncken, the "great pioneer" of the continental European Baptist movement, "attained to Scriptural views on Baptism and the Church of Christ by the simple study of the New Testament."

Lehmann's recital of European Baptist advance was greeted by applause. His speech conveyed to an international audience the growth of Baptist life in Germany and across Europe. Other speakers in London in 1905 were Baron Woldemar von Üxküll from Estonia, and D. I. Mazaev, who both reported on behalf of Russian Baptist communities. They spoke of new freedoms in Russia, but also of many Baptist members who had suffered severely. There was an increased awareness of the need for solidarity. Newton Marshall and James Henry Rushbrooke, two rising British Baptist ministers, contributed significantly to a follow-up Baptist conference, convened by and for European Baptists, held in Berlin in 1908. Both Marshall and Rushbrooke were indebted to the very influential British Baptist, John Clifford, and both had undertaken further study in Germany. The British Baptist Union General Secretary, J. H. Shakespeare, also shared in the organization of this first European Baptist Congress, which attracted 1,800 delegates.

Following the terrible devastation of the First World War, the BWA asked J. H. Rushbrooke and C. A. Brooks, from New York, to survey religious, especially Baptist, life in post-war Europe and to report on what they found. The survey involved a grueling nine-week tour by Rushbrooke and Brooks, taking in Germany, Poland, the Baltic States, Sweden, Czechoslovakia, Ukraine, Austria, Hungary, Romania, the Balkans, Italy, Switzerland, and France. Seventy-two delegates from Baptist unions and conventions in Britain, America, Canada, Australia, and from eighteen continental European countries, then met in London from July 19 to 23, 1920, to hear reports from Rushbrooke and Brooks. There was a determination to give relief aid to the many devastated parts of Europe. A range of matters was discussed and actions were agreed. Among these was a proposal from Brooks and J. W. Ewing, representing American and British Baptist thinking, that Rushbrooke be appointed BWA Commissioner for Europe. This was unanimously and enthusiastically affirmed. A statement was produced on religious liberty, with special reference to Europe: "Religious liberty places all men on exactly the same basis before God and in relation to human governments. We therefore call on the governments of the world to delay no longer in enacting into law this priceless human right." There was evidence of growing European Baptist cooperation.

Further devastation in Europe during the Second World War intensified the desire among Baptists to find ways of working together more effectively. The hope of churches and Baptist unions in Europe to have a pan-European organization with a specific European identity and mission vision was brought into focus in the context of a BWA European Conference held in London from August 13 to 17, 1948. At this Conference a subcommittee was appointed to look at closer Baptist cooperation in Europe, and this subcommittee recommended:

> That the Baptists of Europe be encouraged to plan for a closer fellowship between the various national Baptist bodies, and that the European members of the Executive Committee of the BWA constitute a planning committee to form a European Baptist Committee on Co-operation to further Baptist work in Europe.

In fact, the subcommittee, or the Committee of Seven, as it came to be known, which was established to create the EBF, recommended to the unions in Europe rather more than this. The Committee of Seven (followed by a later group which prepared an appropriate Constitution and By-Laws), proposed a European body with a structure which had obvious resonance with the theology and structures of the national unions. The EBF declares in its statutes that only unions, conventions, or similar Baptist bodies can be members. Here the strongly ecclesial thinking of the EBF has been clearly expressed.

The Committee of Seven was drawn from Britain, Denmark, Germany, Italy, France, Switzerland, and Holland. It represented several significant streams of Baptist life in Europe, including English General Baptists, English Particular (Calvinistic) Baptists, churches across Europe stemming from the work of Oncken, and those who valued the heritage of the Anabaptists, especially the Swiss and the Dutch. The Committee thus reflected the mixed heritage of European Baptist life from the seventeenth to the nineteenth centuries. At their first meeting in Switzerland, on October 8, 1949, it was significant that they moved away from the BWA Conference's suggestion for a European Baptist Committee of Cooperation, and instead proposed that the title of the new organization should be the European Baptist Federation. This clearly expressed their desire, after starting with the local gathering community of believers as the heart of an ecclesial expression, to spread outwards in relationship to other communities. Though the first initiative had, no doubt realistically, come from within the BWA, it was not seen by European Baptists to be theologically correct or appropriate for this new group to be a regional subdivision of the BWA.

It is noteworthy that the three members of the initial Committee of Seven who were asked to meet to produce the final detail of the first Constitution of the EBF included Henry Cook from Britain, who had given particular attention to Baptist ecclesiology. The other members were Bredahl Petersen of Denmark, and W. O. Lewis of the BWA staff. They met in Copenhagen on February 23, 1950 to plan the launch of the EBF. Cook noted the strength of the interdependent (rather than independent) principle elucidated in the Confessions of Faith of the early Baptists, and he commented that both General and Particular Baptists "deliberately linked their churches, both to steady one another in doctrine and explain themselves unitedly to the world, to aid one another in time of need and especially to propagate their views." Further, Cook argued:

It is interesting to note that this sense of unity that was so conspicuous a mark of early Baptist churches in England was even more strongly emphasized by the Anabaptist communities on the Continent. They never were and never sought to be Independents; on the contrary, whenever they were free enough from persecution to create an organization, they never failed to institute, after the example of the Waldenses and the Bohemian Brethren, a system with a general superintendency, an itinerant ministry, and a clearly defined interdependency of the local congregations.

To make the point absolutely clear (and no doubt take the strength of this conviction into the committee which established the EBF), Henry Cook made the following claim:

It comes then to this, that Baptists at the beginning were Congregationalists, but not Independents; that is to say, they believed in the gathered church. . . . But they set their faces against isolationism, and they regarded local churches as livingly related for the common ends of the Gospel.

Cook, Petersen, and Lewis gathered with representatives from ten countries, all Western European, at the Baptist Church in 48 Rue de Lille, in the center of Paris, on October 21, 1950, to take part in the formation of the EBF. Representatives from unions in Spain, Portugal, and Finland had also expressed a strong desire to be present, but had no funds for travel. Exchanging correspondence with the British Baptist General Secretary, M. E. Aubrey, at the end of September 1950, Lewis wrote:

I hope the European Baptist Federation which will soon be launched may contribute to the unification of the Baptist work in Spain as well as in all of Europe. The first meeting of the Council of the Federation will take place in Paris, October 19–22. It is understood that this Federation will be made up of representatives of Baptist Churches of all of Europe when it is fully organized.

Petersen and Cook were elected President and Vice-President respectively of the EBF. The purpose of the EBF was as set out above—the emphases being on evangelism, fellowship, mission, and mutual help. Mission beyond Europe found expression through the European Baptist Missionary Society, later the European Baptist Mission, which was established in 1954.

In the meantime, the Baptist Seminary in Rüschlikon, near Zürich, Switzerland, had been established in 1949. Baptists had for a long time been reflecting on the possibility of founding a theological institution in the heart of Europe. As early as 1908, there was public mention of an international school for theological training. When European Baptists gathered in the Congress in Berlin in that year a resolution was passed unanimously urging the establishment of "an international European Baptist College (*Hochschule*) in a central place." As part of the resolution there was a reminder to Baptists to continue supporting the existing institutions in Europe, to encourage the founding of others, if needed, and to establish a fund to provide scholarships to "allow especially gifted young men" who had completed studies in their own nation's seminaries to study further elsewhere. The resolution was aimed at the BWA as there was no European Baptist body to which the resolution could be forwarded. Speaking at the same Congress, C. E. Benander, Director of the Bethel Baptist Seminary in Stockholm, called for "a great European Baptist University" and opened up the idea that, whilst initial ministerial formation and theological education might be acquired in the home country of the student, there was a case for a Europe-wide institution to which the more able younger Baptists could go.

This vision was not able to be pursued at the time but it came to the fore again during the preparation for the 1920 BWA Meetings on Europe. Rushbrooke believed Prague had considerable potential as the location for a new Baptist seminary. It could serve especially evangelicals among Slav populations. However, at this stage there was little thought of European leadership for any such venture. Rather the establishment of any possible seminary was seen to be dependent on BWA initiative. In the official Minutes of the 1920 BWA Conference it was noted:

> The section regarding Czecho-slovakia [*sic*] is of peculiar interest. Here the Commissioners conferred with President Masaryk and with the Dean of the Protestant Theological Faculty. They find that of all Slav University centers Prague offers the largest opportunity for Baptist students.

The report was positive in echoing the need for a Central European seminary, but the matter was not pursued in the decades that followed. At the BWA Conference on Europe in 1948, which was timed to coincide with meetings of the Executive Committee of the BWA, the Southern Baptist Convention (SBC) took an initiative, reporting: "The Southern

Convention of the USA has voted US $200,000 for a seminary in Switzerland intended to serve the needs of South and Central Europe." A number of possibilities for the location of the seminary were discussed, including Rome, but Rüschlikon, Switzerland, became the location. This was a beautiful lakeside setting.

George Sadler, who was appointed to be the first Baptist Theological Seminary President, on an interim basis, was determined to make the institution useful within the European Baptist community. However, Sadler was approaching the end of his overseas service with the Foreign Mission Board (FMB) of the SBC and the need was for someone younger to take on the Seminary leadership. The person identified was a European, Josef Nordenhaug, then aged forty-seven, a Norwegian with a science degree from the University of Oslo. He had felt a call to ministry and studied at the Southern Baptist Theological Seminary in Louisville, KY, where he had gained a Master of Theology degree and later a doctorate in New Testament and Greek. He had served as an assistant pastor in Oslo, and then held pastorates in Kentucky and Virginia. Nordenhaug was elected and then inducted as Seminary President in 1950, and contributed much to the endeavors made by the Seminary within European Baptist life.

Although the Seminary was not owned by the EBF in its early decades, it helped to reinforce the theme of ecclesial fellowship in Europe, a theme which was central to the life of and developing vision of the EBF. This vision needed to be formulated more clearly. In 1956, at the EBF Council meeting (a Council meeting was convened each year in different places), held that year in Langesund, Norway, a Committee on the Constitution was established. Edwin Bell, from North America, writing to his Baptist colleagues in New York reflected:

> In many ways this meeting of the EBF Council was the best which has taken place so far in that there was the very definite disposition to look at the future of the Federation and its possibilities. This restatement of the functions of the organization came pretty much as the result of a rather long discussion on the future of the Federation and what it really ought to plan to do.

In the achieving of these possibilities, the role of the General Secretaries of the EBF was crucial. The secretaryship of the EBF was initially held by an American, W. O. Lewis, but since then Europeans have been the General Secretaries, as follows:

- Walter O. Lewis, American   1950–55
- Henry Cook, English   1955–59
- Erik Rudén ,Swedish   1959–65
- Ronald Goulding, English   1965–76
- Gerhard Claas, German   1976–80
- Knud Wümplemann, Danish   1980–89
- Karl Heinz Walter, German   1989–99
- Theodor Angelov, Bulgarian   1999–2004
- Anthony A. Peck, English   2004–21
- Alan Donaldson, Scotch   2021–

When he was appointed to the EBF position, Lewis was already an Associate General Secretary of the BWA. The others who followed as EBF Secretaries were to become Regional Secretaries for Europe of the BWA, in each case following the decision of the EBF to appoint them its General Secretary. Erik Rudén and Ronald Goulding were strongly connected to their home unions, in Sweden and Britain respectively. Gerhard Claas, from Germany, went on from the EBF to become General Secretary of the BWA, though his tenure of office at the BWA was tragically cut short by a fatal car accident. After his time of service as EBF Secretary, Knud Wümpelmann served a term as President of the BWA, from 1990 to 1995. Although European Baptists were very conscious of their European identity, this did not mean they wanted to be isolated from the rest of the Baptist world family.

Mission was a major concern for the EBF. In the early meetings of the EBF Council and Executive there are to be found many mission-orientated discussions and examples of hopes regarding mission initiatives. At the 1950 Paris meeting, for instance, the view was expressed that Spain was an open door for church planting and that Baptists in Hispanic America should be encouraged to engage in mission partnership with Spanish Baptists. At the Council meeting in Hamburg in 1951, prioritizing took place, and there was a focus on mission initiatives in Brussels, Iceland, and Greece. This emphasis on mission as a prime motive for local churches cooperating together nationally and internationally is the theme of the Confession of Faith drawn up by representatives of the

Austrian, German and Swiss unions between 1974 and 1977. Section 5, on Spiritual Gifts and Ministries (in translation), reads:

> Each local congregation is understood as a manifestation of the one body of Christ and is responsible for ordering its own life and ministry. These local congregations are bound together, not primarily through organizational ties, but by the one Lord and the one Spirit. The congregations strengthen each other through fellowship in the faith, and by learning from each other, through intercession and by mutual aid. Such things as structure of the congregation and denominational organization, administration and finance, institutions and works, are not ends in themselves, but are instruments of the mission of the church in this world.

The authors, drawn from these different German-speaking Baptist communities, cite passages from Paul's epistles in support of this stand. The language of being "bound together," of strengthening each other in a variety of ways, and of seeing this as being for "the mission of the church in this world" is striking.

It has been the view of Baptists in Europe that their mission involved more than witness to the gospel by word; it also involved witness in deeds and in a concern for a just society. Soon after the formation of the EBF Council and Executive, the issue of religious freedom was on the agenda. Inevitably, this grew in importance with the establishment of the Socialist states of the Eastern European bloc and the work of many Communist governments in the suppression of Christian faith, including Baptists and other evangelical Christians. This became an area that was to develop and was to become a significant feature of the work of the EBF Council and, later, of successive General Secretaries. One initiative that gave help to those in the Eastern bloc was the work of the Books and Translations Committee of the EBF. This provided Bible commentaries and theological books for Russian-speaking ministers. Although much was done by Baptists to support their suffering fellow-Baptists during the "cold war" period, it was only after the collapse of Communism that the EBF Council, meeting in Dorfweil, Germany (in 1994), accepted a recommendation from a Task Force consisting of Thorwald Lorenzen (Germany), Per Midteide (Norway), Ebbe Holm (Denmark), Anatoly Pchelincev (Russia), and Theo Angelov (Bulgaria) to:

- Collect material on human rights' violations in each country;
- Provide prayer information for the unions;

- Organize a consultation for a network of lawyers;

- Provide informational material for an annual EBF Human Rights'
  Day;

- Promote religious freedom for all people.

At that meeting a continuing Human Rights Task Force was established to develop this as an important activity within the overall mission of the EBF.

Across Europe, there was not only Baptist involvement in active mission of all kinds, there was also a concern to articulate Baptist convictions. In the 1960s some discussions took place about the possibility of the EBF establishing a European Baptist Theological Journal, and there was a positive feeling that this could happen, though the project did not get off the ground until some years later. In order to make Baptist convictions and concerns more widely known, from 1969 onward the annual EBF Council began to produce and pass Resolutions on important issues. These were generally facilitated by a Resolutions Committee, formed at each Council meeting, that would work on topics presented to them by member unions, and would submit a proposed text to the full Council. Topics for such resolutions over the years have included consideration of many major issues, for example:

- Peace and Reconciliation among peoples (1969, 1975, 1979, 1982, 1984, 1986);

- Freedom of Religion (1969, 1977, 1992, 1997, 1999);

- Justice and Human Rights (1980, 1984, 1991, 1998);

- Suffering, Dispossessed, and Homeless People in the World (1969, 1975, 1979);

- Rwanda and Burundi (1972);

- The Helsinki Final Act (1975, 1977, 1980, 1984, 1985);

- Migrants and Immigrant Workers (1975, 1987);

- The Evangelistic Task (1975, 1978, 1983, 1990, 2003);

- Nuclear Disarmament (1977, 1979, 1981, 1983, 1985, 1987);

- The Middle East (1978, 1982, 2006);

- The International Year of the Child (1978, 1979);

- International Youth Year (1984, 1985);

- Racism (1985);

- Dignity as Human Beings (1981);

- Unemployment (1983);

- Interchurch Conversations (1982);

- The European Vision and Structures (1979, 1990);

- Women and Christian Leadership (1987);

- Human Trafficking (2003);

- Eradication of Poverty and Forgiveness of Debts of Poorest Nations (1998, 1999, Jubilee 2000, 2005—the Micah Challenge);

- Millennium—Proclamation of the Good News (1998);

- The Caucasus Conflict (1999);

- The Balkan Conflict (1999);

- Terrorist attacks in USA, 9/11 (2001);

- The War in Iraq (2002, 2004).

The EBF Council is the most visible annual expression of the solidarity of Baptist communities of Europe and the Middle East and the gathering is important for fellowship, discussion, and decision-making.

After the retirement of Knud Wümpelmann as General Secretary in 1989, Karl Heinz Walter from Germany emerged as the new General Secretary. Previous General Secretaries had to work in a deeply divided Europe. The challenges for the EBF of operating in a post-communist world became clear at the 1990 EBF Council at De Bron, in the Netherlands, as the EBF faced issues of Baptist identity (which would take up much of the time of the Council throughout the 1990s), and the challenge to adapt EBF life as many new Baptist unions were created in Eastern Europe. The early atmosphere was euphoric, with much talk of a new era of religious freedom and of evangelism. Led by Karl Heinz Walter, the EBF was very active in the provision of humanitarian aid for Eastern Europe. Baptist Response-Europe was formed by the EBF (later renamed European Baptist Aid). In the years following the end of the Communist regimes the euphoria lessened, and the EBF and the unions faced many challenges of post-modernism and of new laws constraining the rights of churches in several countries throughout the region. These challenges were taken up by Theodor Angelov, who followed Karl Heinz Walter and was the first

EBF General Secretary from an Eastern European country, and then by Tony Peck.

In 2003, the EBF launched the Indigenous Mission Project (IMP) to support men and women to plant new churches in their own contexts. By 2008 there were sixty indigenous missionaries serving in twenty-five countries, and since then many others have been added, not necessarily under the auspices of the EBF. Over two hundred missionaries have been supported in total, and a significant number of European Baptist unions have worked with transcontinental mission organizations in North America to take the church planting work forward. Since the inception of IMP there have been, at various times, twenty-three mission partners. In the early years of the IMP, about 80 percent of the funding came from North America, but by 2015 70 percent was coming from Europe. The missionaries have been predominantly serving in Central and Eastern Europe, Central Asia and the Middle East. The project has been overseen by a Polish Baptist pastor, Daniel Trusiewicz, who had earlier studied at Rüschlikon.

In the late 1980s, as the EBF was about to embark on a new phase in its life, a sea change took place with regard to the Baptist Seminary at Rüschlikon which, in retrospect, occurred at the right time. The Foreign Mission Board of the SBC took the decision to hand over ownership of the property of the Baptist Theological Seminary to the EBF. It was a change which helped to bring a new sense of cohesiveness to the EBF and, as can also be seen in retrospect, was an important preparatory move before the collapse of Communism in Europe in 1989/1990. John David Hopper was appointed President of the Seminary in this time of significant change. He was a historian and a linguist with a fine pedigree of service with the FMB, especially relating to Baptists in southeast Europe, including Yugoslavia. FMB president, R. Keith Parks, handed over the keys of the Seminary to EBF General Secretary, Knud Wümpelmann, on May 28, 1988.

However, the subsequent defunding of the Seminary by the SBC meant that staying in Rüschlikon, an expensive location, became financially untenable. The November 1993 meeting of the Seminary Board of Trustees proved crucial in the decision-making process. Here options for a move either to Prague or to Berlin were discussed. It was finally agreed that Prague represented the best future option. There were a number of reasons for this. Prague was a cultural meeting point between the Slavic and Latin worlds. Also, costs would be lower than Berlin. Karl Heinz

Walter wrote to all forty-six member unions and twenty-five replied. Not all were in favor of Prague, but the consensus pointed that way in the light of the considerations that were put forward, resulting in the EBF Executive Committee resolving, in May 1994, that property should be purchased in Prague. The Jenerálka site, in an area of natural beauty on the outskirts of the city, had already been identified as suitable for the needs of the Seminary by a joint Board of Trustees and EBF Executive Committee search group.

As a result of further decisions by the EBF Council, the Prague campus became a center primarily for international post-graduate study. With Keith Jones as Rector, the International Baptist Theological Seminary (as it became), usually abbreviated to IBTS, gained validation to offer post-graduate degrees at Masters and Doctoral level from the University of Wales, and the seminary was recognized as a private University by the Czech Ministry of Education with the Rector becoming a member of the Czech Rector's Conference. This formal level of recognition within the European Union had not been possible in Switzerland. This focus continued until 2014, when the work of the Seminary moved to Amsterdam, where the International Baptist Theological Study Centre, as it was re-named, began to operate as a Centre within the Free University of Amsterdam. In Amsterdam it offered a Master's degree of the University of Manchester and doctoral degrees through the Free University, as well as a Doctor of Ministry degree in cooperation with Acadia Divinity School in Nova Scotia, Canada.

Throughout all the period of the life of the EBF, leadership has been important. Authority does not come down from above, but is found in the life of the EBF itself. As well as the role of the General Secretaries, and the part that has been played by the leadership of the Seminary, the office of President of the EBF carries with it the clear general leadership of the EBF, and the President chairs meetings of the Council and oversees Congresses. The presidency is an honorary and essentially part-time post held for a maximum of two years. Most of the Presidents in the history of the EBF have been senior officers within their own unions or in some cases seminary rectors and they have been unable to devote much time between meetings to the affairs of the EBF. Therefore, the office of General Secretary has had a major role, working closely with others, within the life of the EBF. The holders of this office have been much more than administrators and letter writers, but rather "living letters" (a term from the New Testament that has been used), developing the policies of the

EBF and moving between the unions strengthening the ties that bind together European and Middle Eastern Baptists.

This work of strengthening ties has also gone beyond Baptist life. European ecumenical leadership has had a significant number of Baptists involved, in both national and in pan-European ecumenical work. In ecclesial terms, it is Baptists, more than any other denominational grouping in Europe, who have sought to foster a pan-European ecclesial identity. It is also Baptists who appear to have the greatest spread of any Christian World Communion denominational group across the nations of Europe. This Baptist presence has often been unrecognized in studies of Christianity or of religion more broadly in Europe. Admittedly Baptists cannot claim anything approaching the numerical strength of the Catholic Church, the Orthodox Churches or some of the major Protestant traditions in Europe. However, they have a European identity which is arguably stronger than that of the other Protestant denominations. This is to a very large extent due to the work of the European Baptist Federation.

Bibliography

Jones, Keith G. *The European Baptist Federation*. Milton Keynes: Paternoster, 2009.

Barnes, Irvin. *Truth Is Immortal: The Story of Baptists in Europe*. London: Carey Kingsgate, 1955.

Green, Bernard. *Crossing the Boundaries: A History of the European Baptist Federation*. Didcot: Baptist Historical Society, 1999.

Jones, Keith G., and Ian M. Randall, eds. *Counter-Cultural Communities: Baptistic Life in Twentieth-Century Europe*. Milton Keynes: Paternoster, 2008.

Peck, Anthony A. "European Baptist Federation." In *A Dictionary of European Baptist Life and Thought*, edited by J. H. Y. Briggs, 179–81. Milton Keynes: Paternoster, 2009.

Pierard, Richard V., ed. *Baptists Together in Christ 1905–2005: A Hundred-Year History of the Baptist World Alliance*. Birmingham, AL: Samford University Press, 2005.

Randall, Ian M. *Communities of Conviction: Baptist Beginnings in Europe*. Prague: European Baptist Federation, 2009.

Randall, Ian M., et al., eds. *Baptist Identities: International Studies from the Seventeenth to the Twentieth Centuries*. Carlisle: Paternoster, 2006.

Woodfin, Carol. *An Experiment in Christian Internationalism: A History of the European Baptist Theological Seminary*. Macon, GA: Baptist History and Heritage Society, 2013.

21

The Evangelical Baptist Church of Georgia

An Experiment in Inculturation

Ilia Osephashvili

Introduction

THE EVANGELICAL BAPTIST CHURCH of Georgia has been actively going through an inculturation process during the last twenty years. This process started as a result of church reforms of which Archbishop Malkhaz Songhulashvili is in charge.

The history of the Evangelical Baptist Church in Georgia goes back to German missionary Martin Kalweit, who came to Georgia in the 1860s and set up the first Baptist congregation in Tbilisi. Kalweit was in touch with Johann Gerhard Oncken, who founded Baptist congregations in Germany and other countries on the European continent. Tbilisi was the place from where the Baptist movement spread in the Caucasus and throughout the whole Russian Empire. Many Molokans, who suffered persecution because of their faith, joined the newly founded church, and had, at first, a great impact on its liturgy and ecclesiology. As the Orthodox Church was responsible for the persecutions, the Molokans had a strained relationship with this church and transferred their negative attitude into the newly-founded Baptist Church. The Baptist movement was also culturally isolated. From the day of its foundation the Baptist

Church has been spreading God's Word with great enthusiasm, and because of such active work, the first Baptist martyr, Illia Kandelaki, who had worked in the Baptist Church since the 1920s, was killed in 1926. Kandelaki is considered the first Georgian who founded a Baptist congregation in Georgia, and since then the church felt the need to be close to the local culture.

It must be admitted that the Georgian Baptist Church's identity was based on a negative attitude towards the Orthodox Church and Georgian culture for a long time. Baptists were Baptists because they were not Orthodox. There was a negative attitude towards all kinds of liturgical expressions, and there was a huge wall that separated the church and its surrounding society. As but one example one can remember that Georgia is famous for its grape culture. If, therefore, a Baptist invites a guest and does not put wine on the table or does not dance Georgian folk dances because drinking or dancing is considered a sin, such attitudes dissociate the church from society. Being a good Christian means to live in a society with healthy principles and values; each church is called to be like Jesus Christ. Christ's attitude towards his people, country, society, and culture should be exemplary for any church in any culture. Jesus Christ preached about the kingdom of heaven, but at the same time he fully shared the features of his culture. As related in the Gospel of John (chapter 2) Jesus offered better quality wine to the guests of the wedding party than they had previously consumed. Christ's whole activity is the confirmation that any church can build the Lord's heaven without isolating itself from the local culture of the country it lives in.

The Reforms

The sign of starting reforms in the Evangelical Baptist Church of Georgia was the day when the church leader archbishop Malkhaz Songulashvili appeared in a cassock in front of the congregation. Such behavior caused displeasure in the church. Thus was the logic: "Ministers never wore cassocks at services before, and that's why we can't accept this." But they could not agree on why ministers had to wear civilian clothes. Later, an altar appeared in the church, and then some frescos connected to church holidays were unveiled, which are signs of the Baptist Church's cultural heritage and not so-called "worshiped" icons. Candles have also been used as well as a censer for frankincense, etc. The liturgy has been enriched as there are now elements of both western and eastern Christian traditions. The liturgy had been very simple before the reforms and only featured preaching, prayer and singing. The church elders would lead the service in civilian clothes. Two or three preachers preached during each service, touching many themes in their sermons at the same time, and it was really hard for the congregants to remember and analyze the sermon content.

According to the Baptist tradition, each local church is free to choose its liturgical style. So Tbilisi Cathedral, where the reforms took place, is no exception: The Cathedral started to use a liturgical calendar, which includes Christian holidays (Christmas, the Holy Child's presentation, Baptism, Palm Sunday, Holy Thursday, Good Friday, Easter, Ascension Day, Pentecost) as well as various saints' memorial days. By remembering Basil the Great, Gregor of Nazianz, Thomas Akuinel, Augustine of Hippo, and all God's servants, the Baptist church confirms that it considers itself a part of Christ's whole church. This church has also given the Virgin Mary her rightful place. A fresco of the Virgin Mary and infant Christ hangs in the Baptist Cathedral. The church leaders and bishops wear a Pangaea with Mary's and Christ's image. Before, the Baptist Church looked with suspicion not only at the saints but at Mary as well. This was in reaction to a revival of the cult of folk saints. According to Baptist belief, such a point of view about the cult of Mary and the saints overshadows Jesus Christ and his deeds which was unacceptable, as the Baptist Church is based on Holy Scripture alone. However, since the church began to look more seriously at this issue, it returned Mary and all the saints to their proper place.

The church then started to use a lectionary—i.e., a collection of scripture readings. It is in line with the synagogical tradition which divided the Pentateuch into fifty-three parts for the fifty-three Sabbaths of the year. The first lectionary had been made for the Jerusalem divine service, and it is presumed its Georgian version goes back to the fifth century. The Baptist Church uses a lectionary which was devised by an ecumenical group of students and based on a three-year course of Bible reading. The canonical books are read once every three years. It was also a novelty for the church that the foundation of the ministers' Sunday sermons is the Scriptures as presented in the lectionary for that particular day. The congregation is prepared for the Scripture, and thematic preaching makes it easier to understand separate chapters and verses of the Bible. The church restored a ceremonial reading of Holy Scripture so that God's word and not the preaching or the preacher is at the center of the divine service. Each Sunday and Wednesday, a specially prepared group of readers read God's word according to the lectionary. Preaching, the Litany, and liturgical dance help the Scriptural interpretation. According to this tradition, full concentration is focused on God's word during the service.

As in all other churches, the Eucharist is at the heart of the service in the Evangelical Baptist Church. On different occasions the Eucharist is celebrated according to the ecumenical liturgies of James, Basil the Great, John Chrysostom, Mark and the ecumenical Lima Liturgy. The ministers and the congregation prepare in a special way for the celebration. As a sign of this, special vessels—the Holy Chalice and Eucharist Plate—are used. Not only Baptists but everyone who lives in peace before the Lord and is in good standing in his/her church and neighborhood may receive the Eucharist as the Eucharist Table belongs to Christ and not to any church. Each person who is present at the Eucharist must decide whether or not to participate.

Such an attitude towards the Eucharist may be perceived as unsupportable, but Holy Scripture can teach otherwise. When Jesus had his Last Supper with his disciples, he did not say, "You all are worthy to take part in the Eucharist except Judas." Jesus Christ spoke about the sacrifice he was to make for humankind's redemption and thus explained the essence of the Eucharist to his disciples. Later, he hinted on the expected betrayal, though without naming the betrayer. At last he passed bread and wine to Judas together with the other disciples. After this act of Christ the responsibility of taking bread and wine went to each disciple separately. It totally depended on them with what kind of heart they would receive it.

When the church thinks that it is the host of the Eucharist table, it defines the rules and laws according to its way of thinking who should and who should not take part in the Eucharist. More often than not, these rules do not derive from Holy Scripture. For example, some Baptist churches will not allow people to receive the Eucharist if they were not baptized in the Baptist tradition. A person baptized in the Orthodox Church or other churches would not be perceived as a Christian. They would not allow a woman wearing trousers or having makeup to receive the Eucharist either. In such cases the church will not consider brothers or sisters from a different church as Christians, even though they are also saved by faith in Christ and lead a healthy Christian life. In the church where Jesus is the host, humans are given the freedom to take part in the Eucharist or not, depending on what their hearts tell them and how pure their consciences are before God. These are the guiding principles of the Evangelical Baptist Church of Georgia concerning its Eucharist celebration.

As mentioned before, the cassock was introduced for the ministers, and much could be said about "spiritual clothing" according to Holy Scripture. Here, however, this issue should be looked at from a cultural point of view. Georgia is a country where the clergy have been wearing special clothing for more than fifteen centuries, distinguishing them from the "normal" population. Any citizen in Georgia cannot imagine a minister without a cassock. It was completely strange for our culture in recent years to watch Baptist pastors preach or do wedding or burial ceremonies while wearing white shirts and ties. The cassock and other visual means became a bridge between the Baptist community and our national culture.

Today, Baptist deacons, pastors, and bishops who wear cassocks preach the same gospel as they did while wearing suits and ties. They remain faithful to Baptist principles. All local congregations have complete freedom in choosing to use liturgical clothing or not, or what kind of clothing to use. One can see ministers wearing a cassock or jeans sitting next to each other in the Tbilisi Evangelical Baptist Peace Cathedral, and the congregation listens to their preaching with equal attention. According to the "Liturgical View Document" which was approved by the church meeting in 2005, there are three categories of liturgical clothing: (1) minimal—which means to wear only the minister's white collar (symbol of God's faithfulness); (2) middle—which means to wear the robe, minister's inner clothes, and cross. Bishops bear a shepherd's crozier, cross, and Panaghia; (3) ceremonial—which is worn only on Christian holidays. It consists of the Philon (Chasauble)—symbolizing the vestment in Christ; the Epitrachyl (stole)—symbolizing the yoke of Christ; the Belt—symbolizing a firm standing in Christ; the Epigonation—symbolizing the sword, Christ's word; the Cuffs—symbolizing cleansed hands; the Mitre—symbolizing the guidance of the Holy Spirit; and the Crozier—symbolizing pastoral responsibility.

Baptism by immersion is performed in the church, as in all Baptist churches. People who understand the essence of faith are baptized; the baptism age is not strictly determined, but infants or little children who have no faith perception are not baptized. People of any age who confirm that they received Christ as personal savior and have a vital relationship with God are baptized and anointed with oil. The anointing used to be unusual in Baptist churches, although it is often mentioned in the New Testament.

Other rites include the presentation and dedication of babies, wedding ceremonies, anointment of ministers, and burial ceremonies. On holidays the services are enriched by liturgical dances performed by the dance group. Of course, liturgical dance is unfamiliar to Eastern Christian culture, and consequently there was, at first, not a comfortable attitude towards it in the church. Liturgical dance was unacceptable for some people, because to their minds the church became a concert hall. For some, even Georgian folk dances were idolatry, although liturgical dance has its own place in the Holy Scripture, and it was conducted to worship God. Accompanied by thematic music, liturgical dance brings forth many deep emotions in people and revives episodes of Holy Scripture.

During the reforms, special attention was given to the Eastern tradition of fasting. Besides individual fasting, when a person chooses the day, type and duration of fasting by him/herself, there were introduced Christmas and Easter fasts, when the church pays special attention to care for the ill, oppressed, and socially unprotected people. Also, the church became actively involved in dealing with ecological problems, which indicates that caring of God's creation is part of the church's responsibility as well.

Reforms were implemented in terms of the church's ministries. There had been only two consecrations before—of deacons and pastors. As a result of the reforms a third office, that of a bishop, was added. The bishop is a minister who is responsible for congregations of a particular region in the country. The archbishop is the first shepherd among equals. Of course, this does not mean complete denial of congregational polity and a complete move to an Episcopal structure. Rather some Episcopal principles are added to a congregational structure, which somehow balances the church's work in our culture.

The Place of Women in the Church

A very important feature of the Evangelical Baptist Church of Georgia is the ordination of women to the ministry. To be sure, there are different attitudes towards this issue in different churches of the world. There have been deaconesses and female pastors in the Baptist Church since the 1970s. In 2008 a woman bishop joined their ranks.

The valued service of women has not been unfamiliar to Georgian culture. It is significant that Georgia was converted to Christianity by a woman missionary—Saint Nino, who came to Georgia from Cappadocia in the fourth century and brought the Christian faith. She preached the word of God and healed the sick. As a result of her work, Christianity became the state religion in 337 AD. It is obvious that Saint Nino was a special minister. Her words and acts were blessed and given power by God. Can we forbid Saint Nino, who converted Georgia to Christianity, to serve in her own established church only because she is a woman? The great Georgian poet Shota Rustaveli, in his poem in the twelfth century, said: "The lion's whelp is a lion, be it male or female," and this equality refers to all fields.

Christ has erased the borders not only between nationalities and cultures, but between male and female as well. "For you are all sons of God through faith in Christ Jesus. For all of you who were baptized into Christ have clothed yourselves with Christ. There is neither Jew nor Greek, there is neither slave nor free, there is neither male nor female; for you are all one in Christ Jesus" (Gal 3:26–28). Doing away with borders does not mean to lose one's identity, but complete religious and social equality. We all know that the Lord assigned Peter as the disciples' leader: "I say to you that you are Peter, and upon this rock I will build My church; and the gates of Hades shall not overpower it" (Matt 16:18). It was the apostle Peter who had to lead the church, which was born on the day of Pentecost.

The first mission of the church had to be the announcement of Christ's crucifixion and resurrection. Christ gave this honor first to a woman: Mary. It was a woman who was the first to announce the greatest truth to the world, Christ's resurrection, and it was a woman who brought the message of the resurrected Christ to Georgian civilization for the first time. Could Jesus not have shown himself to Peter at first? Was it not Jesus who assigned him as the head of the disciples? But Jesus showed himself to a woman first and pointed to the priestly anointing of women by this act. Can we forbid Mary, God's first and faithful witness, to do valuable service only because she is a woman? We already see women deaconesses serving actively with the apostle Paul several years after the church's foundation. The apostle Paul mentions a woman minister—Phoebe—who was anointed as a deaconess at Cenchrea, in the last chapter of his letter to the Romans, when he greets the spiritual brothers and sisters (Rom 16).

Changes and the Discerning of Different Traditions

Today's Georgian Evangelical Baptist Church liturgy is a mix of different church liturgical elements, which sometimes causes misunderstandings in society. It has often been said that the Georgian Evangelical Baptist Church lost its face and is trying to imitate different churches by combining diverse liturgies.

As we have mentioned before, there are different attitudes towards the Eastern and Western traditions merging inside the church. All kinds of changes are painful. When a congregation has attended services for many years and is used to a particular liturgy, and on one beautiful day the congregants are presented with a completely new and different liturgy, it will, of course, not be received only with joy. The Baptist community was no exception. The logic is such: When the author of this chapter started attending services, pastors wore suits while preaching, and we sang Protestant hymns; there was only one thing written on the church wall: "God is Love"; we did not have any bishops, let alone a woman bishop; we did not have any special liturgies, and simplicity and modesty were our signature. But now everything is changed head over heels. In reality, a person does not become a Baptist because of accepting or not accepting Orthodox or Catholic, or other churches' traditions or rituals, but being faithful to Baptist principles. These principles include: Freedom of faith and conscience, the separation of state and church, priesthood of all believers, autonomy of the local church, and baptism of believing Christians.

It will be no surprise that there were acute discussions and arguments around the reforms among the clerical and lay people working in the church. A special conference to discuss these issues was held in the small town of Likani, near Borjomi, in 2002, when the Evangelical Baptist Church of Georgia had to make its decisions about the reforms. The European Baptist Federation's general secretary at that time, Dr. Karl-Heinz Walter of Germany, was especially invited to this conference. Almost all the church representatives agreed that the church was there for society and for the people and not only for itself. "The church for the people and not the church for the church only" was the concept which had decisive influence for the Georgian church's identity. Archbishop Malkhaz Songulashvili proclaimed that the content of the church's faith must stay forever, but that expressions of the forms and traditions of this faith must change continually. Since that time, there is only one tradition—that nothing is to become traditional in the church. The church is given complete freedom from God to change traditions and liturgical forms continually to be able to share its faith better among all kinds of cultures, epochs, and generations in languages understandable to them. As the Baptist movement is a fruit of Western reflections and as it must exist in the Orthodox culture in Georgia, its development is impossible without a spiritual bridge. People can be Baptists by faith but Orthodox by culture, and this is quite normal.

Any church must perceive of itself as a part of the universal church, otherwise it will not be a church but a sect which is separated from the one body. In fact, the problem for the Evangelical Baptist Church was in looking at itself as a part of the church universal. The problem was not the liturgical changes which had been difficult to accept. It had been written in the church constitution that the Evangelical Baptist Church of Georgia was the spiritual heir of the Baptist Church which was founded in 1867. But this paragraph was completely changed after the reforms and the church started to see its spiritual heritage from a different angle. During the fifth church meeting on December 16, 2005 the spiritual heritage was thus defined: "The Evangelical Baptist Church of Georgia is an heir of the Apostolic church of Christ and a part of the one universal, indivisible Church. It is a spiritual heir of Eastern Orthodoxy on the one hand and the Western radical Reformation on the other." A special place was given to the Nicea-Constantinople Creed, and the church highlighted its spiritual heritage by this act. As the Evangelical Baptist Church of Georgia views itself as part of the one universal church, it is not difficult for it to combine Eastern and Western Christian traditions and to accept any liturgical framework if it promotes the sharing of the faith.

When addressing the issue of spiritual heritage, the question may be raised how the Baptist Church which has only one and a half centuries of history in Georgia may claim apostolic heritage? Is it not rather a sect with a very short history? The answer appears to be simple as faith in Christ Jesus makes a person the apostles' spiritual heir, and this does not depend on being a member of a church with a ten-century or a ten-year history. A Christian of the twenty-first century is a spiritual heir of the apostle Peter, who himself is a spiritual heir of Christ, Abraham, and all the forefathers, by having faith in the Trinity. Paul states in the letter to the Galatians: "Even so Abraham believed God and it was reckoned to him as righteousness. Therefore, be sure that it is those who are of faith who are sons of Abraham" (Gal 3:6–7). Any person who lives in any epoch (despite his/her nationality, race, or gender) is Abraham's and Peter's spiritual heir if he/she believes in God. That is why it is no surprise if Baptists or members of other churches may claim to be part of the apostles' spiritual heritage.

It is completely different in Georgia. Here, the talk is not about the true faith and healthy spiritual values, but rather about which church is true and which is not. The answer depends on the age of the church and the apostolic succession of the bishops and not on faith in Christ. It should be, however, that all Christians, be they Orthodox, Catholics, Baptists, Pentecostals, Charismatics, or whatever, are brothers and sisters, because they believe in one and the same God and recognize Jesus Christ as their Savior. If we follow this line of thinking, God's heaven is not only what the Orthodox Church does, or what Catholics, Anglicans, or other Protestant churches do, but what these churches do together.

According to this concept, the church is the one body which consists of Orthodox, Catholic, Anglican, and all the other Protestant churches. If this is true, the doors are wide open for Eastern and Western traditions in the Evangelical Baptist Church. Combining different church traditions and liturgical peculiarities is like gathering pearls which only enriches the church and brings no harm. When Jesus was asked which commandment is greater and more important in the law, his answer was: "You shall love the Lord your God with all your heart, and with all your soul, and with all your mind" (Matt 22:37). Mind and heart, intellect and emotion must be fully involved in our faith in and our knowledge of Christ. To serve God perfectly can be accomplished when these two components are combined. When a person listens to the preaching, his/her intellect is being fed. But he/she needs emotionally to feel the preached word for it to be fruitful. And this is where the liturgy comes into play. It is most significant that all five human senses are involved in the worship service. One listens to the word of God, looks at the fresco, smells the incense, feels the oil, and tastes the Eucharistic bread and wine. Saturating the simple liturgy with Eastern and Western Christian traditions only enriches the feeling a human needs for worshiping God.

When we take measures to combine different Christian traditions under one roof, we may encounter some kind of aggressive attitudes towards this move in the church, and each others' traditions may be looked at as radical. As mentioned above, all Christian congregations are assured only of the truth of their own church, otherwise people would not have become members of a particular church. All churches take for granted that they thoroughly fulfill God's will and that their services are held according to what has been handed down to us in the gospel, even though church members may not have read it.

My own experience had been for many years that I considered the Baptist Church with its faith commitment, traditions, habits, and liturgical forms as the only true church and that other churches were in one way or another wrong. The Orthodox service was unacceptable for me because I could not find certain elements of the liturgy in the gospel. It appeared to me as if all that was happening in the Baptist Church had been taken directly from the gospel. In the New and Old Testaments, we encounter only two rules and traditions of worship service, the temple and the synagogue services. Jesus Christ used to go to both temple and synagogue, and this highlights the importance of the two: "When he had come into the temple, the chief priests and the elders of the people came to Him as He was teaching" (Matt 21:23). In the Gospel of Luke it says: "And He came to Nazareth, where he had been brought up; and as was His custom, He entered the synagogue on the Sabbath, and stood up to read" (Luke 4:16). After Christ's crucifixion, resurrection, and ascension we again read that his followers, like their teacher, worshiped God in Jerusalem's temple and synagogue: "And day by day continuing with one mind in the temple, and breaking bread from house to house, they were taking their meals together with gladness and sincerity of heart" (Acts 2:46). Neither Jesus nor his disciples established a new form of a worship service. Christ did not tell his followers, "Do not recognize the temple or synagogue service because I give you a new liturgy and you must follow it from now on."

If we say that the church must depend on the Holy Scriptures for its services and that everything must be done as it is written in God's word, we would have to consider the synagogical liturgy as the only one; hence the church would not have needed to formulate new liturgies. But Jesus Christ foresaw that his church would soon go beyond the boundaries of Judea and Jerusalem and continue its mission in various countries and cultures. This is why Jesus did not pay much attention to certain expressions of faith when he was with his disciples. As believers are justified by their faith before God, this faith experience must be followed by equivalent forms of faith expressions, church polities, etc. Christ himself gave freedom to the church. According to this freedom, the church has two choices: It must directly take, as its model, the synagogical liturgy which is not obligatory in a non-Jewish environment, or it must choose and establish liturgical elements which it considers best for the local culture.

This is why it is meaningless to argue which liturgy or tradition is more "true": Eastern or Western, Orthodox or Baptist, etc. Any kind of liturgy and tradition must be seen as equally valuable for the churches, and they must recognize God's given diversity in them. Therefore, when using the Holy Scriptures as sole criterion, it is acceptable that within one and the same denomination local churches may have different forms of worship services in Georgia, Germany, the USA or any other place. Moreover, it is acceptable that a church in a city may be different from a church in a village because there are completely different cultures and traditions in both places. It is most significant that God's word becomes relevant for the people.

Conclusion

The Evangelical Baptist Church of Georgia is open for all Christian church traditions, and this will help to achieve a better exposure to God's word. It is acceptable for the church to follow Western as well as Eastern traditions and liturgical forms. However, it must be done in such a way that the church does not loose its identity and that it remains faithful to those principles and "distinctives" which are characteristic of Baptist churches. What unites all churches is faith and not liturgical forms or traditions. If this approach is taken seriously, it will help all Christians to see that the different denominations in the world, be they Orthodox, Protestant, or Roman Catholic, have much more in common than what separates them from each other. Each church must remember that it is part of the One, Holy, Apostolic, and Indivisible body of Christ, and that this unity will help each church to build the kingdom of heaven in that part and culture of the world where it serves God by his will and grace.

Bibliography

Songulashvili, Malhkaz. *Evangelical Christian Baptists of Georgia: The History and Transformation of a Free Church Tradition*. Waco, TX: Baylor University Press, 2015.

iv. From Latin America

2 2

Major Moments in the Baptist Story in Latin America

DINORAH B. MÉNDEZ

Introduction

IT IS IMPORTANT TO clarify at the outset that although the title establishes a discussion about major moments in the Baptist story, it is necessary to point out that this expression must not necessarily be understood in a triumphal or uncritical sense. In fact, the development of Baptist life has not always been positive or progressive. Sometimes it has been static or even regressive. At least, this has been the reality in Latin America in the last few decades, especially if Baptist growth is contrasted with the general Evangelical movement.

A case in point is the situation in Mexico which the author knows personally. Not to mention that there has been a profound crisis in Mexican Baptist life would not be honest. In particular, this crisis is evident in the institutional life and on the organizational or structural level. It is difficult to explain the reasons behind this crisis as a number of factors may have caused the situation. On the one hand, it is possible to see cultural customs, but also critical problems in the local churches such as lack of spiritual leadership, doctrinal deviations as well as ethical inconsistencies. On the other hand, many churches or local communities continue to be firm and faithful, but sometimes they display little involvement in the denominational organizations.

However, to examine and to reflect critically and realistically our history does not eliminate or diminish the joy to remember and celebrate the great work that God has accomplished in our midst. The words of a friend seem very appropriate: "The gifts men and women were given by our God produces deep emotions as we reflect the Baptist history in . . . Latin America!"[1] By exploring some examples of the struggles and accomplishments of Latin American Baptists we may recognize both our Baptist heritage and identity and may appreciate them even more as both were developed and communicated in an adverse context: The Baptist movement was a dissident religion. Finally, this essay will at the end explore some ideas as to how Baptists in Latin America can face the challenges and opportunities of the twenty-first century.

Historical Highlights of Latin American Baptists

Latin American Baptists should celebrate the emergence of the Baptist movement in the seventeenth century because they should remember that they have much older roots in history than their own beginnings in the nineteenth century. They should take advantage of this exercise of remembrance to review their history and to value the common Baptist heritage along with the development and challenges they faced in their context. Moreover, a celebration and historical reflection of Latin American processes can be much more enriched if both the similarities and the differences in the development of the stories of Baptists around the world and through different epochs are kept in mind. Then, the analysis of the Latin American Baptist history should be less unilateral and more multilateral. Obviously, to write a history of the Baptists in Latin America is not the purpose here; that is a huge task, and few have risked doing so even after years of continued investigation. The work of Professor Justo Anderson stands out;[2] others are more concerned with a regional or local approach. Therefore, the following section is only a selection of representative cases of a history almost two hundred years old.

The common pioneer of Baptist work in Latin America was the Scottish Baptist Diego Thomson[3] who arrived to Argentina in 1818 pre-

---

1. Clelia Machinandiarena, "El Progreso del Trabajo Bautista en América Latina: Argentina," Personal email correspondence from June 28, 2009.

2. Anderson, *Historia de los Bautistas*.

3. Méndez, "History and Development," 57–58.

cisely during the Wars of Independence (1810–24). Thomson was on good terms with the leaders of the independence movement throughout the continent, such as: José de San Martín from Argentina, Bernardo O'Higgins from Chile, and Simón Bolívar from Venezuela. The liberal ideas of education were very different from those of the colonial period which had been controlled by the Roman-Catholic Church. Thomson worked for the British and Foreign School Society, an educational organization that promoted the Lancastrian or monitorial method which represented an advanced pedagogical system at the time. Thomson was also associated with the British and Foreign Bible Society, so that he promoted the distribution of the Bible simultaneously with his educational projects. Thomson traveled throughout Latin America, from Chile and Argentina to Mexico under the banner of education and with the purpose of forming a Latin American society. Leaders of the independence movement and even some liberal Catholics decided to join Thomson's project. It served as an opening of the Catholic context toward a new reality and was somehow a preparation for the time when the Baptist missionaries started to come in the second half of the nineteenth century.[4] On the other hand, in spite of this common "pre-history," Latin American Baptists have a multilateral origin or diverse sources. It seems necessary to turn now to at least some cases that may exemplify the different origins.[5]

A pioneer of Baptists in Argentina was Pablo Besson (1848–1932), a scholar and pastor from Switzerland, who had studied in Germany. While he was studying the New Testament, he became a Baptist and served as missionary in France with support of the Mission Board of the American Baptists. A great number of immigrants came to Argentina as well as Brazil, and a group of French immigrants wrote to Besson and asked for a pastor. When Besson did not find a candidate and as he was single, he decided to accept the invitation himself. He sold everything to buy his ticket and arrived in 1881 to work among the French colony. He soon encountered Catholic fanaticism and Catholic monopoly in many social spheres, such as the cemeteries which were off-limits to non-Catholic citizens. This confrontational situation motivated him to be actively involved in the fight for religious liberty. He always tried to maintain a

---

4. Cf. Martínez-García, *Escocés distribuidor.*

5. I am grateful to several friends for providing information about the Baptist work in their countries or in the Continent in general: Escobar, "Los Bautistas," 30–34; Machinandiarena, email cited; Moreno, "History and Baptist Tradition"; Scialabba, "La Libertad Religiosa."

balance between his tasks as pastor and evangelist and his outstanding activities as a respected and dedicated politician and journalist.

In the case of Brazil, immigrants from the southern part of the USA came to live in Brazil during the Civil War in their country. In 1871 they asked the Southern Baptist Convention to send missionaries and pastors in order to take care of their spiritual needs and to evangelize them. The Baptist pioneers were the Bagby family who arrived in 1881, to be followed a year later by the Taylor family. The intense immigration since 1892 brought Baptists from Germany, Hungary, Lithuania, and Bulgaria; their churches cooperated with the national churches to form regional associations. In 1901 the publication of the *Jornal Batista* started which met important educative and associative needs. The Brazilian Baptist Convention was organized on July 22, 1907.

Missionaries James Hickey and Thomas Westrup were pioneers of Baptist work in Mexico; they began their ministry before 1860 and founded the First Baptist Church of the country in Monterrey in 1864 during a time when there was no religious freedom. Later, following the passing of new laws, including one on religious freedom (although it supported mere tolerance rather than liberty), missionaries arrived from both the Northern and Southern Baptists to consolidate the work. On September 13, 1903 the National Baptist Convention of Mexico was organized. The Journal *La Luz Bautista* has been published since 1885.[6]

The South American countries of Colombia, Ecuador, Perú, and Bolivia make up a region that was characterized by the presence of an ultraconservative Catholicism and a deeply popular and indigenous religiosity. Canadian Baptists sent the first missionary, Archibald B. Reekie, to Bolivia in 1899. He tried to avoid confrontations with Catholics and started his work as an educator of children and young people who were interested in learning English. This put him in contact with liberal politicians. In other parts of the subcontinent a similar mode of procedure for achieving religious ends was used which was a key aspect for the insertion of Baptists in Latin America. The work of Reekie was well received, and as he never forgot his evangelistic task in the midst of his educational work, new churches began to emerge. An interesting quality of the Canadian missionaries was their great initiative in evangelism and their determination to pass on the vision to the national leaders. Thus, in 1936

6. Méndez, "History and Development," 59–64.

the Bolivian Baptist Union was organized, and one of its first projects was the missionary endeavor in the mineral centers of that country.[7]

Thus, one of the great similarities between the beginnings of the Baptist Movement in Holland and the beginnings in Latin America was its continued struggle for religious liberty that started with the first Baptists in the seventeenth century. It was also a main principle for the first Baptists in Latin America. Many of the pioneers arrived precisely at the same time that the liberal idealism of the nineteenth century encouraged the elite of the Independence movements. Later in different places some of the more radicals of the liberals looked for a limitation, or elimination, of the privileges of Catholicism in the newly independent countries.

This historical view of our origins even though it was presented here in only a few and contrasting cases, demonstrates the common roots that Baptists in Latin America have with the first Baptists in Holland. However, another way to see this connection is to take a look at our Baptist identity and heritage and appreciate both by exploring some of the struggles and accomplishments of Latin American Baptists especially as they developed in a difficult context.

A Review of the Baptist Developments in Latin America

Can a further connection be made between the history of the Baptist movement that emerged in Holland and extended to England over four hundred years ago and the emergence and extension of the Baptists in Latin America?

A tie that binds those histories of different times and places is the common and identical experience of persecution and intolerance, but at the same time the courage to question the socioreligious order with the proclamation of a new life, the practice of congregational democracy and the emphasis on the separation of church and state. All of this enables us to remember and to rescue for our collective memory both where we came from and how we came to be.[8]

As it has been established, in nearly all the countries of Latin America the influence of the Catholic Church has been an undeniable reality since the Spanish Conquest in the sixteenth century until today. The arrival of Baptists and other evangelicals in the nineteenth century met with the

7. Moreno, "History and Baptist Tradition," 2–3.
8. Escobar, "Los Bautistas," 40.

crude reality of intolerance, verbal aggression, and in many cases, as in Colombia, México, and other places, with the physical persecution.

This antecedent has marked Latin American Baptists until today in their struggle for religious freedom, many times evidenced in a profound anti-Catholicism. This author believes it is pertinent to mention that she is conscious of the hope of better relationships with the Catholic Church which some colleagues on this continent have entertained in recent times. For example, through UBLA (the Latin American Baptist Union) and even through the dialogs between the BWA and the Vatican there have been many new approaches. It is also necessary to say that the Catholic Church is multifaceted, and Baptists from other regions have not known the same kind of Catholicism that has been experienced in Latin America, and, perhaps, particularly in Mexico. For example, on one occasion Dr. Paul Fiddes[9] commented that for English Baptists the Catholics have been their allies and even their friends in the history and struggle for religious freedom against the official Church of England. He made this author to see the great difference between his context and hers. At the same time, it is pertinent to mention the curious way in which the Catholic Church has throughout history interpreted the principle of religious freedom. In times and places when and where that church was in power, it has condemned this freedom (Pius IX, 1864) and, of course, denied it to non-Catholics, while in times and places when and where this Church lacked power, it defended the practice, especially for itself. The principle can be summarized as follows: When the Catholic Church is in a majority, it grants as much tolerance to others as absolutely necessary, when in a minority, it demands as much freedom for itself as possible.

Therefore, although it is possible to celebrate especially the interchurch approaches, which produce fraternal relationships as well as a common and genuine struggle in favor of freedom, peace, and justice, it is necessary to recognize that for many Latin American Baptists these relationships are still viewed with distrust. This is especially true when the aggression of the Catholic Church is not only a thing of the past, but is today in many places renovating its force and retaking its economic, political and social power, including its popular and governmental control to obtain its former privileges. At least, this is happening in Mexico and it is from that reality this article is shared.[10]

9. Personal interview with Paul Fiddes, PhD, former director of Regent's Park College, Oxford University, Oxford, UK, September 2007.

10. In February 2016, Mexico, with a long and strong tradition of laity and

Then, this author thinks that when we study the history of the Latin American Baptists in the perspective of the celebration of Baptist history, the Latin American context must not be minimized or diminished, but must be taken fully into consideration. Sometimes the controversy with the Catholic Church is looked upon as something of a bygone era or as if those who remember it are haunted by a traumatic past. In fact, some Latin Americans try to ignore or to avoid the topic and pretend that it never happened. Others think that it is necessary to overcome that past, to forgive and try to imagine that such injuries never occurred; they think that forgiving and forgetting are necessary for the dialog and new approaches. In the humble opinion of this writer, history shows that those who forget it are condemned to repeat the same errors as their forebears. Moreover, it is absurd to deny something that is registered in our history and therefore has affected our identity and has formed the Latin American Baptist heritage; it also connects us with the Baptist heritage of four hundred years as free and dissident churches.

On the other hand, if we are to maintain alive in our collective memory the remembrances of the context in which the first Baptists lived on this continent and the context in which we continue to live today, should this or should it not be an impediment to dialog with people of a different faith? Then again it is indispensable to make constant reevaluations of this context to help us maintain our heritage and identity as Baptists in Latin America; it is of equal importance to ask our fellow Baptists from other regions to understand the particularities of our context when global projects are launched. This is especially true because in many places on this continent the struggle for religious liberty was not only an endeavor of the nineteenth and twentieth centuries, but must continue as it has not been attained because of a powerful and dominating Roman Catholic Church.

---

separation of church and state, displayed a contradiction of principles and practices. It received another visit (February 12–17, 2016) from Pope Francisco, not only in his capacity as the Head of Vatican State, but as the leader of a specific Church. The government was fully involved in the reception, celebration, and funding of this visit. This would be not the worst for religious minorities, but just two weeks prior to the pontiff's visit a group of ten families were persecuted and expelled from their ethnic community in the province of Jalisco for being Baptist believers, while both the local and the national governments did nothing against this violation of human rights and religious freedom as supported by Mexican law. This is a small sample of the lack of respect of minorities and the power of the Catholic Church in Mexico. In spite of the expressed law (spoken or written), the facts spoke loudly.

Another emblematic topic of our heritage has been the principle of separation of church and state. In most of the newly independent countries of Latin America it was possible to include this principle in their civil laws, at least since the second half of the nineteenth century. However, in most cases the separation was never practiced as the alliances between Catholicism and governments of various countries have remained intact since the end of that century until today. For this reason Latin American Baptists should pay close attention to new arrangements between some governments and some churches. Nowadays this is happening not only with the Catholic Church, but with some of the so-called megachurches of the Neo-Pentecostal movement.

In addition to those struggles the legacy of our Baptist heritage in relation to the practice of congregational democracy should be mentioned. The establishment and structure of democratic churches in a context of authoritarianism is a great contribution. Baptists appealed to the free will of the individuals to accept Christ and be baptized as believers and thus gave opportunity for the practice of democracy in the congregations. Congregational democracy generated time for discussion of ideas and projects and provided opportunities for all its members to participate and express their opinions. This practice was not only for the benefit of the church but also for the community-at-large and offered an alternative model from which many of the democratic ideas on the continent were nurtured.[11]

It is necessary to clarify that this congregational model was taught in Latin America by the missionaries who founded churches and thus it was received by the people who joined. However, it has not been applied everywhere in a homogeneous way. The major problem that congregationalism has had in Latin America is the collision with the reality of the context. From colonial times to the present this context was modeled by the close amalgamation of society and Catholicism which accounts for the authoritarianism and hierarchical model of many Latin American societies. Thus, this Baptist distinctive also confronts the tendency towards authoritarian leadership and the minimizing of congregational participation which may seem to be a doctrinal problem, but is, in reality, also contextual where democracy is being restricted or even nullified.

This review of selected elements of Baptist practice in Latin America permits a reassessment of that heritage by looking at its difficulties and its

11. Moreno, "History and Baptist Tradition," 4–5.

progress as examined contextually. It will also shed light on some themes for reflection as well as challenges and opportunities for the development of Baptist work and what it means to be Baptist in the current century. It is important to take into consideration that Latin American Baptists have not always been aware of the perspectives that they are facing in this century and the need to reflect on the current changes that are happening in society and in the church.

Challenges and Opportunities of Latin American Baptists in the Twenty First Century

Pentecostalism, Neo-Pentecostalism, and Post-Denominationalism

One of the main religious movements in Latin America during the twentieth century was Pentecostalism and the most recent religious wave called Neo-Pentecostalism.[12] Pentecostalism achieved its demographic explosion in the decades of the 1960s and 1970s. Nevertheless, during this time it maintained tense relationships with historic and evangelical Protestantism. With the emergence of Neo-Pentecostalism, however, a new way of relating within the Latin American religious setting appeared. Not only are there tensions, but oftentimes these come from those leaders who are interested in homogenizing the religious setting into a proposed "unity of the body of Christ." A similar proposal of the vision of unity is forwarded by Catholics in many meetings and conferences. Thus, Neo-Pentecostalism did not rise up to be another denomination, but rather to be a transversal force that crosses all denominational boundaries. Its influence includes worship and theology with an emphasis on emotions rather than on reason, a simpler and lighter proclamation for the consumer society, a focus on material prosperity for the believers, and an entrenched proposal for political conquest as a means of Christianizing the society.

This kind of religious movement also influenced Baptist churches and elicited opposing reactions. On the one hand, there was the complete refusal to change that brought about a retreat into a kind of traditionalism as a form of protection from change; change is seen as destructive.

---

12. The following insights come from Moreno, "History and Baptist Tradition," 7–8; see also Méndez, "History and Development," 65–67.

These churches do not seem to be desperate about a "boom" in spectacular church growth or changes to contemporary worship; they are congregations with a calm sense of growth, praise, and fidelity to the Lord as ever. On the other hand, there are those who affirm to have received the Neo-Pentecostal wave as a great renovation and a contemporary eruption of the Holy Spirit or as a new great revival. As a result everything changed in those churches. For some even the name "Baptist" is something of the past, the hymnbook is an object of the past, congregationalism is considered an illness that must be removed, the principle of the separation of church and state is irrelevant because it is necessary to be involved in politics and to be part of "the power that be" in society, poverty is a curse, and illnesses are demonic activities. Therefore, many people are attracted to this alternative church because of the immediate relevance it seems to have for the person.

One of the consequences of the Neo-Pentecostal movement with its ability to reach beyond denominational boundaries has been the promotion of a post-denominational era characterized by the use of the name "Christian" without denominational "surnames" (Baptists, Methodists, Presbyterians, etc.). These new churches proclaim to be the "body of Christ" under the unity of a pastoral staff; they promote the presence of the church in society through political action and with the purpose of "Christianizing" the entire society. This movement also is characterized by the Prosperity Gospel and has, therefore, sociological implications such as its insertion in sectors of middle class and the lower upper class, but without abandoning completely their commitment to the poor, although its theology is not compatible with the existence of the poor; they try to overcome this reality in a spiritual way. Moreover, they try to establish specific plans for strategic spiritual warfare and the territorial conquest in the cities. The denominational organizations are left behind because they are considered nonfunctional, slow, traditional, and bureaucratic. Theologically, it emphasizes a simpler theology, without giving much attention to deep and complex doctrinal discussions and controversies. This movement focuses more on experiential rather than on rational theology.

Therefore, the Neo-Pentecostalism and its partner, the post-denominationalism,[13] represent a new scenario and challenge in which is required that Baptist reexamine their own identity. What does it mean to

13. Deiros, *Protestantismo en América Latina.*

be Baptist in a world where this identification is frequently minimized, or completely diminished? It is probable that many of our denominational organizations will not survive much more without making changes, but what kind of changes?

It is important to remember that this epoch in which we live called post-modernity has been characterized by quick changes the effects of which are relative and temporal. Therefore, in these moments of celebration and reevaluation we need to consider the temporary character of our changing reality in order to give answers to the challenges and opportunities that we face, but without diminishing the principles that constitute our heritage and identity.

The Socioeconomic and Political Situation in Latin America

The economic and political situation in Latin America is another reality that demands answers of Baptists as one of the great challenges.[14] The worldwide socioeconomic reality is a crisis that concerns Latin America, but not as a new event, for decades this has been a continent marked by the presence of scandalous poverty and inequality. We live in a continent that has been "Christian" for centuries. As if that were not enough, there are various waves of Christianity that have come one after another to renew the previous setting and its ministry.

Perhaps there are in Latin America more Christian church buildings per square meter and per inhabitant than in other continents, but equally in this same proportion, there are poverty and misery. Here is a mission imperative for Baptists. There is a challenge to practice in daily life our theological identity. This economic reality is accompanied by a political reality in turmoil. As a response to this problem the governmental elite try out one governing model after another. Currently "the strong man" ("caudillo") leader predominates, with even some outbreaks of authoritarianism. Baptists have a congregational heritage that, while it may not solve all problems, it nevertheless carries inherently principles that counteract the concept of "caudillo" leadership and the authoritarianisms that are held so dear at this time not only in society but also in our churches. Therefore, the practice of the model of church government must also be recuperated from our heritage as well as the principles of

14. Most of this section comes from Moreno, "History and Baptist Tradition," 12; See also, Méndez, "History and Development,," 67–69.

equality and justice which should be recognized as basic. In fact, these practices must be logical consequences of the spiritual principle of the priesthood of all believers.

Challenges and Opportunities of Christian Mission in Latin America

A final challenge and simultaneously an opportunity is the mission field. The mission activity in Baptist history has always been one of its distinctives, not only based on our theology but also in our ecclesiastic beliefs. Today the spiritual need and religious confusion is a common reality all over the world, and Latin America is no exception. People are looking for answers not only material but spiritual, for refuge, for restoration, and even rehabilitation to continue living or to find meaning in life.

Thus, it is a perfect time to take the challenge and opportunity to share the gospel in an integral way in Latin America. This means that the whole gospel with all its implications for the whole person must be presented in this context, and the temptation of the proclamation of a gospel of ready consumption, without conversion, without a radical discipleship, and without a social commitment must be avoided. From our Baptist heritage we can learn how to ward off these errors, as since the beginning, the first Baptists tried to proclaim the whole gospel message to a needy spiritual people in spite of material or cultural barriers.[15]

In addition, another factor in this new century is the phenomenon called globalization that implies a planetary culture; in the religious field this has repercussions such as the dialog and analysis of convictions of believers from different faiths and continents. One challenge of this reality is a seeming relativism that comes with religious pluralism. At the same time, however, when we study the mission field and take our Baptist heritage into consideration, we can remember our global consciousness of missions and see in the celebration of the identity of Baptist life a challenge: As Latin American Baptists we must come to understand that the mission is no longer monocentric, coming from Europe or from the United States "to us, the ends of the earth," but rather multicentric, coming from many centers to many "ends of the earth." It is also important to acknowledge that this movement not only has been changing from one center to many centers, but also that the method of doing mission

15. Escobar, "Los Bautistas," 39.

is being changed from one to many methods. Recently, Latin America Baptists have started their own history of sending missionaries with these characteristics and by doing so, it has been possible to participate in one of the emphases of our heritage.[16]

In this twenty-first century many churches are active in the missionary work which is true in Latin America and much more so in Africa and Asia where poverty, inequality, and injustice also predominate. However, in spite of the dire circumstances, new forms of Christian mission have been appearing. To carry the point a bit further, these new missionary endeavors pose a new and real challenge to the former centers of Europe and the United States from where the missionaries were first sent. All indications are that in Europe and to a lesser degree in the USA we find a post-Christian cultural situation where even well-established churches are rapidly losing their influence in their societies. Some observers maintain that in those places a new kind of pagan life with few signs of Christianity is on the rise.[17]

Taking all of this together, it is indispensable that the communication of the gospel be accompanied by a genuine surrender of one's life to Jesus Christ so that each believer may have a new life style in order that non-believers are really attracted and affected by the gospel. We need to recognize that the first Baptists had such a quality of Christian life and their transformed lives led them to be willing disciples, even unto suffering. Again, to remember and to celebrate is a challenge that confronts us with the opportunity to renew our commitment to our heritage.

Conclusions

For Latin American Baptists, the celebration of Baptist history is an opportunity to recognize us in that history, to locate ourselves in it, and to appreciate our heritage and identity as valuable and effective ones.

Baptist testimony for nearly two centuries on this continent has been varied, its impact recognized by many, but valued in different ways. We are recognized as an educated people, with a good organization in our churches, interested in missions, insistent on baptism of believers by immersion, on religious freedom and on the separation of church and state. However, we are also seen as exclusive groups with lack of social

16. Moreno, "History and Baptist Tradition," 10.

17. Escobar, "Los Bautistas," 40.

commitment and an ambiguous political position considering our principle of separation of church and state.[18]

Thus, it seems that even though we have the right to continue to exist as a denomination, we must keep our heritage and identity. At present Latin American Baptists face real challenges, and we must interact in order to prepare ourselves for the current century.

The charismatic characteristic of the Neo-Pentecostal movement is being a danger to our basic principle of the Lordship of Christ. This is because authority is located in the charismatic leadership and the charismatic experience of the believers; the Christ-centered fundamental principle of our churches is automatically lost.

Even some Baptists insist that there is no risk in participating in inter-denominational or ecumenical movements in Latin America. However, Baptists need to continue to be careful that such interfaith approaches do not affect the integrity of the ecclesiastic principle of our heritage in a context where it is still necessary to establish the identity through the contrast with the differences.

It has been said that the cultural context of this continent promotes at large an arbitrary, authoritarian, and hierarchical style of leadership. Therefore, our challenge is to continue to practice the congregational church government based on the priesthood of all the believers.

It has also been said that in Latin America many countries have written constitutions or laws stipulating religious freedom and the separation of church and state. However, it is necessary that as Baptists who participated in the struggle to obtain and maintain these laws, we do not now neglect the current struggle to put the written law into practice, as those principles are violated and denied regularly in many Latin American countries. We should take care that these distinctives of our Baptist heritage be respected not only by the governments but no less also within our churches.

Finally, the Latin American Baptists should grow in fidelity to the missionary principle which is another distinctive legacy. Thus, in the new context of a global world which is desperately in need of the good news, we can not only share the whole gospel on our continent, but we can add our voices to the mandate of going to "the ends of the earth."

18. Moreno, "History and Baptist Tradition," 14.

Bibliography

Anderson, Justo. *Historia de los Bautistas*. 3 vols. El Paso, TX: Casa Bautista, 1990.

Bastián, Jean Pierre. *Historia del Protestantismo en América Latina*. México: Ediciones CUPSA, 1986.

Canclini, Arnoldo. "Aportes del Protestantismo a la Vida Argentina." Unpublished paper.

Deiros, Pablo A. *Historia del Cristianismo en América Latina*. Buenos Aires: Fraternidad Teológica Latinoamericana, 1992.

———. *Historia del Protestantismo en América Latina*. Nashville, TN: Editorial Caribe, 1997.

Escobar, Samuel. "Los Bautistas y la Misión Cristiana." Unpublished chapter.

Martínez-García, Carlos, and James Thomson. *Un escocés distribuidor de la Biblia en México, 1827–1830*. México: Maná Museo de la Biblia, 2014.

Méndez, Dinorah B. "History and Development of Baptists in Mexico." In *Baptist Faith & Witness, Book 4: Papers of the Study and Research Division of the Baptist World Alliance 2005–2010*, edited by Fausto A. Vasconcelos, 57–70. Falls Church, VA: BWA, 2011.

Moreno, Pablo. "History and Baptist Tradition in Latin America: An Indigenous Reading in Recognition of 400 years of Worldwide Baptist History." Unpublished paper presented to RIBET-UBLA Assembly in Lima, Perú, April 2009.

Scialabba, Raúl. "La Libertad Religiosa en la Sociedad Plural de América Latina." Unpublished paper presented in UBLA Assembly, Lima, Perú, April 2009.

23

Challenges for Baptists in Argentina

Tómas Mackey

Introduction: A Brief History

THE FIRST BAPTIST GROUPS who arrived in Argentina came from two main sources: European and American. It is also worth recognizing that from very early in its history Argentine Baptist work had a solid and efficient local leadership. This was crucial for its development. The first Baptist group in Argentina was established in 1865 by Welsh immigrants who settled in the Chubut Valley in the depths of Patagonia, Southern Argentina. Soon after, the group invited Pastor William Rhys Casnodyn who exercised a long ministry and was highly respected by the community. Unfortunately the group had a tragic end during a flood in 1899, and the surviving members dispersed and joined other churches. Hence, no church from that group has lasted until today.

Pablo Besson (1848–1932), a Swiss-French missionary, arrived in the country in 1881. He settled in one of the first colonies made up of Swiss, French, and Germans in Esperanza, Santa Fe province. A few years later Besson would move to Buenos Aires where in 1883 he founded a church which is the country's oldest Baptist church to date. Besson made full use of his excellent academic background and even produced a Spanish translation of the New Testament. He wrote many articles on the issue of freedom of conscience which were published by the most prestigious

336

and important newspapers of his time. He was a tireless fighter for the rights deriving from freedom of religion, making him an agent of major changes in this area.

In 1894 ethnic Germans from Russia arrived and began an intensive work with very good results to this day. A large number of Slavs (Russians, Poles, Ukranians) arrived in Argentina after the communist revolution and, like the Germans, established their churches with their respective languages, styles, and customs. At that time Argentina openly received thousands of immigrants, particularly from Europe and the Middle East; they constituted from then on the majority of the Argentine population. In 1899 Robert Hosford arrived from Ireland.

The first United States missionary to settle in Argentina was Sidney M. Sowell, who arrived in 1903, supported by the Southern Baptist Convention. He soon established churches that are still active today, and he would be the leader to lay the cornerstone for the International Baptist Theological Seminary in Buenos Aires. Subsequently, Southern Baptists would influence Baptist work in the whole country in several aspects such as church organization, pastoral training, church planting, and the provision of seminary professors. It was not until 1957 that a second American missionary organization, the Swedish North American Baptist Convention, sent missionaries who settled mainly in Northwestern provinces.

What Challenges Do Argentine Baptists Face Today?

More than a century and a half elapsed since that first Baptist group arrived in Argentina. Many changes have occurred in the world, in the country, and certainly among Baptists as well. What challenges do Argentine Baptists face today? Is it possible that these challenges faced by Argentine Baptists are coincident with those principles Baptists have had since their origins? At the same time it is possible they are shared by other Baptists from around the world. The most appropriate contextualization for church work should not be detached from the catholicity of the church. An honest search for a relevant application of the mission for the church today must be in continuity with the mission of the "one" church from the New Testament to our days. The challenges to be considered are important and significant, but by no means the only ones faced by Baptists in Argentina.

1. A search for the roots may lead to a relevancy for the present time. It is possible to say that Argentine Baptists are experiencing a crisis of identity. Baptist identity has to do with the way of understanding the mission, organizing the church, guiding the church by its leadership, and making the church relevant for society. Identity not only has to do with the past but with the contemporary way a community portrays itself in relation to its purpose of being and doing. Some of the questions on the subject of identity to be answered by Argentine Baptists today are:

- Is it relevant to talk about Baptist identity today?
- Do we not live in a "post-denominational" time?
- What value can be assigned to "Baptist identity" and what is the degree of commitment and loyalty to the denomination?
- How far is it possible to conceive of a diversity of Baptists?
- How many "other kind" of Baptists may be included within the Baptist associated work at either national or regional level?
- Is it possible to keep doing cooperative work with multiple Baptist identities?
- Is it possible to build trust without some degree of common identity?
- On what basis must this be?
- Is it possible to have unity without identity?

The answer is that it is very difficult to keep the pace of unity in any body without a clear and vital identity through which parties feel connected and supported. There is a risk of appealing to identity as a justification for defensive closure that should be avoided. But it is also true that when those distinctive features are diluted, institutions experience pain, division, and loss of relevance. This has happened to some Argentine Baptist institutions.

2. Difficulties with Baptist otherness. Some degree of fragmentation has accompanied the Baptist people from the beginning, but at certain times unity has sadly experienced traumatic ruptures. Argentine Baptist work is not an exception. Argentina has been enriched for a long time with its conventional work which allowed linkages among the vast majority of Baptist churches in the country since 1909. A number of causes, including a strong charismatization of many leaders and churches, led to a rupture of the associated Baptist work in 2005. Today Argentina has

two national Baptist bodies, the Argentine Baptist Evangelical Confederation (CEBA) and the Argentine Baptist Association (ABA since 2005). Is it possible to heal the fractures and reach unity again among Argentine Baptists? The challenges of Jesus' prayer for unity (John 17), and Paul's teaching on unity (Eph 2:14–22; 4:3–6, 11–13; Phil 4:2–3) are to seek unity without losing the essential truths of the gospel. Reconciliation will take time and effort, and it will be necessary to work on opportunities for reconciliation which, although seemingly fragile, can be the way to obtain deeper and lasting achievements.

3. Serious ethical challenges. Baptists do not have a common hermeneutics regarding moral and ethical issues, but this does not exempt them from always searching for answers. In a sense ethics is in fashion today. So, the big challenge does not rely on the possibility of neglecting ethics, but on its contents. Contemporary ethics tends to be one without transcendence, without compelling values, an ethics of pleasure which often serves unethical interests. The levels of corruption, immorality, and impunity are already inadmissible. It is now strictly necessary that Christians think and act ethically. What are the parameters to determine what is fair, adequate, compelling, or desirable? How much must be mandatory? It is almost impossible to think ethically without some degree of regulation. Ethical issues faced by churches in the world have been abundant from the New Testament to today.

Secularism, for example, is a subject of interest to Christians all over the world, obviously also for Baptists in Argentina. Facing this issue, and many others, means making a larger commitment than just "taking a stand in a debate." It means to consider the patterns of behavior to be evaluated as part of the mission of the church. In addition to the broad range of ethical issues, we must consider the speed with which opinions on these issues change. What happened in Argentina in recent years may serve to illustrate this point. Argentina was one of the last countries in the world to enact a civil divorce law, and is today one of the first countries in the world to enact a civil law for same-sex marriage. Moreover, in 2015 Argentina amended its civil code which had served for decades. This means that new criteria govern the social life of the country, and the question is what should be the participation of Baptists as they face this challenge?

4. Nearness and total otherness as well as liturgical reforms. In recent decades a variety of charismatic forms developed, some of them taking a very intense degree in a number of Argentine Baptist churches.

This made the coexistence with the "otherness" of Baptists which had existed until then very difficult and created serious difficulties in resolving the continuity of working together either at the associated or at the local church levels. Charismatic systems have made a lasting impact and are now a reality in different aspects of Argentine church life. One of the areas where it has impacted the most is worship. This generated a number of questions. For example:

Is there a liturgical form that best captures "the" or "a" Baptist spirit and generates integration without encouraging controversy between Baptist "others"? Forms must be a channel linking the nearness of God with his "full otherness": "There must be both the liturgical presentation of the majesty of God, which reaches out beyond the ages and in the language of tradition transcends the present moment, and that nearness of God in our market places and our highways and hedges."[1] (Thielicke). Community worship provides pastoral work, promotes big changes, facilitates unity and serves as an evangelistic channel.

The Evangelical hymnody is part of the identity. A part of Baptist devotion is channeled in prayer and singing. Part of its theology is announced through hymns. When songs have little or poor biblical contents and are very subjective, theology walks down those same lanes resulting in an impoverishment of personal and community life. It is true that forms are not essential in worship, but they should not be underestimated. Every individual and community expression of worship includes forms. The expression "in spirit and in truth," mentioned by Jesus, is not equivalent to disregarding or disqualifying the forms for worship. Forms can and should also be a vehicle for the best worship. However, forms should not asphyxiate worship and should instead help its implementation. It is possible to say that rigidity in cultic forms is not the most suitable for the freedom that the Spirit brings, but on the other side the laxness in forms does not guarantee the freedom of the Spirit. The solution is to find ways to facilitate the freedom of the Spirit rather than the personal tastes of those who lead the liturgy, and that is something Argentine Baptists should seek.

5. Where are the new forms of preaching? "The promise still stands and the task yet remains, for God ever renews His church through new forms of preaching. . . . Where such proclamation is faithful to the living and written Word of God and enlivened by the Spirit, it is an effective

---

1. Thielicke, *Encounter with Spurgeon*, xxxi.

means of grace and a sure sign of the true church."[2] Argentine Baptist work was enriched by great preachers who marked a path that even spread to neighboring countries. Unfortunately, there may be an impoverishment of this function among Argentine Baptists today.

Surely the role of the pulpit has changed in the world. However, preaching, with its multiple uses (expositional, pastoral, educational, prophetic, and many others) must be considered important by every church and every organization that promotes the associated work. It is possible to wonder whether the mission of preaching has today the relevance it once had. If the answer is negative, it could be important to know the reasons for the absence of such voices, and also to know why it has been supplanted, or what is taking its place, or how this significant task is being performed. If the role played by what was called pulpit is to be relieved, it would be good to ask what will supply it and with what quality. Is there a way to sustain and reform the church without preaching? It is true that the church's mission is not executed only by preaching, but surely it will be done with preaching included.

6. The priesthood of all believers and religious liberty. The priesthood of all believers, soul competency, and religious liberty are different issues, but interrelated. All these have been and continue to be of deep interest to Baptists and, in the history of Argentine Baptists, they were and continue to be a priority.

Argentina is a country where the vast majority of the population holds the Roman-Catholic religion which exerts great power over the various spheres of society; the federal government supports the Roman Catholic religion (Art. 2 of Argentina National Constitution). The introduction of religious education in public schools has added seriousness to the situation. Since the beginning, Baptists have upheld the principle of separation of church and state, lay public schools, freedom of conscience in the country, and equal rights for all. Pablo Besson, the pioneer of Baptist work in Argentina, exercised a key role in the Baptist and evangelical world at large, defending with intelligence and courage the issue of religious liberty. For all these reasons, the relationship of Argentine Evangelicals and Baptists in particular with the Catholic Church has been complex and critical, and it explains the difficulty of arriving at an agreement on the best way to relate to each other. It is difficult to say if having a pope from Argentina will or will not be beneficial to this relationship.

2. George, "Jesus Came Preaching," para. 17.

Churches themselves are at risk of going against their liberty when they are enclosed in four walls (even ideologically), or when they privatize their beliefs and think that they have no place in the public arena, or accept the creed of those who claim that having faith is to discriminate those who do not believe. It is good for Baptist churches to render unto Caesar what is Caesar's, but at the same time not to render unto Caesar what is God's. The issue of religious freedom is imperative and urgent in view of the cruel persecution to which many Christians (and not only Christians but also followers of other religions) are subject, even to death. When this happens, can the issue of religious freedom take second place? The answer must be a resounding "No."

A serious but subtle problem in confronting this issue is the tendency to reductionism, particularly to reduce religious freedom to freedom of worship. This shortens the inherently public nature of biblical faith and it transforms faith into one of closed doors. This reductionism leads to a misconception of the mission of the church because it is then conceived only as a private activity, with no impact on society and without accountability in the public world. In this case faith is pure individualism and subjectivism. Another reductionism is the "dictatorship of relativism" which paradoxically impulses relativism as a universal form.

Finally, within this great theme but from another perspective, it is helpful to note two risks that Argentine Baptists face. The first risk is to close the congregational system on itself with a defensive attitude. When this happens it is a sign of fear rather than one of local responsibility, and it will certainly limit the growth of the congregation and the full use of the potential of all believers. The second risk is that megachurches may ignore both congregational government and the full exercise of the priesthood of all believers.

7. Are we at risk of losing the practice of regenerate church membership? A distinctive Baptist principle is the regenerate church membership. Shades of the same subject can be studied under believer's church, voluntary church, born-again church, fellowship of the redeemed. Several Baptist practices are associated with this issue, such as believer's baptism, congregational government, local church autonomy, priesthood of all believers, church discipline. In 1905, at the first Baptist World Congress in London, J. D. Freeman said: "The principle of regenerate church membership more than anything else marks our distinctiveness in the world

today."[3] Long before Freeman, the Somerset Confession (1656) declared that when admitting a new member the church must have a clear demonstration of his/her "new birth." William R. Estep writing about Baptists in his country said that they "are perilously close to losing their insistence upon a regenerate church membership." That could also apply to Argentine Baptists today and if this happened, it would be a very painful loss.

The above is not intended to lead to elitist churches but to churches that are accountable of exercising good care of their members. Argentine Baptist churches are at risk of running after numerical growth unaccompanied by membership training (pragmatism), not having systematic Bible study programs, or providing counseling with more of a clinical than theological basis. It is important to stress the principle of regenerated membership to promote redemptive discipline, doctrinal purity, sanctity of life, and growing unity.

8. The place of pastoral work. Pastoral work undoubtedly requires an ongoing review everywhere in the world. The definition of the pastoral role, the sense of calling, recruitment, and training of pastors are key issues. These are major challenges for Argentine Baptists. The answer to such issues affects the kind of training future pastors should receive. Also, topics such as the number of pastors needed and pastor's support are also important.

9. The mission of the church. It is always important to remember that there is no church without mission or mission without church. The commitment to the gospel leads the church to be missionary. This also implies that the sense of universality of the mission does not depend on the geographical location of the community, but on the divine intention to reach everyone with his saving love. In recent years Argentine Baptist churches ran several risks. One of them was to become an end in itself, not realizing that the church exists for the mission that transcends it. Another risk was to identify themselves with secular processes to the extent of forgetting they were born by Christ's salvation. Yet another risk was to become a kind of religious movement whose identity is given by following a leader and not Christ. In this context it is important to recover the local church as an agent of God's mission.

10. The social situation. Social issues are multidimensional and of deep interest to the mission of the church. Churches must take preventive and development actions, must anticipate a redemption that is "already

---

3. Shakespeare, *Baptist World Congress*, 27.

but not yet," and have to pay immediate attention to concrete human and social crises. Churches have to serve as agents of change, hope, and renewal.

Argentina is a country of large resources. A variety of climates, all types of soil, freshwater, seacoast, a population enriched by the presence of various cultures and religions coexisting in peace and yet, poverty reaches important and worrying levels. One other complex and destructive problem which aggravates the situation is related to drugs. Argentina is a country with a high level of drug use and drugs production, and has been proven to be home to drug dealers on a large scale. One reason for many of Argentina's shortcomings despite so many available resources relies in the high level of corruption that runs through its political, economic, social levels. It is not only the presence of corrupt individuals but of a corrupt operating system and practices not adequately controlled or condemned. It is impossible not to detect corruption around the world; corruption is part of a fallen humanity. But the difference is in the degrees of corruption and the way families, the educational and judicial systems as well as the church with a mission can work to heal the situation. The work of Argentine Baptist churches has not reached the desired impact on its social context. Certainly we must recognize that it is not easy, but churches can and should be tools for service and channel the light of Jesus.

11. Looking to the future with a sense of expectation and hope. Meeting the challenges which were listed above demands effort and dedication, but they are at the same time very stimulating for Baptist churches in the country. Argentina is a fertile ground for the mission of the church and Argentine Baptists already have a good experience of service in the country and have excellent gifts and resources. For all these reasons it is possible to look at the future of Baptist churches in Argentina with confidence and meaningful challenges.

Bibliography

George, Timothy. "Jesus Came Preaching." *First Things* (blog), June 16, 2014. https://www.firstthings.com/web-exclusives/2014/06/jesus-came-preaching.

Shakespeare, John Howard. *The Baptist World Congress, London, July 11–19, 1905: Authorized Record of Proceedings*. London: Baptist Union Publication Department, 1905.

Thielicke, Helmut. *Encounter with Spurgeon*. The Thielicke Library. Cambridge: Lutterworth, 2016.

v. From the Caribbean Baptist Fellowship

24

Baptists in Jamaica

DEVON DICK

THIS PAPER TRAVERSES A journey from the arrival of American Baptist missionary, George Liele, to the present with special emphasis on church growth, struggle against slavery and colonialism, and development of Independent Jamaica. During this period Baptists in Jamaica played a significant role in nation building and it is therefore not surprising that of the seven national heroes three were Baptists, namely Samuel Sharpe, Paul Bogle, and George William Gordon.

Liele arrived in Jamaica in 1783, the latter part of British colonial slavery in Jamaica, and established a Baptist witness. His was the first successful ministry among the enslaved. Liele and his congregations were of the Anabaptist persuasion. The work grew and the pioneers Liele and Moses Baker needed assistance, and they sought help in the form of English missionaries; the Baptist Missionary Society responded by sending John Rowe in February 1814. This was the beginning of a long list of English Baptist missionaries to Jamaica including William Knibb and James Phillippo. These missionaries facilitated the development of the Baptist work among the enslaved, albeit with a focus of saving the soul, while ignoring initially the context of slavery. The enslaved read the same Bible as the missionaries but had a different interpretation. One such enslaved person was Baptist deacon Sam Sharpe (1805–32) who claimed that slavery was inconsistent with the teachings of the Bible. His desire was to be treated and paid as workers, and the protest was in the form of a passive resistance of a strike. This resistance was the catalyst that led to the Act of Emancipation in 1833.

Apprenticeship followed for four years, and it was a continuation of the exploitation of the Africans. The apprentices believed that the houses they lived in and plots of land they cultivated were theirs. However, when apprenticeship ended in 1838, the emancipated Africans were required by the planters to pay rent or be evicted. It was, therefore, left to the missionaries and the Africans to seek alternative economic solutions. The Baptist missionaries built Free Villages, the first one in 1838 by James Phillippo. These villages consisted of houses, churches, streets, and schools, and they provided economic well-being, facilitated a reasonable standard of living, stable family life and a place to worship. By 1840s the Free Village system had delivered 52,903 lots.

Native Baptists broke away from the English Baptist-dominated church around 1837 when congregations were formed which became the nucleus of the Jamaica Native Baptist Missionary Society (JNBMS) founded around 1839/40. By 1841, they had 13,687 members. One reason for the establishment of JNBMS was to redress the sidelining of persons of African descent who wanted to become pastors and who experienced the prejudice by English Baptist missionaries. They challenged the colonizers' interpretation of the Bible and engaged in what would now be called "hermeneutics of suspicion." They advocated that they were free to have their own interpretation. Native Baptists were incorporated into the English Baptist-dominated JBU by 1883 and are no longer in existence as most of the leaders were killed.

George William Gordon (1815–65) was elected to the House of Assembly in 1863 representing St. Thomas in the East. He won with the help of the Native Baptists. Gordon had estates in many parishes and wherever Gordon had properties, he tried to establish chapels and to promote the gospel in the parishes in which his property lay. Paul Bogle (1820–65) was a close associate of Gordon. Bogle functioned as a pastor organizing baptism and giving oversight of the congregation at Mount Zion and Sunning districts.

Native Baptist leaders Paul Bogle and George William Gordon, now National Heroes, were in the forefront in agitating on behalf of persons who were experiencing economic woes and an oppressive justice system in the 1860s. In August 1865, Bogle and his followers marched approximately 40 miles from Stony Gut to Spanish Town to meet the governor in order to register the gravity of the situation but were not given a hearing.

Subsequently, he and his followers marched to the Morant Bay Court-house to protest continued injustices. They were fired upon and the ensu-ing melee led to the deaths of eighteen persons of the ruling class and thousands of peasants. This watershed event known as "the 1865 Native Baptist War" was followed by better governance and the disestablishment of the Anglican Church.

In 1843, Baptists were the first to establish theological education which also had a teacher training component. In 1912, Calabar, an all-boys high school, was established by Baptists. Baptist life in Jamaica has other significant accomplishments in education. By 2014, Baptists owned schools or leased schools numbering 154, or 10 percent of all schools in Jamaica. They run three high schools, eighty-five early childhood institu-tions, and sixty-six all-age (six to fifteen years old) and primary (six to twelve years old) schools. Baptists introduced a better standard of the educational system, used more indigenous materials, and allowed greater access for the disadvantaged.

In April 1998, the TBC FM 88.5 radio station was formed under the leadership of pastor of Tarrant/Balmagie Circuit of Baptist churches Neville Callam, the first General Secretary of the BWA of African origin. This was Jamaica's first Christian radio station, and it was owned and operated by a Baptist church. In February 1993 there was the formation of LOVE FM, a religious radio station, which included Baptists in the ownership structure. LOVE FM garnered a significant 14 percent of the Jamaican audience at its peak. Normally on a Sunday, unlike many other Caribbean nations, Jamaica would have gospel music played as a matter of course. With the advent of Christian and religious radio stations, more airtime has been afforded gospel music during the week, and gospel art-ists have been given more exposure to proclaim the gospel. These various media outlets offer an opportunity to tell the truths about the gospel and reach more people and much faster with the good news of salvation.

The Baptists have continued to engage in this wholistic ministry even into the twenty-first century. In 2001, the Jamaica Baptist Union had dental clinics and medical clinics operated by seventeen churches in nine of the fourteen parishes. In 2014, Boulevard Baptist Church devel-oped five two-bedroom units as part of its mandate to help citizens with housing.

Today there are approximately 40,000 Baptists in 332 churches with 130 ministers of religion. The Baptist Church in Jamaica is entirely led and staffed by Jamaican ministers who were locally trained. Baptists in

Jamaica are well-respected and well-known for their proclamation of the gospel and engaging in nation-building ministries.

Bibliography

Dick, Devon. "Baptist Life and Religious Freedom in Jamaica." Paper delivered at the BWA Annual Gathering in Jamaica 2013 to the Religious Freedom Commission.

———. *The Cross and the Machete: The Native Baptists of Jamaica: Identity, Ministry and Legacy.* Kingston: Ian Randle, 2009.

———. *Rebellion to Riot: The Jamaican Church in Nation Building, 1865–1999.* Rev. ed. Kingston: Ian Randle, 2004.

Kreitzer, Larry J. *"Kissing the Book": The Story of Sam Sharpe as Revealed in the Records of the National Archives at Kew.* Oxford: Regent's Park College, 2013.

vi. From the Asia Pacific Baptist Federation

25

Growth, Aid and Development, and Education and Training

Baptists in Asia in the Twenty-First Century

ERIN MARTINE SESSIONS

BAPTISTS HAVE BEEN WITNESSING in Asia since 1793 when William Carey began work in India. Since then, countries throughout Asia have been receiving Baptist missionaries from Europe and the United States, with Australia and New Zealand later joining the missionary endeavor. Local churches, associations of churches, and conventions now operate in most Asian countries. This chapter begins with an introduction to the Asia Pacific Baptist Federation (APBF) and its divisions: Asia Pacific Baptist Aid (APBAid), Asia Pacific Baptist Youth (APBY), the Asian Baptist Women's Union (ABWU), and Asia Pacific Baptist Theological Education (APBTE). I then turn to brief overviews of both historical context and the recent work of Baptists in individual countries throughout Asia—from Bangladesh through to Vietnam—highlighting their focus on local and foreign church growth, aid and development work, and education and training.[1]

1. Though APBF membership stretches from Japan to Korea in the north, to New Zealand and Australia in the south and from the Philippines in the East to India and Sri Lanka in the west, this chapter narrows its scope to Asian countries, with the exception of China, central Asia, India, and Sri Lanka.

The Asia Pacific Baptist Federation (APBF)
and its Divisions

Momentum had been building since 1953 for Baptists across Asia to federate and, in 1975, the Baptist World Alliance (BWA) officially formed the Asian Baptist Fellowship. In 2007, at the Seventh Asian Baptist Congress in Chiang Mai, Thailand, the nomenclature was changed to the Asia Pacific Baptist Federation, to reflect more accurately the region's diverse makeup. Over the last forty-plus years, Baptist conventions, unions, and associations from all over the Asia Pacific region have met together to: impart inspiration, promote a spirit of fellowship, serve and cooperate through mission and evangelism, provide relief and development, build peace networks, develop leaders, promote theological education, and to share information and network. APBF now represents over 33,000 local churches and sixty-five conventions in twenty-two countries.[2]

Since Asia is the continent most affected by natural disasters, APBF was strategic in its creation of Asia Pacific Baptist Aid. APBAid's origins stretch back to 1975, as the Aid and Relief Committee. The committee has actively carried out its mission by informing members of humanitarian needs in the region; educating members to offer the gospel in holistic ways, including rendering justice to the poor; and providing training to practice environmentally sustainable development. On the twenty-sixth of December, 2004, the world was shocked by the massive scale of an earthquake, and the tsunami that followed, which devastated countries around the Indian Ocean. The Asian Tsunami triggered a renewed commitment to helping communities hit by disaster and, as a result, APBAid was established, in 2008, to organize and govern the work of the Committee.[3]

The mission for Asia Pacific Baptist Youth (APBY) is to build a comprehensive network among members and to help, support, and train young people to become future leaders. Two recent examples of the kind of work carried out by APBY include responding to the needs of young people in house churches in Vietnam in 2015, and the APBY Conference held in Baguio City, at the Philippine Baptist Theological Seminary in 2019. Young converts in Ho Chi Minh city, Vietnam, had been looking to neighboring organizations for assistance in encouraging and growing their churches, so APBY brought together teenagers from across the

2. Asia Pacific Baptist Federation (APBF), "Who We Represent."
3. APBF, "About APBAid."

district for a time of worship, and with the aim of hosting an APBY Conference there in future. Around four hundred delegates attended, with a further twenty-five young people receiving specialized discipleship training from APBF leadership.[4] APBY continues to take seriously the call to go and make disciples, with the theme of the 2019 APBY Conference, "Making and Multiplying Disciples," seeing youth and youth leaders form over twenty countries commit to growing their church communities.[5]

The Asia Baptist Women's Union (ABWU) has a vision to see women in Asia empowered for leadership, to engage confidently in various traditional and creative ministries, and to bring the gospel to the lost.[6] The union carries out a broad range of work due, in part, to the status of women varying from country to country: the Convention of Philippine Baptist Churches (CPBC) has been ordaining women since 1979 and now almost half their churches are led by women;[7] Indonesia held its first women's leadership conference in 2015; in November 2016, thirty-two women attended the Bhutan Christian Women's Leadership Training conducted by ABWU in Dalsingpara, India—the training covered the role of women in the family, church, society, and ministry;[8] and in September 2018, the thirteenth ABWU Assembly coincided with their sixtieth anniversary.[9] More recently the union has been directing their attention to COVID-19 support work.[10] The purpose of the APBTE, which oversees more than fifty Bible colleges and seminaries, is to equip pastoral and educational leaders through seminars, colloquiums, consultations, and the supply of itinerant teachers.[11] In 2014, APBAid Peace Network and APBTE held a Peace Forum in collaboration with the Peace Studies Center at Myanmar Institute of Theology. Theologians, development workers, and peace-builders reflected on peace and conflict, with a view to drafting educational strategies for equipping leaders and the church with peace-making skills.[12] I had the privilege of joining in APBTE's work in January 2019 at the APBF TEAM (Theological Education, Aid,

4. APBF, "Visit to Baptist Convention of Vietnam Youths."

5. APBF, "Asia Pacific Baptist Youth Conference 2019."

6. Asia Baptist Women's Union (ABWU), "Our Vision."

7. World Council of Churches, "Convention of Philippine Baptist Churches."

8. "In the Land of the Thunder Dragon," 5.

9. ABWU, "13th ABWU Assembly."

10. ABWU, "ABWU Support COVID Third Wave."

11. APBF, "Asia Pacific Baptist Theological Education."

12. APBF, "APBF Peace Forum 2014 Report."

and Mission) meeting in Melaka, Malaysia, presenting on refugees and asylum seekers, among other issues at the intersection of gospel and government.[13] This work remains pertinent, especially considering the vast numbers of internally displaced people in Myanmar.

In order to appreciate this discussion of Baptist ministry in the twenty-first century, it is important to understand that the history of Baptists in Asia prior to the twentieth century was dominated by Western missionaries. However, the narrative changed during the twentieth century, when Christianity in Asia shifted toward indigenization and a more equitable partnership between foreign missionaries and local believers. In turning to the individual overviews of each country, it becomes clear that the recent story of Baptists in Asia in the twenty-first century is characterized by: growth—sometimes unprecedented—in the number of churches and believers; a commitment to aid and development work, especially in the wake of natural disaster; and a focus on education and training, in particular theological education.

Bangladesh

Bangladesh is a young nation with a rich history and a Baptist presence reaching back to Carey. Contemporary challenges include poverty, political and religious tension, and natural disasters like cyclones, flash floods, mudslides, and tornadoes, which ruin infrastructure and leave over one million people homeless per year. Though Bangladesh consists of a population which is 90 percent Islam, 9 percent Hindu, and 1 percent other, Baptists have a considerable presence and make up the largest group of Protestants. The APBF networks are the Bangladesh Baptist Church Fellowship (BBCF), the Bangladesh Baptist Church Sangha, and the Garo Baptist Convention.[14]

The BBCF traces its origins back to the work of the New Zealand Baptist Mission in 1886. It is now a group of five hundred and thirty-five churches (with over forty-five thousand members), which reach out to and serve tribal groups, Hindu communities, and Bangladesh's majority Muslim population. BBCF is focused on: growth—since 1990, two hundred and fifty-nine churches have been planted, which include

13. For the opportunity to present, and her overwhelming support for my writing this chapter, I thank my dear friend, colleague, and APBTE Chair, Dr. Miyon Chung.

14. APBF, "APBF Member Bodies."

thirty-five Muslim-background congregations and there are around thirty full-time evangelists working in remote villages; aid and development—BBCF runs one of the region's most prominent development agencies, providing emergency relief and rehabilitation support, adult- and child-education, primary healthcare, economic development, and promoting justice, human rights and gender equality, improvement of social and spiritual values, and sustainable environment measures; and education—rapid growth has meant that "barefoot" lay-training occurs at a grass-roots level, and a hostel-system ensures children from rural communities receive education, nutrition, and safe accommodation.[15] In 2019, BBCF celebrated their centenary.

The Bangladesh Baptist Church Sangha (BBCS or Sangha), the oldest Protestant denomination in Bangladesh, has its origins in the (West) Bengal Baptist Union and the East Pakistan Baptist Union.[16] The Sangha consists of three hundred and seventy-four churches in total (with over twenty-three thousand members), and focuses on growth: establishing churches among the Santal tribal people and among the Mru in the Bandarban Hills. The Sangha also concentrates its resources on aid and education: supporting various health programs and schools.[17]

The churches in Bangladesh are struggling to equip leaders as fast as the church is growing. Lay-leaders, youth, and women are actively encouraged to participate in the Theological Education by Extension (TEE) program of the College of Christian Theology Bangladesh (CCTB), which is specifically designed to train lay-leaders quickly and flexibly. CCTB was the first interdenominational theological training institute in Bangladesh. The Sangha alone currently has over three hundred students studying at CCTB.[18] Particularly in their aid and educational work, Baptists in Bangladesh often work ecumenically and, more recently, have been participating in interfaith dialogues concerning climate change.

15. Partners International, "Partner Organizations."

16. Bangladesh Baptist Church Sangha, "About Us."

17. World Council of Churches, "Bangladesh Baptist Church Sangha."

18. Asia Theological Association, "Visit to College of Christian Theology Bangladesh."

Cambodia

Baptists have been in Cambodia, in the Batdambang and Siemreap prov-inces, since 1953 and were, of course, affected by the intensely turbulent recent history of Cambodia. During and after Pol Pot's Khmer Rouge regime, from 1975 to 1979, Cambodia was closed off from the rest of the world, its infrastructure ruined, its adult population decimated, and the next generation left illiterate. Missionaries were expelled and Christians were murdered and, by 1990, the evangelical population had declined to no more than six hundred believers. The tides began to turn for Christians, especially Baptists—the leading church planters in Cambodia—in the 1990s.

A Southern Baptist Convention missionary was assigned to be the Baptist's strategic coordinator in Cambodia. He developed a church planting manual in Khmer and began working with six Khmer-national church planters. By 1993, the number of Baptist churches had grown from six to ten. By 1994 that number had doubled. The number of churches grew again to forty-three in 1995, and the leaders formed an association of churches: the Khmer Baptist Convention. In 1996, the number rose again to seventy-eight. By 1997, there were one hundred and twenty-three Baptist churches throughout fifty-three of the country's one hundred and seventeen districts.[19]

Given both Cambodia's calamitous history and their church plant-ing success, there has been a focus on (church) growth. The SBC Strategy Coordinator handed the work over to a team of missionaries and local leaders in 1996, attributing the unprecedented growth to a number of key factors: prayer; rural leadership training programs (RLTPs); mentoring; and indigenization—each church was to be planted by Cambodians. The Khmer Baptist Convention (now the Cambodia Baptist Union—CBU) endorsed the team's aim to church plant in each district of Cambodia.[20] The president of the CBU, Rev. Nhem Nivath, stated that "our 5-year goal is to plant 1,621 churches in Cambodia, 1 per village."[21] So far, five hundred and forty-eight churches have joined the CBU.[22] This model of church planting has been successfully adapted for other countries and contexts.

19. Mission Frontiers, "Case Studies of CPMs."
20. Mission Frontiers, "Case Studies of CPMs."
21. Christians Sharing Christ Film Ministries, "Update by Brother Nivath."
22. Baptist World Alliance (BWA), "Cambodia Baptist Union."

From my own Australian perspective, Baptist agencies like Global Interaction (GI) and Baptist World Aid Australia (BWAA) evidence the need for—and focus on—ongoing aid and development work. As Cambodia continues to grapple with the aftermath of a brutal, genocidal government, Australian Baptists have witnessed firsthand the resilience (and work to heal from trauma) of Cambodian Christians. More recently, GI missionaries have been fostering relationships through addressing issues like "poor health, low literacy rates and high unemployment."[23] And BWAA has partnered with local Christian organizations, like Ponleu Ney Kdey Sangkhum (PNKS),[24] assisting in capacity building and implementing community development projects.[25]

Hong Kong

When Hong Kong was ceded to the United Kingdom in 1842, the Dean and Shuck families both moved to Hong Kong, later founding the Queens Road Baptist Church.[26] The Shucks also established a school, and the long tradition of Baptist education continues today with the Baptist Convention of Hong Kong (BCHK) overseeing upwards of thirty kindergartens, along with seven primary schools, eight secondary schools, and two tertiary institutions.[27] As well as the continued concentration on education, BCHK is working to strengthen mission partnerships, and establish churches in the New Territories.

Hong Kong Baptist University is one of the two Baptist tertiary institutions and celebrated its sixtieth anniversary in 2016. In 1920, BCHK began discussions about a Baptist university, in 1956 the Hong Kong Baptist College was created, and the next sixty years would see the college gain university status, forge international partnerships, and continue to innovate, in particular, in the arts and in Chinese medicine. HKBU aims to provide whole-person education and their vision for 2020 was

---

23. Global Interaction, "Living among the Khmer People."

24. Ponleu Ney Kdey Sangkhum, "Welcome to PNKS."

25. Baptist World Aid Australia, "When Women Keep Raising a Village."

26. William Dean had worked with Chaozhou speaking Chinese in Thailand and pastored the Maitrichit Chinese Baptist Church (the world's first Chinese Protestant church). Reverend Jehu Lewis Shuck, and his wife Henrietta Shuck, had worked with Cantonese speaking Chinese in Portuguese administered Macau.

27. Baptist Convention of Hong Kong, "Ministries."

for continued quality in teaching and learning, innovative research, and dedicated service to the community.[28]

There are many communities within Hong Kong, especially in the New Territories, without a church. Challenges such as the extremely high cost of living and the difficulty missionaries experience trying to enter the Special Administrative Region (since Hong Kong was returned to China in 1997) are a hindrance to establishing new churches. Almost any church-planting work outside of a house-church will require large sums of money. Hence, BCHK is focusing its efforts on supporting local believers to begin house-churches. BCHK also turns its attention abroad, with the Mission Board having ministry partnerships in Japan, China, Mongolia, Burma, Nepal, Malaysia, and Indonesia.

The ongoing tensions between Hong Kong and China have been a particular barrier to the work of BCHK and others in Hong Kong. The 2019–20 pro-democracy protests, sparked by a—now withdrawn—extradition bill, and concerns over the loss of autonomy and rights of people in Hong Kong, have contributed to the former president of HKBC, Rev. Lo Hing-choi's, decision to resign and move to the United Kingdom. He joins the growing list of Christian leaders who are speaking out and responding to China's totalitarianism through the lens of their faith.[29]

Indonesia

Though a majority-Muslim country, Indonesia has the largest Protestant population in Southeast Asia. Baptists have been active in Indonesia since Australians started working in Irian Jaya (now West Papua) in 1956. The current members of the APBF in Indonesia are: the Convention of Indonesian Baptist Churches (Kerapatan Gereja-Gereja Baptis Indonesia); The Fellowship of Baptist Churches of Papua (Peresekutuan Gereja-Gereja Baptis Papua); the Union of Indonesian Baptist Churches (Gabungan Gereja Baptis Indonesia); and Grace Baptist Church of Indonesia.[30]

Late in 2015, the Indonesian Baptist Alliance organized the first Baptist Women's Leadership Conference, which was an historic occasion. It was the first time that women from all over Indonesia, including Papua, and from various Baptist conventions and churches, were able

28. Hong Kong Baptist University, "About HKBU."
29. Kenny, "Hong Kong Baptist Leader."
30. APBF, "APBF Member Bodies."

to come together for a conference. Over two hundred women from all the islands gathered and received training on becoming leaders who are responsive to the changing needs of society and the church, and on the role of the church, government, and society in human development. And in September 2017, Yogyakarta were able to host the Asia Pacific Baptist Congress.[31]

Usually, little information has been made (publicly) available on Baptist activities due to the persecution of Christians. However, we do know that the present strategic focus is on: evangelizing and discipling, particularly among university students; equipping future church leaders, especially with a mission-centered theology, to reach the more than two hundred unreached people groups in Indonesia; and aid and development, through crisis relief, the education of women and children, and enterprise development. Currently, crisis relief efforts are centered on responding to the COVID-19 pandemic, as Indonesia's case numbers have, devastatingly, rapidly surpassed that of any other nation.

Japan

The APBF in Japan is made up of four member organizations: Japan Baptist Conference; Japan Baptist Union; Okinawa Baptist Convention; and—by far the largest—Japan Baptist Convention (JBC). Baptist work in Japan commenced with two Southern Baptist Convention (SBC) missionaries in 1889 and, following World War II, sixteen churches formed the JBC at Seinan Gakuin Church. Their aim was to establish churches in prefectural capital cities and reach out from there. JBC was—and still is—committed to overseas mission, sending missionaries to Brazil in 1965, and later focusing on work in Indonesia, Thailand and Singapore.[32]

"At the end of World War II there were pastors, like Noguchi Sensei, and church members to spare. At one time there were over 29,000 *renmae*, as the Southern Baptist churches are called."[33] As Japan's society

31. APBF, "9th APBF Congress Yogyakarta."

32. Japan Baptist Convention, "Cooperative Missions Pamphlet."

33. I thank SBC missionaries, Marsha and Tony Woods, who were with the International Mission Board (IMB) for close to four decades, for their interview and overview of Baptist work in Japan since World War II, and of coworkers Naoki Noguchi Sensei and Makato Sato. For more on Naoki Noguchi Sensei see: Woods, *Sacrificed, Given to an Empire; Found by God.* For more on Makato Sato: see: Woods, "Trevor & Makato, friends since age 6."

changed and more people claimed to have no religion (even Shinto and
Buddhism are declining), the "old methods" were not working as well as
they once did. The Woods family—former missionaries—experienced an
abatement, stagnation, and then a return to growth, albeit a slow one.
And this is reflected in BWA statistics, too. The difficulty of spreading the
gospel has been attributed to "prosperity and a lack of suitable pastors to
fill the roles of the retiring ones."[34]

Baptists still represent the largest group of Protestants in Japan.
Early work establishing a hospital and a school system set the tone for the
work that continues today. "Kindergartens still remain a huge outreach.
Most Japanese lean toward Christian kindergartens because they believe their children will be well-nurtured before the harsh school system
begins."[35] The Japan Baptist Hospital and Seinan Gakuin University are
two branches of Baptist work continuing to serve the community.[36]

"Today there are many growing and strong churches, with new
progressive pastors, especially in the northern areas."[37] Pastors, like the
Woods's friend Makato Sato, continue to work toward church growth,
support the Disaster Relief Committee, and encourage their congregants
to gain a theological education. Makato became a Christian through the
Woods family and, in 2011, he was ordained and installed as the pastor
of the very church he first stepped into when he was six years old. Their
colleague Noguchi Sensei, when he and his wife were in their eighties,
hosted over four thousand volunteers who had come to Japan to help in
the aid and relief efforts after the 2011 9.0 magnitude earthquake and
resulting tsunami. Makato, too, led his church in disaster relief following the tsunami. Ten years after the "triple disaster" (earthquake, tsunami, and Fukushima nuclear disaster), the Disaster Relief Committee
continues to provide aid, especially in the area of Fukushima.[38] The 7.3
magnitude earthquake which struck northeast Japan in February 2021
galvanized many Christians into action and reminded them that disaster
can be a "catalyst for positive change."[39] Their ministry and cooperation

---

34. Tony Woods, personal interview on November 30, 2016.

35. Marsha Woods, personal interview on November 30, 2016.

36. Japan Baptist Hospital, "Origin of the Japan Baptist Hospital"; Seinan Shin
Gakko (formerly Seinan Baptist Seminary, now Seinan Gakuin University) celebrated
its centenary in 2016, "Message from the President."

37. Marsha Woods, personal interview on November 30, 2016.

38. Japan Baptist Convention Disaster Relief Committee, "Bond of Prayer."

39. Foxwell Duttweiler, "Aftershocks."

continues to contribute to the slow, steady growth of Christianity across Japan.

South Korea

In stark contrast to the slow expansion in Japan, the Republic of Korea has experienced spectacular growth, especially over the last thirty years. The number of Christians, in particular Protestants, has doubled each decade. In recent years, Christianity was growing faster in Korea than in any other country. After Buddhism, Christianity is now the second largest religion with almost 30 percent of Korea's fifty million people identifying as Christian. Catholicism was first introduced to Korea in 1784 and Protestant missionaries followed a century later. Korea Baptist Convention (KBC) is one of the largest denominations, with *well over three thousand churches*, and dates back to 1889, when the Church of Christ in East Asia partnered with Southern Baptists.[40]

Historically, Korea has been vulnerable to both China and Japan, and the impact of World War II and the Korean War, and the modernization which followed, led to a society which was ready for the empowering message of Christianity. Korean Baptist history bears two distinct influences: the conservative influence of the SBC, and the charismatic influence of early pioneer missionary Malcolm Fenwick.[41] In 1978, Korean Baptists took over the leadership of the Convention and responsibility for most areas of denominational life, and their two distinct and differing influences still coexist within KBC today.

Currently, KBC has two main branches: theological education, and church ministry and mission. Korean Baptist Theological University/ Seminary is the largest Baptist Seminary outside of the United States and the largest seminary in Asia. Their programs include: the World Missions Training Center, which has been integral to global mission; the Institute for Life-Long Education, which is an open-education platform for reflecting on the changing demands of society; and the Songkang Social Welfare Community Center, which contributes to local welfare

40. Plenty has been written on the explosive growth of Christianity in Korea, but I am particularly grateful to Kun Jae Yu, who wrote the history of the Korea Baptist Convention, "Analysis of the Historical and Theological Identity."

41. Fenwick was the leader of the denomination until 1944. And from 1945, SBC missionaries were responsible for the formation and development of the Convention's theology.

development.[42] Interestingly, while the theological faculty tend to be more conservative, many of the students are charismatic. The student body reflects the diverse theological colors of the Convention: Calvinist dispensational, Arminian, and charismatic Christians partnering in mission and humanitarian work.

Korean Baptists are the largest contingency of overseas missionaries, sending workers throughout Asia and further abroad: much of the ministry in Mongolia is carried out by Koreans; Koreans have been instrumental in working with internally displaced people on the Myanmar/Thailand border; significant Korean diasporas exist in major Western cities, providing fertile ground for community outreach and church networks; and as North Korea continues to show signs of collapse, anecdotal evidence suggests that an underground Christianity is already taking root among the population.

Malaysia

The first Baptist churches in Malaysia were established by Baptist immigrants from Swatow, China, and SBC assisted the new churches with teaching, polity and ministry. The 1950s were a time of great change, with Malaysia achieving independence, the formation of the Malaya Baptist Convention, and Malaysia Baptist Theological Seminary (MBTS) also being founded. The Convention has long been committed to aid and relief work, to education—investing in MBTS, and growth through mission—especially in central Asia.[43]

When the Boxing Day Tsunami desolated many Asian countries in 2004, MBC urged churches to contribute to the Tsunami Relief Fund, raising a total of RM 1157,525.22. Following this significant effort, they set up the Malaysia Baptist Convention Aid Fund, thus enabling MBC to respond quickly to natural disasters. In 2006, MBC was able to partner with churches and organizations in Indonesia to provide aid after the Yogyakarta Earthquake. They were also able to provide support and relief after the Philippines Typhoon in the same year. The aftermath of the Durian Typhoon continued to plague the Philippines in 2007 and a special

---

42. Korean Baptist Theological University/Seminary, "Mission & Vision."

43. Now Malaysia Baptist Convention, MBC celebrated its fiftieth anniversary in 2003 with the launch of Bobby and Dorothy Evans's book *Great Things He Has Done!*. I am indebted to them and their work.

collection was taken up to support those affected by flooding. Today their disaster relief work is focused on responding to the COVID-19 crisis.[44]

MBTS was established in 1954, and its Singaporean branch (BTS) was founded in 1983. Over the next thirty years MBTS, under the auspices of MBC, cultivated international partnerships with the United States, Australia, and Korea, and co-developed programs in World Christian Foundations, Holistic Child Development, Youth Ministry, Counseling, and a Doctor of Missiology program in Korean.[45] The recent mission of MBTS has been to mobilize God's people to serve as full-time ministers and lay workers, supporting the spiritual leadership of local churches, and equipping students holistically.

Further areas of investment for MBC are: church growth—the Baptist New Work Fund supports church planting; theological education—providing churches with quality teaching and training in the form of seminars and workshops; mission—continuing work in East Malaysia and with their Tamil-speaking ministry, and advancing their work abroad, including a project to get two thousand Bibles into Central Asia; and aid and development work—particularly, helping women break the cycle of poverty in Central Asia through sewing ministries.[46]

Mongolia

The first Protestant missionary to Mongolia was John Gibbens, who had been involved in translation and humanitarian work since the 1970s and, after the dissolution of the Soviet Union, was able to identify himself as a missionary. There continue to be a number of challenges to the relatively new work, including the ongoing popularity of Shamanism, and alcoholism is a problem. There are also challenges for those trying to report on it: Mongolia's definition of church—and loose concept of denomination—make it difficult to clearly discern the Baptist work. However, it is clear that Christianity is on the rise and partnership is key to the progress being made.

---

44. Malaysia Baptist Convention, "Welcome to Malaysia Baptist Convention Online."

45. Malaysia Baptist Theological Seminary, "History."

46. Malaysia Baptist Convention, "Welcome to Malaysia Baptist Convention Online."

Mongolian people are open to the supernatural, and a factor in the reported number of Christians growing from fifty to twelve thousand is their ready acceptance of the resurrection. Their interest in the mysterious has also meant that Shamanism, the religion of Genghis Khan, feels a natural fit to many Mongolians, and this has been difficult for churches to counteract. Many congregations still gather together in house-churches (*ger* church), making obtaining accurate statistics for Protestant churches troublesome. Mongolian church leaders, like Baptist pastor Rev. Oggie Yoshua, have indicated that the formal statistics do not recognize *ger* church numbers, and they estimate there are approximately forty-five thousand members across five hundred churches.[47]

Among the estimated five hundred churches, one fourth of them have been planted by Mongolian national leaders. Mongolia is made up of twenty-one states or provinces (*aymags*), which are further divided into three hundred and thirty counties or districts (*soums*). Of these *soums*, only 40 percent have local churches. There are over five hundred foreign missionaries working in Mongolia, including SBC missionaries, but the vast majority of these cross-cultural workers—around four hundred—are Koreans. They work in partnership with Mongolians, "to set up churches on indigenous, sustainable principles," much like the Cambodian model.[48] There seems to be no clear distinction between missionaries and Christian non-government organization workers, making obtaining accurate statistics difficult. Another difficulty in obtaining Baptist-specific data is the blurry boundaries of denomination.

Missionaries to Mongolia, no matter their denomination, have worked in partnership with one another, and with locals, establishing interdenominational churches. Many churches tend toward a Presbyterian identity—though they do not necessarily name themselves as such—because the majority of Korean missionaries have been sent from Presbyterian churches. In 2015, Mongolia had ten churches which identified as Baptist, including one in the remote Khovd *aymag*. Nine of these churches were being led by Korean missionaries and one church has a Mongolian-national pastor—Yoshua. There are also tens of small churches in Baihangar, which are heavily supported by Suwon Central Baptist Church. Most of the leaders from these churches have visited Korea and

47. The APBF 2017 conference was the first time a Mongolian church leader, Rev. Oggie Yoshua, had attended. Much of this information comes thanks to him.

48. Missionary to Mongolia Robert Keroac quoted in de Bourmont, "Christianity in Mongolia."

participated in leadership training programs held by Suwon. Though they have Baptist distinctives, they hesitate to call themselves Baptist, at least partially due to receiving subsidies from other denominations.[49]

A Baptist Bible School and Seminary, operated by Korea Baptist missionaries, averages five to ten students each year. The total number of graduates, so far, is over thirty. As of yet, there is no organized Baptist association or convention. Yoshua, who is the pastor at Holy Foundation Baptist Church, is forming a Baptist association which aims to join the APBF in the not-too-distant future. He has the respect and trust of Baptists and missionaries in Mongolia, and he indicated that many of the Baptist leaders have felt the need for these kinds of networks.

Myanmar

Myanmar (Burma) has over one hundred ethnic groups, many of which have their own distinct language or dialect. They have experienced some of the longest civil wars in recent history and, following the almost fifty years of military rule from 1962 to 2011, there had been tenuous ceasefire arrangements between the military and various ethnic groups. But military rule resumed in 2021, with a one-year state of emergency being declared. Upwards of three thousand seven hundred villages had been destroyed, relocated, or abandoned since 1996 and, by the close of 2012, conservative estimates put the number of displaced persons at four hundred thousand.[50] While the 2012 reforms, and Aung San Suu Kyi's landmark 2015 election, had meant progress, and that many diplomatic relationships had resumed, the conflict and persecution have not ceased, but they have, in fact, considerably increased after the military coup on February 1, 2021 and San Suu Kyi's imprisonment; Baptists are still working in the shadow of a neglected healthcare system, ethnic strife, and human rights violations.

Baptist history in Myanmar began with pioneer missionaries Adoniram and Ann Judson, and their legacy includes the Myanmar Baptist Convention, formed in 1865, which now records close to two million

---

49. I thank my APBF colleague, Timothy Hyun-Mo Lee, Senior Professor of Missiology at Korea Baptist Theological University/Seminary, for his report submitted to the APBF Executive Committee.

50. Border Consortium, "Changing Realities, Poverty and Displacement."

church members.[51] Myanmar is a predominately Buddhist country with approximately 6 percent of the population identifying as Christian. Around two-thirds are Protestant and half of these Protestants are Baptist. Myanmar Baptist Convention (MBC) has eighteen affiliated language and regional conventions. The centennial of the Karen Baptist Convention, the largest member body of MBC, was in 2013. This occasion was closely followed by the two-hundred-year anniversary of the arrival of the Judsons in Burma. The four-day commemoration was organized by the Myanmar Institute of Theology (MIT). It was remarkable that thousands of Baptists from all over the world were able to meet together in a country where meetings of more than five people were strictly forbidden during the half century of military rule.[52]

The Convention operates MIT, which was founded in June 1927 on Seminary Hill, Yangon. MIT receives enrollments from upwards of twenty distinct ethnic groups and ten different Christian denominations. The Institute originally used the facilities of the Karen Theological Seminary, now known as the Kayin Baptist Theological Seminary. Since the exit of American Baptist missionaries from Burma in 1966, the Institute has continued to flourish and at times has been staffed entirely by Myanmar nationals.[53] Over the last sixty years, MIT has had to navigate the difficulties of a diverse student body and the numerous challenges of operating under a military regime. Based on their experience with MIT, MBC is planning to open a Christian university.

As well as a strong focus on education, Baptists in Myanmar are actively involved in ethnic and community-based health organizations, particularly in conflict-affected and remote regions of Eastern Myanmar, where health and sanitation issues continue to be problem. Dr. Cynthia Maung, Director of the Mae Tao Clinic, is herself a displaced Karen, and a Baptist, who was forced to flee Burma in the pro-democracy uprisings in 1988. For close to thirty years, she has worked in Mae Sot, on the Thailand-Myanmar border, providing health services, and sanctuary, to refugees. The current emphasis of primary healthcare programs offered by organizations such as the Mao Tao Clinic, is reproductive, maternal, and child health services. Baptist health organizations are "dedicated to ensuring that the people of Burma are empowered to advocate for their

51. Baptist World Alliance (BWA), "Myanmar Baptist Convention."

52. Allen, "Baptists Celebrate Judsons in Burma."

53. Myanmar Institute of Theology, "Myanmar Institute of Theology."

own civil rights and to have equitable access to basic services such as healthcare and education."[54] As the horrific treatment of ethnic minorities comes increasingly to light, there has been renewed efforts in strategic humanitarian intervention work.

Following the shocking reinstatement of military rule, MBC has bravely called for the release of the President, the State Counselor, and other detainees, while hoping for the emergence of a democratic republic, which "values and promotes peace, justice, national reconciliation, non-violence, and respect for human rights and dignity."[55] MBC also drew attention to the compounding factor of the COVID-19 pandemic.

Nepal

After the political reforms of 1990, Nepal was more open to the spread of the Gospel. The Nepal Baptist Church Council (NBCC—all the Baptist Churches of Nepal) was formed on the eleventh of April 1992 with eight Baptist churches. When the NBCC is not responding to frequent natural disaster, it is focused on mission, evangelism, discipleship, church planting, leadership development, social works, and equipping local churches to be healthy, sending churches. BWA records NBCC as having two hundred and forty-six churches (increasing from one hundred and seventy-six in 2015) and over twenty thousand baptized members (up from eighteen thousand).[56]

Nepal was ravaged by a 7.8 magnitude earthquake in April 2015. The earthquake claimed the lives of more than five thousand eight hundred people and left thousands more homeless. The aftershocks caused further damage and made coordinating relief work difficult. Local congregations from the Kathmandu area immediately formed a disaster relief committee. Francis Horton, the Central and South Asia area director for Baptist Global Response, ensured committee members received humanitarian crisis training. They then partnered with the agency and other national and international organizations, such as the Cooperative Baptist Fellowship and Hungarian Baptist Aid, to provide much-needed aid, assist with navigation, and assess which major needs had not yet been met by other organizations. Horton recognized that "partnership is

54. Health Information System Working Group (HISWG), *Long Road to Recovery.*

55. Myanmar Baptist Convention, "Statement of the Myanmar Baptist Convention."

56. BWA, "Nepal Baptist Church Council."

a key element—really essential in trying to meet the needs in appropriate ways."[57]

NBCC has set growth goals for the near future: to "mobilize local churches to establish new churches"—the plan is to achieve this through evangelism, discipleship and training; to "develop capable Christian leaders for mission in all areas of society"—again, this will be accomplished through training, as well as founding Bible colleges or centers, developing scholarship programs, and cultivating support for church administration and management; to conduct more humanitarian and social work through community development programs and social services, including income generating projects, health education, responding to natural disasters, climate action, and conflict management; to "facilitate organizational development" by purchasing land, constructing buildings, developing policy, and updating structures and systems.[58] NBCC has been developing strategic partnerships to help reach these goals, and given their rapid increase in churches and members over the last five years, they are well on their way to achieving these goals.

Philippines

After years of Spanish colonial rule, extensive Catholic influence, and the aftereffects of World War II, Filipino pastors and believers needed to rediscover and redefine their identity and their mission. It was becoming increasingly clear that they wanted to develop their own distinct Filipino way of expressing faith. There are approximately four thousand Baptist churches with six hundred thousand members across the Philippines. These are made up of the Convention of Philippine Baptist Churches (CPBC), Baptist Conference of the Philippines (BCP), General Baptist Churches of the Philippines, Convention of Visayas and Mindanao of Southern Baptist Churches, Central Philippines Convention of Southern Baptist Churches, and Luzon Convention of Southern Baptist Churches.[59]

In the 1980s, Pastor Rudy Acosta aptly described the situation in the Philippines as an identity crisis: "Chinese have chopsticks, what about Filipinos? What do we have? We don't know what we are. We're like a

---

57. Baptist Standard, "Baptists Respond to Needs in Earthquake-Ravaged Nepal."
58. Nepal Baptist Church Council, "About Us."
59. APBF, "APBF Member Bodies."

hamburger."[60] Within a society that was still exploring its nationhood after independence, Baptists were also experiencing a period of self-reflec-
tion. The time was ripe for working through what a contextual theology
looked like for the Philippines, and to question the ways in which they
should engage with the changing and developing culture around them.
Pastors were concerned with practical questions from daily life.

Issues of everyday church operations, and how Christians and
the church should relate to their neighbors, were explored. The Director of the Baptist Convention Bible College, Rev. Angelina Buensuceso,
responded by developing new educational and training opportunities,
saying "Culture and Christian spirituality are intertwined. One appears
foreign and unfamiliar without the other. . . . A spirituality detached from
culture develops a (spiritual) life without meaning. A culture detached
from spirituality develops a (cultural) life without firm foundation."[61]
Establishing first their own Filipino Baptist identity, and then earnestly
seeking to connect with their communities, has shaped the life and work
of Baptists in the Philippines today.

Inspired by the work of Buensuceso and others, the CPBC now
places a particular emphasis on educational programs. Its department
of Christian Education is tasked with assisting local churches to develop
a ministry through which "people and communities are continuously
renewed, nurtured, transformed and empowered faithfully to participate in God's redemptive acts towards a fuller manifestation of God's
reign."[62] Furthermore, a department for theological education was set up
to oversee theological schools and Bible colleges and organize continued
training for pastors. CPBC conducts community outreach work including partnering with indigenous peoples, ecological programs, and adult
literacy programs.

The other conventions also continue to be focused on growth, aid,
and development, and theological education: BCP concentrates on overseas mission, sending and supporting forty missionaries to twelve different nations; Convention of Visayas and Mindanao of Southern Baptist
Churches have a dedicated men's ministry and a flourishing youth fellowship; the General Baptist Churches of the Philippines are focused on

60. Rudy Acosta quoted in Jalando-on, *History of Philippine Baptist Pastors 1898–
2002*. Once again, I am indebted to my APBF co-worker, F. Neil Jalando-on.

61. Angelina Buensuceso quoted in Jalando-on, "History of Philippine Baptist Pastors, 1898–2002."

62. World Council of Churches, "Convention of Philippine Baptist Churches."

church planting and the two bible colleges they operate—General Baptist Bible College and Matigsalog Bible Institute; and the Luzon Convention of Southern Baptist Churches is channeling their efforts into social justice, youth ministry, men's ministry, the Women's Missionary Union, global mission, and were instrumental in responding to Typhoon Mangkut in 2018.[63] With the COVID-19 delta variant reaching the Philippines in July 2021, the conventions are redoubling their relief efforts.

Singapore

In stark contrast to countries like Cambodia and Myanmar, Singapore was ranked first in Asia on the UN Human Development Index.[64] Singapore's people fare very well in terms of education, healthcare, life expectancy, housing, personal safety, and general quality of life. By 1970, the original two Baptist churches had turned into eleven autonomous churches. After some deliberation over the use of the term convention, since those churches who had been a part of the Malaysia Baptist Convention—before Singapore exited Malaysia—had negative experiences, the Singapore Baptist Churches' Fellowship was inaugurated in 1971. It took only a few years for the initial concerns over the use of the word "convention" to subside as the various Baptist churches learned to cooperate.[65] The Singapore Baptist Convention now places emphasis on evangelism, church planting, theological education, and foreign mission.

The Singapore Baptist Theological Seminary (SBTS) was established in 1983 as a branch of the Malaysian Baptist Theological Seminary (MBTS), as Singaporean students were having difficulty obtaining visas to study in Malaysia after Singapore's independence. Eventually the seminary became an institution in its own right (under the umbrella of the Convention) and was renamed Baptist Theological Seminary (BTS). BTS offers a Doctor of Ministry through Union University, Tennessee, USA, and overall enrollments have surged from twenty-two in 2004 to ninety in 2016.[66] The English-speaking program has students from Myanmar, the Philippines, Thailand, Korea, India, Indonesia, Vietnam,

63. APBF, "Typhoon Mangkut Shelter Recovery."

64. Now second to Hong Kong, as at 2020: UNDP Human Development Report.

65. Morris, *Singapore Baptist Family Story 1970–2000+*.

66. Baptist Theological Seminary, "History."

and the United States. Local students and students from China make up the Chinese-speaking program.

The first two years after the creation of the Convention were integral to the development of many of the key programs they would undertake over the next thirty years. A strategic partnership with the Southern Baptist Convention, and cooperative relationships with international Baptist organizations have enabled a concerted effort in church growth, mission, the development of new courses and programs at BTS, and fostering cooperation between Chinese Baptists.[67] By 2015, the Convention had thirty-seven member churches with approximately ten thousand baptized believers. Ministries have been focused on: BTS—developing and accrediting new courses; Mission—ongoing work on the Riau Islands in Indonesia and Isaan in Northeast Thailand; working toward uniting Chinese Baptist organizations all over the world (the 2017 Trans-World Chinese Baptist Mission Conference was held in Bangkok); aged and community care—providing financial, spiritual, social, and educational aid to the disadvantaged and specialized care for seniors; aid and development work—Baptist Global Response is a disaster relief and community development organization which supports the work of Southern Baptists worldwide; and several ministries dedicated to training and supporting pastors and lay-leaders.[68] The Convention continues to focus on ministry partnerships and membership growth.[69]

Thailand

There are four member-organizations belonging to the APBF in Thailand: the Twelfth District of the Church of Christ in Thailand (CCT); Thailand Baptist Convention (TBC); Thailand Karen Baptist Convention (TKBC); and Thailand Lahu Baptist Convention (TLBC)—the largest of these being the Thailand Karen Baptist Convention. The ethnic Thai are difficult to convert—since to be Thai is to be Buddhist—with more and easier growth being seen among other ethnic groups, like the Karen and the Lahu. As well as church planting and education, much of the work of Baptists is dedicated to humanitarian aid and development, especially given their proximity to Myanmar.

67. Morris, *Singapore Baptist Family Story 1970–2000+*, 34.

68. Singapore Baptist Convention, "Baptist Publications."

69. Singapore Baptist Convention, "Convention Team."

The Church of Christ in Thailand is the oldest denomination in Thailand, it was established in 1934 by a merger of American Baptist and Presbyterian churches, and is also the largest Protestant denomination, accounting for about half of all Protestants. It now has Thai, Chinese, Karen, Lahu, and English-speaking congregations. The CCT has a focus on both education and aid work. They currently operate: two universities, two theological seminaries, seven hospitals, and in excess of thirty schools. Their aid and development work includes: social work in the slum communities of Bangkok; agricultural and community development in rural areas; in the 1970s their work with Cambodian refugees was crucial; and they continue to work with refugees from Myanmar today,[70] including programs in HIV/AIDS education and prevention, and they provide vocational training for tribal women, giving them an alternative to the sex industry.[71]

TBC is, comparatively, a small denomination of Baptist churches. SBC missionaries laid the groundwork for the convention in the early 1800s and TBC is now one of only five Christian organizations recognized by the Thai government. One of the recent efforts of TBC was to ensure Thai people can easily access information on each of the churches in the convention. This information is also being used to discern where new churches need to be planted,[72] and has become part of a Thai-led, spirit-led revival.[73]

The TKBC is a branch of the Karen Baptist Convention of Myanmar, which is one of the eighteen member-bodies of the Myanmar Baptist Convention. The Lahu are an ethnic group originally from Tibet, with populations in China, Myanmar, Thailand and Laos. TLBC, based in Chiang Mai, celebrated their fiftieth anniversary in 2020, and have a missions focus on China. An overview of Thailand would not be complete without mentioning the remarkable work of the Kawthoolei Karen Baptist Bible School, which is one of the largest seminaries in Southeast Asia. It was founded in 1983 and in 1986 they moved to their current location, in the Mae La Karen Refugee Camp, in the Song Yang District, to

70. World Council of Churches, "Church of Christ in Thailand."

71. Global Ministries, "Church of Christ in Thailand."

72. Thailand Baptist Convention, "Directory"; Tuthai, "Find Churches By."

73. Shellnutt, "Making Missions Count" and "Thai Church Holds Record-Breaking Baptism."

avoid persecution. The Bible School has become a displaced institution, serving and training a displaced people group.[74]

Vietnam

Vietnam is considered one of the least religious countries in the world, with over 70 percent of the population identifying with a nominal form of Vietnamese folk religion—combining elements of Confucianism and Taoism. Despite this, the Baptist Convention of Vietnam (BCV) has over five hundred churches with over forty thousand members.[75] Notwithstanding the beginning of the war in 1954, Baptist work in Vietnam commenced in 1959, and the first church, Grace Baptist Church, was established shortly after in Saigon. Le Quoc Chanh, the first Vietnamese Baptist-convert, became pastor in 1970 and led the church for the next thirty years.[76] By 1975, forty missionary families had joined in the work and were spread throughout Vietnam, discipling local believers.[77]

After two decades of war between North and South Vietnam, Saigon fell in 1975. Vietnam had been ravaged and its people did not know what to expect of the new reunified Communist government. Though the Foreign Mission Board of SBC had decided to pull its missionaries out of Vietnam, Grace Baptist Church kept its doors open and continued to hold services, even with the political climate. It was the only church to do so in the early days after the end of the war.[78] Since then, government restrictions have been placed on public expressions of faith and churches cannot own land or buildings. This means that many Vietnamese Baptists meet in house-churches. People have continued to come to faith through this model, but it has led to dozens of small, disconnected groups.[79] In 2008, largely through Le Quoc Chanh and his son Huy's guidance, a new national Baptist confederation was formed, and Grace Baptist Church was formally recognized by the government.[80] In 2010, Huy followed in his father's footsteps and became senior pastor of Grace Baptist. Grace

74. Kawthoolei Karen Baptist Bible School, "Brief History."
75. BWA, "Baptist Convention of Vietnam."
76. Graham, "New Hope Dawns for Vietnam."
77. Rivers, "Baptists Celebrate 50 Years in Vietnam," para. 11.
78. Rivers, "Baptists Celebrate 50 Years in Vietnam," para. 5.
79. Graham, "Unity for Vietnam's Baptists."
80. Ranish, "Baptist Church Celebrates Vietnam Recognition."

Baptist Church still meets at its original location, and in 2019 it celebrated sixty years of Baptist work in Vietnam.[81]

At the beginning of 2016, there was a renewed effort for the Baptist Churches of Vietnam to form a convention and to obtain further recognition from the government. The goals of the new convention are: to plant new churches, disciple believers, train workers, develop leaders, publish training materials, and meet human needs in the name of Jesus.[82] The national convention also assists in sending missionaries to neighboring Southeast Asian countries like Laos and Cambodia.

Conclusion

Baptist churches and organizations across Asia are overwhelmingly focused on church growth at home and abroad and, while there is a considerable emphasis on education and training, they are less concerned with issues of theology. The catastrophic forces of nature that Asia is prone to, has meant that organizations like APBAid need to be able to respond quickly to disaster and be strategic in their communication, partnership and training. Bangladesh operates one of the regions key development agencies and has experienced rapid church growth. Cambodia's remarkably successful church-planting method has inspired similar models in other contexts. Hong Kong Baptist University carries out innovative research and are world leaders in the field of geography. Indonesia is experiencing increased cooperation across its various conventions. Japan is being reinvigorated by more progressive pastors. Korea's unprecedented growth and commitment to foreign mission is formidable. Malaysia has been instrumental in aid and relief work following multiple natural disasters in the region. Mongolia is striving toward forming an association of churches. Baptists in Myanmar and Thailand, in the face of turmoil and strife, are working to provide holistic care to persecuted and displaced peoples. Nepal, while often earthquake-affected, is dedicated to planting new churches. The Philippines encourages female pastors and educators, and have worked hard to develop a distinctly Filipino faith. Singapore's BTS is growing both in terms of student numbers and courses provided. And Vietnamese house churches continue to prosper despite a lack of religious freedom. The fruit of APBF's spirit of fellowship, service, and

81. Rivers, "Baptists Celebrate 50 Years in Vietnam," para. 6.
82. Rivers, "Baptists Celebrate 50 Years in Vietnam," para. 10.

cooperation through mission, evangelism, relief, and development, and theological education is clearly evident in its member bodies.

Bibliography

Allen, Bob. "Baptists Celebrate Judsons in Burma." *Baptist News*, December 5, 2013. https://baptistnews.com/article/baptists-celebrate-judsons-in-burma/#. UqHSLvRDtqU.

Asia Baptist Women's Union. "ABWU Support COVID Third Wave." https://www. asiabwu.org/covid-19-second-wave.html.

———. "Our Vision." https://www.asiabwu.org/.

———. "13th ABWU Assembly." https://www.apbf.org/blog/post/5520/13th-ABWU-Assembly/.

Asia Pacific Baptist Federation. "About APBAid." https://www.apbf.org/blog/post/5384/ About-APBAid/.

———. "APBF Member Bodies." https://www.apbf.org/blog/post/5339/APBF-Member-Bodies/.

———. "APBF Peace Forum 2014 Report." https://www.apbf.org/blog/post/5241/ APBF-Peace-Forum-2014-Report/.

———. "Asia Pacific Baptist Theological Education." https://www.apbf.org/page/apbte/

———. "Asia Pacific Baptist Youth Conference 2019." https://www.apbf.org/blog/ post/5208/Asia-Pacific-Baptist-Youth-Conference-2019/.

———. "9th APBF Congress Yogyakarta." https://www.apbf.org/blog/post/5512/9th-APBF-Congress-YogyakartaIndonesia/.

———. "Typhoon Mangkut Shelter Recovery." https://www.apbf.org/site_files/4002/ upload_files/blog/TyphoonMangkhut-ShelterRecoveryUpdate.pdf?dl=1.

———. "Visit to Baptist Convention of Vietnam Youths." https://www.apbf.org/blog/ post/5247/VISIT-TO-BAPTIST-CONVENTION-OF-VIETNAM-YOUTHS/.

———. "Who We Represent." https://www.apbf.org/page/about/.

Asia Theological Association. "Visit to College of Christian Theology Bangladesh." http://www.ataasia.com/visit-to-college-of-christian-theology-bangladesh/.

Bangladesh Baptist Church Sangha. "About Us." http://www.bbcs.org.bd/about-us. html.

Baptist Convention of Hong Kong. "Ministries." http://www.hkbaptist.org.hk/acms/. content.asp?site=bchk&op=listbycode&code=Union&sort=EventStartDate&orde r=desc&topn=1.

Baptist Standard. "Baptists Respond to Needs in Earthquake-Ravaged Nepal." https:// www.baptiststandard.com/news/world/17737-baptists-respond-to-needs-in-earthquake-ravaged-nepal.

Baptist Theological Seminary. "History." https://bts.edu.sg/about/get-to-know-us/.

Baptist World Aid Australia. "When Women Keep Raising a Village." https:// baptistworldaid.org.au/2021/05/17/when-women-keep-raising-a-village/.

Baptist World Alliance. "Baptist Convention of Vietnam." https://www.baptistworld. org/baptist-convention-of-vietnam-bcv/.

———. "Cambodia Baptist Union." https://www.baptistworld.org/cambodia-baptist-union/.

————. "Myanmar Baptist Convention." https://www.baptistworld.org/myanmar-baptist-convention/.

————. "Nepal Baptist Church Council." https://www.baptistworld.org/nepal-baptist-church-council/.

Rivers, Tess. "Baptists Celebrate 50 Years in Vietnam." *Baptist Press News*, November 25, 2009. http://bpnews.net/31767/baptists-celebrate-50-years-in-vietnam-with-hugs-tears.

The Border Consortium. *Changing Realities, Poverty and Displacement in South East Burma/Myanmar.* https://reliefweb.int/report/myanmar/changing-realities-poverty-and-displacement-south-east-burmamyanmar.

Christians Sharing Christ Film Ministries. "Update by Brother Nivath." http://www.cscfm.org/from-cambodia-update-by-bro-nivath-cambodian-baptist-union/.

de Bourmont, Martin. "Christianity in Mongolia: A Look at How a Foreign Faith Is Adapting to Mongolian Culture." *The Diplomat*, May 10, 2016. https://thediplomat.com/2016/05/christianity-in-mongolia/.

Evans, Bobby, and Dorothy Evans. *Great Things He Has Done! A Century of Malaysian Baptist History.* Malaysia: Malaysia Baptist Convention, 2003.

Foxwell Duttweiler, Marisa. "Aftershocks: What the Japanese Church Has Learned 10 Years After Fukushima." *Christianity Today*, March 12, 2021. https://www.christianitytoday.com/news/2021/march/japan-christians-triple-disaster-tsunami-fukushima-churches.html.

Global Interaction. "Living among the Khmer People." https://www.globalinteraction.org.au/support/workers/people-groups/khmer.

Global Ministries. "The Church of Christ in Thailand." https://www.globalministries.org/partner/the_church_of_christ_in_thailand/.

Graham, Don. "New Hope Dawns for Vietnam." *IMB Connecting: Commission Stories*, July 18, 2011. http://stories.imb.org/asia/stories/view/new-hope-dawns-for-vietnam.

————. "Unity for Vietnam's Baptists Is Pastor's Next Goal." *Baptist Press*, February 16, 2016. http://www.bpnews.net/46324/unity-for-vietnams-baptists-is-pastors-next-goal.

Health Information System Working Group (HISWG). *The Long Road to Recovery: Ethnic and Community-Based Health Organizations Leading the Way to Better Health in Eastern Burma.* https://reliefweb.int/report/myanmar/long-road-recovery-ethnic-and-community-based-health-organizations-leading-way-better.

Hong Kong Baptist University. "About HKBU." https://www.hkbu.edu.hk/eng/about/abouthkbu.jsp.

"In the Land of the Thunder Dragon." *APBF Digest*, January 2017. https://www.apbf.org/site_files/4002/upload_files/blog/January2017web.pdf?dl=1.

Jalando-on, Francis Neil G. "A History of Philippine Baptist Pastors, 1898–2002." *Baptist Heritage*. http://bwa-baptist-heritage.org/wp-content/uploads/2016/07/History-of-Philippine-Baptist-Pastors-1898–2002.pdf?iframe=true.

Japan Baptist Convention. "Cooperative Missions Pamphlet." http://www.bapren.jp/uploads/photos/536.pdf.

Japan Baptist Convention Disaster Relief Committee. "Bond of Prayer." http://baptist2.exblog.jp/.

Japan Baptist Hospital. "The Origin of the Japan Baptist Hospital." https://www.jbh. or.jp/english.html.

Kawthoolei Karen Baptist Bible School. "Brief History." https://sites.google.com/site/ kkbbsc/home/brief-history.

Kenny, Peter. "Hong Kong Baptist Leader Who Backed Protesters Quits before Abruptly Leaving for UK." *Ecumenical News*, https://www.ecumenicalnews.com/article/ hong-kong-baptist-leader-who-backed-protesters-quits-before-abruptly-leaving-for-uk/60861.htm.

Korean Baptist Theological University/Seminary. "Mission & Vision." http://eng.kbtus. ac.kr/mission&vision.html.

Lee, Timothy Hyun-Mo. "A Report on Mongolia Submitted to Asia Pacific Baptist Federation." Executive Committee, September 3, 2015.

Malaysia Baptist Convention. "Welcome to Malaysia Baptist Convention Online." http://www.mbc.org.

Malaysia Baptist Theological Seminary. "History." http://www.mbts.org.my/en/history.

Mission Frontiers. "Case Studies of CPMs—The Khmer of Cambodia." http://www. missionfrontiers.org/issue/article/case-studies-of-cpms-the-khmer-of-cambodia.

Mission Network News. "Baptist Church Celebrates Vietnam Recognition." https:// www.mnnonline.org/news/.

Morris, Russell A. *The Singapore Baptist Family Story 1970–2000+*. Singapore: Singapore Baptist Convention, 2007.

Myanmar Baptist Convention. "Statement of the Myanmar Baptist Convention." http://mbc-1813.org/2021/02/10/statement-of-the-myanmar-baptist-convention/?lang=en.

Myanmar Institute of Theology. "Myanmar Institute of Theology." https://www.scribd. com/document/6991805/.

Nepal Baptist Church Council. "About Us." http://nbccnepal.org/.

Partners International. "Partner Organizations." https://www.kutoa.org/partners/ bangladesh-baptist-church-fellowship.

Ponleu Ney Kdey Sangkhum. "Welcome to PNKS." http://www.pnks-cambodia.org/.

Ranish, David V. "Baptist Church Celebrates Vietnam Recognition." *Mission Network News*, January 21, 2008. https://www.mnnonline.org/news/baptist-church-celebrates-vietnam-recognition/.

Seinan Gakuin University. "Message from the President." https://www.seinan-gu.ac.jp/ eng/aboutsgu/message.html.

Singapore Baptist Convention. "Baptist Publications." https://www.baptistconvention. org.sg/publications/.

———. "The Convention Team." https://www.baptistconvention.org.sg/convention-team/.

Shellnutt, Kate. "Making Missions Count: How a Major Database Tracked Thailand's Church-Planting Revival." *Christianity Today*, March 15, 2019. https://www. christianitytoday.com/ct/2019/april/missions-data-thai-church-fjcca-reach-village.html.

———. "Thai Church Holds Record-Breaking Baptism Despite COVID-19." *Christianity Today*, September 22, 2020. https://www.christianitytoday.com/ news/2020/september/thailand-largest-baptism-covid-fjcca-reach-village.html.

Thailand Baptist Convention. "Directory." https://thaichurches.org/directory/ denomination/.

Tuthai. "Find Churches By." https://thaichurches.org/directory/area/.

UNDP Human Development Report, "Latest Human Development Index Ranking." http://hdr.undp.org/en/content/latest-human-development-index-ranking.

Woods, Marsha. "Trevor & Makoto, friends since age 6." *Baptist News*, 2011, http://bpnews.net/36309/.

Woods, Tony. *Sacrificed, Given to an Empire; Found by God.* Gold Coast: Marton, 2011.

World Council of Churches. "Bangladesh Baptist Church Sangha." https://www.oikoumene.org/member-churches/bangladesh-baptist-church-sangha.

———. "Church of Christ in Thailand." https://www.oikoumene.org/en/member-churches/church-of-christ-in-thailand.

———. "Convention of Philippine Baptist Churches." http://www.oikoumene.org/en/member-churches/convention-of-philippine-baptist-churches.

Yu, Kun Jae. "An Analysis of the Historical and Theological Identity of the Korean Baptist Convention: An Indigenous Charismatic Movement." A Thesis Submitted to The University of Birmingham, 2014.

26

Baptists in India Today
Tribal, Marginalized, and Independent

Dietmar Schulze

List of Abbreviations
ABC: American Baptist Churches
APBF: Asian Pacific Baptist Federation
BWA: Baptist World Alliance
CBCNEI: Council of Baptist Churches in Northeast India
Crore: Ten Million
KJV: King James Version of the Bible
SC: Scheduled Castes
STBC: Samavesam of Telegu Baptist Churches
TBC: Telangana Baptist Convention

Introduction

There are many books on the history of the Baptists in India, but it is difficult to find a single book in German or English on all Baptist unions in India today. This fact makes this topic very difficult when one considers that there are twenty-one Baptist unions that are members in the Baptist

World Alliance (BWA)[1] in a country with some 1.34 billion people (July 2021, est.).[2] Most unions can be found in the northeast of the subcontinent, a region that is geographically as well as culturally distinct from the rest of India. In addition to those Baptists within unions, there are independent Baptists which make up about half of the 4 million members in churches that have some form of Baptist traditions.[3] Although there is no umbrella organization, many of these churches are connected by a similar confession of faith and by common features. Research must consider that Christian in India face persecution, in some states more than in others. India is number 10 on the 2021 Open Doors World Watchlist[4] and number 6 on the 2020–21 BWS Baptist Vulnerability Index[5]

In this chapter, three different groups of Baptists will be presented as examples of the denominational spectrum in India. The first group are the tribal Baptists in northeast India. Up to the twentieth century, tribes like the Naga people had been practicing headhunting before they converted to Christianity. The tribal culture contributed decisively to the present form of the tribal Baptists. The second group are the marginalized. These Baptists are for the most part Dalits. Many of them are Telugu-speaking people in eastern India, especially in Andhra Pradesh and Telangana. The membership of the Samavesam of Telegu Baptist Churches was under review because of financial irregularities, and it is no longer member of the BWA. In the year 2016, the alternative union Telangana was launched that is still not listed on BWA's member website. Finally, there are about seven million independent Baptists.[6] Some of KJV-only fundamental independent Baptist churches serve as an illustration for the influence of Western congregations and conventions on Baptist churches and that denominational label could have a different meaning in India.[7] The different length of each section is best explained by the amount of information that was available to this author. The focus is on the northeast of the country.

1. Baptist World Alliance, "Member Unions."
2. CIA, "The World Factbook."
3. Johnson and Zurlo, "World Christian Database."
4. Open Doors USA, "India."
5. Baptist World Alliance, "2020–2021 BWA Baptist Vulnerability Index."
6. Johnson and Zurlo, "World Christian Database."
7. Fundamental.org - King James - Fundamental - Independent-Baptist, "India."

The author is an outside observer of these three groups. In his dissertation,[8] he had written about the Baptists in Northeast India. The sources for this chapter are books, articles, messages, personal correspondence, and webpages. Before the reader turns to the three groups, some introductory remarks should bring orientation on the overall situation of the Baptists in India today.

Baptists in India

According to the World Christian Database, there were about 4 million Baptists in India in 2015.[9] More recent data is available for the 2.1 million members in the twenty-one unions that are affiliated with the Baptist World Alliance (BWA).[10] Statistics differ and must therefore be handled with caution. According to JoshuaProject, there are twenty-seven million Christians,[11] according to the World Factbook, there are thirty-one million Christians,[12] and according to World Christian Database, there are sixty-six million Christians.[13] The numbers of the World Factbook are based on the census data. In 2001 and 2011, 2.3 percent of the population was identified as Christian.[14] This is almost the same percentage as in 1991 and less than the 2.43 percent in 1981.[15] The following table shows Christians in India who are somehow related to Baptist traditions.

8. Schulze, *Baptisten in Nordostindien.*

9. Johnson and Zurlo, "World Christian Database."

10. Baptist World Alliance, "Member Unions."

11. Joshua Project, "India."

12. "World Factbook."

13. Johnson and Zurlo, "World Christian Database."

14. Office of the Registrar General & Census Commissioner, India, "Census of India 2001"; Office of the Registrar General & Census Commissioner, India, "Census of India 2011."

15. Verma, "Census of India 1981," 176.

Data source: Johnson and Zurlo, *World Christian Database*.		
Denomination Name	Year Begun	Affiliated 2015
Apatani Baptist Association	1977	44,000
Assoc of Regular Indep Chs of India	1935	8,000
Association of Oriya Baptist Churches	1910	12,000
Baptist Bible Believers Assembly	1968	1,600
Baptist Christian Association	1945	5,500
Baptist Church of Mizoram	1902	164,000
Baptist Union of North India	1947	94,000
Bengal Baptist Union	1935	19,600
Bengal-Orissa-Bihar Baptist Convention	1836	35,000
Conv of Bapt Chs of Northern Circars	1874	280,000
Conv of Baptist Chs of Maharashtra	1950	15,000
Council of Baptist Chs in NE India	1835	1,604,400
Free Will Baptist Conference of India	1935	25,000
Gospel Association of India	1945	14,000
India Association of General Baptists	1940	22,000
India Gospel League	1906	4,800
Karnataka Baptist Convention	1950	79,800
Kuki Christian Church	1943	82,000
Lairam Jesus Christ Baptist Church	1971	38,100
Laymen's Evangelical Union/Fellowship	1935	300,000
North Bank Baptist Christian Assoc	1930	120,000
Rabha Baptist Church Union	1959	14,000
Samavesam of Telugu Baptist Churches	1836	740,000
Saora Association of Baptist Churches	1900	29,000
Separate Baptists in Christ	1917	2,000
Seventh Day Baptist Church	1900	50,000
Siloam Baptist Brethren Fellowship	1975	12,000
Tamil Baptist Churches	1861	2,200
Telugu Baptist Churches	1968	2,600
Tripura Baptist Christian Union	1938	119,000
Zeme Baptist Church Council	1937	40,000
SUM		3,979,600

Table 1[16]

16. Johnson and Zurlo, "World Christian Database."

This diversity is the result of many factors. A decisive factor is the pioneering work of British and American missionaries beginning in the late 1700s. Later, Canadian, Australian, and Swedish Baptists followed and planted churches. The special denominational and cultural imprint that shaped churches for decades, can be recognized even today. The majority denomination in one region can often be explained best by the fact that the first missionaries belonged to this denomination. For example, most Christians in Nagaland are Baptists, while most Christians in Mizoram are Presbyterian.

Other factors that have contributed to the denominational spectrum are the size of the country and the cultural diversity. The population in India is divided into four ethnic groups: "Indo-Aryan 72 percent, Dravidian 25 percent, Mongoloid and other 3 percent (2000)"[17] and several language groups: "Hindi 43.6 percent, Bengali 8 percent, Marathi 6.9 percent, Telugu 6.7 percent, Tamil 5.7 percent, Gujarati 4.6 percent, Urdu 4.2 percent, Kannada 3.6 percent, Odia 3.1 percent, Malayalam 2.9 percent, Punjabi 2.7 percent, Assamese 1.3 percent, Maithili 1.1 percent, other 5.6 percent (2011 est.)."[18] Baptists in the northeast of the country belong to the Mongolian people groups.

The following table shows Baptist unions that are members of the Baptist World Alliance. While the number of churches has declined, the number of members has increased.

BWA Baptist Unions in India					
Sources: http://bwanet.org/about-us2/stats (2015); https://www.baptistworld.org/member-unions/ (2020).	Year	Churches	Members	% Annual Average Growth: Churches	% Annual Average Growth: Members
Arunachal Baptist Church Council	2015	1,024	91,990		
	2020*	1,152	100,397	2.50%	1.83%
Assam Baptist Convention	2015	746	35,169		
	2020*	921	37,410	4.69%	1.27%
Baptist Church of Mizoram	2015	642	116,687		
	2020*	663	122,072	0.65%	0.92%

17. CIA, "World Factbook."
18. CIA, "World Factbook."

Baptist Churches Council of Eastern India	2020*	142	26,513		
Baptist Union of North India	2014	53	14,203		
	2020**	54	15,700	0.31%	1.76%
Bengal Baptist Union	2015	130	14,000		
	2020*	145	7,785	2.31%	-8.88%
Convention of Baptist Churches of the Northern Circars	2004	255	165,400		
	2020*	310	240,000	1.35%	2.82%
Evangelical Baptist Convention of India	2015	199	36,283		
	2020*	207	40,859	0.80%	2.52%
Garo Baptist Convention of India	2015	5,452	295,406		
	2020*	2,619	333,908	-10.39%	2.61%
India Association of General Baptists	2004	121	10,300		
	2020*	121	10,300	0.00%	0.00%
India Baptist Convention	2012	80	8,000		
	2020*	80	8,000	0.00%	0.00%
Karbi Hill Baptist Convention	2015	315	31,746		
	2020*	338	37,515	1.46%	3.63%
Karnataka Baptist Convention	2012	685	56,950		
	2020*	900	72,000	3.92%	3.30%
Lairam Jesus Christ Baptist Church	2015	103	17,766		
	2020*	118	19,822	2.91%	2.31%
Lower Assam Baptist Union	2015	320	36,942		
	2020*	335	38,088	0.94%	0.62%
Maharashtra Baptist Society	2015	253	9,240		
	2020*	413	12,565	12.65%	7.20%
Manipur Baptist Convention	2015	1,303	196,217		
	2020*	1,449	216,429	2.24%	2.06%
Nagaland Baptist Church Council	2015	1,585	586,593		
	2020*	1,615	610,825	0.38%	0.83%
North Bank Baptist Christian Association	2015	1,111	85,901		

	2020*	1,228	109,838	2.11%	5.57%
Orissa Baptist Evangelistic Crusade**	2013	3,421	388,577		
	2020*	34	3,842	-14.14%	-14.14%
Tripura Baptist Christian Union	2015	845	84,795		
	2020*	943	70,604	2.32%	-3.35%
SUM 2015 (or other)		15,885	2,015,660		
SUM 2020		13,753	2,130,630	-2.68%	1.14%
Annual Population Growth in India					1.2%***

*latest available information on https://www.baptistworld.org/member-unions/.

**This data might have an error and will be excluded from SUM.

***Source: https://www.thehindubusinessline.com/news/indias-population-grew-at-12-average-annual-rate-between-2010-and-2019-un/article26803237.ece.

Table 2

"MEGACHURCH: The massive Sümi Baptist Church in Zünheboto is a striking symbol of the imprint of Christianity in the remote state of Nagaland in northeast India. (Photo © Aheli Moitra / The Morung Express)."[19]

19. Jenkins, "Most Baptist State."

Different numbers of members in BWA-affiliated unions and conventions can be found in the BWA Baptist Vulnerability Index: 2.5 million members 14,347 churches.[20] Nagaland remains being the federal state with the highest percentage of Baptists worldwide.[21]

Tribal Baptists

Krishna Chandra Pal, the first Hindu, who was led to faith in Christ by William Carey and was baptized in December 1800, left Serampore for a mission trip to the tribal territories. However, his work was not very successful and did not create a surviving movement quite in contrast to his ministry in Calcutta. Pal was an important pioneer of the Serampore Baptists.[22] From small beginnings, over the course of time and several revival movements later, a large Christian population can now be found in a country that is predominately Hindi. In his thesis, this author identified four conducive circumstances that have contributed to the enormous growth of the Baptists in Northeast India. The following part includes findings of this dissertation.

Firstly, the prohibition of head-hunting resulted in a crisis of identity because the tribes lost an important tradition. The missionaries could help with a new identity through faith. Secondly, the local Christians did the evangelistic work mostly by themselves. It was a movement of young people who went singing and preaching from village to village. Formerly marauding hordes had now turned into mission teams. Thirdly, church structures replaced broken tribal associations. Fourthly, people experienced liberation from spiritual and traditional bondage. It was a process of transformation, in which the culture of the northeast was a suitable ground for the seeds of the gospel. On the other hand, the church changed the culture through the preaching of the gospel. Today there are Christian schools, social services, and Christians in all areas of public life. Depending on the region, the proportion of the Baptists in the society in Nagaland is between 60 to 90 percent.[23]

However, there are also conflicts and problems. Tribes are at enmity, year-long guerrilla war for independence and contacts to the

---

20. Baptist World Alliance, "2020–2021 BWA Baptist Vulnerability Index."

21. Jenkins, "Most Baptist State."

22. Schulze, *Baptisten in Nordostindien,* 49.

23. Lotz, "Who and Where in the World."

independence movement led to a critical observation by the government. Corruption and increasing drug dependency among young people show that each new generation must be won for the gospel. The high number of members in Baptist churches should not conceal the difficulties and challenges like the weakening affinity to the church.[24]

Formerly, British colonization with its ban on the head-hunting contributed to a positive response of Christianity. Today, globalization is reshaping tribal identity. The exchange of worldviews, media, internet, fashion, music, fast food, social networks, etc., are transforming culture and church. The English language connects people who otherwise would not be able to communicate. The rapid growth of the world's metropolises leads to comparable environments. The reactionary efforts to preserve ethnic, linguistic, cultural, and religious traditions are a counter force to globalization. Only a minority of those who answered this author's survey in 2001 referred to themselves as "Indians"; most of them were aware of their tribal identity. By turning to the Christian faith, tribal societies often broke with the old traditions. Today, it seems, cultural forms of the past do experience a comeback. In Northeast India, most people live in the countryside. But even here, many churches operate in an urban context. The comparison of the characteristic groups village/town showed the different influence of this context. Again and again, significant differences were found. The pastors of tomorrow are today's students in the context of the big cities.

Council of Baptist Churches in Northeast India (CBCNEI)

CBCNEI represents those churches that are on the most successful mission field of the American Baptist Churches; their representatives came there in 1836. The Council was founded in 1950. Foreign Mission organizations helped with its formation, especially the American Baptist Foreign Mission Society, which today is the International Ministries of the American Baptist Churches, USA.

The historical connections explain today's ties between CBCNEI and the ABC. "Over the years the CBCNEI has grown to now over 7,000 Churches in 109 organized associations. They are administered under six regional conventions namely, Assam Baptist Convention, Arunachal Baptist Church Council, Garo Baptist Convention, Karbi Anglong

---

24. Schulze, *Baptisten in Nordostindien*, 55.

Baptist Convention, Manipur Baptist Convention, and Nagaland Baptist Church Council."[25] It is the largest denominational body of Baptists in India. More than 1,000 missionaries have been sent by churches and mission agencies. The Secretary General is appointed, the President is elected annually. Rev. Prof. Akheto Sema is the current General Secretary. Prior to him Rev. Dr. Solomon Rongpi served in this position who was the first member of the Karbi.[26] CBCNEI supports annually events for evangelism and charity. There are joint ministry activities with other Baptist associations in India like the Baptist Church of Mizoram and North Bank Baptist Christian Association. Also, a cooperation exists with Presbyterians, the Roman-Catholic Church, the Church of God, and some others. CBCNEI is a member body of the BWA. The following section contains Dr. Rongpi's assessment of theological positions in this convention. His assessment will be compared with the results of the 2001 survey conducted by this author (see second number).[27]

Who Is a Baptist?

Which statements represent best the opinion of most members in Baptist churches that are connected with your organization? Please check the numbers which represent best the importance of the following statements. 0 = not important, 4 = very important.

A Baptist is a person who has been delivered from spiritual burdens (3/2.7), who believes that baptism is as a sign of conversion (4/3), who is a member in a Baptist church (4/2), who regularly attends the church (3/1.8), who believes that the Bible is the only guiding principle of life and faith (3/3.2), who has a personal relationship with Jesus Christ (4/3.5), who gives about 10 percent of his income to the church (3/2), who is part of the priesthood of all believers (4/2.5), who is evangelistic (4/2.4), who supports human rights (4/1.5), who carries his/her cross (4/2.9), who is persecuted (3/no data), who enjoys blessings of health and

25. Council of Baptist Churches in North East India, "Council of Baptist Churches in North East India."

26. KABC Office, "Rev. Dr. Solomon Rongpi."

27. In the first question, the respondents had to weigh of the answers with the numbers 1–16. 16 refers to the most important and 1 an unimportant feature. Dr. Rongpi answered on a scale of 1–4, so that there are two different methodologies. Nevertheless, a trend in the responses can be identified.

wealth (3/0.7), who stands for freedom of faith and conscience (4/2.2), who supports the autonomy of the local church (3/1.6).

Meaning of Baptism

There are different opinions about the meaning of baptism. Which of the following seems to be the majority position among the members in the churches which are connected with your organization? Please select number 5 for the opinion which seems to describe best the view and number 1 that seems to describe least. You may select the numbers more than once.

A. Baptism is a sign of the incorporation into the body of Christ: 5 (4.49); B. only through baptism is membership in a Baptist Church possible: 1 (3.05); C. baptism is an important family ceremony 1 (1.67); D. baptism is a normal step of growing up 1 (2.27); E. through baptism the believer receives the Holy Spirit: 1 (3.42); F. in baptism the old person dies: 4 (3.36); G. through baptism the believer answers the promise of the gospel: 1 (3.48).

Theological Controversies[28]

How do you see most church members positioned in the following theological controversies? Please indicate it by checking the number which represents best the standpoint of most church members. Up to 3 points could be awarded for each side of a controversy.

Fundamentalism vs. Liberalism (2); Calvinism (TULIP) (2) vs. Arminianism; Inerrancy of the Bible (2) vs. Errors in the Bible; Cessationism (miracle gifts have ceased) vs. Continuanism (miracle gifts still exist) (2); Substitutionary Atonement of Christ brings life (3) vs. Jesus's death does not bring eternal life; Eternal hell (3) vs. no eternal hell; Homosexuals cannot be church members vs. Homosexuals can be church members (1); No female senior pastor accepted vs. female senior pastor accepted (3); No remarriage after divorce vs. remarriage after divorce (2); Church has replaced Israel (3) vs. separate future for church and Israel; Only true Christians will go to heaven (3) vs. everyone/None will go to heaven; God created the earth in 6 days (3) vs. God has somehow used evolution.

---

28. There is no corresponding data from the 2001 survey.

Reasons for Membership in the Baptist Church

People have different reasons for their church membership. Which of the following reasons apply to most members? Please answer based on this scale with 7 fields. 1 = not my opinion, 7 = exactly my opinion.

I am member of the Baptist church, because … A. The church is doing good deeds: **1** (4.23); B. The church is good to the poor, old, and sick people: **1** (3.84); C. I am a Christian: **4** (5.05); D. I give my consent to Christian teaching: **1** (4.84); E. I think of the time after death: **2** (4.52); F. The church works for justice in the world and a better future for all people: **3** (5.04); G. The church gives me the opportunity or meaningful work: **3** (4.23); H. I care for my children: **3** (3.28); I. I need the fellowship: **3** (4.87); J. The church gives me comfort in dark hours: **2** (4.79); K. I look for fellowship with people of my caste/tribe:**1** (2.97); L. I want to experience a Christian marriage and be given a Christian funeral service: **2** (2.93); M. I am religious: **2** (3.16); N. The church gives me inner strength: **2** (5.56); O. The church provides answers to the questions about the meaning of live: **2** (5.10); P. My parents were/are in this church: **2** (4.75); Q. It is my place of professional work: **2** (2.83).

What Age Group Is Represented Most in the Majority of Churches?

A. 10 to 20 years_/ B. 20 to 30 years (X)/ C. 30 to 40 years/ D. 40 to 50 years_/ E. 50 to 60 years_/ F. 60 to 70 years_/ G. 70 to 80 years_/ H. 80 years of age and older_/

Number of Active Members in the Average Local Baptist Churches

A. Less than 10 percent of the members of the Church_/ B. 10 to 20 percent _/ C. 20 to 30 percent _/ D. 40 to 50 percent (X)/ E. more than 50 percent (X)/ F. I don't _/.

In summary, it can be said that churches in the CBCNEI are theologically characterized both by the current ABC and by conservative theologies. The influence of the ABC could be conjectured in matters of the ordination of women and remarriage of divorced. On the other hand, conservative convictions can be seen in creationism, inerrancy of Scripture, eternal damnation, and the atoning death of Christ. Churches lean towards Calvinism and replacement theology in view of Israel. It is amazing to see in how many areas the assessment of Dr. Rongpi is like the results of the survey from the year 2001. Some of the variations can be best explained with different methodology. Dr. Rongpi has not assigned numbers that are greater than four in the question on reasons for church membership. In contrast to the Baptist churches in the Western world, the young age of the members and the activities of nearly 50 percent of the members are noticeable. In the twentieth century it was typical for evangelical Christians in the West to go to church almost every Sunday. Today, there are only 58 percent of evangelicals in the USA doing that.[29] In Northeast India, however, the weekly service attendance is still a sign for Baptists.

Marginalized Baptists

The second group which will be presented here as an example of Baptists in India, are the marginalized. These Baptists belong to Scheduled Castes (SC) and Scheduled Tribes (ST) or Dalits. This designation has replaced the terms untouchables or outcasts. In the 2011 Census, 16.2 percent of the population belonged to SC and 8.2 percent to ST,[30] which would be 340 million people in 2021. "According to some estimates, there are 15–20 million Christian Dalits in India."[31]

During the 2017 election of the President of India, the two main candidates were Dalits. Seventy-one-year-old Ram Nath Kovind, from the lowest Dalits group, and a member of the Bharatiya Janata Party, was elected. This encouraging example should not obscure the fact that the Dalits in India are still disadvantaged and discriminated against. In the last decades, the proportion of Hindus who became Christians was higher among Dalits than in the rest of the Indian population. This fact had caused the Hindutva-movement to reach out to Dalits.[32] Their efforts for a re-conversion back to Hinduism include financial incentives and pressure in the form of expropriation.[33] "According to official figures for the year 2020, the biggest gainer—in terms of new converts—was

---

29. Pew Research Center, "Evangelical Protestants."

30. Office of the Registrar General & Census Commissioner, India, "Census of India 2011."

31. International Dalit Solidarity Network, "India: Official Dalit Population."

32. Lazar Thanuzraj Stanislaus, "Hindutva and the Marginalzed."

33. "India: The Politics of (Re)conversion."

Hinduism. People who embraced Hinduism constituted 47 per cent of religious conversions in Kerala during the one-year period under reference."[34]

In the history of the Christian Church in India, V. S. Azaraiah and the Dornakal Revival movement must be mentioned in connection with Dalits.[35] In 1912, Azaraiah became the first Indian Anglican bishop in Dornakal, which belonged to Andhra Pradesh, and is now in the federal state of Telangana. His revival movement contributed directly and indirectly to planting of many Baptist Churches in this region. "There were increasing numbers of people willing to take up Azariah's challenge through innovation. Samuel Stokes, for example, developed with Sundar Singh the idea of a 'Brotherhood of the Imitation of Jesus's, which would plant in India a startling innovation: 'a life of literal obedience and the detailed imitation of Christ.'"[36]

However, the roots of the Baptist churches in this area go back to the 1860s.[37] The marginalized Baptists are Telugu-speaking people in Andhra Pradesh. Over 640,000 Baptists live mainly in coastal areas. Their churches belong to the Samavesam of Telegu Baptist Churches (STBC). The BWA membership of the STBC was suspended in 2004, because of irregularities with denominational property acquisitions, the lack of transparency and accountability. Asia Pacific Baptist Federation (APBF) followed with a similar exclusion in 2005.[38] Fair and democratic elections are the requirement for a review of the BWA membership status.

An alternative to the STBC was a new convention in Telangana. Telangana is the twenty-ninth state of India that was founded in June 2014. On the occasion of the hundred years celebration of the Baptists in Secunderabad, 170 Baptist leaders from all parts of Telangana, especially from the districts of Warangal, Suryapet, Nalgonda, Hyderabad, and Ranga Reddy, came together on January 12, 2016. At this meeting, the Telangana Baptist Convention (TBC) was founded, and Baptist congregations in all of Telangana had been invited.[39] However, in 2021, this author could not find any traces of this convention. This development is

---

34. "At 47%, Hinduism Biggest Gainer."

35. Shaw, *Global Awakening*, chapter 67.

36. Hutchinson and Wolffe, *Short History of Global Evangelicalism*, 168.

37. Taneṭi, "Telugu Baptist Christianity."

38. Lotz, "Who and Where in the World Are the Baptists?," 12–13.

39. APBD News Bureau, "New Day for Telugu Baptists."

important if one considers that these churches were part of the former STBC. Although most of the churches were not involved in this conflict and experienced large growth in various areas of ministry, they were officially isolated from the global and regional communities of Baptists. The new convention was initiated at the request of "thousands of Baptists in thousands of churches"[40] of the former STBC. The TBC should promote fellowship, mission, and evangelism. The APBF was represented in this inaugural meeting by Pastor Edwin Lam, Rev. Bonny Resu, Mr. Bijoy Sangma.

The history of the marginalized Baptists is a history of successful inculturation or according to the terminology of Andrew Walls and Lamin Sanneh, a history of the *re-translation* and *re-transmission* of the gospel. This indigenous history ranges from Indian Anglican Bishop V. S. Azaraiah up to the founding of the TBC which became possible after the foundation of the federal state of Telangana. The attraction of the Christian faith is not only caused by a *social gospel* and a form of liberation theology. According to Mark Shaw, it is a holistic approach that translates the gospel for the poor, the disadvantaged, and discriminated people in India and helps them to accept a new identity in Christ.

Independent Fundamental Baptists

The autonomy of the local church is an important indicator for Baptists. Some churches even reject any membership in conventions or hierarchical structures above the local church. Independent Baptists were formed in the late nineteenth and the early twentieth century, first in the United States and the United Kingdom. Today there are independent fundamental Baptist churches in almost a hundred countries.[41] Of course, not all independent Baptist churches in India are fundamentalists. Despite the rejection of organizational structures, there is a feeling of solidarity and cooperation among independent churches. The phenomenon of independent churches is not limited to Baptists.

> The many independent churches within the area of the Wadiaram pastorate [South India] have all been started since the 1959 study, most of them in the past twenty-five years. Behind them were developments in Indian Christianity that began more

40. APBD News Bureau, "New Day for Telugu Baptists."
41. Fundamental.org - King James - Fundamental - Independent-Baptist, "India."

than one hundred years ago. These were related to revivals in other parts of the world but also to remarkable new movements in India. Many of these movements can be called "Pentecostal" or "charismatic," but there is one tradition that could better be called "independent Baptist," and other strands of modern evangelicalism are also represented.[42]

Independent Baptist churches often can be characterized by a conservative fundamentalist theology (dispensationalism, anti-charismatic, anti-prosperity gospel, etc.), the sole use of the King James Version of the Bible without or with notes of Cyrus I. Scofield (Scofield Reference Bible), formal dress code in the worship services, and a rejection of modern music styles. In South India, most church members are Dalits.

The observer might wonder how it is possible that the KJV of the Bible is still being used in Baptist churches in India in the twenty first century. On August 15, 1947, India gained its independence from the British Empire. In the following decades, policies had been implemented that should erase traces of the colonial period. This also included the renaming of the cities. Bombay became Mumbai, Madras became Chennai, and Bangalore became Bengaluru. In churches, the style of music changed from western hymns to Indian rhythms and melodies. After such transformation, Indian churches stand out when their webpages are accompanied by American hymns in the style of the 1950s, and when their statements of faith emphasize the exclusive use of the KJV, as in the case of the "The Pillar and Ground of the Truth Baptist Church" by Dr. Enoch C. Kumar in Moolekate, Bhadravathi.[43] Once the website visitor starts exploring the other pages of this website, he or she will encounter Christian songs produced by the pastor with Indian melodies and in the south Indian language Kannada. Pastor Kumar came to faith in Christ with the help of American missionaries, and he studied theology in the USA.

The independent Baptists in India are quite a mixed group of churches. Firstly, the directory[44] has not been up to date for the last three years; there are several double entries, and most homepages do not work. Churches with functioning webpages usually are committed to the exclusive use of the KJV. The Heritage Baptist Church of Pastor Adrian

42. Carman and Vasantha Rao, *Christians in South Indian Villages*, 68.

43. Kumar, "Pillar and Ground."

44. Fundamental.org - King James - Fundamental - Independent-Baptist, "India."

Hendricks argues for the sole use of translations based on the Masoretic Text and the Textus Receptus with two Bible passages: "The only translations of the Bible which will be used in the public ministry of Heritage Baptist Church are those which are accurate, word for word translations based upon the Masoretic text and the Textus Receptus (Rev. 22:19; John 12:48)."[45]

This church is very exclusive. On its website it says: "Any associations with other churches and fellowships shall never be anything other than voluntary, and shall continue only so long as these groups are in agreement with the doctrine of Heritage Baptist Church."[46]

The reader might wonder how Bible passages can refer to text versions that are hundreds of years younger than the Bible. The Masoretic text is from the seventh to the tenth century, and the Textus Receptus had been published in the sixteenth and seventeenth century. It also remains unclear to which of the several versions of the Textus Receptus those Bible passages should refer.[47] The author of this article could not find out whether there is a discussion in Indian independent churches about the Textus Receptus. At least, the internet presence of some churches suggests that in addition to the belief in the infallible Sacred Scripture, there is also the belief in an error-free text tradition of the KJV. Perhaps, a critical review of the teachings of the independent Baptists has already begun like in the United States. It is conceivable that there is a traditional theological presentation in English and a different view in a national language.

In an interview with an Indian doctoral student in Texas, this author learned that there are some Baptist churches in India that follow in content and style their supporting churches in the USA. This loyalty has two levels. The first level is the relationship level between the Indian pastor and a church in the USA. The second level is the relationship between the Indian church to her pastor. On the first level, theological training and ongoing donations align the theological profile of the pastor with the church in the United States. On the second level, Indian culture values loyalty. For a visitor of a Hindu temple, it is of secondary importance, which God is venerated there. The choice of God is a matter of tradition in old temples. In new temples, it is a question of the training of the

45. Heritage Baptist Church, "Heritage Baptist Church."
46. Heritage Baptist Church.
47. Ward, "Which Textus Receptus?," 51–52.

priest; and thirdly, it is handled pragmatically. There are gods for sports, business, love, etc. Such a culturally influenced religiosity could be suspected in Christian churches as well. Either there is the local church that has existed for a long time and the pastor has the obligation to preserve tradition, or there is a newly planted church which is shaped by the theological education of the pastor, or there are churches that are very pragmatic according to the proverb: "He who has the gold makes the rules."

Nevertheless, an outside observer has no right to judge Indian churches about their motivations for certain church policies. The level of research does only permit observations and asking questions. It may be true that the beliefs which are described here are deep convictions of most church members. It may also be true that religion follows the money. Ultimately, it is a result of the nature of the independent churches that there is lack of accountability and transparency toward institutions outside of them. This could explain why such a curious case could exist as follows:

The *Rose of Sharon* congregation led by female pastor Soroja in Mumbai is like an Outlier[48] church that is strikingly different from typical independent Baptist Churches. This church is listed on the website of Fundamental.org, but it is anything but a typically fundamentalist, *King James only*, anti-charismatic church which would also reject the ordination of women. The KJV is used on their website as a source for Scripture quotes, but even these quotes are interpreted differently: "We believe that the Lord speaks to us today through his chosen apostles and prophets (Ephesians 2:20; 3:5)."[49] The website says about the pastor and prophetess: "There rests the calling of a prophetess on her life. Just as in the days of old, today the Lord speaks to her in visions and dreams. Every prophecy and revelation has [sic] been confirmed as coming from the Holy Spirit of God."[50]

These statements have surprised this author. The Rose of Sharon Church reminds us that "theological drawers" not always contain what is promised on the label. In his introduction to this author's dissertation, Denton Lotz pointed out the difference between "Walk and Talk." *Independent* is a broad term, especially if there is money involved.

48. See Gladwell, *Outliers*. Outlier is a term used in statistics to describe data that differs significantly from other observation. Gladwell had made this term popular with his book.

49. See the Rose of Sharon Church's website at http://roschurch.org/.

50. See "Pastor."

Fundamental is a term that does not clearly define only one form of theology. *King James only* includes Indian translations when they are based on the Masoretic text and the Textus Receptus. With Mark Ward, this author hopes:

> If I can successfully show a TR/KJV defender that TR editions feature exactly the same kinds of variants as those that occur between the CT and TR—if I can show that our views differ in degree and not in kind—I can perhaps make a small dent in the amount of divisive internet grandstanding in the world, and save a layperson the difficulty of being told by well-meaning brothers that they must call other Christians' Bibles "corrupt." What could be more divisive than telling people who cannot read Greek or Hebrew—and therefore lack most of the capacity necessary to check out the issue for themselves—to disdain each other's Bibles?[51]

India is a large, complex, colorful, and mysterious land, that covers the major part of the subcontinent. It is not surprising that there is no monography on Indian Baptists. This author looks forward to reading it once it is available.

Bibliography

APBD News Bureau. "A New Day for Telugu Baptists." https:/www.apbf.org/site_files/4002/upload_files/blog/January2016web.pdf?dl=1.

"At 47%, Hinduism Biggest Gainer in Religious Conversion in Kerala." *The New India Express*, April 2, 2021. https://www.newindianexpress.com/states/kerala/2021/apr/02/at-47-hinduism-biggest-gainer-in-religious-conversion-in-kerala-2284660.html.

Baptist World Alliance. "Member Unions." https://www.baptistworld.org/member-unions/.

———. "2020–2021 BWA Baptist Vulnerability Index." https://www.baptistworld.org/vulnerability-index/.

Carman, John B., and Chilkuri Vasantha Rao. *Christians in South Indian Villages, 1959–2009: Decline and Revival in Telangana*. Studies in the History of Christian Missions. Grand Rapids, MI: Eerdmans, 2014.

Council of Baptist Churches in North East India. "Council of Baptist Churches in North East India." http://www.cbcnei.in/.

Fundamental.org - King James - Fundamental - Independent-Baptist. "India." https://fundamental.org/kjv-church-directory/wpbdp_category/india/.

Gladwell, Malcolm. *Outliers: The Story of Success*. New York: Back Bay, 2008.

51. Ward, "Which Textus Receptus?," 77.

Heritage Baptist Church. "Heritage Baptist Church: About Us." https://www.heritagebaptist.in/about_us.

Hutchinson, Mark, and John Wolffe. *A Short History of Global Evangelicalism* Cambridge, MA. Cambridge University Press, 2012.

"India: The Politics of (Re)Conversion to Hinduism of Christian Aboriginals." In *Annual Review of the Sociology of Religion*, edited by Michel Patrick and Enzo Pace, 195–215. Leiden: Brill, 2011.

International Dalit Solidarity Network. "India: Official Dalit Population Exceeds 200 Million." https://idsn.org/india-official-dalit-population-exceeds-200-million/.

Jenkins, Philip. "The Most Baptist State Isn't Mississippi. It's Nagaland, India." *Christian Century*, March 2, 2021. https://www.christiancentury.org/article/notes-global-church/most-baptist-state-isn-t-mississippi-it-s-nagaland-india.

Johnson, Todd M., and Gina A. Zurlo. *World Christian Database: India/Denominations*. Leiden: Brill, 2021. https://www-worldchristiandatabase-org.ezproxy.liberty.edu/wcd/#/detail/country/96/-43-denominations.

Joshua Project. "India." https://joshuaproject.net/countries/IN.

KABC Office. "Rev. Dr. Solomon Rongpi; the First Karbi to Hold the Post of General Secretary of CBCNEI." https://web.archive.org/web/20170421053511/http://www.kabc.in/2014/05/dr-rev-solomon-rongpi-first-karbi-to.html.

Kumar, Enoch C. "The Pillar and Ground of the Truth Baptist Church Ministries." http://www.1timothy315.org/.

Lazar Thanuzraj Stanislaus. "The Hindutva and the Marginalzed: A Christian Response." https://www.missionstudies.org/archive/IACM/Papers/Hinduvata%20and%20Marginalised.htm.

Lotz, Denton. "Who and Where in the World Are the Baptists?" *Baptist History and Heritage* 40 (2005) 8–22.

Office of the Registrar General & Census Commissioner, India. "Census of India 2001: Religious Composition." https://censusindia.gov.in/Census_Data_2001/India_at_glance/religion.aspx.

———. "Census of India 2011: Religion." https://www.censusindia.gov.in/Census_and_You/religion.aspx.

———. "Census of India 2011: Scheduled Castes & Scheduled Tribes Population." https://censusindia.gov.in/census_and_you/scheduled_castes_and_sceduled_tribes.aspx.

Open Doors USA. "India." https://www.opendoorsusa.org/christian-persecution/world-watch-list/india/.

"Pastor." http://roschurch.org/pastor.

Pew Research Center. "Evangelical Protestants." http://www.pewforum.org/religious-landscape-study/religious-tradition/evangelical-protestant/.

Schulze, Dietmar. *Baptisten in Nordostindien: Eine Mitgliederstudie*. Baptismus-Studien 11. Kassel: Oncken, 2006.

Shaw, Mark R. *Global Awakening: How 20th-Century Revivals Triggered a Christian Revolution*. Downers Grove, IL: InterVarsity, 2010.

Taneṭi, James Elisha. "Telugu Baptist Christianity: A Religion of the Marginalized." *American Baptist Quarterly* 29 (2010) 63–75.

Verma, V. S. "Census of India 1981: A Hand Book of Population Statistics." https://www.censusindia.gov.in/DigitalLibrary/data/Census_1981/Publication/India/49962_1981_POR.pdf.

Ward, Mark. "Which Textus Receptus? A Critique of Confessional Bibliology." *Detroit Baptist Seminary Journal* 25 (2020) 51–77.

"The World Factbook: India." https://www.cia.gov/the-world-factbook/countries/india/#people-and-society.

27

Australian Baptists

KEN R. MANLEY

BAPTISTS WERE NOT INVOLVED in the beginnings of European settlement in Australia (1788) and have always been a minority denomination, reaching a peak of 2.3 percent of the population in 1901. In recent
decades, Baptists have hovered around 1.6 percent of the population
according to census data. A late emergence as a denomination in the
colony and small numbers has minimized their impact. Moreover, their
voluntarist emphasis generally prevented them gaining financial support
from the various Church Acts, which helped the early expansion of many
other denominations. A few early churches did accept grants of land,
later arguing that the colonial situation was different: aid did not equate
with control.

The first Baptist service of worship in Australia in Sydney, on April
24, 1831, was led by Rev. John McKaeg (1789–1851), who also conducted
the first believer's baptisms in Woolloomooloo Bay (in Sydney) in 1832.
McKaeg's small group was granted a site for a chapel by the Governor.
After some funds had been raised and plans prepared, McKaeg's tobacco
business failed, and he fell into disgrace as a drunkard and was imprisoned for debt. Though he recovered and later became an ardent advocate
of total abstinence, the fledgling Baptist work was left in disarray.

Provision of adequate pastoral leadership was to be a constant
struggle for Australian churches, although their tradition of lay leadership meant that churches could be established and maintained even
if there were no ministers available. Still, the fostering of welcoming

networks assisted Baptist settlers to adjust to the strangeness of colonial life, a strategic role of religion in society. Issues that had caused debate and even division in Britain when transposed into the Australian setting became focal points for tragic dissension. These included subtle theological variations within Calvinism, open or closed membership, open communion, and patterns of church leadership. These divisions condemned many Baptists to struggle in a backwater of introspection and irrelevance for much of their early life in the colonies.

The majority of British settlers were Particular Baptists although mostly in the form of the evangelical Calvinism that had supported William Carey's mission work. Some Strict and Particular Baptist churches were founded from early days but were never numerically very strong, whilst Scotch Baptists, with their rejection of a paid ministry, were another expression of British Baptist life that impacted on churches in the new colony. Some few pioneers came from the General Baptist tradition, but they never formed a rival group, and the British distinctions became increasingly irrelevant in Australia. The various strands of Baptist Dissenting tradition were gradually woven into the national identity of Australian Baptists.

The development of Australia as British settler colonies inevitably shaped the pattern of Baptist life. Each separate colony developed its own life, and although inter-colonial exchanges were encouraged, questions of identity and mission at both a colonial (now, state) and national level have been perennial issues for Australian Baptists. At the same time, some key individual Baptists expressed significant community leadership. This is the dominant pattern of Baptist influence for the first generation. As a denomination, they were for many years not structured to act in a corporate way; any influence had to be through individuals. The earliest denominational structures, called associations (and later unions) were formed principally for mutual support and planning: Victoria (1862), South Australia (1863), New South Wales (1868), Queensland (1877), Tasmania (1884), and Western Australia (1896). Rapid expansion of the population during the gold rush era of the 1850s led to numerous evangelistic endeavors and churches being founded, especially in Victoria.

The economic crises of the 1890s, the federation of a new nation (1901) and the traumas of the First World War were accompanied by a developing denominational awareness and confidence. Baptists increasingly acted in a corporate sense although the impact of key individuals is still crucial to the story. Since the Second World War, Australian

Baptists have acted in a more cohesive and increasingly corporate way in Australian society, especially in evangelism, church planting, theological training, welfare, health, and education.

Outstanding among nineteenth-century Baptists was the pioneer Sydney minister John Saunders (1806–59), who set a remarkable pattern of pastoral and community leadership. Saunders established the first Baptist congregation and opened the first Baptist chapel at Bathurst Street in 1836. He also gave himself vigorously to various religious, moral, and philanthropic concerns. Thus, he opposed the barbarities of the convict system and was a leading advocate for the abolition of transportation. But his public profile in the colony was seen most dramatically in two areas: his unfailing advocacy of temperance and his passionate condemnation of European injustice towards Aboriginal peoples. His sermon of October 1838, delivered at the time of the debate in the colony about the trial and execution of the Myall Creek murderers, attracted notoriety as it was published in full in the colonial press (Colonist, October 17, 20, 24, 1838). He powerfully condemned both the murderers and those who defended them. Saunders's sermon has been described by historian Henry Reynolds as "one of the most eloquent presentations of humanitarian doctrine" from the period.

Meanwhile in Van Diemen's Land, an older pastor, the doughty Calvinist Henry Dowling (1780–1869), had led Baptist work at Launceston and Hobart since his arrival in 1834. He itinerated throughout the colony and acted as a chaplain to convicts, defending his financial support from the Crown for this ministry.

Baptists provided a different kind of leadership in the establishment of the South Australian colony in 1836. The vision and influence of George Fife Angas (1789–1879), an English Baptist deacon and businessman, were significant in forming the South Australian Company. He hoped to establish a free Christian settlement, without convicts and as a base for "the diffusion of Christianity in the Southern hemisphere." Scottish Baptist David McLaren (1785–1850) was the company's colonial manager and also served as a Baptist lay pastor whilst in the colony from 1837 to 1841.

Among the first to migrate from Tasmania to the new settlement at Port Phillip (in what is now Victoria) was Thomas Napier (1802–81), a strong-minded Scotch Baptist who purchased land in Collins Street where the first services were held in 1839. The Collins Street Church was eventually formed in 1843 with a recent arrival from England, Rev. John

Ham (1792–1852), as pastor. Concern with the plight of the Aboriginal population led some Port Phillip Baptists to establish a school at the junction of Merri Creek and the Yarra River in 1845. A leading layman from this period was Henry Langlands (1794–1863), who arrived in 1847 to join his brother, and their foundry was one of the largest employers in the colony. Leading pastors in this formative era included James Taylor (1814–96) and Isaac New (1803–86) from Birmingham in England, James Martin (1821–77), and Samuel Chapman (1831–99). F. J. Wilkin (1845–1940) became a pioneer home missionary leader and theological educator.

In Queensland, controversial Presbyterian cleric John Dunmore Lang (1799–1878) established a united Protestant church of Presbyterians, Congregationalists, and Baptists at Moreton Bay (Brisbane) in 1849. The first minister selected was a young Baptist minister, Charles Stewart (ca. 1820–58), who led what he called "a beautiful experiment" in what became known as the United Evangelical Church. The vision faded, and denominational ambitions could not be restrained. Eventually, Baptist minister Benjamin Wilson (1823–78) arrived in 1858 to lead Baptist work. One distinguishing feature of early Baptist work in Queensland was the contribution of a significant number of German Baptists, who established strong networks of church planting and evangelism among German settlers.

In Tasmania, the work begun under Dowling was greatly strengthened by the generosity of wealthy pastoralists William (1820–92) and Mary Gibson (1811–1903). They were enthusiasts for the ministry of English preacher C. H. Spurgeon and were inspired by visits to the colony of his son Thomas. The Gibsons eventually built fifteen chapels and many manses and brought out a succession of graduates from Spurgeon's College. Spurgeon had a powerful impact on the conservative theology of Baptists, especially in Tasmania but also in New South Wales and Queensland. The best-known graduate of Spurgeon's College was undoubtedly the distinguished essayist and preacher Dr. F. W. Boreham (1871–1959), who had pastorates in New Zealand, Hobart, and Victoria.

Western Australian work did not begin until 1895 when J. H. Cole (1840–1915) led the first church in Perth, but valuable pioneering work by William Kennedy (1868–1929) helped found several rural churches in the colony. The Baptist movement, with its strong emphasis on the role of lay people in its leadership, tended to develop rugged individualists who embraced opportunities to serve in the public life of the growing colonies.

In both Queensland and South Australia in particular, a remarkable number of leading laymen—merchants and manufacturers in the main—gave a certain status to the Baptist cause and made a significant contribution to civic life during the nineteenth century. This included people like Charles Swan (1811–91), owner of the Moreton Bay Courier and mayor of Brisbane (1873–75); Thomas Symes Warry (1775–1864), the first Baptist to sit in the Queensland Parliament (1860–63); and his brother, R. S. Warry (d. 1891), chief magistrate of the colony and a mayor of the city. Baptists were a tiny minority in the colony but had an active role in commerce, politics, and the philanthropic life of the community.

In South Australia even more Baptists were prominent in public life. After his arrival in 1851, George Fife Angas brought together men like William Kyffin Thomas (1821–78), proprietor of *The Register*, and successful businessmen like J. A. Holden (1834–87) and David Fowler (1826–81). They resolved to establish a new church and sent to England for a new pastor. With the formation of the Flinders Street Church and the advent of its founding pastor, the inspirational Silas Mead (1834–1909), in 1861, Baptist work became cohesive and grew rapidly. Other leaders in South Australia included James Smith (1819–1900), chairman of directors of the Bank of Adelaide, G. W. Cooper (1858–1906), managing director of Elder Smith and president of the Chamber of Commerce. John Darling (1831–1905) and his son John (1852–1914) founded of a remarkable dynasty: John Darling and Son became the largest exporter of grain from Australia, both served in parliament, and John Jr. became chairman of Broken Hill Propriety. James Holden was a founder of the South Australian Chamber of Manufacturers, whilst his son, (Sir) E. W. Holden (1885–1947), was chairman of General Motors Holden and served as a Member of the Legislative Council (MLC) from 1935 to 1947. George Swan Fowler (1839–96), with his brother, established the grocery firm D. & J. Fowler—destined to be one of the leading commercial houses in the Southern hemisphere. Sir Charles Henry Goode (1827–1922) was active in almost every evangelical and philanthropic initiative in South Australia. This remarkable group of men brought a sense of stability and status to the Baptists in that state.

In Victoria, an anonymous gift of £25,000 was made in 1884 by the Geelong grazier Silas Harding (1816–94) to establish the Victorian Baptist Fund on condition that the churches could match this amount.

This was achieved, and the trustees appointed to manage the Fund (which founded the theological college and provided for home mission expansion and support for needy ministers) reveal a significant group of lay leaders: William McLean (1845–1905), a wealthy merchant; C. J. Ham (1837–1909), MLC and Lord Mayor of Melbourne (1881–82); T. W. Jackson (1830–1918), Deputy Postmaster General; J. M. Templeton (1840–1908), a colonel of the infant militia and an important figure in the history of life insurance in Australia; and J. M. Bruce (1840–1901), a businessman active in numerous civic projects and father of Stanley Bruce, the later Prime Minister of Australia.

In New South Wales (NSW), a leading layman was Sir Hugh Dixson (1841–1926), the tobacco importer and manufacturer, who with William Buckingham (1854–1928) generously supported the establishment of numerous Baptist church properties and a wide range of evangelical missions.

By the beginning of the twentieth century, Baptists were active in each colony, and their way of being Baptist was largely derived from Britain. The heroes for Australian Baptists were still largely English. In addition to Spurgeon, "Our Heroic William Carey," as he was called by Australian leader Allan Webb (1839–1902), was the inspiration for foreign mission and the impetus to undertake work in India. John Clifford was a more controversial figure but did inspire many to adopt a bold social justice dimension in their ministry. These diverse figures of English Baptist life all found a response in Australia.

However, there was an increasing desire to work together to establish a national Baptist identity, to develop what in 1918 one leader called "our own church in our own land." This was helped by publication of a fortnightly paper The Southern Baptist from 1895, which served Victoria, South Australia, and Tasmania, whilst smaller papers were published in the other colonies. Representative gatherings were convened to promote cooperation across the colonies. Delegates were sent to each other's annual assemblies and as political federation gathered momentum, so Baptists met in Melbourne in 1897 with each colony, and New Zealand represented. Possibilities of a federal theological college, ministerial accreditation, a national newspaper, and a national foreign mission society were explored. Further meetings were convened, and in 1908 hopes were high that a federated Baptist body would be created.

World War I intervened, but the Baptist Union of Australia (BUA) was eventually formed in Sydney on August 25, 1926. New Zealand had dropped out of negotiations although cooperation continued at several levels. Each state union remained an independent body, and the BUA coordinated work in Christian education and publication, home missions, and various evangelistic programs. A national weekly paper, The Australian Baptist, functioned from 1913 until 1991 when it was replaced by various state monthly publications. Baptists did not at first establish their own denominational social programs but had supported a wide range of evangelical mission organizations. Joseph Palmer (1841–1930), for example, was the founder of what became the NSW Bush Missionary Society. George Ardill (1857–1945) established the Christian Sydney Rescue Work Society, whilst a number of Baptist women were active in city mission-type work. Margaret Bean (1854–1940), commonly known as "Sister Grace," ran an inner-city rescue mission for young women in Melbourne from 1912 until 1929. Baptists were key supporters of the social work of these diverse missions.

In terms of influencing public morality, there was little to distinguish Baptists from other conservative Protestants. Moral questions with social implications became political issues, notably Sunday observance, alcohol, and marriage laws. A bewildering range of societies and programs promoted Baptist opposition to liquor. Bands of Hope were found in most churches, and the Blue Ribbon movement was popular in many churches. The Woman's Christian Temperance Union (WCTU) was the most significant of all the temperance movements; Baptist women were especially prominent in each state, and some, like Mrs. Margaret McLean (1845–1923) in Melbourne, became leaders in the international movement.

Baptists shared with other Christians a strong belief in marriage as a divine institution. Unlike Anglicans and some other denominations, Baptists supported the proposals for reform of divorce laws in New South Wales in 1886, which allowed divorce for desertion, drunkenness, repeated assault, and long-term imprisonment. Gambling was not opposed by all churches but was condemned by conservative Protestants; for Baptists, gambling was synonymous with greed and viewed as a vice that hardened the heart. The role of a modern leader against organized gambling, such as that undertaken by Rev. Tim Costello in Melbourne, has continuities with earlier Baptist moral arguments, though Rev. Costello's approach employs hard facts in order to gain widespread community support.

Australian Baptists were aware of international movements for social reform among Protestant Christians. Some ministers strongly supported the workers in the labor disputes at the end of the nineteenth century, notably W. T. Whale at Brisbane, who acted as arbiter in the bitter boot-makers' strike of 1895. Only a few ministers were strong advocates of socialism in a Christian form, most notably A. H. Collins (1853–1930) at Fitzroy (Victoria) and in South Australia. Samuel Pearce Carey (1862–1953) was so identified with John Clifford, the outstanding English Baptist Christian Socialist, as to be hailed as "the Dr Clifford of Australia" during his term as minister at Collins Street (1900–1908). Carey conducted special services for the unemployed and served on one of the government wages board committees.

Early Baptist concern for the plight of Aboriginal peoples was spasmodic, and their awareness was scarcely distinguishable from their evangelical peers. They lamented the injustices committed against Aboriginal peoples and supported evangelical missions to convert them, but in general were as patronizing and as powerless as any others in knowing how best to serve them. Baptists had passed resolutions deploring the racial treatment of Chinese and other ethnic groups during the nineteenth century, and some key leaders were outspoken in their condemnation of the White Australia policy. Only after World War II, when Baptists established their own mission to work among the Warlpiri people at Yuendumu, was there a sustained effort to minister among the desert Aboriginal population. This work has produced some remarkable Baptist Aboriginal leaders and developed striking cultural expressions of Christian communication such as Christian iconography and corroborees. Many Baptists, such as the Northern Territory Baptist Union in 1972, supported the claims to land titles by Aboriginal peoples. During the moves towards reconciliation around the end of the twentieth century, Baptist assemblies issued formal apologies to the Indigenous community and held services of reconciliation. Some well-known Indigenous leaders with Baptist links, such as Lowitja O'Donoghue, brought home the horrors of the "stolen generation" to Baptist people.

Many Baptists opposed the compulsory military training for boys and young men in 1911, but few were active pacifists. During the Great War, Baptists were enthusiastic supporters of the imperial cause, thousands enlisted, and at least 750 connected with Baptist churches were killed during the war. Baptists were firm supporters of the unsuccessful "Yes" vote in the conscription debates of 1916 and 1917 with T. E. Ruth (1875–1956), the fiery pastor of the Collins Street Church in Melbourne, emerging as a vigorous opponent of Catholic Archbishop Mannix.

Baptists shared in the conservative Protestant reaction to socialism and communism that marked the years after the war.

During the depression years, Baptists struggled to maintain their work and to meet the vast needs of the unemployed. Some set up schemes, but the problem was too vast for them to make any significant impact. Still, certain pastors in working class areas, such as J. H. Goble at Footscray in Melbourne, acquired reputations as caring and compassionate servants of a hard-pressed community. When Goble died in 1932, the Footscray community erected a life-size statue of the preacher which still stands on the Geelong Road, a unique tribute to a Baptist minister in Australia.

Many Baptist women played significant community roles during these difficult years of war and depression. Outstanding among these was Mrs. Cecilia Downing (1858–1952). Although extremely active in Baptist women's organizations, she became best known for her civic leadership. She was a long-serving member of the WCTU, on the executive of the National Council of Women (secretary from 1928–36), president of the Travellers' Aid Society, a probation officer to the Children's Court, and a member of the Women's Inter-Church Council.

Throughout these decades, Baptists had also maintained an important social role through providing Sunday Schools and a wide range of youth activities. Baptists have tended more generally to flourish in the middle-class suburbs of the cities. Still, the provision of a wide range of youth leadership activities such as Christian Endeavor, debating clubs, and uniformed groups such as the Boys' and Girls' Brigades, promoted a vision of Christian living that was not without impact on the formation of values in a significant number of the nation's youth. The Sunday School movement largely collapsed from the late 1960s, and Baptists had to find a more varied and less educationally structured way of serving their youth. In Carlton (Victoria), Baptists had commenced a day kindergarten in 1901, the beginnings of the Free Kindergarten movement in the state. Today Baptist churches run numerous playgroups, kindergartens, and child-care programs around the nation.

Baptists have not, however, given themselves as extensively as some other denominations to the provision of schools. The first denominational school was Carey Baptist Boys' Grammar School in Melbourne. Opened in 1923, Carey is now a large co-educational school and one of the leading private schools in the state. Two influential Baptist Girls' Grammar schools have also been developed in Victoria: Strathcona first opened in 1943, and Kilvington began in 1948. In 1924, Congregationalists and Baptists in Adelaide opened a boys' school, King's College, which merged with Girton College to form Pembroke College in 1973. Some Baptists in New South Wales began a new type of Christian school in that state when in 1976 the Christian Community High School, with fourteen scholars, was opened in church properties at Lidcombe and Regent's Park. The Baptist community schools have grown into a large movement, and the Australian Association of Christian Schools now has over 250 affiliated schools. These schools, which receive some government funding, tend to be associated with political conservatism.

During the first half of the twentieth century, a policy of aggressive evangelism was effective, especially in New South Wales where the pastor at Stanmore, C. J. Tinsley (1876–1960), gave a powerful lead to others. John Ridley (1896–1976), who had been seriously wounded in battle at Fromelles, became a dynamic evangelist around the churches, whilst A. J. Waldock (1872–1961) led an expanded home mission policy. George H. Morling (1891–1974), as the NSW College principal, gave a balanced evangelical basis for pastoral work. Other states were influenced by this lead.

The most unifying movement among Australian Baptists has been "foreign" mission work, begun separately in each of the colonies. The first society was established in South Australia, under the inspiration of Silas Mead at Flinders Street in 1864, and in cooperation with the English Baptist Missionary Society supported work in Faridpur (India). The Victorian society was founded in 1865 and sponsored workers in Mymensingh. The first Australian Baptist missionaries were sent from South Australia in 1882 when Marie Gilbert (d. 1926) and Ellen Arnold (1858–1931) began work in Bengal. Arnold returned briefly because of poor health, but traveled around the nation inspiring Baptists with the missionary vision. In 1885, five women were farewelled from Adelaide: Arnold, Martha Plested (d. 1923) from Queensland, Marion Fuller (d. 1897) and Ruth Wilkin (d. 1910) from Victoria, and Alice Pappin (d. 1935) from South Australia. Following Mead's sermon on the feeding of the five thousand, when he had asked what were these few women among so many, they became known as "the five barley loaves." The women led the way and were trusted to commence the work among women. Rosalie McGeorge from New Zealand joined the team in 1886. Arthur Summers (d. 1945), the first male missionary, went to India in 1887.

By 1913, when the state societies federated into the Australian Baptist Foreign Mission, sixty-five persons had been sent from Australian churches. Later known as the Australian Baptist Missionary Society (1959) and since 2002 as Global Interaction, Baptists have been active in vigorous crosscultural mission. After World War II, Australian Baptists began work in Papua New Guinea and subsequently in Indonesia, Africa, Thailand, and several Asian countries. The contemporary vision of Global Interaction is to "empower communities to develop their own distinctive way of following Jesus." Currently, over sixty personnel are working in some twelve countries with nine least-reached people groups as well as continuing partnerships with some places where they had previously served. In 2012, the expenditure was well over $7.7 million.

Five state unions established five independent theological colleges, suggestive of both the importance each state has given to ministerial training and the "tyranny of distance" that has hampered Baptist cooperative work. The first college was started in Melbourne in 1891 and is now named after its founding principal, Dr. W. T. Whitley (1861–1947). Other colleges were formed in Brisbane, now named Malyon College after its founding principal, T. J. Malyon (1844–1921), in 1904; Sydney (1916), now known as Morling College after Rev. G. H. Morling, principal for forty years (1921–61); Adelaide (1952), named after E. C. Burleigh (1901–74), the first principal (although this has now closed); and Perth (1963), called Vose Seminary after its founding principal, Dr. Noel Vose (1921–2016), who became the first Australian to serve as president of the Baptist World Alliance (1985–90). Victorian Baptists shared in the establishment of the ecumenical Melbourne College of Divinity in 1910 (now the University of Divinity), and all colleges are affiliated with degree-granting bodies. These Baptist colleges now provide a wide range of courses for all interested people and not only ministerial candidates. A few Australian Baptists have found international recognition for their scholarship. John Drakeford and George Peck made significant contributions in North American seminaries. John Thompson and Mark Brett, with Terry Falla, an acknowledged Syriac scholar, are well known in Old Testament studies; German-born Thorwald Lorenzen in theology and Michael Frost in missiology are similarly well regarded.

In Australia, ordinations have generally been conducted by the state Baptist unions. Rev. Marita Munro was the first woman to be ordained (Melbourne, 1978), since which time women have also been ordained in South Australia, Tasmania, and New South Wales. Women serve as pastors in Queensland but are not ordained. In Western Australia, neither women nor men are now ordained. Of 1,877 Baptist pastors in 2011, some 415 (or 22 percent) were women.

During the second half of the twentieth century, ties with Britain were gradually broken, and there has been a demonstrable shift from a British Protestant culture to an American Protestant culture. Popular theology was largely disseminated through American publishing houses. Certainly, every state was attracted for a decade or so to Southern Baptist models of education in the All-Age Sunday School and in co-operative budgets. Whilst there is increasing disenchantment with many aspects of American Protestant and political culture, it is probably true that much of our church life remains imitative, especially of "successful" North American evangelical churches. Tensions among American evangelicals have had their echoes in Australia. Fundamentalism has shaped the identity of at least some significant parts of the Australian Baptist community. This is to say that militant anti-liberalism, insistence on biblical inerrancy, millenarianism, and anti-ecumenism are part of Australian Baptist identity, although they have not generally produced the divisions experienced in some other parts of the Baptist world. Australian Baptists have generally rejected participation in conciliar expressions of the ecumenical movement. Yet in other ways, many barriers have been broken down, and most Baptists evidence a "pragmatic ecumenism," which leads to cooperation in a wide range of activities: in theological education, in exploring traditions of worship and spirituality, in evangelism, and in action on social issues.

During the last third of the twentieth century, Baptists shared fully in debate about a wide range of social and moral topics. Tensions between more conservative Baptists, such as those who supported the Festival of Light from 1973, and those who were more radical in their critique of the churches' role in society, became increasingly apparent. This had emerged in Victoria where opposition to the Vietnam War, in particular the method of conscription, had occasioned divisive debate. Peace advocacy has grown among many Baptists, and representative Baptist leaders in both Victoria and South Australia voiced opposition to Australian involvement in the war in Iraq.

Various health and bioethical issues have been reviewed in Baptist assemblies and seminars: abortion, in-vitro fertilization, euthanasia, alcohol and substance abuse, and the tragedy of youth suicides. Family and sexuality debates have been vigorous, and attitudes to homosexuals in particular have engendered considerable tension. Sexual abuse, sadly a phenomenon not unknown in many denominations, has been strongly condemned, and policies for ways in which offending clergy or church leaders are to be treated have been adopted. A wide range of social and moral issues is reviewed constantly: questions of poverty, attitudes to unemployment, and a series of questions on the environment and ecology generally. Human rights abuses, whether among Aboriginal Australians or other peoples, have received regular condemnation. Baptists have also protested against the treatment of refugees by the Australian government.

The most significant institutional community role among Baptists, however, is now played by their provision of homes for the aged and a variety of other community services. Baptists had agreed to accept government funding for their schools, concluding that this did not deny their cherished opposition to state aid since it did not amount to sectarian support but was for a community service. As a result, Baptists have happily received government support for their social service programs. The first Baptist home was opened in 1945 in suburban Melbourne. Similar moves were made in other states, and after 1952 when government funding was received for such ventures, considerable expansion rapidly followed. "Baptist Homes" organizations were established in each state, and although government funding has facilitated much of this growth, the initial vision and provision of resources was from Baptist lay people. Today what is known as "Baptcare" is a large multimillion-dollar enterprise with a wide-ranging program of community services, but still with a major emphasis on aged care.

Preparing the way for these new forms of ministries among Baptists were a number of radical discipleship communities founded by Baptists, notably the House of the New World in Sydney (1970), the House of Freedom in Brisbane (1972), and the House of the Gentle Bunyip in Melbourne (1975). Dr. Athol Gill (1937–92) was a significant leader in this movement, which challenged Baptists to serve in more intentional mission work and often showed a sharp activist edge. Many local Baptist churches now conduct a diverse range of social ministries as a regular expression of their mission: legal advisory services, ministry to street people, youth residential hostels, emergency accommodation or other specialized services, such as care for newly arrived refugees, a center for Alzheimer's Day Care, support for those with mental illness or drug addiction, or teaching English to migrants.

Australia is today multicultural and multiracial and has more Buddhists than Baptists. Accordingly, a feature of Baptist church life has been the growing number of ethnic churches or multicultural congregations. The last census (2011) showed that an increasing proportion (30 percent) of Baptists were born overseas. Among Protestants, Baptists have been perhaps the most successful in establishing these churches. Baptist migrants have come from many of the European nations and, in recent years, from South East Asia and Africa. There are today well over a hundred Baptist "ethnic" congregations, which include Arabic, Slavic, German, Ukrainian, Romanian, Slovakian, Greek, Macedonian, Cambodian, Chinese (many of which are Chinese-Anglo integrated congregations), Estonian, Japanese, Korean, Lao, Spanish, and Vietnamese. Other groups are from Lebanon, Indonesia, Iran, Fiji, Samoa, and Poland. A number of refugees from Latin America, notably from El Salvador, and more recently from Burma (Chin and Karen) and Sudan, have also been welcomed and supported. Nationally, this multicultural ministry has brought an added dimension to Australian Baptist identity. More congregations, traditionally Anglo-Australian in membership and customs, are adapting to the presence and values of migrants who are being integrated into church life—a process not unimportant for their settlement into Australian society.

According to Australian census figures, Baptists reached their peak of percentage of the population in 1901 when they were 2.37 percent of the population. After declining to 1.60 percent in 1933, at the last census (2011) they were 1.64 percent of the population when 352,499 people identified themselves as Baptists. Census figures need to be compared with church membership and attendance figures. In 2011, there were 959 churches (659 in 1966) with the largest number being in New South Wales (350) and Victoria (203). The total number of church members was 62,719, although 141,959 were estimated to belong to the total Baptist community. Whilst there are some who have prominent roles in academic and public life, most have lived unremarked lives but are a part of a church movement that has played a role in shaping modern Australian society, an influence greater than their numerical size.

Outside the Baptist Union churches, there are several small groups. In 2013, there were 196 Independent or fundamentalist churches in Australia, most of them with less than fifty people and a total attendance of about 8,000 people. Some few Baptist Reformed Churches, which hold to a strict Calvinism, formed a fellowship in 1982. Only four Strict and

Particular Baptist churches still survive in Australia, with a total membership of twenty-four. A handful of Seventh Day Baptists are also present in Australia.

Bibliography

Cupit, Tony, et al., eds. *From Five Barley Loaves: Australian Baptists in Global Mission 1864–2010*. Preston, Victoria: Mosaic, 2013.

Hughes, Philip J., and Darron Cronshaw. *Baptists in Australia: A Church with a Heritage and a Future*. Nunawading, Victoria: Christian Research Association, 2013.

Manley, Ken R. *From Woolloomooloo to "Eternity": A History of Australian Baptists*. 2 vols. Milton Keynes: Paternoster, 2006.

———. "'Planted in a New Land': German Baptists in Australia (c. 1860–1914)." In *Gemeinschaft der Kirchen und gesellschaftliche Verantwortung (Festschrift für Professor Dr. Erich Geldbach)*, edited by L. Lybaek et al., 108–23. Münster: LIT Verlag, 2004.

28

New Zealand Baptists
and the Struggle for Identity

Martin Sutherland

Since the beginnings of colonization in the nineteenth century, New Zealand Baptists have struggled to find a sense of identity in a strange place. Successive attempts to build a new home have been abandoned, and Baptist people remain disconnected, spiritually scattered. The vital statistics may be quickly summarized. Baptists have never been a large group. Those who identified themselves as "Baptist" in Government Census returns peaked as a proportion of the population in the 1880s but settled to a steady state of around 1.6–1.7 percent through most of the twentieth century.

The early figures reflected a small population which amplified the effect of a single very large church. The twentieth-century rates have been remarkably constant, somewhat above equivalent figures for Australia and considerably above those in Britain.[1] A different picture emerges when figures of actual membership are plotted. On this basis (which, of course, excludes children) the denomination up until 1990 enjoyed real growth. However, that turned in the final decade of the century, and since then the picture has been one of decline. With statistics, of course, we see only as if "in a glass, darkly." In this short study I will attempt to trace the

---

1. Hughes, *Baptists in Australia*, 38–40.

New Zealand Baptist search for identity and in the process, I hope, add living flesh to the dry bones of these figures.

The Baptist story in New Zealand is not long. The first church was not formed until 1851. Crucially, there was no originating "idea" of being Baptist in the colony. Baptists did not arrive as missionaries as had Anglicans, Methodists, and Roman Catholics. Neither did they organize large-scale religious settlements. Instead they drifted in, mostly from Great Britain, as anonymous individuals and families, scattered across the new landscape. Only slowly did Baptists come to recognize each other and seek regular communion. This disordered beginning and the sometimes surprising nature of colonial life presented unanticipated challenges. Most of the early Baptist leaders arrived with a robust sense of who they were. They were British and they were nonconformist. Culturally self-confident they relished their role within that culture of the religious outsider, the sect, the community of contrast. The first generation imagined they were constructing a new Britain, a "Brighter Britain."[2]

Among the first generation an almost naïve confidence, fueled by the seemingly endless possibilities of life in a new-land-inspired aggressive evangelistic endeavor. There was no greater symbol of this than the New Zealand career of Thomas Spurgeon, son of the famous Charles, who from 1881 had an outstandingly successful ministry in Auckland, eventually gathering the largest church in Australasia. When Spurgeon resigned the charge on health grounds in 1889, he was appointed Colonial Evangelist, holding revival meetings throughout the country until his return to Britain in 1891. The Spurgeonic version of religion dominated New Zealand Baptist life through the 1880s. It both epitomized evangelistic success and served as a direct link to the concerns and controversies of Britain.

British structures were automatically adopted. A Union was constituted in 1882, and in 1885 the New Zealand Baptist Missionary Society was formed to take up opportunities in Bengal. However, neither the Union nor the Missionary Society worked well in their first years. The Union was threatened by two potential splits within its first decade and the Missionary Society, though able to send out a succession of committed young women to Bengal, faced scandal and near collapse on the field by

---

2. The title of a public lecture delivered by Thomas Spurgeon during a visit to Britain in 1884. For the thesis that from the 1880s there commenced a revisioning of the idea of New Zealand which amounted to "recolonization" see Belich, *Making Peoples*, 446–50.

1899. Both had been formed prematurely, and both were barely sustainable in the colony. New Zealand was not Britain. In the new environment few of the old rules applied. In this skinny, mountainous country where communication was difficult, the dynamic of Baptist life was centrifugal, local. The needs of the two central organizations drew too much energy and led to some resentment in the churches. Baptists' sense of themselves and their relationships with others would have to adapt. Mere transplantation of denominational forms was not going to be enough.

There had of course already been concessions to this reality. The exigencies of the colonial environment forced a degree of pragmatic innovation. The traditional 'gathered' church model did not suit the sparsely populated countryside. In response, an early form of church planting was attempted. Many local congregations were formed at the initiative of a few key large churches. Areas of likely settlement or population growth were identified and sites secured, often more than a decade in advance of use. The new causes would often remain closely dependent on the sponsoring congregation.[3] Alternatively, the extension could be managed regionally. A small but vigorous Association was set up in Canterbury in 1873 specifically in order to employ an evangelist.

By 1900 the British influence was slipping. With the death of the father and the departure of the son, the Spurgeonic element waned. The shortcomings of the national organizations—first the Missionary Society, then the Union—became obvious and increasingly pressing. Most fundamentally the sense of being "non-conformist" was found to have little currency where there was no established church. Baptist colonists had arrived with a strong sectarian memory. This had its advantages. It was relatively easy to maintain some sense of identity while they were able to define themselves over and against someone else. But what did it mean to be a contrast community in New Zealand? If Baptists were "dissenters," from whom were they dissenting? The colonial Church of England would not, could not, play that old game, as the New Zealand state was self-consciously secular. Sectarian issues were as a result often distinguished from political questions.

A sectarian identity survived for a time, but it had to find a new focus. The second generation of Baptist ministers, especially those who were shaped and trained in the colonies, marked themselves out as different, not so much from Anglicans or Presbyterians, but from Catholics.

3. For a study of one sponsored congregation see Sutherland, "Cohesion and Conflict," 3–21.

Indeed, anti-Catholicism for a time threatened to define the New Zealand Baptist identity. Its manifestations could be extreme. During the First World War a Baptist minister (Howard Elliot, narrowly defeated for the Presidency of the Union in 1917) formed the radical "Protestant Political Association" with the express purpose of excluding Catholics from power. Elliot became so notorious that the Union had to issue a statement distancing itself from his activities.[4]

The building of central structures became increasingly important from the 1920s onward. A subtle change was taking place. As a third generation emerged the sense of being a contrast community was relegated. A "centripetal" or center-seeking dynamic was taking over. Baptists would make a pitch for the mainstream, to join the Anglicans, Presbyterians, and Methodists with a natural claim to a seat at the Protestant table. For such a tiny group it was in many ways an absurd ambition, but it was attempted with energy and some success. Conservatives were occupied elsewhere; the sterner sectarians were growing old. The way ahead seemed clear. In mid-century New Zealand Baptists must play (and look) their part in wider church life.

The signal for this new era of increased focus on organization and structure was the Baptist Union Incorporation Act of 1923. Primarily a means of safeguarding ownership of property, the Incorporation Act was the most public outcome of a drive to centralization which began in the 1920s. In the next decades a raft of committees was set up to manage more efficiently the work of the denomination. In 1915 the annual assembly had appointed six committees; by 1945 it was appointing twenty-three.[5]

The move to the mainstream had ramifications for relationships with other denominations. This would become a major theme in the 1940s and 1950s. Baptists sought to build a profile which avoided them being dismissed as fringe sectarians. In this they only partially succeeded. There remained a deep stream of Baptist life for whom biblical purity was paramount and who put a greater premium on heart religion than on mainstream acceptability. Nevertheless, the centripetal approach in the middle period of the century was a genuine, if unstated, attempt to construct a new Baptist identity in New Zealand. Baptists continued to champion evangelical enthusiasm and freedom of conscience but it was hoped to achieve this in a way which did not alienate other

4. See the entry for H. L. Elliot in Orange, *New Zealand Dictionary of Biography*, 3; also Beilby, *Handful of Grain*, 96–98.

5. Beilby, *Handful of Grain*, 30–32.

denominations. Baptists too could be regarded as pillars of the Christian establishment.

The 1950s were a period of considerable growth. Those willing to enter formal membership of local Baptist churches increased by over 45 percent. These members also grew as a proportion of the total population. Interestingly, the proportion of the total population which figures of those who listed Baptist as their denomination in the official censuses remained stable. This means that a growing proportion of those total adherents as measured by government census were committed members of congregations, rather than merely nominally Baptist. The relative willingness of those nominally "Baptist" to be committed to denominational distinctives such as baptism and membership might be cited as an indicator of denominational loyalty and a crude guide to the strength of Baptist identity. If so, then the mainstreaming period did not apparently weaken the Baptists' sense of themselves.

By 1964, however, denominational General Secretary Lawrence Alfred North (1903–80) was acknowledging "disturbing questions concerning the life of our Denomination, our objectives and the results being achieved."[6] The charismatic movement was beginning its course. In New Zealand, unlike the situation in some other countries, the greatest effect of what was first termed "neo-pentecostalism" has been within existing denominational structures. Independent churches were formed and small Pentecostal denominations emerged, but otherwise "mainstream" bodies have been greatly influenced by renewal movements. This is certainly the case among Baptists. However, through the sixties the fledgling charismatic movement was viewed with great suspicion by the leadership which regarded it as divisive. This negative response to charismatic stirrings turned largely on a key issue in Baptist life, the locus of authority. Religious authority was assumed to rest with the informed individual conscience exercised within agreed structures. The "work of the Holy Spirit" was to be found primarily in the ordered democracy of the church meeting. The notion that the Spirit spoke exclusively to some was anathema.

For two decades there were attempts to check the spread of charismatic styles and practices. The movement was a challenge to order and, in the eyes of the leadership, threatened to relegate Baptists once more to the fringe. Yet the charismatic movement continued to make ground

6. *Baptist Union Year Book 1964–1965*, 17.

among New Zealand Baptists. The passion and emotional commitment of the charismatic movement fitted naturally with the sectarian enthusiasm of earlier groups. Indeed, among Baptists the renewal movement combined with the Spurgeon stream of Biblical conservatism to create a powerful new force which, by the 1980s, had come to dominate Baptist life.

There were inevitable consequences for denominational organization. The dynamic of Baptist life was swinging back to a centrifugal model. Society was changing rapidly and Baptists like many others were beginning to feel threatened. A series of "restructurings" began which would gather pace in the 1980s. In that decade the whole of New Zealand society was caught up in the reforming zeal of the fourth Labour government. Small government and individual enterprise lay at the heart of administrative and economic reform. Baptists too proceeded to dismantle their central structures. In 1990, reviewing his period as General Superintendent, Gerard Marks identified decentralization as a recurring theme.[7] Increasingly it was argued that the focus should be shifted from the denomination to the local churches. The more naturally sectarian charismatic influence grew. The sense of "contrast" returned. The contrast was vague, however, and the result was a retreat from engagement. The public questions committee was done away with. When a new ecumenical body was formed in 1985 Baptists chose not to take part. In 1992 Marks's successor Ian Brown warned that "our sense of identity and our reason for existence as Baptist congregations—communities of faith—is in danger of disappearing." Nevertheless a renewed sense of identity was to be found, in being a "movement" rather than a "denomination."[8] The 1993 Assembly was galvanized by the notion that "the age of the institutional church is over, and the day of the relational community has begun."[9]

In 1991 a new level of leadership, Regional Superintendents, was introduced. On the face of it, this was clearly devolution. Now significant senior figures would be available to encourage and to coordinate local efforts. The national leadership, nevertheless, remained in place. Superintendents were an additional layer, partly funded from the center. Most importantly, their role evolved. Initially presented as a means of

---

7. *Baptist Union Year Book 1990–1991*, 33.

8. Brown, "River and the Lake" 3.

9. Robertson, "Rediscovering the Dream," 20.

providing pastoral care to local pastors and church leaderships their focus soon became mission leadership. Ian Brown, who succeeded Marks
in 1991, identified a further role. "The Superintendents will certainly give
pastoral care and direction to churches and pastors but equally important
will be their apostolic role."[10]

In talking of an "apostolic role" Ian Brown was looking to a responsibility of care to provide overview and cohesion, rather than an authoritative office in a Pentecostal sense. Nevertheless, the language gelled with
a shift which had been taking place over the previous two decades, in
which some churches and leaders moved towards charismatic styles and
models. These forces—devolution or deinstitutionalization and apostolic
leadership—are clearly not perfectly congruent. This incongruity led inevitably to mixed signals, a confusion of messages as to the way forward.
In 1997, for instance, a new statement of the role of superintendents was
adopted. In this the emphasis shifted slightly, with the key aspects of the
role defined as:

1. Provide spiritual leadership to local church leaders.

2. Ensure ministry staff receive effective pastoral care.

3. Promote healthy churches.

In the same year, perceiving a continued drift in denominational
life, the new leadership core of Ian Brown and the Regional Superintendents called the Assembly to "New Directions," an effort to refocus the
"movement" around mission and evangelism. This proposal was strong
on organizational theory and sentiment but relatively short on concrete
proposals. Though it was adopted by the Assembly, Brown later conceded
that it "did not receive the acceptance we believed it would." Very little
change resulted.[11]

This was a major disappointment to the leadership. Their efforts
seemed to have fallen flat. Yet another start on the issues was made in
1999. At the November Assembly Ian Brown was commissioned to bring
together a process of reflection on the nature and mission of New Zealand Baptists in the twenty-first century and the structures and leadership models required.[12] It was expected that documents for discussion
would be ready by February 2000. This timeline had to be abandoned,

10. *Baptist Union Yearbook 1990–1992*, 38.

11. Brown, "Annual Report," 1.

12. See Brown, "Towards Bethlehem 2000," 5.

as events took an unexpected turn. The previous contact of some leaders with American Baptist leader Paul Borden set up a fact-finding visit of a group led by Ian Brown to the American Baptist Churches of the West (ABCW) in Northern California during February 2000. The visit had a profound impact. The visiting group was struck by the "Growing Healthy Churches" emphasis in the ABCW. On its return this became the focus of reflection on the New Zealand scene. More startling for the churches was Ian Brown's decision, communicated soon after his return from California, to conclude as Executive Secretary a year before the expiry of his term. What was needed, he explained, was "a new style and age of leadership."[13]

In 2001 Paul Borden and John Kaisar from ABCW came to New Zealand to work with the refocused Union, conducting training sessions and church consultations. In this year also, the key appointments of National Consultant and National Leader were made. An appointment was made to the first role without controversy. Moves to appoint to the second position encountered much heavier going. In December 2000, Assembly Council (the executive body between Assemblies) agreed that the position demanded a "practitioner leader"—"i.e. the new national leader would not only be a person with a proven track record in growing healthy churches but also lead the denomination while continuing in their present church-based leadership role."[14] This was a new concept to many and generated considerable disquiet among the churches. It was thus decided to appoint an interim leader through to Assembly 2002, with the model of leadership to be debated at the upcoming Assembly 2001, where it was ultimately approved.[15]

One effect of the restructurings of the final decades of the twentieth century was that Baptists gave tacit endorsement to more "apostolic" approaches to leadership, which placed less emphasis on congregational government. This was true at the local level, with the promotion of the "staff-led" model by which those in ministry leadership roles were given more authority. This led to the inevitable sidelining of the members' meeting. It is even more evident at national level. The result has been a significant shift in ecclesiological practice. Baptists were not alone. A general apathy with regard to denominational structures in New Zealand

13. Brown, "Executive Secretary's Column," 5.

14. Kenning, "Council Comment," 5.

15. Kenning, "Council Comment," 5. See the debate in "Models of Leadership," 16–17; see also Finlay, "New Health Goal," 8; Kilpatrick, "Another Model," 8.

was leading to numerous realignments and the demise of hitherto key bodies. Nevertheless, the effect on Baptists has been particularly profound. The old question of identity was now muddied as never before.

Nowhere has this been more evident than in the struggles of the denomination to develop a response to New Zealand government legislation to legalize same-sex marriage. In 2013 the Marriage (Definition of Marriage) Amendment Act was passed with a speed and level of public support which shocked many in the Christian community. In the face of years of slippage caused by an increasingly secular society, conservative Christians had convinced themselves that at least in terms of "family values" they were in tune with the majority view (albeit often silent) in the culture. They were wrong.

For Baptists, after decades of little engagement with public issues, the problem was suddenly very acute. The 2013 Assembly was presented with proposals to discipline churches and ministers should same-sex marriages be conducted. This engendered considerable angst. Deep uncertainty about Baptist principles was uncovered. What role after all, did the denomination have in disciplining churches? The proposals emanating from the denominational leadership seemed in conflict with the fundamental principles of the 1923 Act of Incorporation. A commission to consider the issues was set up and reported back two years later. The 2015 gathering endorsed measures implying the capacity of the denominational center to call churches and ministers into line on the issue. The question remains untested, and indeed itself represents a test of identity. As New Zealand Baptists face a rapidly changing social structure, they remain challenged by the fundamental debate which has ebbed and flowed for their entire history. What does it mean to be Baptist in this place and time?

Bibliography

Baptist Union Year Book 1964–1965. Wellington: Baptist Union of New Zealand, 1964.

Baptist Union Year Book 1990–1992. Wellington: Baptist Union of New Zealand, 1990.

Beilby, George Thomas. *A Handful of Grain: The Centenary History of the Baptist Union of N.Z.* Wellington, New Zealand: Baptist Historical Society, 1984.

Belich, James. *Making Peoples: A History of the New Zealanders from Polynesian Settlement to the End of the Nineteenth Century*. Auckland, New Zealand: Penguin, 1996.

Brown, Ian. "Annual Report." *N.Z. Baptist*, November 2000.

———. "Executive Secretary's Column." *N.Z. Baptist*, April 2000.

————. "The River and the Lake." *N.Z. Baptist*, December 1992.

————. "Towards Bethlehem 2000." *N.Z. Baptist*, December 1999.

Finlay, Chris. "The New Health Goal." *N.Z. Baptist*, July 2001.

Hughes, Philip J. *The Baptists in Australia.* Canberra: Commonwealth of Australia, 1996.

Kenning, Brian. "Council Comment." *N.Z. Baptist*, April 2001.

Kilpatrick, Rob. "Another Model." *N.Z. Baptist*, July 2001.

"Models of Leadership: Baptist Pastors Voice Their Views." *N.Z. Baptist*, June 2001.

Orange, Claudia, ed. *New Zealand Dictionary of Biography*, vol. 3. Wellington: Allen & Unwin, 1996.

Sutherland, Martin P. "Cohesion and Conflict in 1880s Cambridge." *N.Z. Journal of Baptist Research* 4 (1999) 3–21.

————. *Conflict & Connection: Baptist Identity in New Zealand.* Auckland, New Zealand: Archer, 2011.